Computer Supported Cooperative Work

D0869999

Springer
London
Berlin
Heidelberg
New York
Barcelona
Hong Kong
Milan
Paris
Singapore
Tokyo

Elizabeth F. Churchill,
David N. Snowdon and
Alan J. Munro (Eds)

Collaborative Virtual Environments

Digital Places and Spaces for Interaction

With 87 Figures

Elizabeth F. Churchill, BSc, MSc, PhD
FX Palo Alto Laboratory Inc., 3400 Hillview Avenue, Building 4,
Palo Alto, CA 94304, USA

David N. Snowdon, BSc, MSc, PhD
Xerox Research Centre Europe, 6 chemin de Maupertuis, 38240
Meylan, France

Alan J. Munro, MA, PhD
School of Computing, Napier University, 219 Colinton Road,
Edinburgh, EH14 1JD, Scotland, UK

Series Editors

Dan Diaper, PhD, MBCS
Head, Department of Computing, School of Design, Engineering and
Computing, Bournemouth University, Talbot Campus, Fern Barrow, Poole,
Dorset BH12 5BB, UK

Colston Sanger
Shottersley Research Limited, Little Shottersley, Farnham Lane
Haslemere, Surrey GU27 1HA, UK

ISBN 1-85233-244-1 Springer-Verlag London Berlin Heidelberg

British Library Cataloguing in Publication Data
A catalogue record for this book is available from the British Library

Library of Congress Cataloging-in-Publication Data
Collaborative virtual environments : digital places and spaces for interaction / Elizabeth
F. Churchill, David N. Snowdon, and Alan J. Munro (eds.).
    p. cm. -- (Computer supported cooperative work)
  Includes bibliographical references and index.
  ISBN 1-85233-244-1 (alk. paper)
    1. Human-computer interaction. 2. Virtual reality. I. Churchill, Elizabeth F., 1962- II.
  Snowdon, David N., 1968- III. Munro, Alan J., 1965- IV. Series.
QA76.9.H85 C647 2001
005--dc21   00-058347

Typesetting: Ian Kingston Editorial Services, Nottingham
Printed and bound at the Athenæum Press, Gateshead, Tyne & Wear
34/3830-543210 Printed on acid-free paper SPIN 10749012

Contents

Part 1 Collaborative Virtual Environments (CVEs): Histories, Perspectives and Issues

Part 2 Technical Issues and System Challenges

Part 3   Bodies, Presences and Interactions

Part 4 Sharing Context in CVEs – Or "I Know What I See, But What Do You See?"

8   How Not To Be Objective
Kai-Mikael Jää-Aro and Dave Snowdon   143

9   Supporting Flexible Roles in a Shared Space
Randall B. Smith, Ronald Hixon and Bernard Horan . . .   160

Part 5 So, Now We're In A CVE, What Do We Do?

10   Designing Interactive Collaborative Environments
Adrian Bullock, Kristian T. Simsarian, Mårten Stenius, Pär Hansson, Anders Wallberg, Karl-Petter Åkesson, Emmanuel Frécon, Olov Ståhl, Bino Nord and Lennart E. Fahlén . . .   179

List of Contributors

Steve Benford
Communications Research Group, School of Computer Science and Information Technology, University of Nottingham, Jubilee Campus, Wollaton Road, Nottingham, NG8 1BB, UK
sdb@cs.nott.ac.uk

Ronald Bergquist
School of Information and Library Science, CB 3360, University of North Carolina at Chapel Hill, Chapel Hill, NC 27599-3360 USA
bergr@ils.unc.edu

Sara Bly
Sara Bly Consulting, 24511 NW Moreland Road, North Plains, OR 97133, USA
sara_bly@acm.org

Adrian Bullock
Swedish Institute of Computer Science, Box 1263, SE-164 29, Kista, Sweden
Email: adrian@sics.se

Monika Büscher
CSCW Centre, Lancaster University, Lancaster, LA1 4YL, UK
m.buscher@lancaster.ac.uk

Elizabeth F. Churchill
FX Palo Alto Laboratory Inc., 3400, Hillview Avenue, Building 4, Palo Alto, CA 94303, USA
churchill@pal.xerox.com

Rémy Evard
Argonne National Laboratory, 9700 S. Cass Ave, Argonne, IL 60439, USA
evard@mcs.anl.gov

Lennart E. Fahlén

Swedish Institute of Computer Science, Box 1263, SE-164 29, Kista, Sweden

lef@sics.se

Mike Fraser

Communications Research Group, School of Computer Science and Information Technology, University of Nottingham, Jubilee Campus, Wollaton Road, Nottingham, NG8 1BB, UK

mcf@cs.nott.ac.uk

Emmanuel Frécon

Swedish Institute of Computer Science, Box 1263, SE-164 29, Kista, Sweden

emmanuel@sics.se

Chris Greenhalgh

School of Computer Science and Information Technology, University of Nottingham, Jubilee Campus, Wollaton Road, Nottingham, NG8 1BB, UK

cmg@cs.nott.ac.uk

Pär Hansson

Swedish Institute of Computer Science, Box 1263, SE-164 29, Kista, Sweden

par@sics.se

Christian Heath

Work, Interaction and Technology Research Group, The Management Centre, King's College London, Franklin-Wilkins Building, London, SE1 8WA, UK

christian.heath@kcl.ac.uk

Jon Hindmarsh

Work, Interaction and Technology Research Group, The Management Centre, King's College London, Franklin-Wilkins Building, London, SE1 8WA, UK

jon.hindmarsh@kcl.ac.uk

Ronald Hixon

Sun Microsystems Laboratories, 901 San Antonio Rd. MV29-110, Palo Alto, CA 94303, USA

ronald.hixon@sun.com

Bernard Horan

Sun Microsystems Laboratories, 901 San Antonio Rd. MV29-110, Palo Alto, CA 94303, USA
bernard.horan@sun.com

Roger Hubbold

Department of Computer Science, The University of Manchester, Oxford Road, Manchester M13 9PL, UK
roger@cs.man.ac.uk

Saku Hujala

Department of Computer Science and Information Systems, University of Jyväskylä, PO Box 35 (MaE), 40351 Jyväskylä, Finland
sphujala@cc.jyu.fi

Avon Huxor

Centre for Electronic Arts, Middlesex University, Cat Hill, Barnet, Herts, UK
a.huxor@mdx.ac.uk

Andrew Johnson

Electronic Visualization Lab (M/C 154), Room 1120 SEO, University of Illinois at Chicago, 851 S. Morgan St. Chicago, IL 60607, USA
aej@evl.uic.edu

Kai-Mikael Jää-Aro

Department of Numerical Analysis and Computer Science, Royal Institute of Technology, SE-100 44 Stockholm, Sweden
kai@nada.kth.se

Jonni Korhonen

Department of Computer Science and Information Systems, University of Jyväskylä, PO Box 35 (MaE), 40351 Jyväskylä, Finland
jonkorh@cc.jyu.fi

Eileen Kupstas-Soo

Department of Computer Science, CB 3175, University of North Carolina at Chapel Hill, Chapel Hill, NC, 27599-3175 USA
kupstas@cs.unc.edu

Jason Leigh

Electronic Visualization Lab (M/C 154), Room 1120 SEO, University of Illinois at Chicago, 851 S. Morgan St. Chicago, IL 60607, USA
spiff@evl.uic.edu

Kelly L. Maglaughlin
School of Information and Library Science, CB 3360 University of
North Carolina at Chapel Hill, Chapel Hill, NC, 27599-3360 USA
maglk@ils.unc.edu

Andrew McGrath
Shared Spaces Group, BT Adastral Park, Martlesham Heath, Suffolk,
IP5 3RE, UK
andrew.mcgrath@bt.com
(present contact email: Andrew.McGrath@Hutchison3G.com)

Alan J. Munro
School of Computing, Napier University, 219 Colinton Road, Edinburgh EH14 1DJ Scotland, UK
a.munro@dcs.napier.ac.uk
(present contact email: alan.munro@cs.strath.ac.uk)

Bino Nord
Swedish Institute of Computer Science, Box 1263, SE-164 29, Kista,
Sweden

Jon O'Brien
Xerox Research Centre Europe, 61 Regent Street, Cambridge CB2 1AB,
UK
jon.obrien@xrce.xerox.com

Samuli Pekkola
Department of Computer Science and Information Systems, University
of Jyväskylä, PO Box 35 (MaE), 40351 Jyväskylä, Finland
samuli@cc.jyu.fi

Wolfgang Prinz
GMD – German National Research Center for Information Technology
FIT – Institute for Applied Information Technology, Schloss
Birlinghoven, 53754 Sankt Augustin, Germany
wolfgang.prinz@gmd.de

Elaine M. Raybourn
Advanced Concepts Group, Sandia National Laboratories, P.O. Box
5800, MS 0839, Albuquerque, New Mexico, 87185-0839, USA
emraybo@sandia.gov

Mike Robinson
Department of Computer Science and Information Systems, University
of Jyväskylä, PO Box 35 (MaE), 40351 Jyväskylä, Finland
mike@cs.jyu.fi

Tom Rodden

CSCW Centre, Lancaster University, Lancaster, LA1 4YL, UK
tom@comp.lancs.ac.uk

Markku-Juhani O. Saarinen

Department of Computer Science and Information Systems, University of Jyväskylä, PO Box 35 (MaE), 40351 Jyväskylä, Finland
mjos@cc.jyu.fi

Kristian T. Simsarian

Swedish Institute of Computer Science, Box 1263, SE-164 29, Kista, Sweden
kristian@sics.se

Randall B. Smith

Sun Microsystems Laboratories 901 San Antonio Rd. MV29-110, Palo Alto, CA 94303, USA
randall.smith@sun.com

Dave Snowdon

Xerox Research Centre Europe, 6, chemin de Maupertuis, 38240 Meylan, France
Dave.Snowdon@xrce.xerox.com

Diane H. Sonnenwald

School of Information and Library Science, CB 3360 University of North Carolina at Chapel Hill, Chapel Hill, NC 27599-3360, USA
dhs@ils.unc.edu

Olov Ståhl

Swedish Institute of Computer Science, Box 1263, SE-164 29, Kista, Sweden
olovs@sics.se

Mårten Stenius

Swedish Institute of Computer Science, Box 1263, SE-164 29, Kista, Sweden
mst@sics.se

Tero Toivonen

Department of Computer Science and Information Systems, University of Jyväskylä, PO Box 35 (MaE), 40351 Jyväskylä, Finland
tptoivon@cc.jyu.fi

Jonathan Trevor
FX Palo Alto Laboratory Inc., 3400, Hillview Avenue, Building 4, Palo
Alto, CA 94303, USA
trevor@pal.xerox.com

Anders Wallberg
Swedish Institute of Computer Science, Box 1263, SE-164 29, Kista,
Sweden
andersw@sics.se

Adrian West
Department of Computer Science, The University of Manchester,
Oxford Road, Manchester M13 9PL, UK
ajw@cs.man.ac.uk

Mary C. Whitton
Department of Computer Science, CB 3175, University of North
Carolina at Chapel Hill, Chapel Hill, NC 27599-3175 USA
whitton@cs.unc.edu

Karl-Petter Åkesson
Swedish Institute of Computer Science, Box 1263, SE-164 29, Kista,
Sweden
kalle@sics.se

Acknowledgements

The authors would like to thank FX Palo Alto Laboratory Inc., XRCE Grenoble and Napier University for supporting the work that went into this book. We would also like to thank our authors for all the work they put into their chapters, and their patience as we sent them comments and suggested changes. Our thanks also go to the reviewers who helped us by providing comments on the chapters, and the series editors for their support and comments on earlier drafts of the book. Thanks are due to Rosie Kemp of Springer for suggesting that we do this book and to Karen Barker for her patience, encouragement and advice on the production of this volume. We also owe a debt of gratitude to the many people and organizations who have helped with the CVE conferences – notably Steve Benford for his support and encouragement, the departments of psychology and computer science at Nottingham University for supporting CVE'96 at Nottingham, and Jeni Tennison, Adrian West and Steve Pettifer for helping us with the organization of CVE'98 in Manchester.

Preface

Collaborative Virtual Environments (CVEs) are online digital places and spaces where we can be in touch, play together and work together, even when we are, geographically speaking, worlds apart. We can hang out, present alternative selves, interact with realistic and fantastic objects and carry out impossible manoeuvres. In CVEs we can share the experience of worlds beyond the physical.

This book offers an introduction to up-to-date research in the area of CVE design and development. A reader might feel that, collectively, the chapters in this book beg the questions "What is a CVE?". And, for that matter, "What isn't a CVE?". These are good questions, which invoke many different responses. What is certain is that CVEs are the perfect arena for gaining insights into human–human communication and collaboration, collaborative interaction with (virtual and real) objects, the effect of (potentially differing) embodiments, and the nature of place and space.

Central to our work and to the work of the authors in this volume is the belief that putting people "into the loop" – explicitly considering human–human and human–environment interaction in the design and development process – is central to the design of any technology, and especially to the design of CVEs. In the case of CVEs this means actually putting people into the worlds, and many of our authors talk explicitly about their experiences and the experiences of study participants in virtual environments.

The idea for this book came about when Rosie Kemp of Springer approached one of us, Elizabeth, following CVE'98, the second Collaborative Virtual Environments conference that Elizabeth and Dave had organized. CVE'98 was held in Manchester, UK, in June 1998; it followed CVE'96, which took place in Nottingham in September 1996. These conferences were the first to focus on the collaborative aspects of virtual environments and enabled us to meet many of the authors whose work you will find in this book.

It was at CVE'98 that Elizabeth and Dave had the pleasure of meeting Alan – and our three-way alliance was born. And given that we have been geographically separated while editing this book, we have experienced at first hand the need for good collaborative tools and shared environments. Over the months we have used phones (both fixed-line and mobile), email, text-based virtual environments, online shared spaces (especially eGroups at http://www.egroups.com/), faxes, answering machine messages and good old "snail mail". To date these are in general easier to set up and use than most collaborative virtual environments. But, as this book and the material presented at the CVE conferences testify, this will not always be the case.

We are now poised for CVE2000, which will be held in San Francisco – this time we have the backing of the Association of Computing Machinery (the ACM – http://www.acm.org/).

And now to business. We hope you enjoy the book, and the worlds described herein.

Elizabeth, Dave and Alan
San Francisco, Grenoble and Glasgow
June 2000

Part 1
Collaborative Virtual Environments (CVEs): Histories, Perspectives and Issues

Chapter 1
Collaborative Virtual Environments: Digital Spaces and Places for CSCW: An Introduction

Dave Snowdon, Elizabeth F. Churchill and Alan J. Munro

1.1 Introduction

In the late 1980s Virtual Reality (VR) burst onto the public stage propelled by a wave of media interest and related science fiction novels such as *Neuromancer* by William Gibson (Gibson, 1989). VR promised to revolutionize the way in which we experience and interact with computers, and research into the field mushroomed. More recently, the hype surrounding VR has died down and, although it is receiving less public attention, serious work is continuing with the aim of producing useful and usable technology. At the centre of current work related to VR is the field of Collaborative Virtual Environments (CVEs). This field has as its goal the provision of new, more effective means of using computers as tools for communication and information sharing with others. Many CVE systems have been constructed. Some of these are desktop systems and applications; but large public virtual spaces have also been constructed (such as AlphaWorld at http://www.activeworlds.com/; see Chapter 15). CVEs are also being used to experiment with new forms of art and interactive television (Benford *et al.*, 1997a,b; Benford *et al.*, 2000a).

In 1996 the first international conference on CVEs took place in Nottingham, UK – this received an enthusiastic reception and was followed in 1998 by CVE'98. Two special issues of the journal *Virtual Reality. Research, Development and Applications* on Collaborative Virtual Environments followed, published in 1998 and 1999. At the time of writing, CVE 2000 is being planned and will take place in San Francisco in September 2000, with sponsorship from the Association of Computing Machinery (ACM – http://www.acm.org/). Given this increasing interest, we felt that now is an appropriate time to collect together a book that can serve as an introduction to this broad and rapidly developing field.

In editing this book, we aim to give a broad introduction to Collaborative Virtual Environments and how they can bring people together and allow them to communicate. By communication we do not just mean text or audio conversations, but we also wish to consider how artefacts and embodiments are also an essential aspect of communication, and thus how the representation of people and artefacts such as documents and tools within CVEs can facilitate communication. Our goal is for readers to get a better feel for why CVEs are an interesting subject, where CVEs can be applied to support collaborative applications, the important aspects of the research in these environments, the current state of the art, and where research and technical developments are heading. In addition, this book is multi-disciplinary – that is, rather than focus only on computer science issues, we have aimed to show how the field of CVE design and development is actively informed by other disciplines, such as psychology, sociology, work practice studies, architecture, artificial intelligence and art. We also intend to maintain a broad perspective in our choice of technology – there are many existing books on 3D Virtual Reality technology (e.g. Anders, 1998; Rheingold, 1992; Vince, 1998; Weishar, 1998) and we do not aim to duplicate them. Rather, we will show how other technologies, such as text-based virtual environments, can also be valid and usefully classified as CVEs (see Curtis, 1996; Curtis and Nichols, 1992; and Chapter 14 of this volume). Further, we would like to note that our focus is on the design and hands-on use of specific technologies. There are many fascinating books that theorize about the impact of these (and related) emerging technologies from social and socio-political perspectives (examples include Crang *et al.*, 1999; Porter, 1997; Kolko *et al.*, 2000). We point readers to these volumes for in-depth social and cultural analyses and critiques.

We have organized the book into a number of sections in order to group together related chapters. However, since CVEs are such an interdisciplinary field there are many links between chapters in different sections and the reader should bear in mind that this grouping is a guide and based on our personal judgement. In the remainder of this chapter we will introduce some of the background behind CVEs and the groupings that we have chosen.

1.1.1 What are Collaborative Virtual Environments? A Broad Definition

Information sharing is central to collaborative work. CVEs can help with information sharing and communication tasks because of the way in which they provide a context for communication and information sharing to take place. However, before we go deeper into the nature of CVEs it is first necessary to define what we mean by a *Collaborative Virtual Environment*. Here is one definition of a CVE that probably fits many people's expectations and is in line with the descriptions found in books such as *Neuromancer* (Gibson, 1989):

> Collaborative virtual environments are distributed virtual reality systems that offer graphically realized, potentially infinite, digital landscapes. Within these landscapes, individuals can share information through interaction with each other and through individual and collaborative interaction with data representation.

While this is not a bad definition, we have found it a little restrictive. Here is the definition that we have been using as the introduction to the current CVE conference:

> A CVE is a computer-based, distributed, virtual space or set of places. In such places, people can meet and interact with others, with agents or with virtual objects. CVEs might vary in their representational richness from 3D graphical spaces, 2.5D and 2D environments, to text-based environments. Access to CVEs is by no means limited to desktop devices, but might well include mobile or wearable devices, public kiosks, etc.

This definition makes it clear that although CVEs are normally associated with 3D graphical environments this need not necessarily always be the case. In the next sections we reflect further on what we mean by Collaborative Virtual Environments, focusing on the nature of environment and what it means for activity, and the nature of collaboration and collaborative work. Following this, we will outline the sections of the book.

1.2 Collaborative Virtual Environments: Some Considerations

1.2.1 Virtual Environments as Places for Action and Interaction

CVEs represent a shift in interacting with computers in that they provide a space that contains or encompasses data representations *and* users. Elsewhere we have noted (Churchill and Snowdon, 1998):

> CVEs represent the computer as a malleable *space,* a space *in which* to build and utilize shared places for work and leisure. CVEs provide a terrain or digital land-scape that can be 'inhabited' or 'populated' by individuals and data, encouraging a sense of shared space or place. Users, in the form of embodiments or avatars, are free to navigate *through* the space, encountering each other, artefacts and data objects and are free to communicate with each using verbal and non-verbal communication through visual and auditory channels.

Figure 1.1 shows a virtual landscape that consists of a central circle or platform. Two avatars or embodiments are currently inhabiting the virtual space – an angel and a round, floating, face. Both of the embodiments can navigate through the space; they can see each other and can both see the landscape clearly. They can interact through audio connections and can orient their bodies to each other. Evidence suggests that people often orient their virtual embodiments toward each other in ways that approximate real-life interactions (Smith *et al.*, 2000). A number of chapters in this volume detail issues involved in using such embodiments within virtual space to interact with others and with virtual objects (for example see Chapters 5 and 7).

Of course, being a digital landscape, it is possible for digital embodiments to behave in ways that our physical counterparts cannot: the rules of "real world" physics do not apply here. In Fig. 1.2 we see a number of virtual embodiments that have floated seamlessly through the floor and now reside *below* the ground plane. Much work is currently ongoing considering what the correct models are for designing collision detection between virtual objects including embodiments, walls and floors within virtual worlds. In this volume, Chapter 3 offers a discussion some of the issues involved in creating such virtual world physics.

However, it takes more than provision of the digital landscape to create digital spaces places that are fit for human–human interaction. Indeed, there has been much debate in recent years about the very nature of space and place in physical and in digital settings (Harrison and Dourish, 1996). Although virtual environments are often assumed to be spaces and most utilize spatial metaphors, there is

Figure 1.1 Embodiments in a digital landscape. From the event "MASSIVE" at the Nottingham NOWninety6 arts festival in London. (copyright Nottingham University, Nottingham UK, 1996. All Rights Reserved.)

an important distinction between space and place. A space is a physical (or digital) volume or container that can house artefacts and in which events can take place. However, one physical space can host several places over time; a sports hall can be a place for playing sport, a place for prize-giving, a place for a student play, a place for a jumble sale and a place for a dance class. Although the physical space is the same, there are multiple understandings of how that space is to be used, depending on the occasion. There are also multiple ways of interacting and behaving in that space depending on the occasion or activity for which the space is being used. In contrast to our notions of "space", "place" has inherent within it a notion of the activities that occur there – activities that *take place* there. The space only becomes a "place" when an understood activity is scheduled or ongoing. Thus, space and place do not share a 1:1 mapping (Munro, 1999). A space can also be seen as a different place at one and the same time, depending on how it is "read". For example, inner city gangs use and read graffiti as markers of territories for activity (Munro, 1999). These physical spaces will have entirely different meanings for the different gangs in terms of whether one is in "home" or "enemy" territory (e.g. Armstrong, 1988). The way the graffiti is read is partly to do with its location – if in the territory of the enemy gang, it is regarded as a great success by those committing the incursion

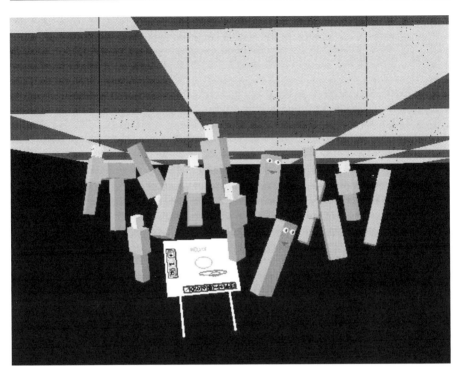

Figure 1.2 Virtual corpses below the digital "land" plane. (Copyright Swedish Institute of Computer Science, Sweden, 1996. All Rights Reserved.)

(Patrick, 1973). Thus a physical space may have many different meanings and modes of inhabitancy depending on one's reading of that space.

Some technologies, such as media-spaces, are focused on connecting different physical *places* without having a corresponding notion of spatiality, virtual or otherwise (Harrison and Dourish, 1996; see also Dourish *et al.*, 1996). Some cases, such as the CAVE system described in Chapter 12, illustrate how spaces and places can be combined in various ways – the CAVE is a real-world physical space that acts as a place in which users can experience virtual spaces and places. In the CAVE, users must negotiate both virtual and real spaces but can share their experiences with others in a way not possible in CVE systems based on head-mounted displays (HMDs), in which the user interface isolates users from the real world. Text-based CVEs can create spaces (rooms) that have only a textual (described) spatial geometry but which are certainly places in which people meet, talk, work and play (Churchill and Bly, 1999a,b,c and Chapters 13 and 14 of this volume). These virtual text-based rooms achieve their sense of place because they are used over time, because inhabitants have both planned and unplanned meetings there and because such meetings have a sense of continuity – the social conventions that make a space a place develop in these circumstances (see Chapter 14). Spaces become places when they are associated with living and lived experiences (Giddens, 1984). Places are imbued with meanings that underpin how we behave there – like the "enemy" and "home" notions above, places can be public or private for example (see de Certeau *et al.*, 1998, on concepts like the "neighbourhood"). Some technologies, such as 3D virtual environments, are inherently spatial, and it could be argued that some 3D virtual environments suffer because they depend too much on *space* without supporting the creation of a sense of *place*. CVEs need to support the *evolution of places for interaction*, and not simply provide spaces where interaction can take place, if they are to be successful in the long term.

Further, if we are to support multiple groups within a virtual space, appropriate landscapes in which varying activities can occur must be designed and developed. These digital landscapes will have many differing places for interaction, supporting many concurrent ongoing activities with multiple groupings of people. Sometimes the places will be bordered by digital walls or separated through the use of distance (see Chapter 15 for a consideration of virtual walls and boundaried digital spaces). That is not to say such places can be reliably *designed* or predetermined. As noted by Roderick Nash (1973; cited in Crandell, 1993) when discussing the evolution of the physical landscape:

> No group sets to create a landscape, of course. What it sets out to do is to create a community, and the landscape as its visible manifestation is simply the by-product of people working and living, sometimes coming together, sometimes staying apart, but always recognizing their interdependence.

Similarly, Harrison and Dourish (1996) note the appropriation of technologies that occurred in many media space experiments. Often in such situations such appropriation means that, in the end, the use of the technologies differs from that which is *intended* by designers at the beginning. We believe that CVEs will evolve through use, and places therein will come and go. This kind of ebb and flow of activity in virtual places has been observed in text-based worlds (Cherny, 1999; Churchill and Bly, 1999b).

1.2.2 Collaborative Work in Virtual Spaces and Places

Elsewhere we have argued that CVE systems and applications must go beyond being "cool" and having aesthetic appeal, and will only become everyday places for action and interaction if they are designed to serve a purpose (Churchill and Snowdon, 1998). Specifically, in order to support collaborative and cooperative activities, it is important that virtual environments offer the means to access (task-) appropriate information as well as communication tools.

Although it is important not to try to simply replicate what we think of as "reality", when designing systems to support collaborative work we can learn a great deal from observations of people working and collaborating together in conventional settings (Bowers and Martin, 1999; Engeström and Middleton, 1996; Moran and Anderson, 1990; Heath and Luff, 1991). In all "real world" domains, collaborative work involves the interleaving of individual and group effort, so collaborative work involves considerable complex information exchange (Bellotti and Rogers, 1997; Harper, 1997; Heath and Luff, 1991; Heath and Luff, 1996; Hutchins, 1990; Hutchins and Klausen, 1996; Suchman, 1996). These interleaved, singular-to-shared activities require considerable explicit and tacit communication between collaborators to be successful. Individuals need to negotiate shared understandings of task goals, of task decomposition and sub-task allocation, and of task/sub-task progress. It is important that collaborators know what is currently being done and what has been done in the context of the task goals. Until recently, most CVEs have been used as meeting places where group activities are the central task (e.g. Greenhalgh, 1997b). Recent work, however, has been aimed at supporting the kind of situation described above, where more complex, interleaved individual and collaborative activities can be carried out within one VE with team members moving continually between individual and collaborative activities (see Chapter 6).

We have noted that such observations point to a number of key features that software should aim to support (see Churchill and Snowdon, 1998). To summarize, these are:

- Shared context

- Awareness of others

- Negotiation and communication

- Flexible and multiple viewpoints

Sharing Context

Shared context is crucial for collaborative activities. "Shared context" can mean many things; it can mean shared knowledge of each other's current activities, shared knowledge of others' past activities, shared artefacts and shared environment. Together, these lead to shared understandings. Shared physical spaces and familiar places facilitate or "afford" shared understandings. As Gaver (1992) states

> in the everyday world, collaboration is situated within a shared, encompassing space, one which is rich with perceptual information about objects and events that can be explored and manipulated

Within these shared spaces, focused and unfocused collaboration is accomplished through alignment towards the focal area of the shared activity, such as a shared document (Heath and Luff, 1996), and through gestures like pointing toward portions of the document for added emphasis and clarity. When artefacts are shared, not only do they become the subject of communication between users, but also the medium of communication; as one user manipulates an object, changes to it are visible to others in an externalization of the processes of change. For the design of systems to support collaborative work, this means that shared artefacts should be visible and available for local negotiation (Dix, 1994; Heath and Luff, 1996) and often the current focus of attention should be indicated. This can drive subsequent activities. Where actions are not physically co-located and co-temporal, providing shared context is more difficult. It is also important to share context in asynchronous work collaborations through meeting capture, version control and so on; such tools provide activity audits and "awareness" of others' activities, which in turn provides a sense of shared context. In many CVEs, it is also possible to leave text, audio or video messages that can be played back.

Awareness of Others

There are several ways of conceptualizing "awareness". For example, Dourish and Bellotti (1992) state that awareness is an "understanding of the activities of others, which provides a context for your own activity". Such a view of awareness centralizes intentional awareness. Tacit or background awareness involves consideration of peripheral as well as focused attention and more accurately characterizes what occurs when team members are engaged in parallel but independent ongoing activities. In contrast to intentional awareness, such tasks often require moment-to-moment peripheral coordination (Kendon, 1990). For example air traffic controllers are not aware of each other's moment-to-moment activities, but peripheral vision and background sound all provide information such that if a disruption occurs, unplanned collaborative activities can ensue (see also Heath and Luff's (1996) analysis of London Underground workers). Some consideration of providing such moment-to-moment awareness or sense of co-presence exists in work on video portholes and video tunnels where offices are linked with video cameras and monitors (Buxton and Moran, 1990; Dourish *et al.*, 1996; Gaver, 1992). Awareness can also relate to activities outside of the current task context where one is interested in the activities of a collaborator who is not currently present and who may not be working on the shared task. Often we need to know where to get hold of someone and/or need to adjust our plans on the basis of when someone will be back. In everyday life, voice mail, answering services, answer phones and vacation email messages play this role.

Negotiation and Communication

Conversations are crucial for negotiation and communication about collaborative activities. Collaborative work requires the negotiation not only of task-related content, but also of task structure in terms of roles and activities and task/sub-task allocations. Further, informal conversations underpin the social fabric that sustains ongoing collaborative relationships. Studies of conversation have demonstrated the extent to which explicit hand gestures and head nods, eye gaze and eyebrow raises determine the way in which utterances are interpreted[1]. As well as these "backchannel" gestures that punctuate and give meaning to many conversational utterances, cues from dress, posture and (often culturally determined) mannerisms provide much of the background context for our interpretations of verbal negotiations (Hewstone *et al.*, 1988; Kendon, 1990).

In graphical CVEs such backchannel gestures are often hard to achieve with embodiments where nuanced subtle gesturing is not easily supported. This can

---

[1] See Cassell *et al.* (2000) for a number of chapters that detail nonverbal channels of communication.

cause disruptions in conversational flow (see Chapter 7). Further, until it is easier for the users of CVEs themselves to fashion embodiments easily, embodiments will not be tailorable and will not offer as many options for giving personalized indications of one's cultural and personal identifications. This has been raised as an issue in the context of representations of gender and race within the broader cyberculture in which CVEs sit (Kolko *et al.*, 2000). In text-based CVEs such cues are often provided explicitly in text (see Chapter 13 for a consideration of cultures in text-based CVEs).

Flexible and Multiple Viewpoints

Tasks often require use of multiple representations, each tailored to a different points of view and different subtasks. For example, Bellotti and Rogers (1997) offer a detailed analysis of the production of a daily newspaper. In this process many different representations are used to design the layout of the paper; these vary from hand-drawn to computer-generated and reflect different task requirements. In certain cases, one individual may require multiple representations to reflect different aspects of their task(s), while in other cases different individuals may require tailored representations to provide information specific to their tasks. In many of the chapters in this volume authors detail provision of multiple views and the support of alternative representations to suit the different roles people are taking and the different information they require (e.g. Chapters 8 and 9; and Greenhalgh and Benford, 1995).

1.2.3 Recreational CVEs

Although our main focus in this book is on collaborative and cooperative work within CVEs, of course CVEs can be used for recreation too. Multi-user games such as Doom and Quake (by id software) provide some of the most effective (and violent) demonstrations of the use of commodity hardware to produce an immersive experience. Watch someone playing Quake and you will see them move their body in an attempt to dodge fire from their opponents even though this (physical) action has no effect on their virtual body. Tap such a person on the shoulder and they will typically almost leap out of their seat – such is the shock of the forced transition from being absorbed in the virtual world to being dragged into the real world. Not all recreational CVEs need be violent though – Chapter 10 describes how "the blob", an amorphous pulsating virtual object, can provide a way to help young children create stories.

Another example of a recreational but non-violent CVE is the "Second World" (Le Deuxième Monde), the first European 3D virtual community, which is hosted on CANAL+'s Web site (http://virtuel.cplus.fr/). The Second World takes the form of a virtual Paris rendered in photo-realistic quality (see Figs. 1.3 and 1.4). Access to the Second World is open to everyone, requiring a simple download of a Web browser plug-in from Blaxxun. The Second World already has more than

Figure 1.3 Paris from "Le Deuxieme Monde" (the Second World) views of virtual Paris. (Copyright Canal+, All Rights Reserved.)

Figure 1.4 Paris again, from "Le Deuxieme Monde" (the Second World) views of virtual Paris. (Copyright Canal+, All Rights Reserved.)

22 000 "citizens" who meet daily, participate in discussions and benefit from events staged in the environment. Users have a free choice of the appearance of their avatars. More than being simply visitors, the citizens can build their own personal spaces while CANAL+ takes care of the representation of the principal districts of Paris. Celebrities are regularly invited to take part in events in the Second World, such as games, quizzes and discussion forums. There are also clubs organized by the inhabitants of the Second World and exhibitions organized by other organizations, such as the galleries of the Louvre in 3D created by employees of the museum.

The Second World is interesting in another respect because the community created is not simply virtual. Second World citizens regularly stage meetings in the real world and can travel large distances to take part. Such crossover is often seen in communities that build up over time and where interactions are ongoing (e.g. Mynatt *et al.*, 1998, 1999; Preece, 1999).

1.3 Themes Covered in the Book

1.3.1 Bodies, Presence and Interactions

In a spatial CVE it is almost a given that a user is represented by an avatar; however, there are many problems which may not be obvious at first, such as how well users can understand someone's actions and point of view judging solely by their view of that person's avatar. Chapters 6 and 7 highlight some of the problems with avatars in collaborative spaces and show two differing ways in which to control one's avatar. In Chapter 7, the user deals at a fine-grained level with every aspect of his or her avatar, and we can see both the opportunities and difficulties inherent in this approach. Granted, one has fine-grained controllability, but in the circumstances, owing to a number of factors such as lack of view, this is not as powerful as it might be.

We can see from Chapter 3 that it is almost an impossibility to get true real-time pictures of one's own and another's avatar. If it were possible, we would in effect be breaking the physical limits of the speed of light and consequently electrons travelling in a network. Any solution to this in terms of software fixes, such as anticipating user behaviour, will have, as Chapter 3 points out, implications for the granularity of our control of the avatar, whether physical (e.g. a robot in the real world) or virtual. Chapter 3 points out the very real implications for other fields, such as tele-robotics.

Chapter 6 addresses this question from a different angle, asking, in effect, why we would want to control our avatar closely in the first place. The authors liken the avatar to a motor vehicle, and note that when we drive, our cognitive processes are largely taken up with driving. It is often difficult, they say, even to hold a conversation with another person in a car if one is driving at the same time. Looking at it this way, they wonder how we are meant to "drive" avatars *and* also do a number of different things in the space, such as the banal everyday tasks of holding conversations or collaborating on a piece of work. The solution is, in their words, to "let the system do the walking". The user's responsibility for controlling their avatar is removed and made a task of the system. In their general contact space, and in their meeting space, users do not have close control of their avatars. Rather, if they wish to do certain things, like leave, the system makes the avatar go through a series of stereotyped preparatory behaviours, such as gathering papers together, lining them up on the desk, and then getting up.

In allowing the system this control through scripting of stereotyped behaviours, it takes the onus off the user for fine-grained control. Thus it should be possible, the authors suggest, to access such a system from both a high-end machine and also a lower end machine with a modem, or even some kind of mobile device.

This solution has a number of implications: it allows a certain freedom of the user from the basics of interaction, but creates a number of burdens on the design of the repertoire of behaviours. The behavioural repertoire will have to be flexible, or limited to a small number of domain-specific behaviours, which could limit the system's usefulness. At the moment, this system is not yet in serious use, so it will be interesting to see what issues come up. Would such a solution even work in a more "spatial" CVE like MASSIVE, where the user is required to do a more spatial task? How would one begin to design a putative system that had the sort of repertoire of behaviours needed for a more spatial CVE?

We also need to pose the question "are avatars always the best way to represent a user?". In Chapter 11 it is argued that there are cases in which avatars simply get in the way and a simpler representation is more effective. The authors also argue for the use of additional media such as video running in parallel with the CVE to give a richer understanding of the actions of remote participants. This argument is further reinforced in Chapter 2, in which the authors argue that it is necessary to provide a stronger integration between CVEs and the use of other media.

1.3.2 I Know What I See, but What Do *You* See?

In the real world people have very sophisticated spatial reasoning skills. These are used to allow people to perform tasks effectively but also to enable social situations to occur smoothly with the minimum of explicit (verbal) negotiation. In comparison with the real world, virtual environments are impoverished in terms of the information that they feed to our senses – a person in a virtual environment is reduced to "tunnel vision" and sees a much simplified world without many of the cues that are (unconsciously) so helpful in the real world, such as shadows, subtle sounds, rich lighting and colours, and proprioception. This sensual lack can lead to a number of problems for the virtual inhabitant that may not be obvious at first glance. Chapters 5 and 7 highlight some of these problems and the ways in which people attempt to cope with them. In this section we have two chapters that consider these issues from a more technical viewpoint. Chapter 9 describes Kansas, a flat 2D world in which the presentation is so ordered that it is easy for people to deduce what is seen by others – in fact the views of others are superimposed on the world in a 2D equivalent of the visible view frustums proposed in Chapter 7. Although in Kansas some users can see objects not available to others, when users' view areas overlap it is clear who can see what and that all users see the objects in the same way.

However, given that virtual environments are not constrained by the real world there are cases in which it might use useful to take advantage of the fact that users don't necessarily see the same things – something which is usually explicitly minimized in CVE systems. Chapter 8 demonstrates how subjective elements can be explicitly added to CVE systems in order to let people customize their view while still remaining in contact with other people – who, except in the case of people suffering from sensory dysfunction, does not occur in the real-world. This theme of subjectivity is also taken up in Chapter 12, which also illustrates that it is not always desirable for every user to experience the world in the same way.

1.3.3 Technical Issues and System Challenges

Unfortunately we must live in a (real) world with imperfect hardware and physical constraints. The speed of light imposes a minimum time to send a message to someone – while we normally do not notice such delays, if the person is on the other side of the world these delays can become perceptible. Even worse, we are not just limited by the speed of light but by network performance, which means that we will often experience delays far worse than simply those imposed by the speed of light. And this is not all: the real world is of such richness that a computer does not yet exist with the performance to even approach a realistic modelling and rendering of it. Finally, despite the hype surrounding VR current interface devices are often anything but *natural* to use; our day-to-day skills from interacting in the physical ("real") world do not easily transfer to interactions with and within VR worlds. With all these limitations where does that leave us? How can we make the best of what we've got? Given that we can't have perfection, can we at least choose where to have the imperfections? It is these and other similar issues that the chapters in this section will try to respond to. Chapter 3 provides a road map of the way ahead for CVE systems and indicates where designers need to focus their attention in future. Chapter 4 shows us how, in a world of imperfect networking, we can choose where to make our trade-offs.

Historically, VR systems were conceived as being worlds apart, not only in what they presented to the user but also in the ways they interacted with the rest of the user's computing systems. If you wanted to discuss a document in a meeting taking place in a CVE then that document had to have an application that could represent it in the CVE. This is one factor implicated in the slow uptake of CVE systems in general use, and Chapter 2 shows why this way of organizing a CVE system is such a mistake.

1.3.4 So, Now We're in a CVE What Do We Do?

So far, the chapters in this book have presented a number of features of CVEs, both negative and positive, and shown some of the impact that the underlying system can have on the user's experience and how user requirements drive systems design. In this section we would like to present some applications that illustrate why we should go to all this trouble and what people gain from using CVEs.

Generally, there is an impetus for considering the use of CVEs for work. As noted above, many studies have pointed out many examples of co-located work that is achieved by the participants communicating with each other, and able to look at and manipulate some mutually available workplace artefact. These artefacts can be as diverse as timetables, displays of train lines or of stock movements in the stock exchange, or even parts of a person who is being operated on by diverse medical and nursing professionals. As Chapter 7 points out, the promise of a CVE is the ability to manipulate these virtual objects and share them with remote partners.

We may, then, be able to utilize and share "physical" or, as Chapter 7 points out, *visual* elements of our work – such diverse things as architectural visualizations, whiteboards, X-ray slides, video images and even "3D objects and animations intended for the 3D world itself". In each case, there are supporting arguments for the benefits of the ability to collaborate around these artefacts while geographically remote.

However, this may not be all we can do. If we incorporate physical objects in some way into the CVE we can actually manipulate them. Such an object-focused element in a CVE promises much. An example of an early version of such a CVE is that discussed in Chapter 11. This chapter describes how a hybrid CVE/media-space system can allow scientists to collaborate in ways similar to how they would naturally collaborate around rare pieces of equipment in the real world. Given that a particular country might only have a very small number (if any) of certain types of exotic equipment, this illustrates how CVE systems can fulfil a real need. Continuing on the scientific theme, Chapter 12 illustrates how CVEs can be used for scientific visualization and education and Chapter 10 shows a 3D interface to support Web browsing.

1.3.5 Emerging and Existing Virtual Cultures

While it may be a truism that, deep down, people are all the same, it is also true that people act differently in different situations. A typical example is how a person will behave at home, at work and at a football match. Each situation lends itself to a different behaviour. Also, each situation will often be experienced with different people. People's behaviour may (will) evolve over time as they grow accustomed to a situation and group of people – for example the newcomer in the office may be quieter than normal until he or she learns how to get on with their new colleagues. As we have noted above, social activity depends on place, people and time and combinations of these will gradually evolve a set of (normally) unspoken and implicit rules that demarcate regions for activity and govern conduct (Giddens, 1984; Harrison and Dourish, 1996; Munro, 1999; de Certeau *et al.*, 1998).

Since CVEs construct places and involve multiple people, it is perhaps not surprising to see customs and cultures emerge that are built around virtual places. For a simple proof of this, one only has to sample some of the mailing lists and

USENET newsgroups available on the Internet – each group has its own customs and accepted behaviours (e.g. Mynatt *et al.*, 1998, 1999; Preece, 1999). Given the richness of a CVE (text or graphical) compared to a mailing list or newsgroup we should expect to see cultures form in long-lived CVEs, and this indeed proves to be the case. Chapter 14 illustrates how a work-related CVE supports social interaction that in turn supports collaborative work. Chapter 15 describes how a virtual office allows the author to make himself available to others in ways not previously possible. Finally, Chapter 13 describes an experiment in which people are assigned specific roles in a virtual culture and given the chance to experience life from a viewpoint that might normally be unavailable to them.

1.4 Summary

In this chapter we have tried to provide a basic introduction to some of the issues that we consider are most important for CVEs at the current time. We have not tried to discuss virtual environments in general, since there are already many good books on the subject. Instead, we have focused on the challenges required to go from a single user environment to one that can actually support rich and meaningful communication and collaboration between groups of people. We have divided the book into a number of sections, each of which represents a particular theme, such as representations of self and other, understanding the viewpoints of others, technical challenges, applications and emerging cultures in CVEs. We hope that the following chapters prove useful and informative.

Part 2
Technical Issues and System Challenges

Chapter 2
Extending the Limits of Collaborative Virtual Environments

Mike Robinson, Samuli Pekkola, Jonni Korhonen, Saku Hujala, Tero Toivonen and Markku-Juhani O. Saarinen

2.1 Introduction

This chapter is about extending CVEs to include more people and more objects in more media. Fundamentally the story goes like this.

More people. Current generations of CVEs are limited by server capacity to between 8 and 20 mutually aware participants (up to 64 in the latest version of Quake). Peer-to-peer and multicast systems, such as MASSIVE I and II face similar limits from bandwidth capacity (Greenhalgh and Benford, 1995). In the latter case, the communication service degeneration is worse as numbers exceed the limits, so we will confine our explicit remarks to server-based systems. Larger numbers of people may be graphically represented (e.g. as a crowd in the distance), but are not participants. The problem is a long pause in service while a participant is switched from one server to another. Where many participants are split over several servers, a pause problem occurs when a person on one server wishes to interact with someone on another server. The worst case is when one or more people wish to address people on several servers in quick succession. The interactions intended by the circled character in Fig. 2.1 just cannot be done. While this seems like a technical issue, it means that events such as large auctions, festivals or rock concerts have limited interactive potential. We suggest one method of overcoming this restriction, under the heading "upward scalability".

Once upward scalability to thousands of people can be achieved, another very interesting story opens – "sideways scalability". In everyday life, at any moment, we are usually aware of a small handful of people – a tiny subset of the total number of colleagues, contacts, acquaintances, friends and family. But we move easily and fluently between such socialities. We reconfigure our people awarenesses on the fly. Current generations of CVEs are not good at this. However, upward scalability can achieve a more meaningful representation of thousands of people in a much wider sense than the crowds at festivals. The thousands might be the many layers of employees and customers in a large e-enterprise. All can be brought into the "same" CVE in the way that small numbers can now. The trick here is not just to support very large worlds, although this is a worthwhile technical achievement in itself. We can now move through the large world, reselecting people, constructing a new momentary sociality, and reconfiguring our people awarenesses on the fly.

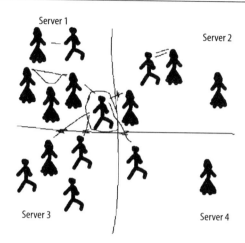

Figure 2.1 Falling between servers.

Upward scalability (*more people*) is a precondition of sideways scalability (*different people*).

More objects. Current generations of VR CVEs provide varying degrees of richness. Some worlds are exquisitely detailed, while others are relatively bare. Sometimes there is provision for creating and adding artefacts to the world. However, the artefacts are, with the exception of documents and CDs, VR artefacts. They have no connection to or counterpart in the real world. We stress that we are talking about VR CVEs here. Non-CVE VRs are often renderings of objects (buildings, landscapes, molecules etc.) in the world. Similarly, some non-VR CVEs (e.g. virtual offices) are about handling objects, documents etc. We propose augmenting the ability to handle external objects in VR CVEs – partly because we believe CVEs are a natural home for the avatars of net-connected fridges, cookers, heating and lighting systems, printers, cars, phones etc. In brief, CVEs need *more and different* objects.

More media. VR is VR is VR (Fig. 2.2). With a few exceptions, such as the mixed reality work at Nottingham, other media are not considered. Where they are

Figure 2.2 A VR-centric view.

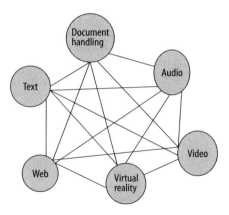

Figure 2.3 A media-centric view.

considered, VR tends to be the access point for moving into other media, e.g. opening a video stream from a video icon in the VR. Similarly, audio, where available in CVEs, tends to be audio *within* the CVE. This leads to a vision centred on VR, which forms the interface, navigation and transition point between media and communication modalities.

This picture should be revised in the light of lessons from Computer-Supported Cooperative Work (CSCW) and, it must be said, some common sense. VR is one medium among many. Any user may start from *any* medium that they happen to be using and wish to add or move to *any* other (Fig. 2.3).

We believe this design emphasis shift will lead to much more useful applications.

More awareness. The combination of more objects and more people and more media means more awareness. This will be considered at length later. For the moment it is enough to say:

- Foreground and background awareness of other people, their activity, and the objects on which they act is central to competent action in everyday life, at work, at leisure and at home.

- Awareness of other people is supported and amplified in CVEs – but the objects of the activity are largely missing. (*More objects*)

- Awareness of objects is supported and amplified by many computer applications, Internet and otherwise – but other people are largely absent. (*More people*)

- The same strange bifurcation (either people or objects) is found generally in media-mediated awareness. Texts and Web pages do not let us know who else is reading them. Videoconferencing has notorious difficulties in sharing views on objects. Audio communication applications generally have no ability to view the objects being talked about. VR and other interactive CVEs (as we have noted already) lose many classes of significant objects. (More objects and people *together*)

- People communicate through the most convenient medium at hand, and move to others as and when convenient. This is not a call to include more media within VR. It is a note that people have *no fixed (media) starting point*. CVE environments (and hence architectures) should allow people to move in from and out to other media at will. (*More media*)

More technology? Most of the technology needed for more people/objects/media is already with us. Some redesign is needed to pull them together in the sense we are already familiar with from awareness and competent action in everyday life. In the following sections, based on our experiences in the VIVA Core Project,[1] we sketch one possible architecture to approach the above targets.

The story and the telling. That was the story we wish to tell. The order of the telling will be different.

Section 2.2 deals with awareness of other people, something CVEs are already fairly good at. We will give an example of how people-awareness can be extended to another medium – the Web. The general lesson is that there is no other-than-technical reason why any medium should not become a CVE. This provides a *prima facie* reason for considering a multimedia architecture for CVEs.

Section 2.3 considers the question of multiple media in work practice, and with respect to CVEs. We give an example of the VIVA general architecture for CVEs in multiple media. This is followed by a brief comparison with other VR-CVE architectures.

Section 2.4, building on Section 2.3, shows how the architecture can be made upwardly scalable to arbitrarily large numbers of users. We then offer some speculations about how upward scalability may be the transitional step to two other desirable features. The first is sideways scalability, or the ability to move easily and fluently between social contexts, work and leisure environments; the ability to reconfigure (the CVE supporting) our people-awarenesses on the fly. The second is downward scalability, or the ability to extend the CVEs to include artefacts of low processing ability, such as mobile phones and net-connected fridges.

Section 2.5 reviews the above stories, moving to the desiderata for CVE design as a universal, scalable, interoperable, multiple-media option in all applications and communications media.

2.2 Support for Awareness of Other People

2.2.1 Understanding People-Awareness

The history of computer support for awareness of and communication with other people is littered with the corpses of "good ideas". For instance, the first visionary prediction for videoconferencing was by Arthur Mee in 1898:

> If, as it is said to be not unlikely in the near future, the principle of sight is applied to the telephone as well as sound, earth will be in truth a paradise, and distance will

---

[1] We gratefully acknowledge support from Nokia, Sonera, TEKES, and Jyväskylä Science Park.

lose its enchantment by being abolished altogether (The Pleasure Telephone, in *The Strand*, pp. 339–69).

The "Picturephone" has been part of the work at Bell Labs since the 1920s (Ives, 1930). In the early 1970s, forecasts were made that by the end of the decade a full 85% of meetings would be electronically mediated (Snyder, 1971). Egido (1988) lists dozens of optimistic projections for videoconferencing from the 1970s and 1980s – and contrasts them with the extremely small installed base and usage levels. In particular, she points out that, contrary to the claims of all vendors, *videoconferencing does not save travel costs or replace face-to-face meetings*. Where videoconferencing is successfully used, she found: "not a reduction in the amount of travel, but, rather, an increase in the number of meetings". The latest addition to the vision is the Microsoft freeware NetMeeting. Anyone with an Internet connection can have free international videoconferencing for a minimal outlay. Yet phone and email use continue to expand exponentially, while video connections remain flat – one is tempted to say, flat on its back. Designing communication and awareness media is trickier than it seems.

In an excellent paper appropriately titled "Turning away from talking heads" Bonnie Nardi and her colleagues (Nardi *et al.*, 1993) note the numerous ways in which video links are used in the real world. Video is extensively used for *providing data* in many industrial and medical settings. Video is used, for instance, to monitor plant and machine operations in remote locations (Tani *et al.*, 1992; Auramäki, 1996), in telerobotics and in remote surveillance (Milgram *et al.*, 1990).

Nardi *et al.* (1993) look at one particular use in the neurosurgical ward of a hospital. The operations take between 5 and 24 hours, and involve teams of neurosurgeons, nurses, anaesthesiologists, neurophysiologists, students and others. The operation itself is microsurgical, and the surgeon uses a microcamera inside the patient and 3D goggles to "see" what she is doing. The TV picture is relayed to monitors inside and outside the operating theatre. The monitors – the view of what is happening inside the patient – play a crucial coordinating role for the various staff involved in the operation. It allows smooth coordination between the surgeon and the nurses (e.g. which instrument is needed next, and when); with the anaesthesiologist (e.g. a change from working inside the head, where there are no nerves, to drilling bone calls for a change in the anaesthetic level); and with the neurophysiologist (e.g. to make better inferences from live graphs in the light of surgical events, changes in anaesthetic levels etc.). Several instances were observed in which participants used the video link in preference to physical presence (e.g. it was possible to hear what the surgeon was saying over the link, but not in the theatre; or it was only possible to monitor neuro-graphs and the operation simultaneously outside the theatre).

We can note several points from this and other studies.

- The account is based on a careful study of what people actually do, and how they appropriate and modify technology to support their work.

- The video is not used to look at the communication partner, but at the object they are communicating about.

- The video image is not self-evident, and considerable skill is needed to read it.

- Considerable time and care was needed in setting up the video equipment.

As Hollan and Stornetta (1992) note:

> ...a better way is not to focus on the *tele-* part but on the *communication* part. That is, to make the new medium satisfy the needs of communication so well that people, whether physically proximate or not, prefer to use it.

In the current climate of NASDAQ fever, "Picturephone" stories of user rejection are less widely told than they might be. One repository of such stories is CSCW. Here the combination of ethnography and technological experimentation has yielded many powerful lessons on computer-supported awareness with relevant others in work processes. We referenced the Nardi study above as our dream would be to construct a CVE that worked as well and as usefully as the home-made CVE in the hospital. The general lesson we draw is that people-awareness is a subtle issue in need of subtle treatment. "In your face" awareness of others is not often useful (a lesson videoconferencing and, dare we say, CVEs, should learn). We need to be aware of objects *with* people. The people *are* essential, but backgrounded, somehow on the periphery of awareness, available but not dominating.

A classic CSCW example is Heath and Luff's (1996) study of London Underground control. They described the fluent and skilled, but near subliminal, ways in which staff coordinated with each other in managing multiple technologies and keeping the train network safe and punctual. The study was the first to introduce the idea of "peripheral" or "out of the corner of the eye" awareness. Staff did their own work, apparently individual tasks, but were constantly using background awareness of others (visual or audio) for coordinating activity. Similar results have been reported by many researchers in many different work situations (e.g. Kasbi and Montmollin 1991; Suchman and Trigg 1991; Harper 1998; Patterson *et al.* 1999). These are convincing demonstrations that work practice involves background and foreground communication with others *woven into* the very fabric of "individual" work.

Despite this wealth of rich evidence, most applications, even "net-aware" applications, deal brutally and simplistically with communication *or* work objects/documents. The Web is a superb way of accessing and handling documents. But the communications facilities of the Net, from Internet Chat (IRC) to telephony to video, are *separate* applications. The lesson of CSCW for architecture and applications is that both objects (including documents, and representations of net-connected artefacts) and conversation about them (in whatever medium) need to be together, need to be seamlessly connected. We refer to such objects of conversation as "shared material" (for richer descriptions see Sørgaard (1988) and Robinson (1991)).

CVEs in general, whether VR (e.g. Becker and Mark, 1998) or text (e.g. Churchill and Bly, 1999a) potentially provide background awareness of/communication with others. Multi-user dungeons (MUDs) and object-oriented MUDS (MOOs), and a very few VRs (e.g. DIVE; Hagsand, 1996) provide some limited text/document accessing ability. The best CSCW attempt to provide a "virtual office" model that combines awareness, activity, and content has been provided by Berlage and Sohlenkamp (1999). Drawing on Robinson's (1993) notion of "common artefact", they develop the ACCT model, which identifies actors, contents, conversations and tools as the central components of a common artefact, arranged on a shared background. The elements of a common artefact provide both a background visualization of the activity, but also permit dynamic notification of particular events (Robinson, 1993, p. 207).

We draw on this thoughtful work in our own VIVA model to be considered later. Here the specific issue is the provision of background awareness of others with the possibility of communication in areas where it is so far lacking.

2.2.2 Support for People-Awareness

One feature of the VIVA virtual office, like the "Internet Foyer" (Benford *et al.* 1996a), is connectivity to the Web. Since Web protocols are designed to distribute documents across multiple platforms, there is no means to connect users with each other. Put simply, one does not know who is on the same page at the same time, and there is certainly no way of conversing with them. We wished to add people-awareness functionality to the Web, learning from CSCW and from earlier attempts to reach the same target. Among these were ICQ and Gooey, both of which show the presence of other people wherever they are in the Web. The disadvantage of both is that other visitors to the same pages are rarely seen, since to be visible requires a download which most people do not have. Another way of achieving people-awareness and possible conversation is provided in BSCW (Trevor *et al.*, 1997). From our point of view, this has the disadvantage that it is only available from, and requires pre-registration on, a BSCW site. It does not generalize to any Web page or set of pages.

We have utilized the CRACK! PeopleAwarenessEngine[2] (Robinson and Pekkola, 1999; Yu and Pekkola, 2000) to provide awareness of others on the same Web page/site at the same time. In this case, it is the page itself that is communication-enabled. No special effort of download or registration is required from the user. From the user's point of view, a simple counter (illustrated at the start of this section) shows the number of people currently on the page or set of pages (depending on the server configuration). People-awareness is provided as "peripheral awareness" that can be drawn on where relevant and ignored where not.

If the user clicks the counter, a list of concurrent users and related sites opens, from which the user may choose to "talk" with some, several or all other visitors. CRACK! is now on public release with these basic functionalities, and even in its current form enables any Web page to become a CVE. Exactly the same technique is used to support awareness of net-connected artefacts (printers, cars, fridges etc.) that are available for interaction. Recursively, clicking an artefact also shows the people connected to it.

---

[2] The CRACK! PeopleAwarenessEngine was developed independently of VIVA by @it Ltd.

Although background people-and-object-awareness/communication has so far only been implemented for the Web and an experimental net-connected artefact, we plan to extend the technique to documents and video. It is, for instance, one of the few features missing from the Nardi *et al.* hospital scenario, and we speculate that it could add unobtrusive but useful functionality to such systems. Nevertheless, the existing technique enables us to link Web pages directly to VIVA VR worlds, and vice versa. Those in the Web can be aware of each other, and of VR participants, and those in the VR can aware of Web users, as we mention again in the next section.

2.3 Support for Multiple Media

In this section, we briefly harness some lessons and theoretical grounding for multiple-media applications, and present an architecture that builds on them. An important feature is the presentation level integration. This supports new approaches to collaboration, involving arbitrary combinations of documents, people, media and access devices. The media for various types of communication, collaboration, work and play are the technological givens. Generically, although they come in many flavours, the media are documents, text, audio, video and virtual reality (VR). The ways in which the media can and should be combined have not yet been decided, or even widely debated. There are no standards. Most of the offerings on the Internet are single media, e.g. documents (Web pages), text (IRC), audio (telephony) and some *ad hoc* combinations of documents and conferencing (e.g. NetMeeting).

Historically, the VIVA project was in the fortunate position of starting from a blank slate of all media and a research request to define an appropriate architecture for commercial working in offices and warehouses over ATM. Our core belief was that a full collaborative system is multimedia *by definition*, since each medium has its own unique affordances. For instance, a phone call or an email can be more effective/appropriate than a visit to another's office or a conversation. The overall principle was theoretically identified by Hollan and Stornetta (1992). They argued that *simulating face-to-face co-presence* (approximating "being there") was the objective of most tele-application designers. This does not parallel experience. Each medium has its own affordances. Mere approximation to face-to-face is a bad design objective. The corollary of this is that each unique medium needs to be included in a full collaborative system.

Further drawing on CSCW, VIVA includes the notions that:

- there will be no fixed starting point for users (i.e. a central medium or application or access device). Here we moved from a VR-centric to a media-centric perspective.

- that even when working in tightly defined legal and organizational frameworks, people will combine media in effective, but idiosyncratic and unpredictable ways.

2.3.1 No Fixed Starting Point

In the first months of VIVA we believed in and designed for a VR world as the centre of a multiple-media world. It would be the application from which documents, video, audio etc. were opened. It soon become clear that VR was one medium among several. Where users were concerned, there was *no fixed starting point*.

An early CSCW finding that points to this is Reder and Schwab (1990). They recorded how real-life activities move seamlessly between media (computer, fax, phone, face-to-face). This observation was taken seriously in the development at Xerox and by Bill Buxton of "ubiquitous computing" (Weiser, 1991; Weiser *et al.*, 1999). This visualized the disintegration of the PC into a host of special-purpose devices, such as Ishii's ClearBoard, Buxton's videoconferencing dollies and intelligent notepads. While the PC remains central to much networking, the coming diversification to WAP and Bluetooth mobile devices and to interactive television will almost certainly realize the idea of "ubiquitous computing". Thus a true document-handling and communications infrastructure cannot make any assumptions about which application or device or medium a user will employ at any moment. What is clearer for infrastructure design is that there will be a demand for all, and all combinations of, services realizable on the current device and medium.

Hence we surmised that what users of video, documents, or the Web needed was not VR itself as another medium, but its affordance of ongoing background awareness of others. It should not be necessary to "go into" the VR for this, although it could be supported by an appropriate use of the VR part of the underlying system.

2.3.2 Formal and *Ad Hoc* Working Practices

CSCW emphasizes the way in which formal objectives and methods in organizations are realized and supported by *ad hoc* repairs and fixes (e.g. Suchman, 1983, 1987; Dourish and Bellotti 1992; Button and Sharrock 1997; Bowker and Star 1999). Even (and especially) in tightly defined legal and organizational frameworks, people will combine media and applications in effective but idiosyncratic and unpredictable ways. Space precludes summaries of the many studies that show this. The point can be made by looking briefly at Button and Harper (1996).

They tell of a factory manufacturing foam composites (seating, cushions etc.) for the furniture industry. It had purchased a tailor-made sales and order system, following a sequential process. Orders generated order forms, which initiated production, which resulted in delivery and an invoice. The system was built on a careful examination of documents and records (analysis), visits to the factory shop-floor and offices (observation), interviews with managers and potential users (participants' accounts), and design discussions with the same people. Sadly, it *had nothing to do with the way the work was actually done*, and was rejected. Staff worked round it, not through it. What went wrong? Button and Harper (1996) argue for "an analysis of the practices through which the participants organize their work in the face of the contingencies that unfold as part of the working day".

The context of manufacture was that customers themselves produced to order, and were always under pressure for fast delivery. Thus it was normal, even mandatory, for the factory to fulfil orders on the same day the order was received. This resulted in (good) working practices to meet the same-day target and avoid clerical delays. Orders were often accepted and then produced for same day delivery *without* an agreed price. They were phoned by the customer direct to the works manager on the shop-floor. Thus it was normal for the shop floor to receive orders, start production and then notify the front office that an official order and price was needed. As Button and Harper (1993) say, "these practices involved the *interweaving of ordering and invoicing into the very production process*". The sequential order system simply could not deal, for example, with processing orders without prices.

Button and Harper (1993) make some design recommendations. Since production and accountancy are intertwined, the technology should be distributed, not isolated in the front office. It should be available as a set of tools based on function (e.g. ordering, pricing, distributing) not on process models. We concur, and add media tools – phone, fax and (probably now) email – to the story. Work-practice interweaves the formal and the *ad hoc*, and the weaving is often done in multiple media. Systems need to take account of this enrichment and provide cross-media accesses. These in turn could lead to further enrichments, such as document awareness from continuous media (e.g. phone) and people-awareness from documents as we discussed earlier.

Mandviwalla and Khan (1999) have explored issues of integrating documents, common views, and some (text) communication. Others have explored multiple-media CSCW architectures (e.g. Benford *et al.*, 1998; Trevor *et al.* 1998), though without specific identification of multiple-media as an issue. Our task is now to sketch a full multiple-media architecture that does not assume a fixed starting point, central medium, application or access device.

2.3.3 VIVA Architecture for CVEs in Multiple Media

VIVA takes CSCW lessons into a scalable architecture for combining multiple media, supporting movement between media and not assuming any fixed starting point, application or device. The VR elements of VIVA attract most attention, so we need to state some differences between VIVA and "traditional" virtual reality applications. It goes almost without saying that many VR-CVEs support more than one medium, such as audio plus VR. Nevertheless, we believe that addressing CVEs from a multimedia perspective has not been done. For instance, others concentrate on supporting interaction that takes place *inside* the VR (Hindmarsh *et al.*, 1998; Smith and O'Brian, 1998), while VIVA supports interaction *either through or outside* the VR interface. As noted, VR is one medium among several. Here, for reasons of space, we describe the VR architecture, but stress its affordances and support for *ad hoc* combinations of shared material and awareness/communication are mirrored in our overall "separate channel architecture" and server/client configurations for each medium. On any local site (but not in telecom pipes) each medium runs in, and devices connect to, separate channels. This is necessary for modularity (each medium has its own specialized servers), and means that low-power devices like mobiles need not receive useless (to them) high bandwidth transmissions.

To support office work, we identified the following general requirements for any VR or mixed reality applications (Benford *et al.*, 1998), as well as for multiple media communication through a virtual office (Robinson *et al.*, 1998).

- Ability to open multiple simultaneous, interactive video/audio/text/graphics windows/channels with other people/places through, within or without the VR. (Note that text "chat" is not a poor relative to audio or video. There are occasions when text is better – e.g. documentation, or when people have different mother languages and little speaking practice in the language being used (Robinson and Hinrichs, 1997)).

- Ability to maintain and move between multiple simultaneous media streams and file accesses.

- Ability to attach comment (text, audio, video, VR) to objects (documents, drawings, photos etc.; Gronbaek *et al.*, 1992).

- Independence of hard and software platforms

- Scalability upward (large numbers of users), downward (e.g. to mobiles) and sideways (re-grouping people and objects, ignoring some etc.).

- Ability to set personal "boundaries" for each medium; e.g. in general, video "glances" are relatively widely acceptable (Dourish and Bly, 1992), while open video or audio links are much more sensitive.

In VIVA, the communications modalities (media) are available separately, and can run within or outside the VR interface, allowing maximum flexibility, while (partially) retaining support for peripheral awareness and shared material. Multiple media are available to support different interaction styles, so architectural questions of the boundaries and accesses to each channel, and the possibility of maintaining, switching between, and managing multiple peripheral awarenesses, need to be answered. Basically, the architecture divides all tasks and work across multiple servers and service providers, and defines generic interfaces and protocols between servers. These are outside the scope of this chapter, but can be found in VIVA Technical Report VIVA/1/2000 (Robinson and Pekkola, 2000).

However, distributing tasks across the network obviously increases the network traffic, usually seen as a bottleneck and limiting factor for CVE applications (Greenhalgh, 1997b). We have taken this into account, and are minimizing traffic by dynamic partitioning to minimize the server transitions, as discussed later. Figure 2.4 illustrates the VIVA architecture and connections between different servers and clients.

The master server is central to VIVA. It connects new clients, VIVA servers and other parts of the VIVA system together. It provides awareness of other services

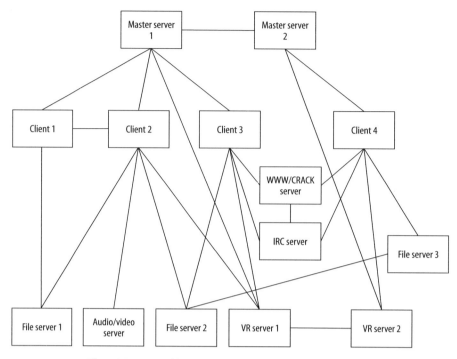

Figure 2.4 VIVA architecture supporting scalability and flexibility.

and servers, and information about each client's status (location in VR or in any other media, available communication tools, etc.). Clients and servers are not connected to the master server continuously, but request information as needed. In general, all servers and clients are free to use peer-to-peer communication from any point to any point, but must keep the master server informed of any changes in client or server status. Another master server function is as a gateway for new clients. For a user to enter VIVA, only the master server address is required. The master server redirects users to the appropriate server by providing data necessary for a new connection from its list of services, servers and users.

From a VR point of view, the most important server is the (set of) VR server(s) (for a full description see VIVA/1/2000). VIVA VR servers are "traditional" (similar to MASSIVE or DIVE), with the difference that they are dynamically linked, in that they reallocate clients between themselves, so they can handle a large number of cooperating users in any space. VR servers are in charge of processing the spatial data (locations and objects' geometrical properties) of the environment. They provide traditional services, such as collision detection, awareness and authorization services, and more unique services such as partitioning the environment. This takes care of dynamic repartitioning of the environment between VR servers according to network loading and user activities. Dynamic repartitioning gives VIVA its (future) ability to scale to very large numbers of users, and support combining, reconfiguring and repartitioning of whole worlds. The partitioning service in each VR server is responsible for communication with adjacent VR servers, so that the users are unaware of transitions or the VR server to which they are currently connected.

While the VR servers take care of calculations over actions occurring in the VR, the file server(s) store and distribute static data (appearance etc.) of any object or document linked to the VIVA system. They distribute VR-related information (environment, object, avatar data), and store all other documents and objects and any changes to them to provide persistence. From a technical point of view, file servers are similar to FTP or HTTP servers.

Communication between users may utilize audio, video or text channels. Clients may establish direct point-to-point connections for private discussions (analogous to ordinary telephone conversation), but to save network bandwidth, and to allow spatial audio, dedicated servers are provided. Media servers (audio, video or text/IRC) mix continuous media streams together and forward the combination to all receiving clients. In contrast to ordinary audio mixing algorithms, where the mixing is achieved by the client, VIVA transfers the task to dedicated servers.[3] To provide spatial audio in VR, the audio server cooperates with the appropriate VR server. The selection of a server is based on the user's VR location.

Another feature of VIVA is connectivity to the Web, discussed earlier, which enables users in the Web to be aware of others in the VIVA-VR and vice versa. Since the Web protocols are designed to distribute documents across multiple platforms, there is no means to connect users with each other. We utilized the CRACK! PeopleAwarenessEngine to provide awareness of others on the same Web page/site at the same time. Because the CRACK! server runs in parallel with, but independently of, the HTTP server, the master server in VIVA can act as a client to the CRACK! server, and vice versa. Practically, this means that users in the Web can be aware of others in the VIVA-VR, and users in any part of VIVA system can be aware of those using the Web – thus achieving interoperability between different platforms.

VIVA client applications are connected to appropriate servers. If users wish VR or video, they are connected to VR or video servers respectively. *The integration of different media channels is accomplished at the presentation level at the client.* A document can be presented in different ways (views), but the data level of the document remains the same. For example, a paper lying on a desk in the VR environment can be seen through the VR interface, or through a different application (e.g. a Web browser). Users may see someone accessing the document no matter what medium the other is using, or what medium they are using themselves. Obviously there are presentational limitations (e.g. video in mobile phones; bandwidth restrictions) that make some cross-platform presentations difficult or impossible.

In general, the integration of different channels at the presentation level makes it possible for client applications to run on a great variety of different platforms. VIVA allows the use of small handheld communicators (downward scalability) and dedicated media devices, while taking full advantage of heavy-duty workstations.

---

[3] Performance aspects of this solution are outside the scope of this chapter.

2.3.4 Comparison With Alternative VR Applications

We will use Snowdon *et al.*'s (1996a) Reference Architecture for distributed virtual reality systems to make a brief comparison with other VR applications. The architecture describes a generic set of components and functions to support distributed VR, but does not cover issues of multiple media applications. Therefore we suggest some additions and modifications to the original. We then use the modified architecture to analyse DIVE, MASSIVE and VIVA. We do not extend the analysis to other VR systems (Spline, RING, NPSnet etc.), since these are adequately covered in the original paper.

2.3.5 Snowdon *et al.*'s Architecture

The Snowdon *et al.* (1996a) reference architecture for distributed VR consists of six basic components and numerous supporting libraries and services.

- *Distributed system services* comprises four specific services: name server, trader, time service and resource discovery agents.

- *Security services*: authorization and authentication services.

- *Object support services*: object managers, compute servers.

- *Core VR services*: collision detectors, spatial traders, gateways, world servers and builder.

- *Non-core VR services*: application objects.

- *User interface services*: visualizers, auralizers, textualizers, input objects and user objects.

- *Other supporting services and libraries*: event management, database support, persistence, continuous media services, synchronization, 3D graphics and multicast.

2.3.6 Proposed Changes

Since Snowdon *et al.* created their reference architecture especially for VR systems, some changes are essential to allow for multiple media systems. Allowing multiple media centres leads to an extension of the *User interface services* module, which now becomes the centre of the architecture. The extension includes *Awareness interface* and *Core VR module* as output drivers, with other communication tools such as video, document handling and Web extensions.

Minor changes include issues like generalizing *Non-core VR services* to *Application-dependent services* (which they are anyway), transferring world builder from *Core VR* to supporting libraries and adding an Awareness service to *Distributed system services*. The Awareness service supports awareness of other users' presence and actions across different communication tools and services. This information is presented through the awareness interface.

2.3.7 Comparison of Applications

For reasons of space we limit our comparison to DIVE, MASSIVE and VIVA. Snowdon *et al.* (1996a) provide a comparison between a wide range of VR systems, and extensions of our analysis to video, audio and text conferencing systems (e.g. COWS), and hybrids such as DIVA and NetMeeting can be found in VIVA/1/2000.

DIVE (Hagsand, 1996), one of the most popular VR applications, is a loosely coupled heterogeneous distributed system, which combines audio, document handling and the Web with VR. DIVE supports peer-to-peer network communication without any central server, and a basic 3D user interface in which users are represented as simple avatars. Awareness of other users arises directly from the VR environment and through audio channels. Awareness information is limited to users present in VR.

In MASSIVE versions 1 and 2 (Greenhalgh and Benford, 1995; Benford *et al.*, 1997) explicit awareness support services have been implemented. However, since MASSIVE is a VR application, not a multiple media system, awareness information is only provided about users inside the VR environment. MASSIVE supports audio communication and multiple output and input devices, but basically all actions take place either in or through the VR environment. Therefore there is no need to support awareness *between* different media, although some experiments in combined VR/stage performances and inhabited TV (Benford *et al.*, 1997; Benford *et al.*, 1999a) have shown a need for awareness support across physical and virtual spaces (e.g. a performer in physical space needs awareness of the VR).

Compared with VIVA (see Table 2.1), both DIVE and MASSIVE support *some* aspects of multiple media awareness. We believe there is space for reworking such systems in a wider media base, with broader awareness support.

2.4 Support for Scalability

2.4.1 Scalability

CVE scalability is usually thought of in terms of the intriguing technical problem of appropriate and smooth representation of large (e.g. football) crowds (Benford *et al.*, 1997). This is an area on which ethnography has little to contribute, and other sociologies can only make a conceptual or speculative contribution. We will therefore only note that crowds do seem to play an important role in human affairs, and that it may be worthwhile experimenting with large-scale CVEs, if only to provoke more empirical investigation.

We also note that the issue of scalability may run deeper, and be connected with reconfigurability of worlds. Current CVEs usually offer the ability to *move between*

Table 2.1. Comparison of DIVE, MASSIVE and VIVA

			DIVE	MASSIVE 1 and 2	VIVA
UI	Media	Video			✓
		Audio	✓	✓	✓
		Text	✓	✓	✓
		VR	✓	✓	✓
	Awareness interface				✓
	Input objects		✓	✓	✓
	User objects		✓		
VR services	Collision detector		✓	✓	✓
	Spatial traders			✓	✓
	Gateway services		✓	✓	✓
	World servers		✓	✓	✓
Application services			✓	✓	
Distributed system devices	Name server		✓		✓
	Trader			✓	✓
	Time service				
	Resource discovery				✓
	Awareness server			✓	✓
Security services	Authorization				
	Authentication				✓
Object support services	Object manager				
	Compute servers		✓		
Support libraries and services	Event management		✓	✓	✓
	DB management		✓		✓
	Synchronization		✓		✓
	Multicast			✓	
	Persistent data				✓
	World builders				

worlds. We believe a truly flexible CVE environment would allow users to create new worlds by forming partial joins. The joins of course need to be made as partitions or selections from a combination of two or more worlds. Scalability is thus directly implicated in the user's ability to reconfigure and create new worlds. Here ethnography does tell us, as we noted in the introduction, that we move easily and fluently between socialities, reconfiguring our people-and-object-awarenesses on the fly. Such sideways scalability is connected with multiple media and awareness issues considered earlier.

There is a last issue of downward scalability, of the sort anticipated in the MASSIVE 1 2D or "textie" feature. Variants of the same CVE need to be available to devices of differing computational power, connection bandwidth and quality of service (e.g. mobiles). We believe upward scalability to large numbers of objects is a precondition of coming down to differing configurations of devices of varying power.

2.4.2 Spatial Server and Environment Partitioning

Some virtual reality systems connect all clients with avatars in the same virtual environment to one central server (e.g. Community Place, RING). The server's communication and processing capacities impose an upper limit on the number of clients that can be in the same virtual space. Other VR systems try to avoid this bottleneck by using alternative approaches, e.g. peer-to-peer architectures, where clients communicate directly without a central server (e.g. DIVE, NPSNet). In this case, network capacity sets the limit. As the number of clients approaches either of these limits, the quality of service tends to decrease. Our approach is to use spatial server partitioning to distribute the tasks dynamically to many servers. In this way, a client is connected to one server, but all servers form a net which dynamically changes its shape.

Typically, most communication (speech, video, any interaction requiring data transfer) will occur between adjacent clients in a virtual world. Assigning these clients to the same server minimizes communication between servers. It also saves network capacity if only servers with adjacent "areas of service" are allowed to communicate.

Since a design objective is that the system should be transparent to users, the spatial server partitioning process should not require any specific actions from them, nor cause unnecessary or obtrusive delays, nor limit activity. Our approach does not fall into any of the standard categories presented in Macedonia and Zyda (1997). The most fundamental difference from other multiple server systems, such as SplineVE (Barrus *et al.*, 1996b) and MASSIVE-3 (Greenhalgh *et al.*, 1998a) is that the locale boundaries in these systems are fixed, whereas our spatial server partitioning is a dynamic process.

2.4.3 Performance

Any algorithm which assigns users dynamically to different servers, and also switches users between the servers, has a number of distinct and partially conflicting goals. It is difficult to set a single value that measures its efficiency. However, performance can be measured in achieving each particular goal, followed by solving a multi-criteria optimization problem.

Our approach was to consider a number of typical and extreme usage scenarios (e.g. typical audio traffic patterns generated in a meeting, problems caused by very crowded spaces or by rapidly moving avatars, etc.) and to consider various parameters that affect the overall quality of service:

1. Number of server switchovers per time unit
2. Total network traffic
3. Number of hops when transmitting broadcast traffic to recipients
4. Average latency in client to client connections
5. Average delay caused by a server switchover
6. Robustness and reliability: number of server splits (and possible unrecoverable client errors)

The lack of data from large-scale user experiments (sessions with hundreds or even thousands of simultaneous participants) made definitive judgement of the relative quality of various candidate algorithms difficult. As a partial solution we developed *ad hoc* simulations of mass user behaviour and then observed the performance of the candidate partitioning algorithms in these simulations.

2.4.4 Outline of the Algorithm

A space (e.g. a closed room) is dynamically divided into convex polygons, each representing an area served by a particular server. Clients (users) are located inside a convex polygon, and connected to an appropriate server. Since each borderline is shared only by a limited number of adjacent servers, any modification to a partition is possible to accomplish without centralized control, by negotiations between relevant servers.

Figure 2.5 illustrates part of a virtual space, divided into several regions using a two-dimensional hexagonal mesh. The vertices of the mesh are moved dynamically in order to even out the distribution of users in the whole environment, not just in that small region. In this example, each corner point is shared by exactly three servers, so the corner's new position can be safely determined with a three-party protocol.

The algorithm assigns a weight W_s for each server s. The weight is affected by the number of "excess" users located in each server. "Excess" is the estimated number

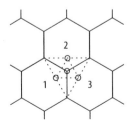

Figure 2.5 A centre point can be moved by common agreement between servers 1, 2 and 3 without affecting the shape of areas served by surrounding servers.

of users who, if moved to another server, would create the best possible quality of service for the remaining users. If each server already has an optimum number (or fewer) of users, the borders are not moved and the algorithm is terminated at this point.

For stability reasons, it is essential to ensure that the hexagons remain convex (within the area surrounded by dashed line in Fig. 2.6) when moving the corner points. In the hexagonal model we propose, the centre point's new position can be computed by assigning "extreme" points for each server area (see small circles in Fig. 2.6), which we denote by two-dimensional vectors V_S, so the new corner point P can be derived simply as the weighted-sum:

$$P = \frac{\sum_{i=1}^{n} W_i^* V_i}{\sum_{i=1}^{n} W_i}$$

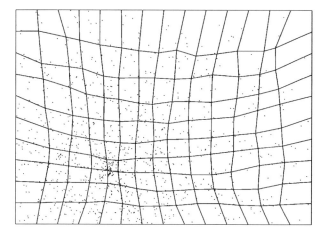

Figure 2.6 Mesh with the point of interest in the middle of the area.

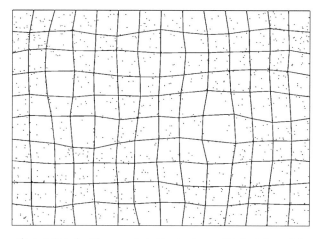

Figure 2.7 Mesh with no central attractor (users distributed evenly).

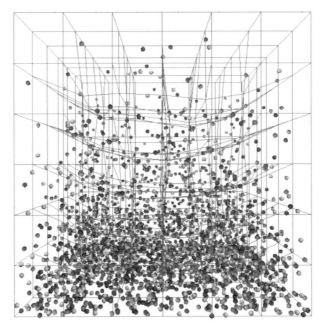

Figure 2.8 Three-dimensional partitioning experiment.

Hexagonal partitioning is an iterative approximation method. An optimum server configuration is never archived on a global scale, since users tend to move around (Bowers *et al.*, 1996b), producing server switchovers. Locally (within adjacent servers) our experiments with the algorithm have shown mostly positive results (see Figs. 2.6 and 2.7 for 2D simulation results), with the occasional exception of some stability problems ("jiggly" behaviour). However, we believe that this can be overcome by applying simulated annealing techniques to the (non-linear) computation of the server weights.

A 2D hexagonal method can be applied in three dimensions by using a three-dimensional cubic lattice as a basis for partitioning. Figure 2.8 illustrates (a bird's eye view of) one resulting configuration of an experiment, in which a point of interest located on one wall attracts users (represented with small spheres).

The details of the three-party protocol are outside the scope of this chapter. We only note here that the protocol can be initialized by a server whose load becomes excessive, and that the protocol is scalable to arbitrary numbers of servers.

2.5 Summary and Conclusion

Our theme was extending CVEs to include more people and more objects in more media, summarized as providing more awareness. A brief gloss of existing applications shows that there is support for one or many media, some level of people awareness and some sort of scalability. However, there is no application, which supports:

- multiple media in the full sense

- awareness of others and their activities across media

- scalability

Some examples are:

- DIVE combines audio, document handling and VR, but only provides visual or audio awareness of users in the VR itself. MASSIVE (Greenhalgh and Benford, 1995; Benford *et al.*, 1997) also supports VR, audio and multiple input and output devices, but basically all actions take place either in or through the VR environment. Therefore there is no need to support awareness *between* different media, although some experiments in combined VR/stage performances and inhabited TV (Benford *et al.*, 1997; Benford *et al.*, 1999a) have shown a need (e.g. a performer in physical space needs awareness of the VR).

- NetMeeting, CUSeeMe, IRC, MUDs/MOOs and other conferencing applications, as well as shared whiteboards and co-authoring systems, support one or sometimes more media, but provide awareness only for that designed application. Awareness across media cannot be claimed to exist in the sense we are advocating. Document repositories (e.g. BSCW) seldom support real-time communication, although awareness in the sense of notification services may be provided.

- Scalability has been addressed in many applications. For example, MASSIVE-1 supports a 2D view for vt100 terminal users and a 3D user interface for users using powerful computers; NPSNet (Zyda *et al.*, 1993) is intended to support hundreds of users; and DIVE allows VR objects to be programmed so that (in principle) they could act as gateways to other applications.

Limiting services to resolving one of these issues runs contrary to findings from CSCW, namely that users move between media and devices promiscuously; combine applications and media in effective, but idiosyncratic and unpredictable ways; and need awareness of others and their activities for successful accomplishment of much work. Awareness, whether backgrounded or foregrounded, needs to be constantly available/present. Satisfying all these requirement is a major technical challenge for CVEs.

Section 2.2 dealt with awareness of other people. We argued from CSCW that people-awareness, whether backgrounded or foregrounded, needs to be constantly available/present. We briefly presented a Web application (CRACK!) that provides people-awareness in the Web, and between the Web and VRs, and which should be extensible to other standard document-handling programs, such as word processors and spreadsheets. We concluded that there is no other-than-technical reason why any application should not become a CVE.

There are some technical, design and aesthetic challenges to this imagined future. How, for instance, do we include a document, its icon or trigger, in a phone conversation? How far do we want to share awareness of the index or contents of our phone answering machine/voicemail?

Section 2.3 considered the question of multiple media in work-practice, and with respect to CVEs. We argued that many media are needed for collaboration, since each has its own special benefits and affordances. We added that work practice normally involves a multiplicity of media and devices, and shifts between them. For this reason, no one application or device can, in future, be regarded as a natural starting point or home for users. This provided a *prima facie* reason for considering a multimedia architecture for CVEs. We then suggested a possible architecture for handling VR, video, audio, text and documents where awareness of others and their activities can generally be provided across media. Important features were *presentation level integration* and choices between media channels. These support new approaches to cooperative situations. Multiple collaborations involving arbitrary combinations of documents, people, media and access devices can be achieved.

Again this imagined future raises serious issues. The mechanisms we have proposed are generally symmetrical, and the arbitrary combinations of people, documents etc. could be configuring their own arbitrary combinations of people etc. There are social and legal implications of this that we have not even begun to indicate within the chapter.

Section 2.4 showed how the architecture, using a dynamic partitioning algorithm, can be scalable to arbitrarily large numbers of users. We regard this as a significant technical achievement in itself, and also as a challenge to ethnography to make closer studies of large organizational and social settings. We then offer speculation about how upward scalability may be the transitional step to two other desirable features: sideways and downward scalability. The ability to reconfigure the people and object constellations in a CVE on the fly seems to us an exciting challenge. The second challenge is the ability to extend the CVEs to net-connected artefacts, such as mobile phones and fridges.

Adding net-connected artefacts to CVEs seems to us a very natural next step, and one that would take VR-CVEs from a slightly eccentric plaything to a commonplace application. We have treated this more speculatively than multiple-media and people-awareness. However, the drive from both vendors and end-users to find a way of domesticating e-commerce is likely to propel it to the forefront. Probably the process will start with the simpler option of Web pages laid out by home appliances. A little later comes (communicative) sharing of the page with the family. Then comes the need to admit local stores to some of the artefacts, like the fridge. And from here, from the ground up so to speak, will come the dynamic of self-fuelling social and technical evolution. Who can be (partially) admitted, and who not, and to what, and how? There will be many competing social and technical and legal solutions to the ensuing game of redefining the very meaning of "home".

We only remark, humbly, that we have tried to suggest some fairly obvious challenges and next steps in the development of CVEs. Meeting these challenges could move CVEs from the periphery to the centre of Internet use. This will not be free of controversy or risk.

Chapter 3
System Challenges for Collaborative Virtual Environments

Adrian West and Roger Hubbold

3.1 Introduction

According to Professor Fred Brooks, virtual environment (VE) research has reached a point where it "barely works" (Brooks, 1999). We interpret this to mean that, although the technology has advanced to a point where many things are possible, there are still inadequacies which prevent its application to real-world problems. This difficulty of getting virtual reality (VR) to work adequately is due to a wide range of things: some are hardware-related, some depend on better algorithms and techniques, and yet others are related to human factors issues. This very diversity has led to some fragmentation in research: different groups study focused, tractable problems; solutions for one problem do not necessarily integrate easily with others, and technological limitations often frustrate attempts to scale up the results for larger real-world tasks. Gluing together the solutions for individual components of the problem is not guaranteed to work, and we can see evidence that the overall task is hard from the lack of convincing industrial-strength examples. Finding a solution for a real-world problem requires that diverse ideas and solutions be combined in some way. Before VR can move from a research-based subject into mainstream applications, ways must be found to integrate ideas from the contributing disciplines into a coherent architectural framework, designed to support systematic application development. Our own work, which is briefly touched upon in this chapter, is concerned with deriving such a system architecture.

The development of any system targeted at widespread use must also take due account of the very diverse requirements of its users. Combined with the wide range of purely technical problems, it is perhaps not surprising that VR "barely works". Brooks was referring primarily to single-user VR applications. For distributed collaborative VEs we add a plethora of new problems which piecemeal development cannot really address. It is here, in our view, that a systems-oriented approach becomes essential. Interestingly, when approached in this way, new areas for research open up. For example, it is self-evident that we cannot totally remove latency from networks; therefore it might be instructive to design our system on the assumption that latencies will be inevitable, and to consider how best to deal with them from the user's perspective.

In this chapter we outline a number of key challenges for designers of collaborative virtual environment (CVE) systems to support real-world applications. These are based on ideas we have been developing for several years, and which are beginning to come to fruition in the Deva and MAVERIK systems (Hubbold *et al.*, 1999; Pettifer and West, 1999). We mention these systems primarily to show that our ideas are grounded in practical experience. Our canvas is broad, and inevitably covers a wide range of topics. We fully acknowledge the excellent work of other groups but, with a few exceptions, we have deliberately not attempted to describe or reference this. The issues we raise are general and not intended to demonstrate why one system is better than any other; rather they are intended to demonstrate why a systems approach is essential, but also difficult to get right.

We begin with a section describing what we mean by a CVE. We use two examples from our own work to illustrate this. We then consider the problems of customizing the way in which VE data is stored for different applications, followed by a discussion of how to describe behaviours. Next, we discuss the problems of distribution and latency. Finally, we consider briefly how to put these different parts together.

3.2 Collaborative Virtual Environments

What do we mean by a CVE? One interpretation is environments in which *people* collaborate. Another is *environments which themselves cooperate* by exhibiting interesting and useful properties and behaviours, which help us to get a job done *and* solve problems collaboratively with other people. This latter view admits all kinds of possibilities – agents, for example, to make interaction easier. It can be difficult to describe ideas in abstract, so we'll use examples from our own work and outline ways in which CVEs are applicable.

3.2.1 The Distributed Legible City

The first example emphasizes social encounter and interaction. CVEs allow participants be aware of each other, in a manner potentially far closer to our real-world experience of a shared environment than can be achieved by other forms of human–computer interaction or computer-mediated communication. A CVE is quite different from using an Internet browser, in which one is essentially unaware of others sharing the resources. If the shared environment is good enough, there is the possibility of using the setting for generalized social interaction and exchange, rather than just task-specific applications. This shared social environment for the general citizen is at the heart of many CVE research projects, which is one reason why the discipline spans arts, education, media, entertainment and government. Achieving such aims raises challenges for our understanding of social interaction, but also pushes the boundaries of our system architecture capabilities, involving as it does real-time interaction for geographically dispersed participants in complex virtual environments.

One example of this kind is the Distributed Legible City, which is a preliminary study of shared electronic spaces for the general citizen. The piece is a distributed version of a multimedia artwork originally created by Jeffrey Shaw in 1991 (Shaw, 1998; Schiffler and Pettifer, 1999). The basis of the work is that buildings of a cityscape are replaced by extracts of social and historical texts and commentary from the localities, projected in 3D. Participants view the work by cycling through this literal cityscape using a modified real-world exercise bicycle (Fig. 3.1).

In the shared version, participants see each other riding cycles within the cityscapes, and can communicate via an audio link. Using an immersive interface makes it possible to look around the scene, for example to face another person cycling alongside. A common criticism in shared VEs is that there is nothing to do or talk about within them; setting this CVE within an artwork attempts to utilize the artistic context to promote discussion and interaction between participants.

One challenge for such CVEs is thus to make them engaging and bring them to life. In part this relies upon good ideas for content and activities, but it ultimately depends on techniques for coding complex behaviours and managing the interactions between participants, and between participants and the environment. Where large numbers of users are involved these techniques must scale to accommodate them. There are additional architectural challenges in managing the distribution of the model and maintaining synchronization in the face of real-time interactive demands. If participants are geographically dispersed, then there are increasing concerns in coping with the perceptually disturbing effects of communication lags and delays. On a desktop presentation, such discontinuities may be acceptable, but in the immersed environment where the VE composes the entirety of the user's experience, such defects cannot easily be ignored, and can render the system unusable.

3.2.2 A Complex Real-World Application

Our second example is the development of CVEs for an engineering application – the design of complex process plants, such as petrochemical installations and offshore drilling platforms. Such installations are massively complicated – both geometrically and in terms of structure and function. A typical offshore installation absorbs over 40 person-years of design effort, requiring the coordination of a large team of engineers, safety experts and operations staff. CAD tools are routinely used for design, and the output of these feeds into structural engineering, process engineering, materials scheduling, construction scheduling and planning, and safety assessment.

The role of the CVE is to support decision making during the design process, to facilitate interaction between experts from different specialist areas, and to enable the operational impact of alternative designs to be assessed. Tasks to be supported include editing the models, simulating construction operations, and simulating subsequent operational aspects, including safety, requiring that users can interact *with the model* and *with each other*. A specific example is seen in Fig. 3.2, which shows a simulation of two users carrying an injured person on a stretcher from the site of an accident to a helicopter landing pad. Such simulations pose major challenges to the designer of a CVE software system.

Figure 3.1 The Distributed Legible City. **a** Two participants wearing HMDs cycling around three inter-linked shared virtual cities. **b** A typical view of a street, with a map of the three cities of Amsterdam, New York and Karlsruhe overlaid. © Jeffrey Shaw. Reproduced with permission.

Figure 3.2 Carrying a stretcher during an emergency evacuation on an offshore gas platform, requiring real-time collision detection, forces to assist navigation, and display of a massive model. **a** A general view of a stairway. **b** A close-up view of the stretcher being lifted over a handrail. (Model data courtesy of CADCentre, Brown & Root and Conoco. Reproduced with permission.)

First, these models are geometrically complex and have myriad rules about how and where different components can be placed. The largest model we have processed to date contains the equivalent of over 108 million triangles when rendered at a single moderate level of detail. Furthermore, this complexity results from *real geometry*, which is fundamentally different from the *apparent* visual complexity of textures. Apart from the significant challenge of rendering such massive models in real time, all of the components in the model have some function relating to their identity and purpose, and the data describing these resides in the native CAD database. In a design context, we expect all of these components to behave correctly – to obey placement rules, to have simulated gravity (if appropriate), and to be subject to constraints such as collision detection during manipulation. A component which is subject to gravity on land may behave differently when submerged and supported by a flotation device.

Second, we must be able to see other users in the shared model and to see what they are doing. This applies particularly to simulating operational or safety procedures. For example, observing other users manipulating parts of the model requires a believable portrayal of what they are doing and a correct simulation of the objects they are interacting with. Our current stretcher simulation uses precise geometric collision detection and force-guided navigational assistance (Dongbo and Hubbold, 1998), but is controlled by one user, rather than two. Extending this to manipulation, by two or more geographically distributed users, of a shared object (the stretcher) remains a challenging problem.

The social setting of the Distributed Legible City and the CAD environment of the stretcher simulation illustrate the kinds of task that a general-purpose VE architecture must aim to support. With these illustrations in mind, we now turn to consider specific challenges for CVE systems architecture.

3.3 Structures for Modelling VEs

Creating rich environments with which users can interact in useful ways is an area requiring research. Advances in rendering and the reducing costs of graphics hardware have made it possible to display visually rich environments, and yet the ways in which we can interact with those environments remain woefully inadequate. In part, this has to do with technology – a keyboard and mouse do not afford rich interaction and manipulation of synthetic worlds. Improved speech technology and multi-modal interaction are required, as are improvements to tracking technologies to enable unencumbered interaction in 3D. But a major part of the problem has to do with improvements in software support for modelling environments in order to support richer forms of interaction.

Commercial pressures for standardization tend to push software designers towards a "one size fits all" approach, in which the goal is to design a single system which can support myriad applications and environments. What results from this, in general, is the derivation of a lowest common denominator in which the data describing an environment, and the means for interacting with it, are the same – or at least very similar – for quite different applications. Is it really possible to use the same modelling techniques and modes of interaction for a surgical simulator, an architectural modelling system and an abstract data visualization task? If we consider these activities in the real world the answer would seem clearly to be "no". And yet, too often, we are expected to believe that these very different tasks and environments can be modelled in the same way – using VRML scene graphs, for example.

Standardized representations, such as the scene graph, cannot conveniently support physical simulations of the kind required to make environments come alive. A consequence of this is that *two models* must be implemented to support the behaviours in an environment: one for the graphical presentation (the scene graph), and the other to perform the application-specific modelling. Worse, these two representations must then be kept synchronized.

The challenge, therefore, is to design software systems which support different modelling techniques within a single framework. These must scale up to realistically large, real-world problems, such as the Legible City and CAD examples outlined previously, and support application-specific methods of interaction and manipulation. Designing solutions for CVEs, in which models must be distributed and shared by multiple users, would therefore seem to require a fundamentally new approach to the problem.

3.3.1 How to Describe Realities?

> ...virtual reality research is still preoccupied with image generation... [which] merely provides the interface – the "connecting cable" – between the user and the true virtual-reality generator... (Deutsch, 1997)

With the ability to interactively render environments of reasonable complexity, the focus begins to move away from the "what" to the "why"; towards consideration of what it is we are striving to simulate – how things really are, rather than just how they appear to be. This distinction is readily apparent in popular computer games, in which the illusion of a sophisticated environment replete with possibilities for interaction is achieved by techniques such as texture mapping in which little of the reality presented is really "available" for use – the simulation knows nothing about them. VEs exhibit increasing presentational richness, but are behaviourally severely challenged.

In attempting to model the behavioural complexity of VEs we face substantial challenges. Behaviour of any significant complexity is extraordinarily difficult to simulate and code – witness the state of the art in AI or robotics, physical simulation, or even the common or garden word processor. So perhaps this task presents an enormous simulation challenge facing computer science, not just VE researchers. Looked at in this way it is not surprising that the common approach of VE systems vendors is to provide the applications developer with hooks to attach code or scripts to the individual objects in the VE system, and leave it at that. Can any more be done? Is it possible to provide more assistance than this to the specification of the reality behind the presentation?

For any particular complex behaviour associated with an object – for example a robot or "intelligent agent" in the VE – then we can do no better than call upon our best AI techniques for help and resort to conventional coding practice. However, the behavioural quality lacking in VEs is often more to do with simple everyday behaviours, but made available to large numbers of objects. In the everyday world of experience a simple environment has hundreds of objects available for inspection and manipulation, conforming to common behavioural characteristics of the environment such as gravity and solidity. In addition, each item exhibits its own peculiar properties, such as the content of a notepad, the communicational affordance of a telephone, or the capability of a light switch. Programming these by attaching scripts to each of those objects is not really satisfactory. Coding these kinds of properties as part of an "application" is certainly possible, though surely this kind of thing properly deserves more support from the VE system.

A key observation here is that many of the properties we associate with everyday experience are most naturally regarded as properties of the environment itself. Gravity would be the simple yet classic example, where all objects experience a downward force in proportion to an attribute of mass, which all objects in that environment possess. Different environments can have different properties that they impose upon their contents; for example in an undersea construction scenario the notion of buoyancy is appropriate. In addition to such environmentally oriented behaviour, individual classes of objects have behaviour and attributes specific to themselves, such as the light switch above. With a simple model such as this, objects placed in the environment automatically attain a degree of sensible behaviour.

This kind of model can be implemented straightforwardly with a multiple inheritance language (one class hierarchy for environmental behaviour, and one for the object specific behaviours). A benefit would be the creation of a range of environments that act as good starting points to situate common kinds of applications.

If we desire to have multiple applications and environments active, however, then we must face the problem of moving objects from one environment to another, detaching their original environmental component and mediating the adoption of behaviour for the new environment. A person moving from the oil rig construction environment to its undersea counterpart will now need some new attributes for the calculation of buoyancy. In a large-scale enterprise in which the VE system is responsible for migrating objects between processors, it makes sense to build support for this kind of behavioural mechanism into the framework of the system itself.

The hierarchy of environments and behaviours is at the core of the Deva VE system we are developing (Pettifer and West, 1999), and is one approach to easing the task of specifying behaviours for VE applications. Whether this helps in practice will probably only be discovered after a number applications have been constructed. Whether that particular scheme works or not, behavioural paucity and limited ability to work with higher level descriptions are limiting factors for VEs, and must ultimately be addressed as a systems/infrastructure issue.

3.3.2 Supporting Distribution

For a VE to be collaborative it must be distributed between the participants who wish to share it, and this brings its own challenges for the VE system. Often it is the mechanism of distribution which is the most visible defining architectural characteristic of a CVE. At a base level, the choice is between the traditional peer-to-peer or client–server architectures. This is parametrized by the degree to which the data structures representing the VE are replicated or cached between the computing nodes, and the underlying transportation technology – for example the use of multicast protocols, or reliance upon guaranteed bandwidths/latencies, as in the case of ATM.

However, whatever the technology, communication latencies are ultimately insurmountable. For geographical distribution on the Earth, the speed of light alone gives a best case terrestrial one-way pole–pole delay of some 60 ms. In practice, using mass communication media the latencies are rather worse than this, as the experience of retrieving pages from the Web illustrates (commonly even where the server is nearby), and this is especially so where many users are concerned. For many applications such delays may not be significant – for example in the Legible City the cyclists do not need to share dextrous manipulation of a common object – but real-time shared interaction is particularly sensitive to lag, especially so in the case of immersive interfaces. The application's sensitivity to such lag depends upon the degree of genuine shared interaction required. For example, in a passive walk-through of a model small temporal discrepancies between participants' experience of the world may well go unnoticed. Multi-user games are to some degree immunized against problems of lag because users are for the most part interacting indirectly – shooting or being shot at. At the opposite extreme of the interaction taxonomy, the two people manoeuvring a stretcher through the confines of an oil rig will find coordination difficult or impossible with any appreciable lag – the effect is analogous to riding a bicycle with loose handlebars as a collaborative task. In the face of such latencies, the simulation cannot be mistaken for its real world counterpart.

What can be done for shared applications dependent upon direct interaction, such as some popular visions of Virtual Surgery? One solution is to use predictive techniques to smooth out temporal idiosyncrasies. This is helpful where events and actions are likely to be predictable or smooth, but must ultimately fail where they are not. Activities directly controlled by human operators that involve rapid changes in velocity (dextrous manipulation for example) will be very hard to predict reliably.

A similar technique is to find ways of distributing descriptions of behaviour to each of the client machines – for example downloading scripts that describe behaviours of objects, or by filtering events at the server to produce parametric descriptions of activity (Marsh *et al.*, 1999). Again these are useful techniques, but they do not in themselves solve the problem of shared direct interaction in the face of latency.

If we cannot achieve adequate synchrony, we can at least attempt to focus resources upon those activities which are most sensitive to lag, that is to say those which produce the most pronounced discontinuities of perceptual experience when lag is present. This involves determining a metric of significance and prioritizing urgency within the communication infrastructure accordingly. One way to view this is analogous to a graphical Level Of Detail (LOD) optimization, but in this case involving the *activity* within the environment – a *Causal* Level Of Detail (CLOD). This does not solve the worst-case problem for our stretcher bearers either, but at least it makes the best of the worst case, and offers hope of rendering other large classes of use viable, gracefully degrading the quality of experience as a complex environment suffers from temporary deficiencies of resource.

If we cannot ultimately solve the problem, then we are forced to admit that we cannot simulate the real-world scenario in sufficient detail for all cases. A number of options present themselves: (a) ignore the problem, and accept the inadequacy; (b) identify when the problem arises (it may be permanent in some situations), and alert the participants to its extent – at least this provides explanation; (c) find new metaphors and ways of working in the shared environment that are effective in the face of latency and resource limitations, even though they do not correspond directly to the real-world task. For example, some real-world situations solve synchronization tasks by passing a physical token, such as a balloon on a stick, between the workers.

In all these cases what we are really striving to achieve is an experience of the shared environment that is, for each participant, perceptually continuous and coherent. Perhaps we simply do not yet understand enough about what aspects of the perceived environment contribute to this perception. For example, it is clear that the experience of the everyday world as perceptually smooth and continuous is to some degree a fiction of the human perceptual system, and that the raw data of perception is commonly far coarser than the subject believes. The blind spot is one example of this, but classic psychological experiments demonstrate a range of such illusions, including the reordering of temporal events in the mind in order to present a plausible story of perception (Kolers and von Grunau, 1976). In effect, it is precisely this task that the VE system is undertaking: to try its best to present to each user a plausible presentation of the underlying reality in the face of often inadequate data.

For experiments using local equipment and guaranteed resources, these issues are probably of less concern. A general-purpose CVE system, however, must sooner or later face them. Our argument here is that distribution raises far-ranging questions that go beyond the low-level networking infrastructure. Furthermore, as they are at the very core of what a CVE system provides, they are quite appropriately issues of system architecture.

3.3.3 Putting it All Together

Software structures for modelling VEs, the issue of "behaviour" in bringing VEs to life, and the demands of distributing complex environments for interactive use, are three intriguing challenges facing VE system architects. "Putting it all together" is the final "meta-level" challenge central to delivering more ambitious CVEs into common use. As with any complex system, addressing each issue experimentally may yield partial solutions, but experience suggests that these cannot simply be plugged together to form a coherent whole. As with buildings, architecture does not seem to work like that. Careful thought is required to find overarching frameworks and principles capable of simultaneously accommodating the technical requirements that we are slowly understanding through smaller scale use. These are quite difficult issues to convey succinctly: high-level views of system designs, such as those presented at conferences, all tend to appear to be much the same – collections of boxes and arrows. The devil, however, is in the detail, and the real merit is often only really understood when we try to put them to serious use ourselves.

Our own effort at addressing these challenges centres on two complementary systems, MAVERIK and Deva, under development for the past four years. MAVERIK is designed to support easy customization for widely differing applications. Rather than *importing* data, the system itself can be programmed to operate *directly* on application data structures. This core concept allows us to break the performance bottleneck and inflexibility inherent in approaches that force models to be imported into an alien environment, often as a "polygon soup".

We refer to MAVERIK as a micro-kernel, using operating system parlance, because it supports a core set of functions from which higher-level systems can be constructed. It provides a framework and mechanisms for defining different classes of application-specific objects, methods for spatial management and culling of large models, and a wide range of default classes and methods for display management and interaction. MAVERIK is specifically concerned with supporting the perception and interaction of a single participant interacting with complex environments with application-specific behaviour. In a multi-user context, it is used to *support* each user's view of, and interaction with, the environment.

Deva is a meta-level system which places emphasis on the environments themselves – the "reality" – rather than each individual's experience of them. It provides the mechanism for managing the content and behaviour of CVEs. A Deva stub client mediates between this underlying reality and a participant's individual perception of it. It is this stub that strives for a coherent interpretation of events, in a manner analogous to the task undertaken by the human perceptual and cognitive systems. On the human side of that stub, the actual rendering, spatial management and interaction are managed by MAVERIK.

This particular division allows Deva to focus upon the problems of supporting multiple, concurrent, persistent environments, which can be shared by geographically dispersed users. Formally separating reality, and the perception of it, provides an appropriate structure for experimenting with the higher level concerns of perceptual coherency in the face of network and resource limitations. Pragmatically this means managing parallelism and the distributed execution environment. To aid the programmer Deva must provide transparent distribution with low overhead. These and other issues of detail are challenging, particularly when brought together under one roof. If the requisite functionality can be attained, however, then it is the conceptual model presented to the application developer upon which the merits of the design will be judged. Though we strive for that conceptual clarity, success can only be meaningfully assessed through the experience of putting the system to use in challenging applications.

MAVERIK and Deva complement each other to form a complete "VR operating system", supporting the dynamic construction and use of CVEs. MAVERIK has been extensively tested and is now being used freely by other groups under a GNU General Public License. It is an official component of the GNU project, and so is more correctly referred to as "GNU Maverik". Deva has been extensively prototyped and a number of the key ideas shown to work. A full implementation of Deva is now under way and will be released under a GNU GPL.

3.4 Conclusion

We have outlined four areas which we believe still present unsolved problems for designers of CVE software systems: software structures for modelling VEs, specifying "behaviour" to bring VEs to life, distributing complex environments for shared interactive use, and "putting it all together". Our list is not exhaustive: for example, we have not addressed the issue of audio communication, which is known to present major technical challenges because of its bandwidth requirements and the problems of synchronizing sound to other actions within an environment. What we have tried to illustrate is that a system architecture approach to the problems is needed, and that this opens new lines of enquiry and experiment.

How well these ideas will work in practice – the extent to which they really *support* and assist the VR application designer – is something that can only be discovered by implementing and using them. Much remains to be done.

Chapter 4
Understanding the Network Requirements of Collaborative Virtual Environments

Chris Greenhalgh

4.1 Introduction

Collaborative Virtual Environments, like almost all distributed systems, are complex and encompass a broad range of interrelated concerns. In this chapter we focus on the network and communication requirements of CVEs in relation to several aspects of their design, implementation and use. We cannot cover the relationships between these various aspects comprehensively in this chapter; rather we will give a framework and a number of key illustrations which will equip the reader with a general understanding of the issues and the typical patterns of influence which are embodied in CVEs.

In this chapter we concentrate for the most part on updates, i.e. changes in the virtual environment, such as user movement or audio. We give less consideration to state transfer issues, i.e. obtaining initial information about the content and definition of a virtual environment. In our experiences to date updates have comprised the majority of the network requirements, at least in part because the CVEs used were media-rich, including real-time audio and/or video.

We cannot understand the network requirements of CVEs in isolation; rather, we need a model of CVE operation which encompasses user, software and hardware concerns. The model that we will make use of (based on Greenhalgh, 1999) is shown in Table 4.1. For the most part, we will consider the way in which the higher layers of this model (closer to the user) influence what happens in the lower layers (closer to the network). For example, consider a CVE being used to hold a distributed meeting.

Table 4.1. A layered model of CVE network requirements

Area	Layer	Question addressed
Users	Task/application/collaboration requirements	What do people want or try to do?
	User behaviour	What particular actions do people do and when?
Software	Process behaviour	How does the application respond?
	Distribution architecture	What communicates with what?
	Communication protocols	How is information exchanged?
Hardware	Network communication	What actually happens in the network?

In this application users may primarily be using audio communication (for speech-based communication), with limited navigation (to form groups and orient to activities and others) and gestures (for referencing and other non-verbal communication – see Chapter 7), and occasional manipulation of virtual objects (e.g. to interact with embedded presentation tools). This defines the top layer, "task/application/collaboration requirements". Within this common context, all users have their own unique ways of working, which will affect exactly what they do and when they do it. This is reflected in the second layer, "user behaviour".

If we assume that users are distributed, then all of their interaction (as perceived by remote users) will be mediated via the particular application(s) they are using. For example, their application will have particular methods for navigation. Certain information must then be communicated to the other users if they are to see this navigation. This is reflected in layer three, "process behaviour".

Different CVE systems handle distribution in different ways, for example structuring their virtual worlds in different ways (dividing them into rooms etc.). Layer four, "distribution architecture", reflects these elements of system engineering. The CVE must then pass this information to standard network services and protocols so that it can be communicated to remote parts of the system. How this is done depends on choices such as whether to use unicast (one-to-one) or multicast (one-to-many) methods of communication, and the level of reliability required (i.e. whether every single message must reach its destination, or whether some loss of messages can be tolerated). This is reflected in layer five, "communication protocols".

Finally, these messages will actually reach the physical network and move towards their destinations. The details of the network (e.g. exactly how machines are connected together, and the technologies used to connect them) will contribute a final determining factor to the system's network requirements. This is reflected in layer six, "network communication".

It is apparent that the network requirements of a CVE (such as the network bandwidth required) depend on all of these factors, and also on others which are beyond the scope of this chapter. As well as flowing from task to network, influence also flows in the other direction, from the final network requirements back up towards the software and the user. We will give some examples of these influences later in this chapter.

In the remainder of this chapter we will examine each of the layers of this model, using examples from real use of CVEs to illustrate the issues. We will consider in turn: elements of user behaviour and the potential effect of tasks and roles; a simple approach to quantifying process behaviour; examples of distribution architecture; choices of communication protocol; and the influence of the underlying network shape (i.e. its topology).

4.2 User Behaviour

It is important to consider user behaviour when trying to understand the network requirements of CVEs because almost all of those network requirements derive directly from what the users choose to do and when they choose to do it. For example, if users spoke only rarely, and never at the same time, then the network requirement for audio would be very limited – enough bandwidth for a single audio stream – and even that would not be used more than a fraction of the time. On the other hand, for some scenarios of use (e.g. OOTW, described below) there must be enough bandwidth for every user to speak at the same time, and this bandwidth is likely to be used for a significant fraction of the time.

From a system perspective, most CVEs allow users a restricted range of possible actions. The users may appropriate and adapt these basic actions to their own ends, but the system itself will continue to observe only the basic actions. Typically, the actions available to a user include entering a virtual world (either by starting the CVE system, or by moving from another virtual world); leaving a virtual world (either by stopping the CVE system, or on moving to another virtual world); moving about within the virtual world; speaking (using networked audio, if available); typing text messages; pointing or gesturing within the virtual world; and picking up, moving and otherwise manipulating objects within the virtual world. In addition, a video-based representation of the user may be embedded in the virtual world, allowing the user to convey information about their identity, physical presence, facial expression and limited (real-world) movements.

If a user's action is to be perceived by another (remote) user then it must be input to or detected by the application software they are using, and ultimately converted into a message on the underlying network that will be received, decoded and displayed (in whatever way) by the other user's application. Consequently, every significant action that a user performs has an impact on the system's network communication. So the first step in understanding the network requirements of a CVE is to understand something of what the users are currently doing, and what they are likely to do in the future.

4.2.1 User Behaviour Measurements

We have been involved in several networked trials of CVEs in which we have had the opportunity to monitor and record what the users are doing (recording this information from within the CVE system itself). These networked trials were:

- "Inhabiting the Web" (ITW) (Greenhalgh *et al.*, 1999a), a series of wide-area project meetings (and other related events, such as an end-of-project disco) involving six to ten participants, held in a network of audio-graphical virtual worlds, which used the MASSIVE-1 CVE system. These meetings comprised primarily audio-based activities such as presentations and reporting sessions, plus informal (audio) chat before and after the main meetings. The trials used a small number of linked virtual worlds, with participants moving between worlds (generally as a group) during the course of the meeting (e.g. to view a visualization in a particular virtual world). There were also a number of staged games, for example a balloon debate.

- COVEN project phase 1 wide-area trials of Division's dVS system (Greenhalgh *et al.*, 1998b) (using UCL's RAT audio tool for networked audio); the trials analysed were based on a four-user collaborative 3D business game. The users assembled around the representation of the game, which was in the centre of a virtual room. Each user had to manipulate a number of virtual widgets in order to maximize the total (group) output of an underlying simulation. They had to talk to each other in order to coordinate their activities, for example brokering available resources.

- COVEN project phase 2 wide-area trials of SICS DIVE system (Frécon *et al.*, 1999), with 16 users, playing a clue-based game similar to the board game "Cluedo". This game and trial is also described in Chapter 10.

- "Out Of This World" (OOTW) (Greenhalgh *et al.*, 1999c), a live multi-user virtual game show with three performers and eight members of the public (in two teams), staged using the MASSIVE-2 system. This was a relatively tightly scripted event, in which the teams were taken (forced) through a virtual world and released at different points to play collaborative games. Three of these games were based on movement (e.g. chasing after "space frogs"), and one was a quiz. All of the games encouraged coordination between the team members via the audio channel.

Table 4.2 summarizes some of the user activity data that we have derived from these trials. For example, the first entry in the table records that the average fraction of time for which any given user was moving in the ITW trials was 19.6%, i.e. on average every single user was moving about one fifth of the time. Ranges, where available, show the variation between users. Interaction with virtual objects was only a significant element (and analysed) in the COVEN phase 1 trial. The "mouth" figure for ITW speaking is an alternative estimate of the amount of speaking derived from the appearance of a virtual speech balloon when users were speaking.

From Table 4.2 we can see that there is considerable variation in activity between the various trials, and between users within a single trial. In these figures we are seeing a combination of the effects of the top three layers of our model. Firstly, the task can have a significant impact. For example, the OOTW event was a game show in which the users had to move about a lot in order to play the games. It was also quite fast-paced (for a CVE, at least) and chaotic in places. This may explain (in part) the high values for the percentage of time spent moving and speaking in this event. Secondly, there is considerable variation between users (see the ranges for each value). This may reflect their role within the trial, their natural disposition

Table 4.2. Summary of levels of user activity from past trials

Trial/system	% move	% speak	% interact
ITW/MASSIVE-1	19.6 (7.2–28)	26.4 (mouth 7.2)	–
COVEN1/dVS/RAT	15.6	5.2 (1.3–10.7)	6.8
COVEN2/DIVE	26.3 (17–37)	8.1 (0.1–19.9)	–
OOTW/MASSIVE-2	44.5 (24.2–82.2)	29.3 (11.9–62.7)	–

(e.g. preference for text communication over audio), and simply what happens in that particular trial. Thirdly, different applications will respond differently to users, and may make some things easier or harder. For example, the OOTW trial used joysticks for movement, whereas all of the other trials used the mouse; this may contribute to the large amount of movement in that trial. Similarly, we believe that the audio application used in the ITW trials (part of MASSIVE-1) was probably more sensitive to background noise than those used in the other trials, and this may have inflated the apparent amount of speaking in that set of trials.

We have also looked at the correlation of activity between users, i.e. the extent to which users will move or speak at the same time as each other. In the first three trials we found very little correlation between the activities of different users, i.e. they did not appear either to deliberately move or speak at the same time as other users, or to avoid moving or speaking at the same time as other users. This already contradicts a common intuition or expectation about audio communication: that users will avoid speaking at the same time. This quote is from an Internet standards document on RTP, a protocol for networked media including audio.

> For example, in an audio conference the data [audio] traffic is inherently self-limiting because only one or two people will speak at a time... (Schulzrinne *et al.*, 1996, section 6.1)

We have not found this to be true for the applications that we have considered. (NB: All of the systems analysed relied on automatic silence detection rather than an explicit "push-to-talk" interface.)

When we consider the OOTW event the picture is considerably more extreme. In each of the four OOTW sessions we find that *all eight* normal users are moving simultaneously for about 4.5 minutes and speaking simultaneously for about 30 seconds in each half hour-long show. From our previous experiences we would have predicted a couple of seconds of simultaneous movement and a fraction of a second of simultaneous audio. The staged nature of this event, with its coordinated group activities, clearly has a large influence on what people do and when they do it (as we would expect).

4.2.2 User Behaviour Implications

We have already observed that almost all network requirements derive directly from what the users choose to do and when they choose to do it (e.g. speaking or navigating). When considering network bandwidth, two key measures are the *average bandwidth* and the *peak bandwidth*. The peak bandwidth is the largest bandwidth required at any single moment. For example, if everyone speaks at once this will require a peak bandwidth sufficient to cope with that number of audio streams. The average bandwidth considers the bandwidth requirement over a longer period of time (e.g. minutes or hours). If users speak only occasionally, then the average bandwidth will be lower than if they speak more often, although the peak bandwidth may be the same. In some situations the peak bandwidth is the main limiting factor. For example, on a small network connection, such as a dial-up modem, there is not much bandwidth available, and if everyone speaks at once most of the information will be unable to get through the network and the audio will be unintelligible. In other situations the average bandwidth is more important. For example, if the networks are all relatively high-bandwidth (compared with the peak requirement) and the other network users are all doing their own thing independently of the CVE then the average bandwidth will be a more accurate indication of the resources being used by (and required for) the CVE.

Relating this to user behaviour, we can see that if users are more active then the average bandwidth will be higher (more movement messages, more audio messages per second, and so on). On the other hand, the peak bandwidth will be higher if users' activities are more highly coordinated, as in the OOTW example, above. If we can make reasonable guesses about the activity of users in an anticipated application then we can make better predictions about the network resources that they will require.

We have also found other implications that follow from task or user behaviour. For example, the OOTW event had users playing three distinct roles: host, team captain and team member. When analysing the resulting network requirements we found that each role had different requirements, independent of the particular person playing that role. For example, the different roles had different navigation and interaction facilities: the team captains had tracked immersive interfaces (head-mounted display plus electromagnetic tracking for head and two hands), while the team members had joystick-controlled desktop interfaces. This is a significant issue to consider, both when designing and implementing the system itself (what range of roles will it support and how?) and when considering the network requirements of the system in use (how many users will be present in which roles?).

4.3 Process Behaviour

Every CVE system has its own set of capabilities and its own ways of representing users and virtual worlds. For example, each system will support a different subset of possible user actions. Each system will then communicate each of these actions to the rest of the system using slightly different information in a slightly different form. For a given system it is possible to identify the core set of available actions, and to perform each in relative isolation. By monitoring the rest of the system (e.g. tracking network packets) it is then possible to identify the basic system characteristics of each action.

For example, the MASSIVE-1 system has three key actions: user movement, user audio and learning about a "peer", i.e. a new object or user (e.g. on joining a new virtual world). Each of these component activities has a characteristic communication requirement, as shown in Table 4.3 (based on the analysis in Greenhalgh, 1999, Chapter 6). For example, each time a MASSIVE-1 user takes a step there is a certain amount of communication with the system itself (1.2 kbyte), and an additional communication (2.1 kbyte) which must reach every other user if they are to see the user's movement.

These intrinsic system values must be combined with information about actual user activity in order to predict what will happen in practice. For example, based on

Table 4.3. Characteristic communication requirements for MASSIVE-1 actions

	Movement (kbyte/step)	Audio (kbyte/s)	New peer (kbyte/peer)
To system	1.2	0	2.1
To each observer	2.1	8.3	13.2

Table 4.4. Characteristic communication requirements for a specific MASSIVE-1 user activity scenario

	Movement (kbyte/s)	Audio (kbyte/s)	New peer (kbyte/s)	Total (kbyte/s)
To system	1.4	0	<0.1	1.4
To each observer	2.5	2.1	0.2	4.8

the ITW trials we might take an average speaking rate of 25% (i.e. each user speaks on average one quarter of the time), a movement rate of 20% (i.e. each user moves on average one fifth of the time) and a step rate of 6 Hz (i.e. the user application moves 6 times per second when the user is moving). This would allow us to derive the expected average communication requirements shown in Table 4.4.

These values are specific to each CVE system. For example movement in MASSIVE-1 is rather inefficient compared with many other systems: for DIVE we might expect 0.75 kbyte/s (to the system and any observers), while for MASSIVE-2 this could be as low as 0.05 kbyte/s for the same levels of user activity. How these values translate into actual data on the network also depends on the choice of distribution architecture, communication protocols and network topology, as considered in the remaining sections.

4.3.1 State Versus Updates

Note that, as in this example, we can normally identify two distinct classes of communication requirement which can be characterized as "state" and "updates". Their typical characteristics are as follows.

State completely describes a virtual object at a single moment in time (e.g. the representation of a user, or a virtual object). It may include position information, geometry, text attributes and other components. Typically, when a user first discovers another object or user (e.g. when they join a new virtual world) they must obtain its initial state. The size of an object's state can vary enormously according to its media components and complexity.

Updates describe only the changes in a virtual object's state. In many systems they are significantly smaller than the initial state because they reflect only that portion of the state that has changed. In a few systems state and updates are (largely) equivalent; for example, the IEEE Distributed Interactive Simulation (DIS) standard (IEEE, 1993) defines update and state to be equivalent, although it does this by making the 3D geometry of the object external to its state and therefore largely fixed. Continuous media streams (e.g. audio and video) also appear as a form of updates, since they have little or no lasting value to the system, but simply reflect what is being said or is visible at that moment.

We have found that updates comprise the majority of the network traffic in the trials that we have analysed. This is partly due to their inclusion of real-time audio and/or video. Partly because of this we have focused on updates in this analysis. However, note that there is also typically more flexibility in how updates can be distributed and which protocols can be used (i.e. it is often more interesting to design for updates). State transfers on the other hand tend to require some kind of server-type component, and unicast (i.e. direct process-to-process) communication (see below).

4.3.2 Application Behaviour Implications

The application behaviour, as we have considered it here, sets the base-line for a CVE system in two respects: it determines the basic quantities of information which need to be communicated in order for the CVE to operate; and it determines the capabilities of the CVE, i.e. what is possible within the CVE (since if something cannot be communicated then it cannot be seen by a remote user, and if it cannot be seen then there is little point doing it in a collaborative system – see also Chapters 5 and 7).

There are several fairly standard trade-offs that must be made at this level when designing and implementing a CVE. For example:

- Using small messages to communicate user activities will reduce the final network requirements of the system, and may make some parts of the system more efficient. However, smaller messages can contain less information, so that the capabilities and flexibility of the CVE may be limited. Also, smaller messages may require more processing to get the necessary information from them (e.g. consider the use of compression).

- Using many different specialized messages may allow each message to be as compact as possible (similar to the above point). However, it will increase the complexity of the system and therefore the time taken to create it and perhaps the likelihood of it containing bugs.

- Using just a few very general kinds of message may make the messages larger, and may increase the processing required for each message (by introducing more levels of indirection between the message itself and the final result). However, it may also allow the system to be simpler and more general-purpose.

Excepting specific applications with extreme demands, a good design heuristic is: design a system to be as general as possible, and then optimize only the most heavily used parts of the system. Typically, this approach gives a flexible system which is also reasonably efficient, and in a reasonable amount of (programmer) time.

4.4 Distribution Architecture

So far we have established that user activities give rise to information to be communicated between parts of the distributed CVE system. The choice of distribution architecture determines which information must be communicated to which parts of the system. Among other things, the distribution architecture will therefore determine how virtual worlds are organized and divided, which users can communicate with each other, and whether or not there are any central coordinating processes or servers. All of the systems which we have studied use a peer-to-peer distribution architecture in which every user application is responsible for communicating with every other user application which it can see or that can be seen by it. However, there are also significant differences between their architectures, which are outlined below.

In MASSIVE-1 there is a server called the "aura manager" or "spatial trader" which introduces user applications to each other when they are close in virtual space. Consequently users can only interact when they are in the same virtual world and close enough in virtual space.

dVS does not have an aura manager component; rather, all users in a given virtual world can always interact with each other. Also, a single process is responsible for the world as a whole. This means that MASSIVE-1 can (in principle, at least) cope with very large virtual worlds better than dVS, since MASSIVE-1 will only require communication between "nearby" users (this issue is considered in Section 4.5.2).

DIVE, unlike dVS, has some general-purpose facilities which programmers can use to divide a single virtual world into smaller units, and to restrict communication within these regions. Like MASSIVE-1, this allows it (in principle) to support very large virtual worlds more efficiently. However, these facilities must be used and managed explicitly by the world programmer. Note that DIVE is the only system considered here which has absolutely no application-level servers, although it does have a network-level system bootstrap server and also makes use of standard WWW servers to serve static data files. In principle this should make DIVE more resilient to program and network failures since there is no single point of failure for a virtual world.

MASSIVE-2 has a concept of "regions" (also known more generally as "third-party objects") which can be used to subdivide a large virtual world and to introduce additional communication constraints. For example, the walls of a room (a region) can be made impervious to a medium (e.g. audio), thereby restricting communication within the virtual world. The implementation of regions requires the use of limited server-type processes to manage those regions.

Many other systems employ client–server architectures rather than peer-to-peer approaches. In this case most or all communication between user applications occurs via one or more centralized server processes which are responsible for that virtual world, e.g. Deva (Chapter 3), NetEffect (Das *et al.*, 1997), CommunityPlace (Lea *et al.*, 1997). Client–server and peer-to-peer approaches are considered further in Section 4.6.1.

The reader should not place undue emphasis of issue of client–server versus peer-to-peer approaches; for example, several systems allow a flexible combination of client–server and peer-to-peer communication, mixing the advantages and disadvantages of both approaches, e.g. SPLINE (Barrus *et al.*, 1996b) and DIVE when used with the DiveBone (Frécon *et al.*, 1999).

4.4.1 Distribution Architecture Implications

The choice of distribution architecture is the main factor determining much of the multi-user "feel" of a CVE. For example, the distribution architecture will typically determine:

- The possible structure of a virtual world, e.g. whether it can cope well with large outdoor spaces or with complex building interiors. For example, MASSIVE-1 and MASSIVE-2 can both cope with large outdoor spaces by allowing each user to experience only a nearby portion of it. However, MASSIVE-1 cannot take account of additional constraints such as rooms when managing distribution – it would require that they be made separate worlds.

- The number of virtual worlds, and the relationships between them, e.g. whether there is a web-like network of virtual worlds which users can teleport between (as in DIVE or MASSIVE-1), or a smaller number of isolated environments (as in dVS or MASSIVE-2), or one essentially seamless but very large virtual world (as envisaged in some popular works of science fiction).

- Who can see what and whom in a virtual world. For example, a user might choose only to see and interact with nearby objects and users in MASSIVE-1, whereas they could not make this choice in dVS.

- How many users can share a single virtual world. Typically if every user – or any other single part of the system – has to be able to cope with knowing about everything in a given virtual world (as in dVS) then this will limit the size of the world, whereas a system which allows each user and server to restrict its knowledge to only part of the virtual world (as in MASSIVE-2) should support larger virtual worlds containing more users.

- The dynamics of the virtual world, including the ways in which behaviours can be realized (e.g. see Chapter 3) and what things can and cannot be changed. For example, it is extremely hard to dynamically change basic geometries in some systems (e.g. dVS and almost all DIS-based systems), whereas it is relatively easy in others (e.g. DIVE).

- The extensibility of the virtual world. For example, some systems will allow completely new objects or applications to be introduced into a live world (e.g. DIVE object behaviours written in the scripting language TCL), whereas other systems would require applications to be recompiled and re-run in order to add new behaviours (e.g. MASSIVE-2).

From a distributed systems perspective this is probably the most interesting part of designing and implementing a CVE system. There are already many options and approaches, and more appear all the time. Further examples and discussion relating to the first four points can be found in Section 4.5.2.

4.5 Communication Protocol

The distribution architecture determines, logically, which parts of the distributed CVE system should communicate with each other. However, even within a given distribution architecture there remains a choice of final protocol to be used. For example, protocols can be either *unicast*, where each network message (packet) is sent to exactly one other application, or *multicast*, where each network packet can be sent in a single operation to an entire group of applications.

In addition, protocols can be either *unreliable*, where a given message may or may not reach its destination (depending on what is happening in the network and the applications), or *reliable*, where a given message is guaranteed to reach its destination (eventually, and assuming that no critical application crashes or terminates). Generally, reliable protocols introduce additional traffic to ensure reliability and, when packets are lost, additional delays before the data is finally delivered. On the other hand, reliable protocols often include some form of flow and congestion control to limit the rate at which messages are actually sent so that the receiving applications and the network can cope. This is often missing from unreliable protocols and can make their use problematic in some networks.

Of the systems we have considered, MASSIVE-1 and dVS use unicast protocols, while DIVE and MASSIVE-2 use multicast protocols (both over IP multicast; Deering and Cheriton, 1990). All of the systems use *un*reliable communication for audio, because it is generally considered that low audio delay is more important that a certain amount of audio message loss. The DIVE and MASSIVE-2 systems both use forms of selective reliability. For example, normal user movement messages are sent unreliably, on the assumption that they will soon move again, thereby bringing everyone up to date. Most other messages are sent reliably to ensure that everyone has approximately the same view of the virtual world.

4.5.1 Communication Requirements Example

Let us consider the total communication requirements of MASSIVE-1. We already know (from Table 4.4) what the basic communication requirements are. We will choose to restrict our consideration to application domains in which users comprise the majority of (distributed) world content and activity. From this, using what we know of MASSIVE-1's choice of distribution architecture (localized in virtual space by an aura manager) and communication protocol (unicast, peer-to-peer) we can predict the total communication requirements for MASSIVE-1. This will depend both on the number of simultaneous users and (because it is unicast) on the number of observers that each user has. We will denote these parameters as

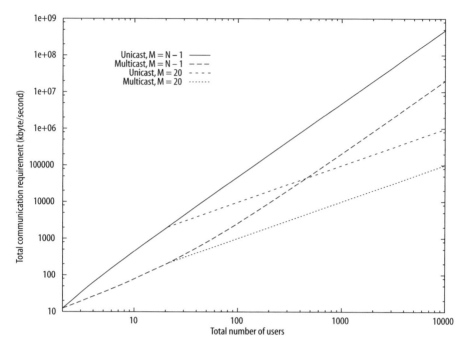

Figure 4.1 Total communication requirements for MASSIVE-1, showing the effects of aura management (i.e. $M < N - 1$) and choice of unicast/multicast.

N and M, respectively. The total communication requirement (typically the average bandwidth) is then (in kbyte/s):

$$B = N(4.8M + 1.4) \tag{1}$$

For a constant number of observers per user, M, (i.e. for a constant size of interacting group) this is proportional to N, the total number of users (see Fig. 4.1). However, if every user is observed by every other user (as would be the case in dVS) then $M = N - 1$, and the total communication requirement would be (in kbyte/s):

$$B = 4.8N^2 - 3.4N \tag{2}$$

In this case, the total communication requirement would be proportional to N^2. To illustrate the effect of the choice of communication protocol, we can image what would happen if MASSIVE-1 could be modified to make ideal use of multicasting (which is actually extremely problematic in general, because of the number of different multicast groups that would be required). In this case, each message sent by a user application would only need to be sent once by multicast, rather than M times by unicast (once to each and every observer of that user). In this case, the total communication requirement would be reduced to (kbyte/s):

$$B = N(0.2M + 6.0)$$

And the worst-base bandwidth (with $M = N - 1$) would be reduced to (kbyte/s):

$$B = 0.2N^2 + 5.8N$$

In the limit, as N tends to infinity, this is a 24-fold reduction. The remaining N^2 term – which limits the potential reduction – is due to the requirement to inform an observer when they discover a new user or object. With some additional optimizations (and in some alternative approaches, such as DIS's heartbeat method; IEEE, 1993) this term can be significantly reduced, or even eliminated for certain applications.

Figure 4.1 illustrates the variation in bandwidth requirements for MASSIVE-1 as modelled here. Note the significant (potential) benefits of subdividing the virtual world, i.e. using virtual locality to reduce the number of observers for each user, M. Note also the large difference between the use of unicast and (ideal) multicast protocols. This kind of comparison has motivated many practitioners to use multicast communications protocols for CVEs which are intended to have large numbers of users. Note, however, that protocols and network provision for multicast is still a research area, especially for applications with large numbers of active senders (as is the case in a CVE) – multicast communication can cause considerable additional complication, and is not universally available (e.g. between many network operators on the Internet at large). Multicast versus unicast is considered further in Section 4.6.1.

4.5.2 Issues for Interest Management

Given this simple analysis we can now revisit some aspects of distribution architecture in a more quantitative way. Interest management is a role of the distribution architecture and is concerned with determining which processes (especially clients) receive which information. This determines several characteristics of the system, such as the nature and structure of virtual worlds. It also has a major influence on system scalability as measured by the potential sizes of virtual worlds, and the numbers of users that they can contain.

The analysis in the previous section was concerned with the total bandwidth requirements for the whole system. When considering interest management we consider instead the network traffic being received and handled by a single user client program. For MASSIVE-1 this analysis gives approximately (in kbyte/s):

$$B_C = 4.8M + 1.4$$

This is proportional to M, the number of observers per user (defined above). This assumes that observers (users) are the main distributed entities in the virtual world, and that observation is approximately reciprocal, i.e. on average a user with M observers will be able to observe M active virtual entities (those same observers). From each entity users will receive initial state information when they first come into range, and thereafter will receive movement and audio data (and any other updates) from those entities. It is relatively straightforward to include non-observer (passive) objects into the model, although this will introduce additional terms into all of the equations (e.g. M_P the number of passive objects in range of an average observer).

In the case of MASSIVE-1, the aura manager is responsible for interest management: "interest" is defined in this case as "within aura range", i.e. nearby in virtual space. If a user had an extremely large aura then all of that virtual world would be considered to be of interest to them, and their value of M (above) would tend towards N, the total number of users (or other active entities) in the virtual world. On the other hand, a user with a very small aura would tend to have a correspondingly small value of M, i.e. very few other users or entities in range.

Note that this *received* bandwidth is the same, irrespective of the communication protocol used (multicast or unicast), although the bandwidth *sent* by the client is much lower in the multicast case (equivalent to $M = 1$, i.e. 6.2 kbyte/s). Note also that every received message is different and has to be processed and handled, whereas in the unicast case each outbound message is simply sent M times, which is a much less CPU-intensive task.

The goal of interest management is generally to ensure that each process receives precisely the information that it needs, and no more. For example, it is not usually necessary for a process to receive geometry updates from an entity that it cannot see (because it is too far away, or beyond a wall), or to receive audio packets from an entity that it cannot hear (because it is too far away, or inside a soundproof room). MASSIVE-1 allows processes to use aura to describe how far they want to see or hear. In addition, MASSIVE-2 allows regions to be specified which modify interest (more accurately, "awareness"). For example, a soundproof room can be represented by a region that blocks audio awareness in and out. MASSIVE-2's interest management system uses this information to avoid sending audio from inside the room to processes that are outside it, and therefore could never hear the audio.

Interest management is a complex area, however some general observations can be made (see also Greenhalgh, 1999).

Firstly, different interest management schemes express "interest" in different ways, e.g. distance, awareness, visibility. Each definition of "interest" will be suited to particular kinds of virtual worlds and applications, and may be quite unsuitable for others. For example, a simple distance measure is a very poor way of determining visibility in a complex interior environment (e.g. an architectural walkthrough).

Secondly, interest management can operate at a range of typical granularities, or levels of detail. For example, MASSIVE-1 performs interest management on individual virtual entities. This is potentially accurate, and may be appropriate for highly active objects (e.g. video avatars, as in Nakanishi *et al.*, 1998). However, it incurs significant management overheads, especially in worlds containing many otherwise simple objects. At the other extreme, dVS can be regarded as performing interest management on entire virtual worlds – you simply join a particular world. Several systems use intermediate forms of interest management, including MASSIVE-2 (regions), SPLINE (Locales) and DIVE (lightweight groups). This is a good compromise approach for many applications.

Thirdly, whenever a new entity becomes of interest to a process, that process must obtain initial state information describing the entity. If interest changes rapidly then the requirements for state communication will be correspondingly greater. This may be the case because the virtual world content is volatile (i.e. many objects are arriving and leaving), because the user is moving rapidly, or because interest is defined in a very discontinuous way (e.g. strict visibility in some types of complex environment). In such cases it may be appropriate to impose additional constraints to limit the rate of change of interest (e.g. a speed limit, a quarantine period on entry), or to design the interest management system to be less accurate but more stable (e.g. by including additional leaving delays).

Fourthly, processes may not be able to cope with what is nominally of interest to them. For example, if a MASSIVE-1 user entered an extremely crowded area, then the same size of aura would suddenly give a much higher value of M and correspondingly more communication and information to cope with. A robust interest management scheme would require a significant degree of adaptation or active management to deal gracefully with situations like this. A simple approach used by Das *et al.* (1997) is to have access controls which prevent too many people entering a world or region at the same time. In MASSIVE-1 the user could adaptively reduce their aura to maintain an acceptable value for M. In dynamically regioned systems (such as MASSIVE-2) it would be possible to automatically subdivide the virtual world into smaller sub-regions, to try to maintain acceptable levels of M. A complementary approach would be to use some form of adaptive group control (comparable to that used in RTCP; Schulzrinne *et al.*, 1996), to reduce network traffic for larger values of M.

Fifthly, in some applications it is also appropriate to consider fidelity: some interest management systems allow the same underlying information to be provided in different forms. For example, MASSIVE-2 allows regions to act as "abstractions", providing a summarized or otherwise simplified representation of what is happening inside them. One example is the "crowd" region, which represents a group of users via a single composite geometry and audio stream. For some observers this abstraction will provide all the information they need, without the full communication and processing costs of receiving information individually from every user within the crowd (i.e. effectively reducing M). Other users may require fuller information, and choose to observe the contents of the crowd directly.

4.6 Network Topology

Based on the factors considered so far, we have built up an understanding of what parts of the CVE communicate, and how much information they exchange. In the last section we were able to form a model of total communication requirements for an example CVE. However, the final network requirements will depend on exactly where in the network each application is running, and how the network is connected (i.e. its topology). For example, if the network is a local area network (LAN) such as an Ethernet, formed using a shared coaxial bus or a central hub, then every machine on the LAN will observe every packet, and the total network requirements will simply be the total communication requirements as in the previous section. However, if the CVE is running over a more complex network, such as a number of LANs connected by a wide area network (WAN) then the actual bandwidth in different parts of the network will vary.

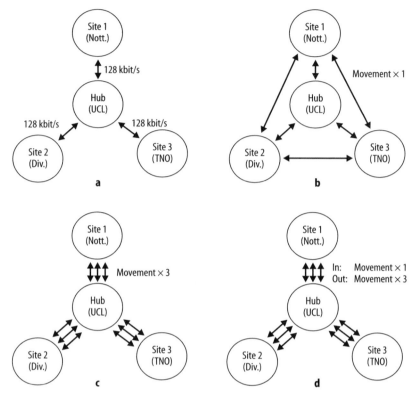

Figure 4.2 Mapping logical communication to network topology for the COVEN dVS trials. **a** Physical network topology. **b** Logical communication. **c** Resulting actual network requirements. **d** Multicast or client–server network requirements.

For example, the COVEN phase 1 trials with dVS were conducted over a dedicated WAN created using ISDN modems. The network was a physical star network (see Fig. 4.2a), with a central hub, and three outlying networks each connected to the hub via its own dial-up ISDN connection with a bandwidth of 128 kbit/s. As already described, dVS has a peer-to-peer distribution architecture which uses unicast protocols. The logical communication between the four applications is therefore as shown in Fig. 4.2b. However, because of the underlying network topology, the only way for messages to get from the user at site 1 to any other user was via the hub. Consequently, the CVE communication was concentrated on these underlying network links, as shown in Fig. 4.2c.

4.6.1 Multicast, Peer-to-Peer and Client–Server Revisited

The scenario in Fig. 4.2 allows us to make an informative comparison between unicast peer-to-peer, multicast peer-to-peer and client–server distribution and communication architectures. We consider each in turn, focusing on the network requirements imposed on a single link (e.g. between site 1 and the hub).

First, we can consider unicast peer-to-peer communication, as shown in Fig. 4.2c. Suppose that there are M observers for a user's action: the hub and the other sites, i.e. $M = 3$ for Fig. 4.2. With a unicast peer-to-peer approach the user's application has to send M copies of each message over the network connection to the hub. These all represent the same user action, and so must all be sent at the same time. This makes the traffic highly correlated (all M messages are being at the same time), and means that we must consider the peak bandwidth requirements rather than the average bandwidth requirements on this connection. This is typically the first major bottleneck in a scenario such as this, and limits the number of users who can be aware of each other in a virtual world (i.e. $M + 1$).

The traffic coming back from the hub has a different composition: there is one copy of each message from each other user (typically also M). To a first approximation, the peak and average bandwidth requirements *from* the hub are the same as those *to* the hub. However, there is only a limited probability that all M other users will move or speak at the same time, and therefore the peak bandwidth is less likely to occur in practice. With enough users and the right kind of application it may be sufficient to consider the *average* bandwidth requirements from the hub and to ignore the *peak* requirements (implicitly assuming that when one user is more active, many others will be less active).

Second, we can consider multicast peer-to-peer communication. In this case the hub will have a multicast router. Each user's application sends only one copy of each message to the hub. The hub then copies this single message and sends it to each of the other sites, as well as making it available to the hub network. This removes the first bandwidth bottleneck, which was due to sending multiple copies of the same message(s) over the link to the hub. This can be seen in Fig. 4.2d.

The next bottleneck is then likely to be the traffic coming back from the hub. This will be exactly the same in the multicast case as it was in the unicast case because it was already free of duplicate packets. The only exception to this is if there are multiple users at a single site, in which case there would have been duplicate packets on the connection (one copy for each local user); using multicast would remove these duplicates.

In terms of network requirements, multicast is a clear winner over peer-to-peer unicast. However, it currently has additional operational problems. For example, flow and congestion control are much easier with unicast protocols than with multicast protocols, and multicast may not even be available on a given wide area network. Using multicast also sacrifices the flexibility to send different versions of a message to different observers. For example, FreeWalk (Nakanishi, *et al.*, 1998) sends video using peer-to-peer unicast so that it can tailor each video message to exactly match the requirements of each observer.

Third, we can consider unicast client–server communication. A simple client–server system will actually look the same as a multicast peer-to-peer system when used over this network topology (provided that the server is located at the hub). This is because client–server communication is logically a star topology, which fits exactly with the network shown here, whereas multicast is logically a bus topology (all machines connected directly together) which has to be mapped onto this underlying star topology. In a simple client–server system the server takes over the multicast router's job of copying and forwarding messages at the hub.

Disadvantages of the client–server approach are as follows. The server will have to do more processing on each message than a multicast router would, and is less optimized for this task. Depending on how the CVE is organized (e.g. if it enforces virtually local interaction) the server may also have to deal with more clients than any single client has observers. Thus communicating via a server almost always increases the minimum delay between one user application sending a message and it being received by another user application. Some practitioners argue that the server(s) are always inherent bottlenecks which limit the scalability of the system, however, in our experience other factors are at least as likely to be the immediate limits to scalability (e.g. user application CPU load, rendering). The client–server approach will always be a logical star, irrespective of the underlying network topology. In other kinds of network this can be highly inappropriate. For example if the server was placed at site 2 (making a tree rather than a star) then messages from site 1 to site 3 would have to travel to the hub, then to site 2 (the server), and then back to the hub before finally reaching their destination.

Advantages of the client–server approach are as follows. All communication with a given user application can take place over a single unicast network connection. This makes it relatively easy to include effective flow and congestion control, so that the system will work more reliably over a range of network bandwidths and conditions. Using a single network connection also allows some of the overheads of network communication to be avoided. For example, messages from several users can be combined by the server into a single network packet, which is generally more efficient (Das *et al.*, 1997). A server can perform additional processing and filtering on messages which a multicast router would never do. For example, a server could summarize a sequence of related messages into a single message to be sent to a client. A server could also be more selective about which messages are sent to which clients than could a multicast router-based system. More generally, client–server systems tend to offer greater control and easier management than peer-to-peer systems.

It should be clear to the reader at this stage that there is no universal choice of distribution or communication architecture, but rather a range of trade-offs in performance and deployment issues. At the present time a reasonable heuristic is to use multicast for unreliable communication (e.g. some updates, audio, video) between system components on a common LAN (e.g. within a server cluster), to use peer-to-peer unicast for highly tailored inter-peer communication (as in FreeWalk) and to use client–server communication for everything else. Note, however, that multicast may well increase its scope of use over the next few years.

4.6.2 Implications of Network Requirements

Now that we have finally arrived at a (relatively complete) understanding and model of network requirements for a CVE we can apply it in three ways.

Firstly, for a particular CVE, application and network we can predict how many users the system should support. We can also address similar questions, such as how active they can be. For example, from the analysis of MASSIVE-1 we expect that a dedicated 10 Mbit/s Ethernet (say 1000 kbyte/s data) could support around 14 mutually aware users (Equation 2).

Secondly and similarly, if we have a particular application and scenario (including a required number of users) then we can predict the network requirements and hence the size and type of network that we will require. This gives us a powerful planning tool when we are considering deploying and using a CVE "for real". For example, again for MASSIVE-1, if we require a system an application to support 30 users, each having 10 observers (i.e. roughly in three groups) then the expected network requirement would be about 1500 kbyte/s (Equation 1).

Thirdly, the complete model gives us an analytical tool that allows us to perform thought experiments with a complete CVE design. This may allow us to identify critical design choices for our particular application, and to prioritize work on enhancing or evolving a system. For example, the theoretical consideration of the use of multicast rather than unicast communication for MASSIVE-1 (above) was a key factor in selecting multicast communication as the basis for MASSIVE-2.

4.7 Conclusions

In this chapter we have laid out some of the many factors which together determine the network requirements of a particular CVE system in use. We have shown, using data from a number of networked trials, that changes to any of these factors can have a significant impact on the final network requirements of the CVE. These factors include the task, application and collaboration requirements; the individual users; the behaviour of the particular applications that they use to access the CVE; the distribution architecture and communication protocols used to implement the CVE system; and the underlying network over which the system is used, especially its topology (shape). We have also indicated how influence can flow both up and down within this model. For example, different tasks or applications can give rise to radically different network characteristics. On the other hand, designing for a particular network or other limitation can constrain design and implementation choices at every level within the system.

We have spent some time considering basic communication and distribution architectures, giving particular attention to issues of interest management.

Designing and implementing CVE systems remains an interesting and challenging exercise and research area; there are many interrelated choices, and many possible approaches and partial solutions. Because of the vast range of choices and possible domains of use, no single system or design is likely to provide a universal solution to distribution and network communication for collaborative virtual environments. Elements of typical "best practice" are beginning to emerge, but this is still far from a solved problem. To echo West and Hubbold in Chapter 3, it is to be hoped that the next few years will produce a growing body of common practice and reusable and combinable resources.

Acknowledgements

We would like to thank the many people who have taken part in the various trials which have informed this work, and projects and sponsors which have supported them, including British Telecommunications (the ITW project and OOTW), the UK's EPSRC (OOTW), and the EU ACTS program (the COVEN project).

Part 3
Bodies, Presences and Interactions

Chapter 5

"He's Behind You": The Experience of Presence in Shared Virtual Environments

Monika Büscher, Jon O'Brien, Tom Rodden and Jonathan Trevor

5.1 Introduction

In this chapter we seek to develop an understanding of the nature of presence in virtual environments from a real-world exploration of first, how presence is manifest in practice within virtual environments and second, the means by which everyday users experience virtual environments. The ethnographic study presented in this chapter is part of a multidisciplinary approach to the design of online large-scale collaborative virtual environments (CVEs) undertaken by the authors in a range of projects. Over the last few years a large number of systems to support online virtual worlds and CVEs have emerged. These include 3D environments: MASSIVE (Greenhalgh and Benford, 1995), DIVE (Dix, 1997), AlphaWorlds, Blaxxun, VWWW; 2D graphical systems: ThePalace; and textual environments: MUDs (Edwards, 1994).

The popularity and diversity of these systems provides us with one of the main motivations for the study and our particular exploration of presence. Existing views of electronic environments have tended to adopt an insular stance with considerations of the virtual environment focusing on the nature of a single environment with little or no regard for the ongoing existence of other virtual environments and systems. Thus users are considered to inhabit a single virtual environment and considerations of presence have focused on the user embedded within that single environment. We wish to broaden this stance to consider these environments in relation to those around them and consider how people manage presence when they are involved in more than one environment.

While the need to consider users' involvement with multiple environments has driven a number of approaches to standardization (most notably in the case of VRML) this has tended to focus on the structure and nature of the worlds and the transfer of different world formations. We wish to consider much more dynamic support for translation between environments. Essentially, we envisage an "e-scape" – an electronic landscape or universe – as a "container" where a diversity of "worlds" and users can meet. We can consider an e-scape as a technical "common ground" and, at the same time, a "physical" space where people can move around and gauge some information about a world before entering it. This information may include world-specific information, such as the quality of display available from the user's respective platform, the structure and appearance of worlds, and the current population of, and activities in, different worlds. It could also include information about the relationships between different worlds (expressed, for example, through their position relative to each other in the e-scape) and the orientation of people inspecting these worlds. Such information provides users with a sense of overview and transition and improves on the current abruptness of teleporting between environments and seeks to maintain a much more continuous notion of presence.

However, it is important to facilitate movement between "worlds" in a way that is socially and aesthetically rich, intuitive and pleasurable. This is particularly critical in view of the fact that the aim is to make online worlds available to the general citizen. The heterogeneity of this audience in terms of "virtual" literacy and technical equipment require a constructive approach to the design of large-scale CVEs. Building on the experience of CSCW, where ethnographic studies of the sociality of work have been used to inform the design of collaborative systems, we have undertaken ethnographic studies of the social organization of space in real and virtual environments and combined this with artistic expertise, praxis and theory to inform the design of electronic landscapes.

The study of interaction in real-world situations has been particularly useful in shedding light on the richness of interactional resources and practices (e.g. Heath and Luff 1992, Suchman 1987, Hughes *et al.*, 1992). For a number of technical reasons, this richness cannot be realized in electronic environments, especially in the context of screen-based versions with their limited field of view and restrictions on interaction. While in some respects this is a problem, in others our research suggests it need not be one, which indicates that users can exploit the features available to them within the environment to develop a sense of presence. In this chapter we wish to report an ethnographic study of visitors' experiences to a multimedia art museum where they encounter a range of different virtual environments.

5.2 The Ethnographic Study

Our exploration of presence draws on fieldwork undertaken in the media museum of ZKM, where a number of interactive art works made shared electronic environments available to the public. The Centre for Art and Media Technology (ZKM) in Karlsruhe, Germany, was founded as a new type of institution that brings together art and technology in an unprecedented and unrivalled way. It combines two research institutes (the Institute for Music and Acoustics, and the Institute for Visual Media), a Media Library and three museums: the Museum for Contemporary Art, the City Gallery and the Media Museum. 12 years after its conception, ZKM was opened to the public in October 1997. This event was celebrated with a number of events and the 5th Multimediale (a biannual exhibition organized by ZKM since 1989). Permanent and temporary exhibitions at the Media Museum contain around 30–40 works. The ethnographic study reported on in this chapter was carried out over a total of 9 weeks, covering the whole of ZKM's opening, and 3 weeks of "normal" opening time in December 1997 and March 1998.

One means of informing an intuitive and legible design of CVEs and to allow people to experience a sense of presence within them are studies of the strategies people employ in moving around real-world space. We draw upon observations from these studies here, but note that such observations in physical space settings alone do not suffice to inform the design of CVEs. Mediating technologies, while in many respects extending the possibilities for human interaction, inevitably alter and impoverish the richness of interactionally relevant information we take for granted in our everyday face-to-face interactions. Therefore, it is necessary to observe people's interactions in and with such environments. However, despite the emergence of online electronic environments these still remain a specialist concern and are seldom used by general citizens – there are few opportunities to observe real-world situations in which people begin to inhabit electronic spaces. To overcome this problem, we undertook a series of studies at ZKM. Field notes derived from participant observation, and documentation of people's engagement with the art works in audio and video recordings were transcribed and analysed.

In our analysis we explore a set of issues that emerge from our observations of the sense of presence experienced by museum visitors using electronic environments. Essentially, video, audio and observational data suggest that a sense of presence is not an individually owned, private quality, but rather one that is embedded in the sociality of our existence in the world. People adapt familiar practices and interpretations entwined with a sense of presence to the affordances of electronic environments. Everyday practices of orientation, movement, and interaction in space are drawn upon, but transposed rather than transplanted in order to fit in with the affordances of the environment. Moreover, a sense of presence is not "split off" from presence in the "real world" but, rather, extended from the real to the virtual space. This means that the practical engagement with electronic environments is one in which activities in the real space are relevant to the activities and events in the virtual space, and vice versa; and that in practice the interface and the screen merge into an instrument with which the electronic space is seen and experienced. Some of the practices involved in the management of this relationship between activities in the physical space and those in the electronic space will be addressed. However, the main issue we are concerned with here is the question of how people adapt to the affordances of the electronic environments.

5.3 Presence in Electronic Environments

In this section, we explore interactional presence – how we are present as participants in interactions with others – and a sense of presence in relation to objects and spaces in electronic environments. In the following examples taken from four distinctive environments studied at the ZKM we present these two experiences of presence and suggest that each environment reflects different facets of our overall experience of being in the world.

5.3.1 Labyrinthos

Labyrinthos (Frank den Oudsten; see Figs. 5.1 and 5.2) is a collaborative environment. It is a game reminiscent of Midi-Maze, the first networked game for home

Figure 5.1 Y, T and O at their terminals.

Figure 5.2 Y bending to see O's screen.

computers, which allows eight players to move through a model of the exhibition space and "shoot" each other. Each player controls a coloured sphere through a simple control (Fig. 5.3). The terminals have different colours that correspond to the colours of the avatars. If an avatar is repeatedly hit, its face changes expression. Eventually it becomes transparent and immobile. The successful "hunter" on the other hand gets a crown. Here, three boys are hunting in a "pack". Y is sitting at the yellow terminal, O at the orange one to his right, and a third boy (T) is moving from one to the other (Figs. 5.1 and 5.2)[1].

---

[1] Most of the transcripts presented in this chapter are translated from German. Therefore, some expressions and overlaps ([xx]) do not exactly correspond with the original.

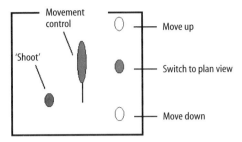

Figure 5.3 Labyrinthos interface.

 1 O: hey I'm alive again!
 2 T: eh cool (d'y' know)
 3   [where you are right now?)]
 4 Y: [eh? Where are you?] (0.) eh ((glances across)) where are you::?
 5 O: I don't know either I'm back at (the square there)
 6 ?:   (xxx face)
 7 Y: WHERE?
 8 O: there comes purple
 9 T: ah!
10 O: eh!
11 Y: ((bends across and back while saying)) I I'm coming where are
12   you? Oh there
13 ?:   (xx)
14 T: blue!
15 Y: I've got gre- I see red I SEE RED I I'm coming to help you I've
16   got green under attack ((starts shooting))
17 O: me too I'm shooting=
18 Y: =eh? (xx but you said xx)
19 O: sh*t
20 T: he! (xx)
21 Y: die you (sh*t)
22 ?:   attention!
23 T: eh! Red is behind you
24 O: red is behind you (0.)
25 Y: where? (.) ni- attention (.)

Y and O are moving their avatars through the space. In order to be able to play successfully, they need to know where they are, in relation to potential targets and each other. At the start of this excerpt of talk, O's avatar suddenly responds to his manipulations of the control after a period of immobility. Immediately, he makes public that he is once more an active player in the game. Now his position in the space becomes an issue. In order to "attack" their opponents effectively, the three boys need to assume strategic positions and coordinate their actions. In their approach they take advantage of the fact that they are distributed across a large distance in the electronic space, yet co-located in the real space. Y asks "where are you" while moving his avatar forward, but the answer is too vague for him to find O. His third request "WHERE?" is cut short by the fact that O discovers "Purple" and is put on the spot. Shots are exchanged and help seems required. Y, in one move, bends across, glances at O's screen, and states "I'm coming to help you". Having seen what O sees, Y is able to work out where he is. However, on his way he encounters first "Red", then "Green". He attacks "Green". What he fails to realize is that meanwhile "Red" has begun to shoot at him from behind. The others can see "red" attacking Y on O's screen. They warn him. A little later on in this game, O "kills" purple. He switches to plan view, where the avatars are represented as coloured arrowheads, and notices that Y is being attacked by "Green".

Reciprocity of Perspective and the Intersubjective Organization of Interaction

Y's move in line 11 rightly assumes that the space of the game is the same for everybody involved and thus projects a principle we routinely apply in our everyday actions into the electronic space. As a "hunter" in the game Y does (and in fact needs to) take for granted that views from different positions in the game are interchangeable. The space must be the same for everyone, otherwise one would not be able to aim at targets. This is necessarily reflected in the visual display on the respective players' screens. Y exploits this fact. Glancing at O's screen he assumes that "if I change place with him so that his 'here' becomes mine, I would be at the same distance from things and see them in the same typicality as he... does" (Schutz, 1970, p. 183). Seeing what O sees allows Y to locate O on his own screen. If the game took place in physical space, Y would not be able to put himself in O's place so easily. Here he makes use of the affordances of the situation and transposes his knowledge of the interchangeability of perspectives.

Such "reciprocity of perspective" is one aspect of a more general principle of intersubjectivity that underpins interactions between people and between people and their material environment. What we say, perceive or do is part and parcel of a world known in common (Schutz, 1970). In our actions, we assume that others know the world and the situation at hand in ways that are similar to how we know them, and we assume that the material world is arranged in a way that draws on and refers to such common knowledge. Thus, for all practical purposes, we assume that we see the same objects and events that others see. This includes people's distribution, appearance and activities in space. Usually we have a whole host of clues that indicate at a glance "what sort of people" there are and "what they are doing", ranging from clothing to movements, gestures and facial expressions. We use this information to categorize what we see and insert our own actions into the whole (Garfinkel, 1967; Sacks, 1992, Vol. 1, pp. 81–94).

In this instance, position, colour, "shooting or not shooting" are the only clues available. However, within the flow of the game this information is sufficient to allow the players to monitor the state of affairs. Looking at the view of the space, T points out to O that "red is behind you" (lines 21–23). Treating the electronic space as an extension of the real space, governed by the principle of reciprocity of perspective, he mirrors everyday practices of seeing. Later on, similar information is gained in a different way. Switching to plan view, O discovers that Y is being attacked. Here, O does not see the bullets hitting Y's avatar, but a semi-circular configuration of coloured arrowheads pointing at Y. Such an abstract, animated, real-time plan view is a device usually unavailable to us. It is an affordance that exceeds everyday environmental conditions. O transposes competencies of categorizing people ("hunter", "target", "us" and "them") drawing on a minimal and abstracted set of clues, and his knowledge of real-world plan views to fit in with the game.

5.3.2 The World Generator

The "World Generator" (Bill Seaman) combines a video link to visitors at an exhibition in Nottingham and a networked electronic environment that invites people at both sites to choose three-dimensional objects and fragments of text, music, film or photographs from a menu and to place them into an electronic plain – a large projection screen in a darkened room. In front of it at some distance is a table with navigation tools. The viewer uses a *spacemaster* (a kind of three-dimensional mouse) to control their movement in the space (Fig. 5.4).

The configuration of the World Generator allows two people – one in each location – to navigate through the space, to select objects in their vicinity, and alter their appearance. Each of them is represented on their remote partner's screen through a tower-shaped avatar. At the same time, a videophone provides a visual and auditory link (Fig. 5.5).

The World Generator allows two participants to arrange and explore their joint "exhibitions". However, at the same time, the World Generator explores the experience of multiple perspectives onto the shared space. The following excerpts of talk between a visitor at ZKM (K), the artist (A), and visitors in Nottingham (N, N1) shed some light on the difficulties experienced and the strategies employed to work around them:

Figure 5.4 The setting of the World Generator.

Figure 5.5 The videophone at the desk in the World Generator.

1 A: so he's actually looking this way
2 K: I see I I didn't- I thought he has the identic- ((speaking into telephone receiver)) OK
3 A: so if you want you can kind of come up next to his avatar
4 K: how could I how could I get his perspective?
5 A: ehmm OK

...

6 A: where did he go? There he is. OK we'll just chase him. OK he's up there. ((quietly)):
       what does he see? He's looking off into nothingness
7 K: what do you see? Tell me, describe it
8 N: (a flying object on the right side of the screen ... possibly walking sticks (hats) (0.3)
9 K: pretty good
10 N1: (it's coming round)
11 N: that?
12 N1: yeah
13 N: looks like a tree ((K looks at the videophone screen))
14   that looks like a – a light a – a streetlight that way round
15 N1: (xx) yeah a streetlight (0.4)
((K turns to A, then to controls, switches to full screen menu and chooses textures))

...

17 N1: (I'm off) see you later
18 N: (xx) (0.4)
19 N: Hi here's Chris back

20 K: hi (0.4) hi how's the life?
21 N: (xx)
22 K: nice. (xx) everything's lost
23 N: have you got my viewpoint yet?
24 K: I can't see in the moment anything but I am on the way (0.8)
25 K: what can you see now?
26 N: err (xxx) I can see a oilrig on the right hand side of the screen going up
       and down
27 K: right
28 N: and the (0.3) errm (0.3) over on the left side of the screen I can see a tree
29 K: tree?
30 N: (floating around)
31 K: a tree?
32 A: [try to (xxx)]
33 N: [(xxx)] (xxxx) turning round
34 K: you said tree?
35 N: (xxx)
36 K: a tree yeah mhm I wonder what what you see really. (0.3) I see something
       too but it
37   doesn't look like a tree but maybe

In this example, the nature of N's presence is a source of interactional trouble, as it is difficult to determine his position and his orientation to objects in the electronic space, and his engagement in the interaction. K assumes that N sees the same part of the environment as he does. However, this is not the case. When this surfaces as one of the reasons for the difficulties the two have in coordinating their activities, K asks "how could I get his perspective" (lines 2, 4).

Cooperative activities in our everyday life that parallel this situation provide us with ample information about the task at hand and the nature, course and potential future development of the interaction in a way that is taken for granted. We can see what is going on between us and others, whose turn it is in the talk, where the other person's focus of attention is, whether they see what we see or their view is obstructed. The lack of information of this kind in the World Generator is made explicit in the above stretch of talk. In order to find some common ground K needs to find an answer to "where am I?" and "where is he?". Finding out what N sees is an approach that, again, relies on the principle of reciprocal perspectives. Two strategies are employed to repair the problem. In the absence of a plan view and given the small field of view, the artist helps K to "catch" N's avatar. However, even once it is found, its shape gives no indication of what he might be looking at, and K asks "what do you see?" (line 7). In order to make this a useful strategy, K would have to determine what N is seeing and bring his viewpoint into a position that is parallel to, or behind, N's point of view. Then they could place objects in front of them in a way that both would be able to see. But a cooperative engagement in arranging objects making use of the space would require N to shadow K or vice versa, a task that is beyond K's level of familiarity with the spacemaster. As another means of establishing at least some workable level of common ground, K asks for descriptions of what N sees (line 25), without trying to shadow his avatar. But this, too, turns out to be a difficult task, because the shapes do not readily conform to categories of objects in our everyday experience. What shapes could be seen as is a matter of negotiation (lines 8–15, 28–37). A further means of dealing with this problem, observed on a different occasion, was to turn the videophone around to capture the local screen, allowing the remote partner to see what was seen in Karlsruhe.

The videophone is usually used as a resource for interactional coordination in a different way. K and N look at each other while talking, and they can see who else is involved in the interaction and how (see, for example, K pointing at A in line 8). A little later on, N1 gets engaged in determining what exactly a shape on the screen looks like (lines 10-18). K looks at the screen of the videophone. Having seen N and N1's orientation towards each other on the screen, K treats this as a private conversation and turns to the people around him, then to the controls where he switches to menu view and begins to choose textures. However, N's next turn is addressed to him, and he quickly switches back to the view of the space. Such a window onto the physical surroundings in this mixed reality environment (Benford, 1996) prevents problems such as the "corpsing" experienced as a source of confusion in MASSIVE (Bowers *et al.*, 1996a). There, avatars whose "owners" were engaged in activities in their physical environment or for other reasons unavailable for interaction in the virtual space (they could even have left the room) showed no sign of their owner's lack of involvement. In the World Generator the videophone prevents such difficulties. However, the information it allows a remote partner to gauge is limited. The camera only captures a fraction of the space that is potentially relevant, and the quality of the picture is affected by the poor display and the timelag in the transmission. The fact that it is possible, but difficult to judge what is happening from the video image alone is acknowledged through N's announcement that he is now back "for real" in line 19.

Different ways of adapting everyday practices to the affordances of this environment can be seen here. Essentially, these all focus on conveying to others the perspective they are experience by mapping one's own point of view onto that of the remote partner. In the description above users seek to achieve this by locating the other's avatar and orientating towards it or by describing verbally their location and even sending the view of the screen through the videophone. What we are seeing here is the importance of an awareness of the perspective of the other and the importance of intersubjectivity in the cooperation between the users.

The activities discussed in this section also suggest that the environment does not provide adequate support to allow users to develop an awareness of the perspective of others and techniques to convey this to others. Rather, users are left to develop strategies to compensate for this shortcoming and none of these strategies succeeds in creating a rich enough surrogate of reciprocal perspectives to allow for cooperation between those using the environment. In seems that we need to consider the development of additional supporting information to allow those using the environment to develop an understanding of these differences in perspective in order to provide practical support for intersubjectivity in practice.

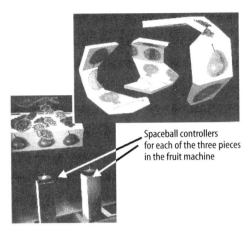

Spaceball controllers
for each of the three pieces
in the fruit machine

Figure 5.6 The Fruit Machine.

5.3.3 The Fruit Machine

The "Fruit Machine" provides a different environment for cooperative action. A three-dimensional octagonal shape is cut into three pieces and suspended in an electronic space (see Fig. 5.6). It can be put together through the coordinated actions of three players, each controlling one piece via a "space mouse". The space mice corresponding to each of the pieces are on a podium placed in front of a projector screen. The order of the podiums correspond to the order of the pieces. The image is projected in stereo and players (and observers) wear glasses to see the pieces.

Here a family with two young children (extract 1) and a group of three adults (extract 2) are engaged with the work:

Extract 1

1 V: you're probably the one at the back (.) Laura
2 L: yes but I'm not doing anything (0.4)
3 V: that's me (.)
4 L: the one at the front that's me
5 M: no that's Dad (0.4)
6 K: which one am I?
7 L: you're tha that one (.) and I'm the [biggest one]
8 K: [which one?]
9 L: you're that one that's just coming to the front (.) no that's me. That's me.

Extract 2

1 C: there is there is one (.) and and if we
2   [got those together now]
3 A: [wait I'm coming] wait
4 B: ah I have bananas too

The children and their parents in Extract 1 squabble about who "is" who in the jigsaw. L assumes that she can just "pick" the shape that appeals to her most ("the biggest one"), while the others are trying to determine which control, and thus whose actions, are related to which piece. K moves her piece in the course of finding out which one she "is", prompting vehement protest from L, who has decided that this is the one she wants to "be". The conversational reference to the space on the screen and the objects in it resembles that of talk around a board game.

To illustrate what we mean by conversational reference in terms of a board game let us use the following extract from fieldwork undertaken in a pre-school centre. Consider this stretch of talk between pre-school children and their nursery nurse over a game of "Winnie the Pooh":

1	ChildA:	that means he's in [front of me]
2	Nurse:	[he's in front] of you see if you can beat him now (.) go on then, how many have you got?
3	ChildA:	four
4	Nurse:	four.
5	ChildA:	one two three: four
6	Nurse:	no: they're there where Ben is. Right James your turn.
7	ChildB:	so I chase the butterfly as well
8	Nurse:	you must have been chasing Ben I think. How many have you got?
9	ChildB:	I (wanted) to be chasing Ben

This extract presents parallels between conversational practices around board games and virtual spaces like the one presented in the Fruit Machine. These children can be seen to use referential expressions that place them "inside" the space of the game – thus applying a "grammar" of playing board games. In the course of the game, they are further instructed in this grammar. The way in which action is projected to the "there" of the space of the board game does resemble the way in which this occurs in the Fruit Machine. This similarity is also amplified given the environment is constructed as a game with three players who have to solve a puzzle to win a prize.

In the second example (Extract 2), the players also employ a referential grammar reminiscent of board games: "wait I'm coming, wait". In both examples people thus anchor their actions in the electronic space to that particular piece by "identifying" with it. This strategy of placing oneself "inside" the electronic space could also be observed in the Legible City, where people said "I am on the market square" or "I'm in Manhattan". However, rather than experiencing presence in the sense of disembodied immersion in a new element, of "being there", where " 'the body', as a sense apparatus, is nothing more than excess baggage for the cyberspace traveller" (Balsamo, 1995, p. 229; see also Heim, 1993, 1995), we would argue that people begin to inhabit these spaces through active involvement with the objects and people they find there. Objects that a person controlled, avatars, or simply one's position in the electronic space (determined by one's point of view), were referred to as representations of one's point of action in this place, at this moment in time. They were "a way of making oneself present there as well as here. And, in the process, the indexical references to there became here" (Tolmie, 1998). This ties people's responsibilities and accountabilities into the electronic environment and becomes a means of achieving intersubjective availability of one's position, orientation and focus.

Interaction with Objects and Spaces

The examples above show that finding answers to such questions as "where am I?" and "where are (what kinds of) others?" is of crucial importance to interactions in electronic environments. Equally important are clues about others' and one's own activities in relation to the "material" environment. Visual clues alone do not seem to be sufficient for a sense of presence. In the above example of large-scale spatial information woven into the interactions between different players in Labyrinthos, for example, T's question in lines 2–3 indicates that despite having access to both screens, he is unable to determine the two players' positions in relation to each other and possible targets. This is puzzling. T seems to be less able to transpose everyday competencies than the other boys. One of the reasons for this may lie in the level of his engagement with the game. He is not a player, but an advisor, monitoring the state of affairs rather than being part of them. The next examples look in detail at the question of how people find their way around in the "material" arrangements of electronic spaces.

The group from example (2) above have just sat down at the space mouse controls of the Fruit Machine (Fig. 5.6):

```
 1 B:   eh I can't see anything ((said quietly, in a laughing voice))
 2 A:   which one are you now
 3 B:   I think the bottom one (.) yeah
 4         (0.3)
 5         do they fit into each other somehow? (yeah or this way) na:: not quite
            ((laughs))
 6         ((A&C laugh))
 7 B:   those [fit]
 8 C:   [(come] further to the front)
 9 B:   they probably don't fit together at all (.) what'd'y mean further to the
         front?
10 C:   you can't you turn em can you?
11         (0.3) ahh
12 A:   ooh now there's one really (.)
13 C:   oh yes
14 B:   [hey look]
15 C:   [heyheyheyhey]
16 A:   we're nearly there
17 B:   but that doesn't [that doesn't work for some reason]
18: C:              [little closer little closer a:nd]
```

Two very different levels of engagement with the installation are documented in the talk and the activities of A, B and C. While A and C discover the task posed by the installation through moving the pieces and take it at face value, B is more detached and critical. Here, and throughout the whole duration of their engagement with the Fruit Machine, she doubts the fit of the pieces. At one point she reveals one of her reasons: "I think they're having us on y'know". She insinuates that the artist elicits a response like A and C's under false pretences, that the "message" of the art work must be something more intricate than what can be perceived at first glance. As a result, she holds back and only halfheartedly involves herself in the task. This in turn, closes off some of the qualities of the electronic space that are discovered tacitly, through "doing" by the others (lines 8–9). She does not perceive the space as a space and only much later concludes that it must be three-dimensional: "they [the pieces] are always in different planes somehow".

A and C, on the other hand, focus on the events on the screen. Their utterances have the character of a running commentary rather than reflections on the nature of the game. This becomes clear *inter alia* through the intonation of their talk which is linked to the events on the screen. These different levels of engagement with the installation result in visibly different levels of dexterity in, and understanding of, the electronic space.

5.3.4 The Legible City

In the Legible City a single visitor can cycle through representations of three cities (Amsterdam, Manhattan and Karlsruhe) projected in front of them (Fig. 5.7). Each city is based on the street plan of the respective real city, while the buildings are made up of letters and words. An LCD display of a street map with a blinking dot indicating the user's position is mounted onto the real bicycle (Fig. 5.8). The following excerpts from the field notes illustrate how a succession of people moved around the Legible City:

> A is cycling. B, C stood in the back, laugh when he can't stay on the street. A: "where am I?". Checks on plan. B, C leave. A evades letters, gets off, leaves. Two women take over, one cycling, one checking where they are on the display. A couple come in, stand back at the wall. A woman (D) and boy (E) enter. She explains what can be done in this installation to the boy, referring to what a friend told her yesterday. A couple and another boy. The boy wants to try, but his father (F) gets to the bike first, gets on and cycles really fast, switches to Manhattan, cycling. D comments: "there's going to be a storm" ((referring to the gloomy atmosphere over Manhattan)). E: "it's not raining" D: "mhm seems to just stay the same". F cycles up closely to letters, then goes through.... A boy gets on, goes through letters carefully, then backwards, then goes through the letters again... a girl, audience laugh when she goes through letters. When she comes to a row of red letters, she can't get through. Turns round, goes through blue letters opposite, then tries the red ones again.... A small child and father. Father doing the pedalling: "No not there it doesn't go anywhere, don't go through letters, stay on the road... this is Karlsruhe, let's go to the castle, past the tax authorities, that's where the castle is.

There are a number of issues relevant to the experience of presence and practices of orientation that can be drawn out from this extract. Firstly, people were

Figure 5.7 The Legible City.

Figure 5.8 The map display on the bicycle.

concerned with finding answers to the question "where am I?", which in the course of movement through the city turned into "where have I been and/or where am I going?". Material markers were practically employed as orientational aids. They range from urban elements such as roads, junctions, buildings and landmarks, to natural characteristics such as the weather, to physical qualities such as the solidity of materials. In our everyday interaction with the material world, these features are mainly understood and interpreted tacitly. Some of the features in the Legible City give rise to puzzlement and thus draw to our attention, not only what kinds of material features form part of our tacit interpretation of the physical world around us, but also point us in the direction of how such features are employed differently within electronic environments.

The combination of the bicycle as an interface and the roads and buildings on the screen that adjust to the moves of the bicycle in real-time offers the user the opportunity to travel through the cities. People readily recognize this as the function of the installation. Whether people recognized the cities as based on the ground plans of real cities or not, the urban metaphor allowed them to see at a glance what the rudimentary workings of this piece of art are. Most carried an urban interpretation further by initially trying to stay on the roads in the environment. This is an interpretation sanctioned or even enforced by the audience. The father instructing his daughter not to go through the letters but to stay on the road makes public just how strong the thrust of such an interpretation is. Similarly, the laughter that greets the difficulties people have in staying on the roads or the first swerves into the letter-buildings indicates that there is something "wrong" in deviating from these paths "meant" for traffic.

However, most people inevitably overshoot junctions and pass through a row of letters sooner or later, as the speed of movement is high and the corners narrow. Thus the lack of collision control within the Legible City is discovered as the result of "accidents". It proved a source of enjoyment: after having crossed through letters once, people visibly and audibly enjoyed cutting through them. This was pleasurable for its own sake, but also had practical consequences. It meant that different types of journey through the cities were possible. While slow movement along the roads allowed people to read the text that stretched alongside them, they could also decide to "just go" or orient with the help of the street plan and steer towards their destination regardless of the "buildings". The degree to which the immaterial character of the letters is taken for granted once it has been established is illustrated through the fact that when a row of letters is discovered that is impenetrable, people react with disbelief. Several trials are made to establish that this row (which is the end of the model) is not like the others.

Other features of urban environments that people used were landmarks. This is most pronounced in situations where visitors who are familiar with Karlsruhe choose this city in the Legible City. The castle, as the main architectural focal point of the city, is sought out and located with the help of other landmarks in the above example. Other, more sculptural, landmarks in Karlsruhe, which are set (in the real and the simulated city) in the middle of major lines of sight, helped people locate themselves within the whole of the environment, and were also used as short-term navigational aids: people cycled through them to stay in the middle of the road.

The "weather" is another resource for orientation. A woman states "there's going to be a storm", as a cyclist is proceeding towards a vista of dark clouds on the horizon. However, the fact that "the weather" does not worsen even though they should be getting closer to the centre of the storm exposes it as governed by different physical laws than weather in our familiar physical environment. In this case the everyday practice of reference to large-scale orientation clues in the sky fails, because the way the storm follows the cyclist makes it unusable as such a resource.

In our everyday life we handle a myriad of objects and move within spaces, mostly without being consciously aware of the factors that are involved in their being ready-to-hand. These activities are ordered through our perception. But how? And how do we deal with the impoverished or altered sensory affordances of electronic environments? One fairly obvious factor people could be seen to rely upon was the sequence of action and events in the environment. In the Fruit Machine, one of the pieces moves of its own accord unless it is controlled via the interface. This means, for example, that this piece cannot be placed somewhere and held static in order for the others to "dock" onto it. It has to be the last piece to be "docked". It also revealed that people relied on the sequence of "action on the controls movement on the screen", because the self-generated movement caused puzzlement, as one visitor states: "from one terminal it was running out of control maybe that was intended, I don't know, in order to make it more difficult" (interview 13 December 1997). Other factors are: the continuity of material arrangements – do things stay where they are and what they are? The continuity of one's own actions – do actions have lasting effects or are they reversible or only temporary? And the consistency of those actions – do the same actions cause the same events every time? Some of these factors have been discussed in, for example, Sheridan (1992) and Ellis (1996). However, the examples described above illustrate that such criteria within the electronic environments – whether they are interactional clues or clues relating to the affordances of the "material" environment – are perceived with reference to the physical "world known in common" but submitted to review and learned about in light of the experience of moving around in the environment. In the final section we will provide an account of presence based on these observations and suggest some implications for the design of large-scale CVEs.

5.4 Supporting Presence through Intersubjectivity and Learnability

On the basis of our analysis we would like to offer an account of presence that is achieved through the engagement with resources provided within the environment. Perception is tied to "grammars" of human interaction and sense making. It is a social phenomenon, embedded in our being, continuously and inescapably, a member of a social world – like any other knowledge, practice or habit, perception is intersubjective.

Put crudely, the more we find out, the "better" we are able to interact both with respect to people and with a view to the material world. But the ways in which people do find out through the transposition of everyday practices implies that they can interpret a diversity of environments. As long as a sufficient degree of intersubjectivity is facilitated, we are flexible with regard to the visual appearance and "material" structure of an environment, its physical laws and the affordance it provides with a view to our own presence and that of other people. Some of the main issues are the following:

5.4.1 Reciprocity of Perspective

In order to be able to coordinate actions, people must be able to assume that others see the same space and the same objects as they do. But this does not mean that the principle must not be relaxed under any circumstances. It can be relaxed – as long as this is made available as a feature of the environment – or provided for in ways that are unfamiliar, such as making people's positions and activities available through, for example:

- an abstracted, animated, real-time plan view

- a screenshot of "this is what I see from where I am"

- a vehicle into which others can be invited to share a particular perspective onto a joint space

5.4.2 Designing for Two Worlds

There are two different ways in which the real and the electronic spaces are linked. Firstly, the practice of seeing and experiencing the electronic space with or through the fusion of interface and display into an instrument that becomes "ready-to-hand" does mark out a route for the development of more sophisticated equipment. However, increased sensory richness (through for example, force feedback and proprioceptive devices) is not necessarily the only direction such development could take. Although the spaces seen are not "real" spaces, the sense of presence in electronic environments is a version of "telepresence" (Sheridan, 1992) in that it provides a sense of control over remote events. The sequence, continuity and consistency of actions and the events they cause, if stable and intelligible, seem to provide "enough" information for a rudimentary sense of presence. They do not have to mimic real-world forms of sensory perception.

Secondly, the context of interaction in the physical space is relevant to the activities in the electronic environment and it should be possible to make available at least some crucial information about it. We would argue that interaction with the virtual world is strongly situated in the everyday world and that people manage their interaction across and between these two worlds. This point has also been made strongly by researchers such as Bowers *et al.* (1996b) and is a dominant theme of Chapter 7. It is clear that designers need to consider this boundary between the real and the virtual more closely and provide techniques to manage the relationship. This effect is currently noticeable in the development of augmented reality environments and the construction of mixed reality boundaries (Koleva *et al.*, 2000) that link between the real and the virtual. The need for support as we cross boundaries between these environments and match our interaction within the world with the real world also underpins the development of engagement properties presented later in this chapter.

5.4.3 Material Markers

The observations presented in this chapter suggest that in designing and developing virtual environments we need to consider how factors that influence a sense of presence are made available to people using these environments. Uncovering and presenting these features of these environments allows us to make resources available to users that they can in turn exploit to develop a sense of presence across a wide range of different presentation techniques and devices. In addition to developing different mechanisms for presenting these properties to users we need to continue an investigation of how people make use of different properties of virtual environment to construct and generate a sense of presence in these environments.

5.5 Developing Engagement Properties

In this chapter we have presented a set of studies showing the various ways in which users made sense of their presence within a wide selection of virtual environments. Emerging from these studies was a recurrent theme of notions of presence being worked up in practice and of users understanding the differences between users as a means of supporting cooperation. It was also clear that difficulties arose when users had little or no sense of the capabilities of other users.

We wish to directly address this shortcoming by outlining a framework to allow the explicit representation of engagement information and to allow this information to be used as resource by those using the environment. We seek to represent the different arrangements we have seen across these studies and to develop a vocabulary to allow these to be expressed and shared between users. In order to do this we have sought to move beyond the current view of interaction and presence based on a fixed arrangement of interaction devices. Rather, we wish to consider how to reflect the means by which users interact with a virtual environment and present this to others. The consideration of this information directly reflects the need to provide cues to allow users to manage their relationship with these environments.

The starting point for our consideration of engagement is the work on action points and viewpoints initially undertaken by Benford and Fahlén (1994). We represent the manner in which users can engage with a virtual environment in terms of three different characteristics for determining interaction and presence within the space.

- View of the environment – This conveys the particular views offered by an environment. Depending on the environment users can have multiple points of view. At any moment in time each point of view will have both a location and a direction.

- Action point in the environment – This conveys the point (or points) of interaction a user may have in the environment. This is the means by which objects are selected and acted upon.

- Position in the environment – This conveys the presence of users within the environment and the means by which this position depends on the other points.

The aim is to convey the relationship between the user and the environment in terms of how they interact with it. These three engagement properties convey the affordances for engagement offered by an environment. They also allow users access to information about the relationship and means of engagement being exploited by other users. For each of these different properties we also encode the control details and they can also be linked together to show different restrictions in engagement enforced by the nature of the environment.

As an example consider the arrangement offered by a simple virtual world provided by the DIVE described in a previous chapter in this book. Within DIVE users are represented in the world as simple embodiments. Each of these embodiments conveys position and orientation to others sharing the environment. Essentially, a user's viewpoint is linked to the orientation of this embodiment while their action point is independent of this. This provides the engagement properties suggested in Fig. 5.9.

In Fig. 5.9 each of the View, Action and Position properties encode the relationship between the user and the environment. These properties can then be conveyed to other users using a set of attribute value pairs such as those shown in the box in the figure.

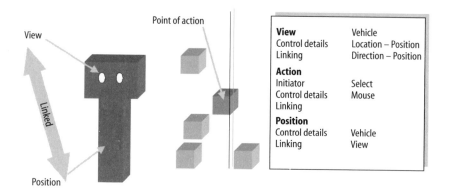

Figure 5.9 Engagement properties for a DIVE world.

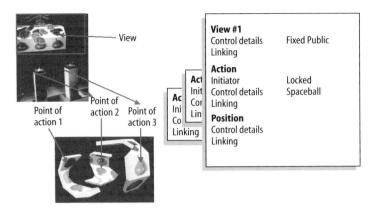

Figure 5.10 Engagement properties for the Fruit Machine.

Engagement properties can also be used to describe more radical worlds with a different range of interaction affordances. Consider for example, the Fruit Machine exhibit described in the study. Here three different users are offered independent action points to rearrange pieces in the environment. The environment is presented using a single fixed viewpoint and no means is provided to represent users in the environment. Rather, they are considered external to the shared environment. This arrangement is shown in Fig. 5.10.

As in the case of the DIVE environment we can encode the engagement properties using a set of attribute value pairs and where appropriate these different engagement properties can be made available to users of environments. The engagement information we may encode using engagement properties represents only a small part of the interaction offered. In fact, we can consider a user's interactional affordances with a given virtual environment as a combination of three things:

- Engagement properties of the CVE – This is essentially represented in terms of the action point, view point and position offered by the environment.

- Capabilities of the interaction device – What the user's current interaction hardware/software allows the user to do. For example, a user interacting at a desktop computer may have multiple windows (allowing many views on the same CVE simultaneously), but can only physically interact in two dimensions using a keyboard or a 2D mouse. However, a user within the same world may be wearing VR goggles, which allow only a single view but can interact with the CVE in three dimensions using a 3D mouse.

- Capabilities of the user vehicle – Users within a virtual environment often exploit some form of vehicle that provides a mapping from the capabilities of an interaction device to movement in the environment. Vehicles allow a range of different navigation profiles to coexist in the one environment. For example, the default avatar may restrict a user to movement in a 2D plane, whereas a helicopter vehicle may also allow the user to move up and down.

The types of interaction that a user can perform within a virtual environment at any given moment are a combination of these three capabilities. Externalizing these capabilities to the user (or making them accessible to other applications and CVEs) allows us to present to users their current interaction capabilities. This will help them to understand what is possible, how the CVE may be interacted with and the manner in which they are present within the environment. In addition, the capabilities of users can be made available to others allowing inferences to be made about their experience of the environment and some sense of intersubjectivity to be build up across the environment. This allows users to develop a sense of the manner in which other users are present in the environment and provides them with the resources needed to support the practical presence strategies reported in this chapter.

5.6 Summary and Conclusions

In this chapter we have presented a set of studies of users' experiences of being present within and across different virtual worlds. We have presented an analysis of a set of different studies of users in different virtual environments and the means by which they made sense of their presence in these environments and the presence of others. These studies suggest that users actively develop a sense of presence through an understanding of the nature of the environment and the effects that their interactions have on these environments.

Drawing upon these studies, we have developed a framework to help present the relationship users have with these environments as a means of supporting how they manage their presence within these environments. The core of our approach to supporting users' management of presence is the representation and externalization of the nature of their engagement with the virtual environments. The use of these properties as external cues aims to support users as they interact with and are present in a collection of virtual environments. The distinct aim here is to provide these cues as resources to allow visitors to virtual environments to establish their relationship with the environment in practice. By offering engagement properties we wish to provide a prop in this activity rather than to propose the development and introduction of an abstract analytical device or theory.

Chapter **6**
All That Is Solid Melts Into Software

Andrew McGrath and Wolfgang Prinz

6.1 Collaborative Virtual Environments Using Symbolic Acting

> All that is solid melts into air, all that is holy is profaned, and man is at last compelled to face with sober senses his real conditions of life and his relations with his kind. (Karl Marx and Friedrich Engels, *Manifesto of the Communist Party*, 1848)

6.1.1 Real Conditions of Life in Co-located Working

Imagine the activities that occur when we are working in an office. We may describe our use of the computer or the phone, but we will also remember the chance meetings, the recruited conversations and the sense of seeing what people are doing and of seeing when people are available. We might smile at memories of the unplanned, unforced social interaction that we engage in. We might also remember that when we are busy we have the ability to ignore people politely when passing them in the corridor or when they seek to engage us in conversation at our desk. All of these situations occur naturally when sharing a real space with people and are either absent or rare in online collaboration tools. Although a body of work acknowledges that these effects of collocation are important – especially to those who are knowledge workers – it is rare to find someone who would realize emphatically the importance of "bumping into someone in the corridor", or who would describe it as part of their job. In fact, these activities are not your job, but they do help you to do your job. In other words we don't consciously feel the need to have them to achieve our tasks, but the reality is that we will find achieving our tasks more difficult without them. As such, these examples of interaction are rarely catered for or fostered in off-the-shelf tools, and even if they were catered for we do not expect to "drive" such interactions and do not want them to interfere with our efficiency on the desktop. These interactions that we would like to put back into online collaboration tools require little mental effort to set up in co-located working; however, the reality of adding such interaction opportunities to online tools would be to add to the features that need to be consciously utilized. There have been those who have observed that since such interaction occur in spatial arrangements then if we create spatial metaphors for collaboration tools then we will re-create the conditions necessary for such desirable. Examples of these include Holodek, Blaxxun interactive, DIVE and MASSIVE (Benford *et al.*, 1994a). These collaborative worlds have generated a large body of knowledge about the qualities of spatial online collaborative worlds, but none has successfully become a pervasive business tool. In fact, the recent trend in the 3D spatial community has been to move away from the 3D aspects of their work in favour of "toolbar" and 2D community products. This would seem to be an acknowledgement that the initial dream of using spatial metaphors to create online collaborative spaces is fading.

6.1.2 Problems and Opportunities with Spatial Metaphors

Those companies and researchers who are working in shared spaces now know that the past hype surrounding "cyberspace" has hidden problems that have become increasingly obvious and which now seem insurmountable. There was the oft-mentioned "intuitive" nature of using 3D space to navigate and communicate. The reality is that navigating such worlds has proved to be problematic and there are signs that this navigation may in fact inhibit the person's ability to do the "business" of communication. Navigating 3D spaces (in fact "driving" most computer applications) can be compared to talking while trying to reverse a car – we *can* do it but we have to concentrate on the navigation so hard that our speech slows down. For business applications in particular we need a collaboration space that has less navigation and more concentration; more concentration on the reason we are in the collaborative space – communication. The communication can be synchronous or asynchronous but it has to be easy to listen and to talk, easy to understand what is happening or has happened between us, our colleagues and our information resources. We have a conundrum to solve: we need to put people and information together in collaboration spaces that inform people about what is happening, but which do not impact on our ability to perform what we call our "work". If we solve this conundrum then surely we can we create an online space which can be "read" (and manipulated) by a user in a similar way to which they read and manipulate real spaces.

If we can solve this conundrum then we can use the affordances of the spatial metaphor that may have hitherto being masked by the "navigation effort" problem. Strengths we want to exploit include people's ability to "negotiate communication" in a space. That is, we know how to "look busy" and thus control our communication subtly and easily, with little mental effort. We are all familiar with the person who we cannot get rid of when busy, and we have developed skills to deal with even those hard situations. In space we can talk to others when we meet them, or are located with them. If we want, we can move towards them or veer away, we can say "Hi" and move on, or we can say "Hi" and then ask a question. Can we use 3D shared spaces with a spatial layout and expressive avatars to negotiate this communication online?

This chapter describes a technique called Symbolic Acting that we believe solves this conundrum, and we describe the implementation of Symbolic Acting in prototype environments and some early results on the usefulness of the technique.

6.1.3 Symbolic Acting – Let the System Do the Walking

In business applications we cannot rely on the "Gee this is fun!" factor of 3D applications such as gaming and interactive simulations. As we have described, one of the biggest difficulties with spatial metaphors appears to be the effort of navigation. If we recreate a "chance meeting" between two people online we want to do that with the simplest navigation system while still using the affordances of the spatial metaphor. Symbolic Acting goes about this by taking your normal desktop activity (activity that you already do, that already happens) and uses it to drive an avatar that represents you to others. The representation of you is *symbolic,* i.e. your avatar acts out the symbolic meaning of what you are doing and does so in a mutual way, in symphony with the avatars of those who you are collaborating with. In addition, symbolic acting can be manifest as implied navigation. Implied navigation is where the users' avatars, and their subsequent views of the world, are moved based on changes in the subject they are writing or reading about or changes in the applications they are running on their desktop. This means movement or navigation without additional user input other than that which they already employ. The idea is to keep cognitive load to a minimum, and we hope to achieve the effect of being able to talk *and* reverse one's car. The "theatre" for your symbolic actor is a spatial metaphor that hopes to create a sense of presence – a sense of being with others and working with others – without any additional effort on your existing desktop commitments. In essence, we believe that Symbolic Acting lets the system do the walking (and acting) for you.

6.1.4 Silence Is a Quality of Presence

With the "theatre" we create for our symbolic actors we aim to create a sense-making collaborative environment that can be filled with the information and communication affordances familiar to us in co-located communication. Communication in co-located spaces is characterized by its analogue nature – communication eases between none and full on. Between saying nothing and talking to someone there exists a continuum comprising mutual sense of presence, body movement, mutual gaze awareness and the trajectory of body motion. The model of technologically mediated communication is characterized by its digital nature – I am either on the phone to you or I am not. I am either sending you an email or I am not. This has partially been to do with the way that communication has been commercially realized. The model for communication charges has been a per-use basis, and communication costs make silence seem like a waste of money. In addition, there has been no way of communicating the continuum between verbal or textual communication in an acceptable way. The development of "always on" communication allows new ways of bringing those important "spaces between the communication" into online collaboration tools. Intranets are "always on" and broadband flat-rate communication channels delivering a continuum of information and communication simultaneously are being implemented now. With these technologies and an appropriate way of expressing presence and awareness we can build online collaboration tools that support the continuum of analogue communication, from "presence with silence" through awareness tools into full verbal and textual communication via email, audio conferencing and IP telephony.

6.2 Symbolic Acting in Action

The following sections describe different systems that apply the symbolic acting idea. This includes the Forum developed at BT Adastral Park and the Nessie World developed at GMD-FIT.

6.2.1 Synchronous Symbolic Acting – the Forum

Helping People Who Cannot Be Together Work Together

The Forum project is a prototype collaboration environment designed and built at BT Adastral Park in Suffolk. As part of the research and development arm of a global telecommunications company the research conducted within Adastral Park is concerned with securing the interests of the company, improving quality of online communication and broadening the spectrum of people who can telework. Despite the increasing bandwidth available to customers, the research community at Adastral Park is always seeking to achieve these ends with a viable mixture of bandwidth, processing power and usability. The Forum project was a direct response to issues raised by our flexible working trials and marketing directives that were concerned with increasing the envelope of occupations that could be achieved online. In addition, the isolation that teleworkers can feel and the lack of tacit knowledge and social navigation options available for flexible workers needed to be addressed. It was to address these issues that the Forum was conceived. There are two parts to the Forum prototype: the Contact Space and the Meeting Space. The Contact Space corresponds to the informal shared office environment, while the Meeting Space is for formal "round the table" meetings. The Contact Space itself does not include any conventional desktop work tools; it is not an application in which you do you work. Rather, it is a space for "hanging out" in, a place to manageably meet your colleagues or people you "ought" to interact with if were conventionally co-located. The Contact Space visualizes activities that we believe will help knowledge workers to do their jobs but which would not be what those users would call their jobs, as such. In fact, the Contact Space makes use of desktop activity to visualize sense making and communication cues that are not easily presented via online collaboration tools. The Forum Meeting Space is similar in its approach to the Contact Space, but is focused more on synchronous meetings and is based round audio and data conferencing. The Meeting Space is a graphically mediated audio conferencing tool that integrates with the Contact Space using the same server architecture and platform.

Let the Forum Envoy Do the Walking

In order to drive the symbolic acting in both parts of the Forum we have built an agent called the Forum Envoy that takes information about your desktop activity and interprets it into a symbolic action or movement. For example, in the Forum Meeting Space, when you have a window obscuring the visualization of the space your avatar is seen to be looking at a document because the Envoy interprets that desktop situation into a symbolic action displaying that your attention is elsewhere. In this way everyone knows who is looking at the reviewing document without users having to control both their desktops and their avatars in the space. It is like having your own method actor. More information on how this works can be seen in the scenario below (see Table 6.1).

Similarly, in the Contact Space, if you are writing a document on, say, JavaScript, the Forum Envoy looks at the keywords in the document, recognizes the approximate subject matter being aired and puts your avatar in the "JavaScript" interest area in the visualization on your desktop. This will put you in "visual proximity" with other people in your Contact Space system working in a similar area (who you can speak to, or politely ignore) without you having to navigate your avatar. Put simply – you let the system do the walking.

This process will put people together based on their subject matter. We also put people together based on their activity. This is to address the "Meeting by the Photocopier" effect or the conversation on the way back from the restroom! Of course nobody photocopies online and nobody goes to the restroom online, so we have to look for the conceptual equivalent of these activities. This will be workplace specific, but examples we have considered include, retrieving project-related information from the Internet or intranet, doing a search, writing project proposals or closing a deal on an account.

The Forum Contact Space and Meeting Space Working Version

Figure 6.1 shows two illustrations of the Contact Space. The left picture shows the ground plane of the Contact Space – the circles with pyramids represent all the Interest Groups belonging to the working group as gathered by the Contact Space Agent (known as Jasper). You can see avatars located in the space, positioned by the system depending on their desktop activity and subject matter. The semi-transparent layers above the avatars represent the "action" layers, where specific job-defined activities (for example, writing a project plan) are treated as special cases to position people on these planes when conducting these activities. Three avatars in one of the "action" layers can be seen in the right-hand picture. The "action" layers open up the users to "meeting" others through a common activity even though they have differing subjects. As the system moves the avatars around it orientates the viewpoint or direction of view of the avatar towards other people in the space who have similar long-term interests; this knowledge about the long-term interests of the users is gathered by the Jasper Agent. In the right-hand picture one of the

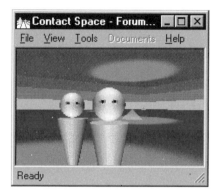

Figure 6.1 The Contact Space.

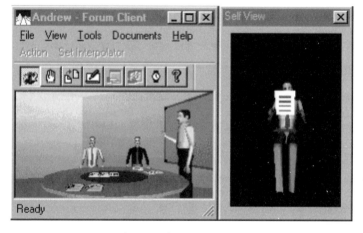

Figure 6.2 The Meeting Space.

avatars is shown in "sleepy" mode: where the user's machine has been inactive for some time the avatar's head shrinks into the body.

Figure 6.2 illustrates of the Forum Meeting Space. In it we see four avatars (one visible in the self view) representing people present in an audio conference. Spatial navigation is turned off in this application as the system handles the users' transspatial movements. Documents can be dragged from the computer desktop and placed on the desk visible between the avatars. To share a document the person drags the icon onto the centre of the table. Others at the meeting see your avatar slide the document into the table. More detail of this is given in the scenario below.

Scenario

As part of the conceptual design process a scenario was created. This is shown in Table 6.1 and illustrates a nominal "day in the life" of a Contact Space user. This

Table 6.1. Scenario

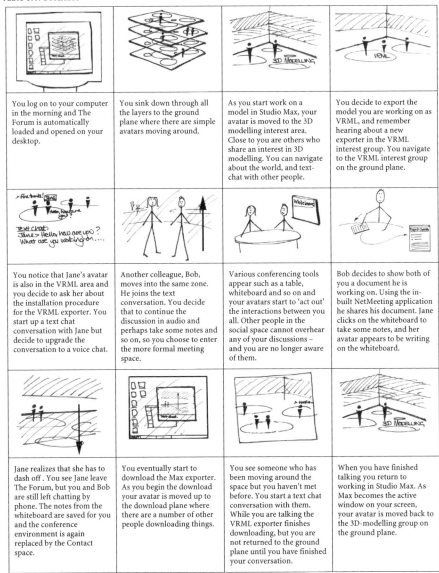

You log on to your computer in the morning and The Forum is automatically loaded and opened on your desktop.	You sink down through all the layers to the ground plane where there are simple avatars moving around.	As you start work on a model in Studio Max, your avatar is moved to the 3D modelling interest area. Close to you are others who share an interest in 3D modelling. You can navigate about the world, and text-chat with other people.	You decide to export the model you are working on as VRML, and remember hearing about a new exporter in the VRML interest group. You navigate to the VRML interest group on the ground plane.
You notice that Jane's avatar is also in the VRML area and you decide to ask her about the installation procedure for the VRML exporter. You start up a text chat conversation with Jane but decide to upgrade the conversation to a voice chat.	Another colleague, Bob, moves into the same zone. He joins the text conversation. You decide that to continue the discussion in audio and perhaps take some notes and so on, so you choose to enter the more formal meeting space.	Various conferencing tools appear such as a table, whiteboard and so on and your avatars start to 'act out' the interactions between you all. Other people in the social space cannot overhear any of your discussions – and you are no longer aware of them.	Bob decides to show both of you a document he is working on. Using the in-built NetMeeting application he shares his document. Jane clicks on the whiteboard to take some notes, and her avatar appears to be writing on the whiteboard.
Jane realizes that she has to dash off. You see Jane leave The Forum, but you and Bob are still left chatting by phone. The notes from the whiteboard are saved for you and the conference environment is again replaced by the Contact space.	You eventually start to download the Max exporter. As you begin the download your avatar is moved up to the download plane where there are a number of other people downloading things.	You see someone who has been moving around the space but you haven't met before. You start a text chat conversation with them. While you are talking the VRML exporter finishes downloading, but you are not returned to the ground plane until you have finished your conversation.	When you have finished talking you return to working in Studio Max. As Max becomes the active window on your screen, your avatar is moved back to the 3D-modelling group on the ground plane.

scenario was used in the design phase to generate early feedback from focus groups prior to implementation.

Working versions of both the Forum Meeting Space and the Contact Space were built and trialled to generate user feedback and information for a re-design. The results of these trials and the subsequent re-design are included later.

6.2.2 Asynchronous Symbolic Acting – Nessie World

At GMD-FIT we have realized the Nessie world, a multi-user 3D environment that plays out the activities of users in a shared workspace system. The system is based upon the integration of the internet based event and notification infrastructure Nessie (Prinz, 1999) and the 3D multi-user environment SmallTool (Broll, 1998).

Nessie is used to recognize the activities of users in their cooperative environment. This includes activities in shared workspaces of the BSCW system (Bentley *et al.*, 1997), on shared documents, on Web documents, or the movement of people within office rooms. These activities are captured by software or physical sensors that signal activities to the Nessie server using events. The Nessie server transforms these events into symbolic acting commands for the SmallView 3D browser of the SmallTool environment. This transformation includes the mapping of the originating user to the appropriate avatar which can be done in a straightforward way. In addition, the location where the avatars' symbolic acting within the 3D world is visualized must be determined. This is based on the working context in which the user activity took place. Only user action in public spaces (e.g. shared document bases, public file directories and project-related intranet Web spaces) are recognized and processed by Nessie. All events that are caused by other actions are deleted and no symbolic acting takes place.

The Nessie world uses rooms to distinguish the different working contexts of its users. Each working context is associated with a combination of a shared workspace, a real office room, or a set of arbitrary documents. The events that are raised by user activities on these artefacts are mapped onto the appropriate locations, i.e. rooms in the Nessie world, by the Nessie server using transformation rules.

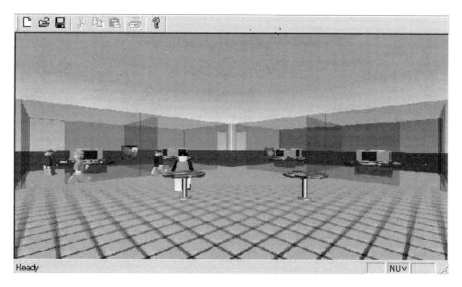

Figure 6.3 The Nessie world.

Figure 6.3 shows a view into a Nessie world with four rooms and a central plaza. Each of these rooms is associated with one or more BSCW shared workspaces or a set of documents that relate to the projects associated with the workspaces. The activities of users in these workspaces or documents are mapped onto corresponding gestures of the users' avatars. We distinguish visit, read, modify and move activities. The read and modify activities are mapped onto reading and writing gestures of the avatar in front of a computer monitor. If a user moves from one context to another the avatar walks into the corresponding office. All avatars own the same body, and they can only be differentiated by their different colours, since each colour represents a different user. The central plaza space is used to visualize movements and noise in a real coffee room. Since these activities cannot be assigned to a specific user, the avatars to indicate these activities are all coloured in black.

In addition to avatars that play out symbolic actions we investigate the use of agent avatars and active virtual furniture. The agent avatars are used to signal the daytime or certain daily events. For example, the appearance of waiters or cleaning personnel indicates that it is time to go for lunch or to go home. Active furniture is used to indicate the state of external values and activities, e.g. temperature or stock values.

The Nessie event and notification infrastructure provides a history mechanism that stores and aggregates events. This is used in combination with the Nessie world to play back past activities. This enables users to review past activities in a fast forward mode to become up to date with activities after an absence from their office.

The problem with 3D indicators is that the amount of required screen space is higher than the space that is normally left when users run their everyday applications. Thus we envisage an office scenario with peripheral monitor screens or projections onto the background of the users monitor. These displays provide a virtual window on the cooperative 3D space. Figure 6.4 illustrates the projection of the Nessie world into the user's workspace ambience and the combination with ambient displays (Wisneski *et al.*, 1998) such as the activity balloon or the bubble lamp.

Figure 6.4 The display of the Nessie world in the user's work ambience.

Ambient displays are used to signal important events in the Nessie world. They are used to attract the user's attention to the world display or to display a general state of the world, i.e. the presence of a certain colleague or the happening of a meeting. The events to which ambient displays shall react are configured individually by the users using Nessie.

WAP mobiles can also be used to interact with the Nessie world. The WAP interface enables users to retrieve information from the Nessie world, such as "who is where", but also to control the location of the user's own avatar within the world. This allows users to place their avatars at places in the 3D world that represent their actual location in a symbolic way, e.g. in a meeting or on the road.

6.3 Results and Re-Design

The development of working prototypes incorporating Symbolic Acting techniques presents an opportunity to assess the usefulness and effect on users and communities. Both the Forum Meeting Space and the Forum Contact Space were implemented and trialled with a number of users over a number of months. The feedback is summarized below and has furnished the development team with opportunities for a re-design although as some of the Contact Space users were closely involved in the development process the results from that trial have to be considered in that light.

6.3.1 Meeting Space Trial

The Meeting Space was trialled and the results based on a mix of formal meetings, informal meetings and test sessions with other trial participants. The maximum number of meetings that interviewees had participated in was 20. All users interviewed were keen to use the system again. Technical problems experienced during installation, while rather demotivating at the time, did not put users off as long as they had participated in one successful meeting. The results of the interviews and video observations can be broadly categorized into two themes: avatars and issues around the interpretation and reaction to the symbolic actions. Broadly speaking, the Meeting Space is a focal point at the start and end of meetings. During the core of the meeting there is less evidence of people looking at or interacting in the Meeting Space window – they tended to concentrate on shared text documents as they were being discussed. This would seem appropriate, as the purpose of the Meeting Space is to help facilitate effective meetings, not to "hog" the proceedings through overly emphatic symbolic movements or sound effects.

6.3.2 Avatars

The majority of interviewees liked the animated avatars and several have suggested that the introduction of animated avatars has made the experience more like attending a "real" meeting – it is worth noting that these users were predominantly working in remote locations from the rest of their team. While the avatar customiz-ation tool in the Forum allows some limited changes to be made to the avatar prior to a meeting, all interviewees wanted the avatars to have more choice in terms of customization, i.e. they wanted to be able to add things such as glasses, more hair-styles, facial hair and skirts for women. Interviewees have suggested that they want the avatars to be a closer representation of themselves but *not* as good as a photo-graphic/video image. It would be interesting to know if this was because the avatar allows a certain "ironic distance" to exist between the users and what their avatars are up to. Some people may not be happy to admit certain physical attributes and may feel more comfortable being limited by the tool to explain the discrepancy between their customized avatar and their "real" appearance. All interviewees except one "dressed" their avatar in similar colours/clothes to those they were wearing at the time or typically wore. One male interviewee changed his avatar to look more casual than the other participants because he always looked noticeably more casual than the others in real life. One female interviewee said that she found black made her look slimmer, wore black in real life and tried to slim down her avatar in black. Users are still commenting (after three months) on the female form of the avatar. It has been described as everything from amusing to offensive. It has been suggested that it is treated lightheartedly by meeting participants who know each other, but could be viewed inappropriately by "strangers" in a meeting envi-ronment. This raises the interesting idea of meeting spaces for "inside" teams and alternative meeting spaces with more "public facing" avatars and actions. One female interviewee suggested that you could have body shapes to choose from as well as head types. In creating the avatar design some aspects of the physical appearance were emphasized because subtle changes in appearance were difficult to detect within the small window on the screen that the Meeting Space occupies. Some accentuation may have been too exaggerated – one interviewee said she dressed her avatar in black because she was slimming, and she felt this also took the focus away from her avatar's large chest.

6.3.3 Symbolic Acting

The most frequently requested symbolic action is one to indicate who is talking. Users have suggested moving lips, moving the head, movement of the arms and on two occasions simply an icon above the user's avatar. The original design of the Meeting Space used body language to discern this information, as the small size of the window and the notoriously difficult problem of realistic lip-synching made lip movement as an indicator unrealistic. Unfortunately, the audio bridge utilized in the trial could not discern which person was talking, so this information could not be displayed. If this could be displayed and combined with more realistic avatars it would help users to identify who is talking, especially when in a meeting with either more than five participants or with unknown participants (or "strangers"). Several users also felt wary of the symbolic action which showed their avatar to pick up and read a document if they opened another application/window in their screen. They suggested that this should be controlled by the user: if they wanted to switch this action off and on they should be able to. They felt there were circumstances where they would want to look at a document without letting everyone else in the meeting know that they were doing so. On the other hand, several users also liked the inclusion of this action because they felt that if someone's attention was wandering they could see this and could bring them back into the meeting, e.g. by asking them to contribute to the conversation. The "raising of the hand" and the "looking at watch" actions were the most commonly used, but these were not used frequently. All interviewees understood the purpose of these actions. Some interviewees thought that looking at the watch was quite formal – one described it as a bit like being at school, but still used it in a meeting environment. Several users were worried that this might be viewed as rude by other users, in particular "strangers" in the meeting.

The most misunderstood animation was the "engaged" action. It ranged from meaning "I am away from my desk and my speaker and microphones are both automatically muted" to "I'm really interested in what everyone else is saying" to "I'm bored – I'm indicating I'd like to finish now".

6.3.4 Contact Space Trial

The contact space was analysed at all stages of its development and has been assessed through one video ethnographic study and two interview assessments. The assessments consisted of one-on-one interviews with the participants; focus groups consisting of a cross-section of the Forum users; and pencil-and-paper diary recordings by participants. The quantitative analysis of individual user activity consisted of data such as login/logout times, duration of time within the Forum and peak use times. In addition, prior to implementation the design storyboards and animations were used in focus groups with different sets of workers. These were students, knowledge workers and flexible workers.

These different groups had very different opinions and concerns regarding the concept and the design of the Contact Space. The younger participants seemed more experienced in Internet communication media such as mailing lists, newsgroups, chat-rooms and buddy lists (ICQ/PAL). As a group the students were very much at ease with the concept of a work-orientated virtual social area. Older respondents were more reluctant to vary or add to their favoured (and established) communication media of email, telephone and face-to-face contact. The younger respondents were also less concerned about any overheads involved with using the system, (for example, setting one's state or avatar to "busy"), and were more confident that desktop activities could be successfully used to represent some sort of contextual accessibility information. There was also a noticeable split between job types, as the need for communication and the role of communication varies depending on what sort of job a person does. For instance, people whose work was quite independent and could rely on documented support felt that the communication channels offered in the Contact Space were too different from face-to-face contact in the way communication is initiated and negotiated. Those people who felt a need to discuss ideas or informally review work perceived a potential benefit in having new channels available to approach sets of people.

For the Forum Contact Space trial, 35 BT Adastral Park colleagues, both on-site and distributed (London, Felixstowe) participated, in which the methodology was qualitative (focus groups, interviews, personal diaries, two-week Contact Space video diary) and quantitative (data logs of dates, communication and movement within the Contact Space).

Two aspects of the investigation were communication and user representation. Communication using text chat functionality occurred between dyads and small groups. Remembering to speak to someone was sometimes triggered by seeing them in the Contact Space, which then led to a text chat. Rather then send an email or phone a colleague, participants stated that they would also check to see if the person was in the Forum to send a text chat to. Interaction with strangers did not occur.

With respect to user representation, adding a wave feature could be a visual cue when greeting another before a text chat or as a casual hello. Communication might also be better streamlined if people were able to phone or email one another by clicking on their avatar, in addition to text chat. The ability to tell what another avatar is doing (i.e. in a text chat, in the meeting space or on the phone) is functionality that should occur automatically when initiated.

Participants feel that the concept of the Contact Space has been nearly realized, although a greater population within the space and greater geographical distribution among the participants would provide more significant findings. An example of the success of the Contact Space in fostering chance encounters occurred when a participant "Sue" saw "Bob" in the Contact Space just before lunch. She opened up a text chat and invited him to lunch; however, he stated that he would be attending a lunch-hour presentation. She then remembered that she also wanted to attend but had forgotten. Five minutes later they met at the presentation. If they hadn't met in the Contact Space, the real-world interaction would never have occurred.

The importance of boundaries was clear. As most use of the Forum occurs in-between working on other documents or programs, the Forum is used often as work is loading up or to give the user a break. Peripheral awareness involves real-world awareness translating into virtual awareness. The "navigate to" button is key to this theme. As the Forum moves from a peripheral to a core tool, new rules of use are adopted as the Forum affects real-world communication; for example, real-world conversations are minimal and blunt. The integration of the Forum with other tools also changes with the move from core to periphery, as other tools cannot be used. The importance of the issue of surroundings was introduced, as was the overriding aim to make the Forum as comfortable as possible.

6.3.5 Nessie World Trial

The Nessie world and the integration of the 3D environment with ambient displays has not yet been evaluated in a systematic way. Thus we can report only anecdotal results on different aspects of the system.

The design of the avatars as Lego puppets that can be distinguished only by their colours was primarily determined by technical arguments. The simple avatars guaranteed the necessary performance of the system. However, we expected users to complain about the avatars since they are used to more sophisticated ones. However, users reacted positive to the avatars and their abstract appearance. They could identify themselves more easily with these simple abstract avatars than with more realistic avatars that cause reactions like "I don't want to look like that avatar". Discussions on how an avatar should look like or what parts should be adaptable, as we experienced with the Forum trial, did not happen.

We also expected that the Nessie world would be more useful when displayed on an additional monitor (Fig. 6.4), since it will be overlaid frequently by other windows when running on the user's main monitor. However, even when this happens the Nessie window comes into the user's view from time to time when other windows are closed or rearranged. This is similar to a user's glance around an open-plan office or out of the office door when one changes from one task to another. Probably it is even better for the Nessie world not always to be in the user's sight, to avoid distraction from the user's actual work.

6.3.6 Redesign

The results of the trial informed a broad redesign of both the Meeting Space and the Contact Space. Some of the main problems are concerned with issues beyond the control of the Forum implementation group. For instance, the ability to collaborate effectively can be stymied by the best efforts of IT professions concerned with security. Since collaboration requires data-sharing and awareness, these need to be transferred through firewalls without compromising the security of intranets. Another major problem is that conferencing has been costed commercially as higher value communication. The contact space relies on a model of conferencing that puts it on a cost par with point-to-point telephony. Unless the cost of conferencing matches the ease of availability in the contact space, no one will want to use it. The obvious problems of installation and the desire not to have another account to log on to were features that could be improved. In addition it became clear that while the Contact Space ought not to occupy the space taken up by tools such as email, telephony and scheduling, it ought to integrate more easily with these other tools. Avatar design was deemed to be crucial, in particular the design of avatars in the Contact Space; the small window makes it difficult to identify people and there is a question of whether the avatar should be more abstract, displaying role and skills rather than shirt colour. In the meeting space this was not felt to be the best way forward, with most people favouring a more sophisticated range of customization options without any attempt to achieve realism. Rather than see someone and then "call them up" on the phone, it was felt that a voice over IP solution might be more instantaneous and therefore more useful. A user would see someone and simply speak to them over the network connection. As people often spend a large part of their day away from their desk it is recognized that there needs to be a way of putting tools such as the contact space onto mobile devices such as WAP-enabled phones and PDAs. Such small devices will not sensibly display a Contact Space rendering, so a more appropriate interface that still allows continuity across interfaces needs to be designed, including 2D and 3D interfaces, more awareness and integration between synchronous and asynchronous awareness tools.

The static layout of the Nessie world hinders the adaptation to a more dynamic working context. It is therefore necessary to allow for a dynamic creation of the virtual environment based on the information and real spaces populated by the users in their everyday work. This also requires new mechanisms for moving the avatars around in the virtual space based on the users' changing between different working contexts. Since the avatars in the Nessie world walk from one place to the other instead of being teleported, the world needs to know the semantics of the spatial layout. This will allow for a computation of a sensible route from one place to the other avoiding avatars that bump into each other or buildings.

6.4 Conclusions and Future Work

The use of the systems presented in this chapter extends beyond what people actually comprehend: one participant stated that he had only used the Forum once all day, but when the actual video was studied it was clear he used the Forum a great deal for short glances and observational purposes, but that he had only registered one task.

The significance of the Forum seems to extend past merely the "chatting" ability and includes the ability to comfort, monitor, increase awareness and observe, all of which are often not easily recognizable by the participant. However, these are the social foundations upon which any use of the Forum depends.

As organizations become increasingly fragmented and their personnel more dispersed, the demand for tools such as the Forum will inevitably increase. The Forum will allow dispersed personnel to stay in more direct contact, not just through text-chat, but through the feeling of "presence" that it gives to users who do not occupy the same physical space. Real-world behaviour that occurs in an office is being replicated in the Forum, in a virtual world. This allows users to carry out observations of who is around when they return from a break, as close as possible to the way in which they could carry out real observations in an office. The trial group has shown that the transfer of practices occurs easily from the real into the virtual world and the importance of subliminal aspects such as awareness cannot be underestimated for distanced workers. Any opportunity to carry out real-world practices which are lost when workers are not co-present is a positive step which will decrease the problems of isolation and loneliness that often accompany teleworking. In addition, a tool such as the Contact Space or Nessie world can be designed to include cultural cues that might allow distributed groups to work together more effectively. Intercultural communication techniques may be brought to bear on the design of online collaboration spaces. The relationship between intercultural communication and online collaboration spaces is further explored in Chapter 13. It may be possible to help online users to get a sense of how a remote organization works via self-created narratives of the user groups themselves.

The ideas presented in the chapter will be further developed towards a Theatre of Work. Both approaches presented here are static systems with respect to the spatial layout of the 3D environment. Future work will concentrate on the dynamic creation of the spatial environment based on the information spaces that are used by the cooperation partners in their daily business. It is necessary to experiment with different visualizations of the information spaces such as standard architectures or artificial spaces. Spaces should be dynamically created and should adopt themselves to changes in the real world to visualize the status and history of the shared collaboration process. Another interesting research issue is the transformation of sequences of event notifications and history information into a narrative of the past cooperative activities to allow users a view back to recent activities and to catch up on events.

Future work on Symbolic Acting needs to address a number of cross-cultural issues. There is the obvious and important area of national or ethnic cultural differences to be addressed in a system that attempts to interpret casual interaction into symbolic acting. An avatar should not misrepresent a user's culture or confuse another through conflicting interpretation of meaning. In addition, there is an issue of bringing together cultures, not of national origin, but of organizational origin. Working together can be made easier or made worse depending on the organizational cultures of the groups working together. Part of the quality of being together physically is the development of a shared communication language and shared understanding of "how we do things here". We spend time with others and learn to see their world, see what is accepted and what is not. The social interactions that often underpin working activities encourage an understanding of the deeper reasons for simple differences. Without this spatially afforded intercultural dialogue, how can we be sure that a productive working environment can be created?

Acknowledgements

We would like to thank Alison Willard, Peter Platt, Amanda Oldroyd, Michael Jewell, Andy Mortlock, Phil Sheppard, Nick Kings and John Davies at BT; and Wolfgang Broll, Wolfgang Gräther, Karl-Heinz Klein, Sabine Kolvenbach, Eckhard Meyer, Uta Pankoke-Babatz and Leonie Schäfer at GMD-FIT. For the analysis of Forum usage the authors are much indebted to Holly Ward, Jon Duhig, Phillip Jeffrey and Bev Wright.

Chapter 7

Virtually Missing the Point: Configuring CVEs for Object-Focused Interaction

Jon Hindmarsh, Mike Fraser, Christian Heath and Steve Benford

7.1 Introduction

In this chapter, we focus on collaborative virtual reality systems that use a combination of 3D graphics and audio to enable people to interact within a virtual setting and to discuss, fashion and manipulate their common environment. The emergence of these systems introduces unique opportunities to develop new sites of sociality and to support distributed collaborative work and interaction. Indeed, as 3D visualizations and single-user VR technologies become increasingly adopted within numerous industrial and entertainment domains (Schroeder, 1996; Stanney *et al.*, 1998), there are heightened opportunities for associated collaborative applications to emerge (Biocca and Levy, 1995). Most successful thus far have been the entertainment applications, such as online gaming, inhabited TV, artistic installations and museum exhibits (see Benford *et al.*, 1997a,b, 1999a; Greenhalgh *et al.*, 1999b,c; and Chapter 5 of this volume). However, here we are particularly concerned with the potential for collaborative VR to provide support for remote working – a relatively under-explored area.

If we consider VR as a potential workplace, then the ability to engage with and share "physical" (or rather, "visible') elements of the world will be critical to its success. The "objects" within the 3D world that might be relevant to working contexts include such things as visualizations of buildings and scenes for architects and their clients to explore and discuss; whiteboards, which often form the focus of multi-party meetings; 3D objects and animations designed for virtual worlds themselves; X-rays or representations of human bodies for medical professionals to plan and debate surgical procedures; video images for film editors to discuss and arrange; abstract data spaces for colleagues to navigate and analyse; and so forth. In each example, a case can be made for the need for, or benefits of, digital workspaces in which colleagues may collaborate around "artefacts" while geographically remote.

Thus our aim is to focus on support for co-participants to be able to discuss, share and manipulate virtual objects and visual aspects of the virtual scenery. Such a focus demands a much richer range of communicative resources, to support actions such as demonstrative reference in all its forms (see Streeck, 1996; Hindmarsh and Heath, in press) and means for participants to cluster around and view relevant objects together. As yet, however, we have little understanding of the ways in which people interact within collaborative VR and the problems they encounter, and whether these innovative technologies will provide a robust forum for work and interaction.

In this chapter, we report on our initial attempts to develop VR environments to provide enhanced support for object-focused collaboration. In particular, we consider the design and development of the most widespread and accessible form of VR technology, namely "desktop" collaborative VR. This can be seen as most accessible, as it does not require specialized hardware of the kind used in "immersive" interfaces (e.g. head-mounted displays, large-scale projection screens). Moreover, for working environments, it provides users with the opportunity to interleave tasks and interaction in the real-world workplace with communication through the virtual world.

To illustrate our work, we will present two extracts of interaction in VR drawn from experiments undertaken using our prototype system. In part, this will demonstrate our approach to the study of interaction through collaborative VR, but more importantly it will reveal the kinds of findings and issues that have emerged from our work. We conclude by exploring the implications that these findings have for new kinds of avatar design to support remote work and collaboration.

7.2 Objects, Interaction and VR

It may be worth briefly charting the provenance of our concern with object-focused interaction through a discussion both of recent naturalistic studies of the workplace and the relative failures of distributed communication "solutions", such as media spaces, to support this kind of work activity.

In their wide-ranging investigation of organizational conduct, "workplace studies", Luff *et al.* (for a review see Luff *et al.*, 2000) have powerfully demonstrated how communication and collaboration are dependent upon the ability of personnel to invoke and refer to features of their immediate environment (e.g. Goodwin and Goodwin, 1996; Heath and Hindmarsh, 2000). Studies of settings such as offices and control rooms have shown that individuals not only use objects and artefacts, such as screens, documents, plans, diagrams and models, to accomplish their various activities, but also to coordinate those activities, in real time, with the conduct of others. Indeed, it is found that many activities within co-located working environments rely upon the participants talking with each other, and monitoring each other's conduct, while looking at and using some workplace artefact.

An essential part of this process, is the individual's ability to refer to particular objects, and have another see in a particular way, what they themselves are looking at (Hindmarsh and Heath, 2000). For example, in our own studies of a telecommunications control centre, we charted how various objects, mainly documents and computer screens, or, more accurately, features of documents and computer screens, form the focus for collaboration and coordination at different times within the working day. Indeed, we noted how these kinds of objects routinely form "organizational hubs", over which colleagues come together to discuss plans of action, to organize *ad hoc* divisions of labour, or to debate the efficacy of current practice (Hindmarsh, 1997). During these moments, it is critical for colleagues to be able to establish and maintain common reference towards (features of) the objects at hand, such that they are secure in the knowledge that they are talking about the same "thing', at least for all practical purposes. If this was not possible, then colleagues would be much less able to subtly and seamlessly exchange information and coordinate their activities.

These kinds of issues provide insights into the demands that will be placed on technologies that aim to provide flexible and robust support for remote working. Interestingly, systems to support distributed, yet synchronous, collaboration are increasingly attempting to meet these needs. Rather than merely presenting face-to-face views, conventional videoconferencing systems are now often provided with a "document camera", and media spaces and related technologies are increasingly designed to provide participants with access to common digital displays or enhanced access to the others' domain (e.g. Tang *et al.*, 1994; Yamazaki *et al.*, 1999; Gaver *et al.*, 1993). However, it is not clear that such systems provide adequate support for object-focused collaboration. Even the straightforward ability to reference (features of) objects is often rendered highly problematic.

A good example is provided by the MTV II system (Heath *et al.*, 1997), which was used in an experiment undertaken by one of the authors, along with Bill Gaver, Paul Luff and Abi Sellen. In these experiments, remote participants were provided with various views of each other and their respective domains on three separate monitors, including a "face-to-face" view, an "in-context" view (showing the individual in the setting), and a "desktop" view (allowing access to documents and other objects). Participants were asked to undertake a simple task which necessitated reference to objects in, and features of, each other's respective environment. Despite providing participants with visual access to the relevant features of each other's domains, participants encountered difficulties in completing the task. In general, individuals could not determine what a co-participant was referring to, and, more specifically, where and at what the person was looking or pointing. This problem derived from participants' difficulties in (re)connecting an image of the other with the image of the object to which they were referring. The fragmentation of images – the person from the object and relevant features of the environment – undermined the participants' abilities to assemble the coherence of the scene (Heath and Hindmarsh, 2000; Hindmarsh, 1997). This undermined even simple collaboration in and through the mutually available objects and artefacts (for similar findings, see Barnard *et al.*, 1996).

In the light of these findings we decided to consider the kinds of support for object-focused work provided by CVEs. Of course CVEs enable participants to work with shared access to objects located in the virtual environment, while media spaces endeavour to provide participants with the opportunity to work on "real, physical" objects. However, we believe that CVEs may provide a more satisfactory method of supporting certain forms of distributed collaborative work. Firstly, the use of VR technologies in a range of pursuits could well involve collaborative work over and around virtual objects, designs and scenes in their own right. Secondly, CVE developers are refining techniques for integrating information from the physical world into virtual environments, for example in the form of embedded video views that are displayed as dynamic texture maps attached to virtual objects (Reynard *et al.*, 1998).

Should CVEs prove to provide effective support for object-focused collaboration with virtual objects, then such extensions might allow them to provide similar support for remote collaboration with physical objects in the future.

Although the problems associated with establishing what another can see or is looking at are well recognized for media spaces, it is often argued that problems of recognizing what views and scenes are available to the other are "naturally" overcome in 3D worlds (e.g. Smith *et al.*, 1998). These would seem reasonable claims, especially because:

- even though the actual users are located in distinct physical domains, the CVE allows participants to share views of a stable and common virtual world consisting of the same objects and artefacts.

- the use of embodiments located in the virtual world, provides the participants with access both to the other, and to the other's actions and orientations in the "local environment". The embodiments can be seen alongside the objects at which they are looking and pointing. In this way, and unlike media spaces, (representations of) participants are visibly "embodied in", and "connected to", the common world of objects.

Therefore we set out to explore the extent to which these factors might mean that collaborative VR could provide robust support for object-focused interaction. We proceed by outlining our general approach to the study of interaction in collaborative VR, before discussing two initial experiments directed towards the study of interaction around objects. These will illustrate our approach and the nature and character of our findings.

7.3 Approach

In recent years, there has been a notable shift in emphasis within human–computer interaction (HCI) to incorporate naturalistic research in addition to more traditional experimental approaches. For example, the emergence of workplace studies within Computer-Supported Cooperative Work (CSCW) has revealed the benefit of examining the *in situ* production of work and the practical concerns of workers using technologies. These studies have been highly effective at revealing the taken-for-granted, tacit competencies of coordinating and organizing collaborative work. As an example, such studies have even revealed how the seemingly individual task of typing computer commands can, at times, be seen as produced, shaped and timed with regard to local interaction with colleagues (Luff and Heath, 2000).

It is the approach used in these kinds of studies that we aim to draw from in two key ways. Firstly, we use the examination of "real-world" work and interaction as a basis from which to compare and contrast observed interactions in virtual worlds. They provide a stock of knowledge with which to explicate the problems and difficulties faced by participants in collaborative VR. They also enable us to consider the nature of the interactional resources that are absent for co-participants in collaborative VR as compared with co-present interaction.

Secondly, we will draw on the analytic orientation used by many of these studies, namely those engaged with interactional analyses of embodied work and communication (cf. Chapter 5), and in particular those that use conversation analysis to analyse video records of workplace activities (for example Goodwin and Goodwin, 1996; Heath and Luff, 2000). Although a thorough description of the methodological orientation is beyond the scope of this chapter (for which see Sacks, 1992; Heath, 1997), it may be worth highlighting one of the key resources that we bring to bear in analysing video data – a concern with the "sequential organization of interaction". This highlights the ways in which individuals display their understanding of others' conduct, step by step, turn by turn, and even moment-by-moment. This turns on what Heritage calls the doubly contextual nature of interaction, where the conduct of participants is both "context shaped and context renewing" (Heritage, 1984). Each action, as a matter of course, embodies and displays an understanding of the immediately prior action(s) and provides the context in which the next emerges. Thus, participants routinely display their understanding of prior actions, in and through the nature of their subsequent contributions. This provides a unique resource for researchers to assess how particular actions are treated, understood and used by participants themselves, in the context of their ongoing activity.

In studying collaborative VR, we focus on the use of talk and the manipulation of the avatar in interaction. In doing so, we look at the audible and visible conduct produced by participants. Thus we consider the ways in which individuals encounter the other and the virtual environment, and how they experience and attend to actions produced by their co-participant(s). In such a way, we are concerned to explore some of the very resources that they have at hand to make actions intelligible and to contribute to the emerging course of interaction.

To do this, we capture audio-visual recordings of the events. Video has a series of benefits over standard observational data. For example, video accesses details of interaction that would be unattainable through real-time observation alone. To hear and see participants to the degree captured on film would mean standing so close as to become a critical part of the activity itself. Moreover, an observer could not possibly record the details of those activities in anything like as much detail as the camera. While noting down one utterance or gesture, for example, the next would come and go. In such a way, video records in detail a version of an activity that is then available to the analyst for repeated scrutiny. This is a critical resource, given our interests in the moment-to-moment sequential organization of interaction. It also provides a stable data source that can be analysed and re-analysed in more and more detail or even with different concerns at hand, and also to facilitate and support discussions between social scientists and designers.

In the past, this kind of approach has not only been used to inform studies of everyday work and interaction, but has also contributed to studies of interaction through prototype media space systems (Heath and Hindmarsh, 2000; Hindmarsh, 1997) and indeed through multi-user VR (Bowers *et al.*, 1996a,b). In terms of the work on VR, Bowers *et al.* have undertaken interactional analyses of meetings involving real-time interaction between participants located at five sites and in three countries (UK, Sweden and Germany). One of their studies (Bowers *et al.*, 1996b) describes the interactional use of simple embodiments in virtual collaboration by showing how changes in the orientation and movement of the embodiments is coordinated with emerging features of the talk. These authors have also discussed the ways in which actions in a virtual world, especially those that seem somehow odd, can be related to activities within the users' real-world environment; that is to say, how ongoing activities and interactions involving participants in their physical environment can impact upon the ways in which their actions appear and are treated in the virtual world (Bowers *et al.*, 1996a).

Although studies drawing on conversation analysis are traditionally associated with the examination of naturalistic interaction, the prototypical nature of collaborative VR raises a series of pragmatic barriers to the collection of naturally occurring materials. The key constraint is that there are very few environments in which collaborative VR is used as a matter of routine, except maybe by CVE designers themselves (as with the studies by Bowers *et al.*). One of the few ethnographic studies of a "community" in collaborative VR can be found in the studies of AlphaWorlds by Schroeder, but he focuses neither on the details of communicative practice nor on a VR system that supports "real-time" audio[1] (Schroeder, 1997). In Chapter 5, Büscher *et al.* examine a range of collaborative VR exhibits in the ZKM centre for art and media technology (in Germany), and thus were able to collect naturalistic materials of museum visitors encountering and experiencing, and communicating through, VR "worlds". However, such studies are very rare. Indeed, even Bowers *et al.* only had access to quasi-naturalistic data drawn from meetings held by the research team themselves, and thus featuring the analysts as participants.

Our research materials have been drawn from artificial or experimental situations. As stated, our concerns are with collaboration over and around "objects" and features of the local (virtual) environment and, at present, collaborative VR systems, if they provide support for this at all, provide it through avatar position or orientation, talk and the ability to manipulate objects. However, we wanted to provide additional support by allowing avatars to gesture and so forth. Thus, we did not have access to any system that provides enhanced (or dedicated) support for object-focused interaction *and* that is currently used in a real-world context. Therefore we developed our own system and organized some experiments with individuals interacting through that system.

However, we must stress that our data are better described as "quasi-experimental", as our approach did not adopt the procedures associated with classical experiments with human subjects. Nevertheless, our use of this quasi-experimental approach is necessary, in part because our interests are to engage in design and development work, and as such we are constrained by the demands of rapid prototyping and redesign. Additionally, however, we know very little indeed about the organization of interaction "through" this communication medium and thus it would be premature to build hypotheses or to undertake large-scale experimental studies. Indeed, there is extremely little human factors or naturalistic work on

---

[1] AlphaWorlds supports text chat, rather than full auditory connections between users, so it uses only graphics and text media. See http://www.activeworlds.com/.

collaborative VR. Another complication associated with full-blown experimentation with prototype collaborative VR applications has been noted by Tromp *et al.* (1998, p. 55):

> The prototypical nature of the applications becomes another methodological issue because it's often not feasible to create different conditions for experiments. Therefore, the given state of the applications at the time of testing constrains the scientific inquiry process.

As a result, our approach is designed to explore and uncover the kinds of interactional phenomena, practices and problems that may be of particular relevance to both participants and designers. In this way we aim to begin to sensitize ourselves to the key issues that impact upon the ways in which individuals interact and discuss objects in collaborative VR.

7.4 Furniture World: An Initial Investigation

To investigate object-focused interaction in CVEs, we adapted a task from the previous studies of the MTV media space system (Heath *et al.*, 1997). Participants were asked to collaboratively arrange the layout of furniture in a virtual room (consisting of two plug sockets, a door, two windows, a fireplace, and a number of items of standard household furniture) and agree upon a single design. They were given conflicting priorities in order to encourage debate and discussion. We implemented this "Furniture World" using MASSIVE-2, a general-purpose collaborative VR platform that has been developed at the University of Nottingham (Benford *et al.*, 1997a).

MASSIVE-2 allows multiple participants in a shared virtual world to communicate using a combination of 3D graphics and real-time audio. Participants are also able to grasp and move virtual objects in the world. The participants in our experiment used Silicon Graphics workstations connected via an Ethernet, with speech being supported by headphones and a microphone.

In order to conduct our experiment, we extended the capabilities of the default MASSIVE-2 embodiment and simplified its default interface. The revised embodiment and interface are shown in Fig. 7.1. Our aim in altering the embodiment was to enhance support for referencing visible objects. The guiding principle behind our design was that the embodiment should broadly reflect the appearance of a physical body. Although photo-realism was not possible for performance reasons, this meant that the embodiment should be generally humanoid (i.e. have a recognizable head, torso and limbs). We adopted this approach because we felt that it is the most obvious choice and indeed, is one that has been widely adopted by CVE designers. One goal of our work is therefore to provide some insights as to the utility of pseudo-humanoid embodiments in CVEs.

Our avatar design supported pointing as one way of referencing objects. This was in addition to referencing them in talk or by facing them, already supported by MASSIVE-2. A participant could choose to point at a target (an object or a general area of space) by selecting it with a mouse button. The avatar would then raise its

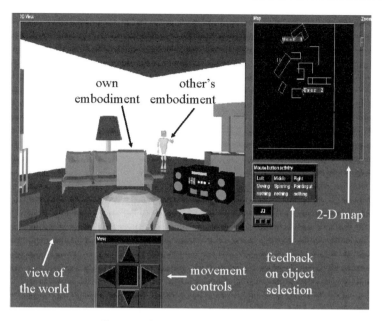

Figure 7.1 The Furniture World interface.

nearest arm to point at the target and would also incline its head towards it, as shown in Fig. 7.2. The field of view provided in our application was 55° horizontally and 45° vertically, in order to minimize distortion on the desktop interface. To simplify usability, we also fixed the viewpoint so that participants could not toggle between different perspectives on the world.

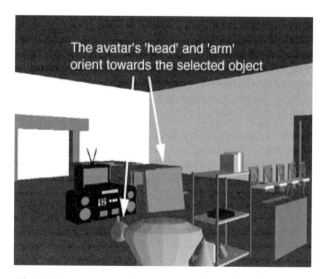

Figure 7.2 A user points at the stereo (view from behind the avatar).

7.4.1 Trials

It should be noted that the adaptation of a task from the previous media space experiments was not intended to facilitate an evaluation of the relative success of the two systems. Indeed, a direct comparison would be rather deceptive, as the technological differences make the tasks quite distinct – in MTV the participants have asymmetrical access to the model, whereas in the virtual environment all participants have equal access to the virtual furniture. Rather, this simple design task encourages (even demands) that the participants discuss and differentiate features of the virtual world. Nevertheless, we have found it useful to reflect upon the differences regarding problems faced by users of the two systems.

Six trials of two participants and two trials of three participants were performed. Most participants were students (twelve male and six female), with a broad mixture of previous acquaintance. None of them had a background in CVE technology. Each trial took about an hour and consisted of ten minutes for participants to get used to the system, approximately half an hour to perform the given task; then to conclude, we interviewed them about their experience of using the system. The principal data were audio-visual recordings of the participants' on-screen and at-screen (or "real-world") conduct.

A more comprehensive discussion of the observed problems and difficulties participants encountered when interacting through the system can be found elsewhere (Hindmarsh *et al.*, 1998). However, within the scope of this chapter we will briefly outline one of the key observations and its implications for redesign and further experimentation. The issue revolves around the seemingly trivial activity of referencing an object in the room.

In a virtual environment, an avatar, its pointing arm and the referent being pointed at can potentially be seen alongside one another. Thus many of the documented problems of referencing in media space (e.g. related to the separation of faces, gestures and objects onto different monitors) are assumed to disappear. However, problems still emerge. Like most "desktop" virtual environments, Furniture World only provides a 55° horizontal field of view, in order to minimize distortion on the desktop interface. This field of view restricts participants' opportunities to see embodiments in relation to objects. When an utterance is produced, individuals are rarely in an immediate position to see the embodiment alongside the referenced object. It turns out that it is critical that they do see them in relation to one another. So, they firstly turn to find the other's embodiment and then look for the object.

To illustrate, consider Fragment 1, in which Sarah asks Karen about the "desk-thing" in the room. Before they can discuss where they might put the desk, they need some 25 seconds to achieve a common orientation towards it (square brackets indicate overlapping utterances; a dot in brackets indicates a short pause in talk).

Fragment 1
S: You know this desk-thing?
K: Yeah?
S: Can you see what I'm pointing at now?

((K Turns to Find S))

K: Er I can't see you, but   [I think

S: [It's like a desk-thing.

K: Er-where've you gone?   [heh heh heh

S: [Erm, where are you?

K: I've. the. I can see

S: Turn (.) oh, oh yeah. you're near the lamp, yeah?

K: Yeah.

S: And then, yeah turn around right. (.) and then it's like (.) I'm pointing at it now, but I don't know if you can see what
[I'm pointing at?

K: [Right yeah I can see.

When Sarah asks if Karen can see what she is pointing at, Karen starts to look for Sarah's embodiment and her pointing gesture. She is actually facing the desk very early on in the sequence, but ends up turning 360°, via Sarah's gesture, to return to the very same desk. See the sequence of images in Fig. 7.3.

In co-present interaction, when an individual asks a co-participant to look at an object at which they are pointing, that co-participant can usually see them in relation to their surroundings. They simply turn from the body of the other to find the referenced object. In this CVE, participants often do not have the other's

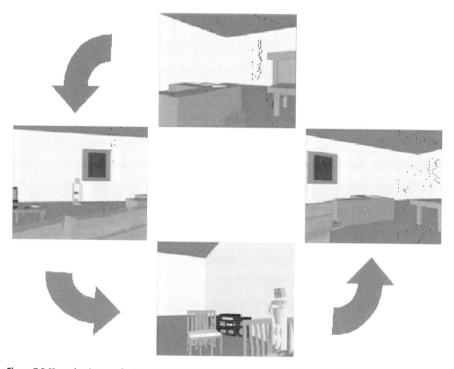

Figure 7.3 Karen's view as she turns 360° to find Sarah's avatar and then the "desk-thing". Look at the images anticlockwise from the top and notice the similarity between the first view and the last.

embodiment in view during an utterance. They might turn out to have initially had the referent in view, but without seeing the object in relation to the pointing gesture they have little information with which to assess if they are looking at the appropriate object. In other words, they may see a "desk-thing", but is it the relevant "desk-thing"? In some cases, then, they cannot be certain that they are looking at and discussing the same object without seeing that object in relation to the other's embodiment.

Participants find the relevant object by following a particular sequence. First they turn to find the gesture and then they use this as a resource to find the referent. Even in short and straightforward instances, participants can be seen to turn away from an object to find the other's avatar gesturing, only to subsequently return to face that object. Participants may, however, need to engage in an extensive search for their co-participant's embodiment before being able to see the relevant object. This problem is compounded by the slow speed of the system.

In real-world co-present environments, the local constellation of objects and artefacts provides a resource for making sense of the actions of others. The production of action is situated in an environment and its intelligibility rests upon the availability of that environment (Heath and Hindmarsh, 2000). However, participants in CVEs only encounter a fragment of the visible world. Separating an embodiment from the objects on which they are acting creates difficulties for participants, as their overall sense of the action is impoverished. As they are rarely in a position to see both object and embodiment simultaneously, they have problems in relating the two. Critically, the sense of talk or action is based upon the mutual availability of that relationship.

Not only does the field of view then cause problems for the person trying to find an object being referred to, but it also raises difficulties for the person doing the referring – in this instance, Sarah. Note how she asks "Can you see- what I'm pointing at now?" and then part way through the fragment, she says "Erm, where are you?" before turning to look for her colleague. In everyday environments, referrers will routinely shape, time and organize their talk and bodily conduct *for the recipient*, even to the extent of delaying the production of a pointing gesture for a few moments while a colleague gets in a position to see more clearly (Hindmarsh and Heath, 2000).

In VR, referrers are often not in a position to be able to see both the other and the object, and therefore attempts to produce actions that are subtly sensitive to the visual conduct of the other are rendered highly problematic. In this instance, at the start of the sequence, Sarah can just see Karen's avatar on the edge of her screen. However, within moments Karen's avatar slips out of view as she is turning to find Sarah. At this point, Sarah explicitly asks whether Karen can see where she is pointing and then later turns to find where she is in order to provide her with directions to the "desk-thing".

This example highlights a more general concern for participants collaborating through virtual worlds. The organization and coordination of much co-present work is facilitated by individuals configuring their actions for another at specific moments within the course of an activity. This sometimes rests on the ability to see the emerging visual conduct of the co-participant. The narrow field of view in VR, however, can often cut out the visible features of the other avatar's orientation, actions and movement while a participant is focusing on an object under discussion. The talk of participants does reveal elements of their conduct, but there is a much greater reliance on the talk than in everyday workplaces. This leads to much cruder and less flexible practices for coordinating and organizing collaborating. Whereas they would normally be able to talk and simultaneously reveal other "information" via visual conduct, almost all their actions are (principally) revealed through talk.

Of course, participants are sensitive to, and have ways of solving, the problems of working in this kind of "blinkered" environment. However, these "solutions" do damage to common patterns of working – an added sequence is inserted into the emergent activity in which participants must establish the common referent before continuing. An illustration is provided by Karen's quest for Sarah's gesture, in which a 25-second search for the desk takes place prior to a discussion about where it could be moved. The problem is compounded by the slow speed of movement in the CVE, preventing quick glances to find the other and the object. Therefore these referential sequences can last longer than the very activities that they foreshadow – for example, the length of time it takes to establish some common orientation towards an object or location can be much longer than the simple query that follows.

Unfortunately, the additional time involved in establishing mutual orientation is not the critical concern. This prefatory sequence actually disrupts the flow and organization of collaborative activities. In co-present interaction, participants are able to engage in the activity at hand, while assuming that the other can see or quickly find the referent. Within the CVE, participants become explicitly engaged in, and distracted by, the problem of establishing mutual orientation. Indeed, it becomes a topic in and of itself.

In Furniture World, participants cannot assume the availability of certain features of the environment and so attend to making those features available to the other. Rather than debating where an object should be placed or whether to remove a piece of furniture altogether, participants are drawn into explicit discussions about the character of an object. This inhibits the flow of collaborative activity and introduces obstacles into collaborative discussions. If collaborative VR technologies do not wish to impede the expedient production of work in the modern organization, it is suggested that these issues are important for the design of systems to support synchronous remote working.

7.5 Duplication World: Extending Actions and Views

Our observations of interaction through Furniture World raise a series of possible avenues of development and possible ways in which we could address the observed difficulties. In particular, in this chapter, we focus on two issues of critical concern related to the limited horizontal field of view available on the desktop system:

- The inability to assemble and understand the actions of others – for example, because it is difficult to simultaneously view the source (i.e. avatar) and target of actions such as pointing.

- The inability to design actions to be seen by others – for example, a lack of information about others' visual actions makes it harder for individuals to coordinate and organize their own conduct for the other to see.

Here we will concentrate on two design decisions generated from these issues – to extend the visibility of pointing gestures from the avatar into the environment; and to utilize "peripheral lenses" to extend the participant's field of view. We subsequently discuss a "follow-up" experiment in which we explored the implications of these decisions for interaction through collaborative VR. Note that elsewhere we provide a comprehensive discussion of the design considerations that emerge from our initial experiments with Furniture World (Fraser *et al.*, 1999; Hindmarsh *et al.*, in press).

Our first proposal focuses on the issue of providing better information about others' actions. Developers of 3D spaces tend to represent actions on the source embodiment alone in a "quasi-naturalistic" manner (e.g. raising an arm to show pointing). However, given the problems that arise because the source embodiment and target object are rarely simultaneously in view, we propose that the pseudo-realistic approach of showing actions solely by moving a pseudo-humanoid source embodiment is too understated. Indeed, we intend to enhance the availability and visibility of key actions by extending them into and through the general environment. For instance, we have chosen to enable participants to extend their pointing gestures out towards the object being referred to, making it more likely that the other can see it. This extension of the arm is triggered through operation of all three mouse buttons. The left button raises the arm in the direction of the mouse cursor and then the other two buttons extend or retract the arm.

In terms of field of view, we wished to investigate possible ways in which the horizontal field of view rendered on a desktop display might be increased. To reiterate the problem facing designers: the limited horizontal space available on a desktop display means that rendering wide views causes perspective distortions in the virtual world.

Distorted displays of the world are likely to compound difficulties with navigating through, and manipulating objects in, the world; problems already evident due to the limitations of input devices, displays and control mechanisms. Moreover, distortion would certainly hinder applications designed for medicine, architecture or the military. In these cases, as with many VR applications, realistic visualizations of the world are essential – imagine, for instance, the potential implications of a surgeon working on a distorted visualization of a real human body! As a result (and as with the Furniture World interface), CVEs usually display a view of the virtual world with a horizontal angle of around 55–60°, a third of a human perceptual capability. Head-mounted interfaces may provide more rapid and "intuitive" viewpoint movement but often suffer from (and are limited to) similarly reduced viewpoints through which problems in fragmenting views of object, action and avatar of the kind discussed in the previous section have also been noted (Fraser and Glover, 1998).

Therefore we decided to explore the benefits of "peripheral lenses" for collaborative VR. Peripheral lenses (Robertson *et al.*, 1997) consist of two additional windows (at either side of the standard focal view), which render peripheral views of a virtual environment on a participant's desktop display. Placed to the left and right of the main view, lenses with increased distortion allow more visual information to be displayed in a reduced horizontal space, such that both the lenses and the focal view fit onto the desktop display. Robertson *et al.* introduced this interface technique primarily as a navigation aid. Providing peripheral vision was intended to enhance the ability of single users to perform spatial search tasks. Their conclusions stated that search times were not statistically improved by the use of peripheral lenses, and they note that "Further studies are needed to understand exactly when Peripheral Lenses are effective". We suspect, however, that an implementation based on this approach might prove more successful at supporting awareness in collaborative situations. Therefore their use might alleviate the kinds of problematic interaction noted in Furniture World and provide further support for awareness of others' actions with respect to the virtual environment.

Figure 7.4 shows a peripheral lens interface displaying a virtual environment used in a second collaborative task. It can be seen that the detail of the focal view is preserved and, conversely, the peripheral lenses use distorted views to provide visual information at the sides of the desktop display.

Our system differs from that of Roberston *et al.* in that participants are unable to alter the horizontal "lens angle", which is fixed at 60° for each view, effectively providing a constant view of 180°.

In addition, we decided to provide the user with the ability to decide to change the focal view between different lenses. Through a technique which we term "peripheral glancing", the interface allows users to momentarily swap distortion between the default focal and peripheral views to "glance" left or right. Interestingly, Pierce *et al.* (1999) address the limited capabilities in single-user 3D systems for accessing tools and information on one's own avatar through a "glancing" metaphor. They describe the limitation in both field of view and viewpoint manipulation techniques and, while not providing explicit peripheral visual information, they note that glances may be a useful technique because "by combining glances

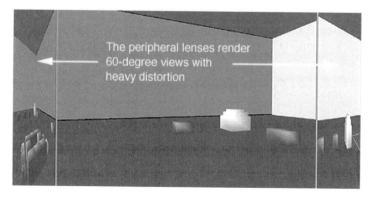

Figure 7.4 Peripheral lenses in MASSIVE-2.

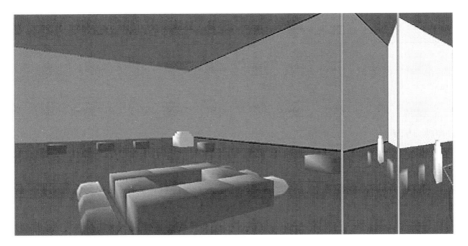

Figure 7.5 Peripheral glancing to the left.

and more traditional 3D navigation, we create a new metaphor for viewpoint control that includes both a virtual head and virtual body".

When designing peripheral lenses for monitoring object-focused actions, we anticipated difficulties in assessing actions depicted in the distorted views. Hence the glancing facility was provided to try to enable users to resolve these problems. "Glancing" begins on depressing a button placed below the relevant peripheral lens. Distortion is removed from the peripheral lens and added to the central view, and releasing the button reverses the process. Thus the peripheral lens momentarily becomes the user's focal view. An example of a user "glancing" to the left (on the same scene as in Fig. 7.4) is shown in Fig. 7.5.

7.4.2 Trials

Through this system, pairs of participants were asked to collaboratively *duplicate* a virtual structure. A large virtual environment was designed with two main areas – one area containing an abstract layout of blocks, and a second area containing all the "building blocks" required to reconstruct that layout. Participants were asked to reorganize the latter half of the world to conform to the same pattern and symmetry as the former. The environment was considerably larger and the task more complex than in the Furniture World trials, in order to exacerbate the problems associated with a "fragmented workspace". The idea was that the larger and more complex world would make it more likely that co-participants would be out of a participant's focal view at the onset of object-focused sequences. In addition, the use of abstract blocks made it harder for participants to distinguish one artefact from another (especially, for example, when viewing them through distorted lenses). Six pairs of participants performed the task and each experiment lasted approximately one hour.

Fraser *et al.* (1999) discuss a range of data fragments which reveal the relative successes and failures of the system redesign. Here, however, we aim to concentrate on one instance that reveals some of the unanticipated problems associated with the possibilities for action provided by peripheral lenses and extendable pointing gestures. In it, Gemma and Barbara are selecting blocks to place in the corners of the structure. This fragment is taken from early on in their task, and the area is still somewhat cluttered with similarly shaped blocks. Having started to talk about one block, they move on to discuss the "one next to it".

Fragment 2

Gemma:	there's also one next to it
	errm (.) hang on
Barbara:	*((B points to a block))*
	just there
Gemma:	err nope further (.)
	((starts to point)) errrr (0.5)
	hang on oh oh oh oh
	ooohhh [hhhh
Barbara:	[oo there's your arm
Gemma:	that one (.) can you see what
	I'm pointing to?
Barbara:	um (.) yeh I think so

Barbara is in close spatial proximity to the block in question, and therefore is able to extend a pointing gesture to the relevant block fairly quickly and during her utterance. However, Gemma is unable to see where Barabara's avatar is pointing. This is due to the occlusion of the gesture by other blocks, and may also be because the point is not extended far enough to touch the relevant block in a crowded scene of similar artefacts, hence Gemma's "further" comment. Gemma then proceeds to attempt her own referential gesture.

Our particular interest here is the attempt by Gemma to point to a block that is some distance from her avatar. Partly due to the distance between avatar and block, she extends the gesture further and further. When pointing out an object for the other, one might expect that the actual production of the gesture is quick and straightforward. However, with this design, extending an arm can take a few moments. The potentially large virtual distances involved and the slow speed of the system mean that it may take some time before the gesture reaches its target. Were these trials to have been conducted over wide-area networks, this situation would have become more conspic-uous, due to additional network delays – consider the various reports of communica-tion difficulties associated with lags in both video conferencing systems (Ruhleder and Jordan, 1999) and indeed collaborative VR (Vaghi et al, 1999).

Gemma displays these difficulties through her talk, in some ways vocally "animating" her virtual arm as it moves towards the target object ("hang on, oh oh oh oh ohhhhhhh"). It is noticeable from the video data that Gemma is using these noises to display an unfinished action; a gesture still in progress. Moreover, as the pointing arm extends, it produces a jerking movement rather than smoothly flowing outwards (see Fig. 7.6).

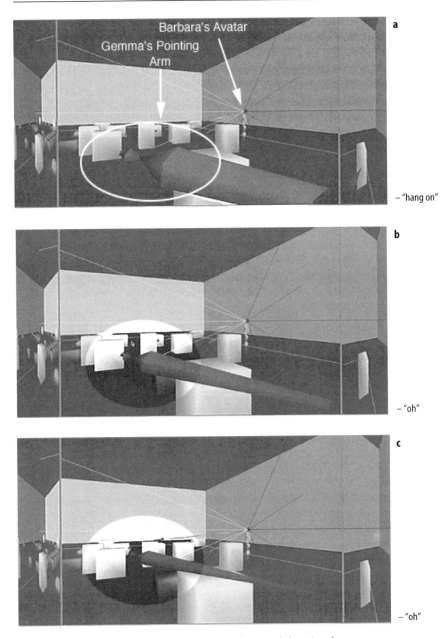

Figure 7.6 Gemma's view as she extends her virtual arm.

At each jerk, the arm momentarily comes to rest by different blocks that lie between Gemma and the target block. She uses each "oh" noise to show that these blocks are not the relevant blocks, and the pointing gesture is still on its way. So each "oh" sound displays that, while an object could be a target for this point –

because it is an object, and because it is an object of the kind being discussed – it is, in fact, not the relevant one for this gesture. Therefore, Gemma attends to the jerking movement produced by the system by using her voice to portray to Barbara that the gesture is still in progress.

So, Gemma goes to some trouble in her talk to display the trajectory of her point towards the relevant block and she marks the gesture as "in progress" as it stumbles and stutters through the field of other nearby blocks.

Unfortunately, Barbara cannot see the arm jerking past a series of candidate blocks; indeed, she does not see the arm moving at all. Her utterance, "oo there's your arm" marks the moment when the gesture "arrives" in her focal view, but prior to that moment the peripheral lens renders it barely perceptible (Fig. 7.7). The virtual arm is too thin to be noticed in the distorted condition of the peripheral lens.

Thus, Barbara only has access to Gemma's action through her vocalizations (cf. Hindmarsh *et al.*, 1998). The peripheral lens interface provides Barbara with the potential resources to see Gemma's arm in more detail through the use of a peripheral glance. Yet the problem is that if the participant cannot see something happening in the peripheral lens in the first place, then the ability to glance at it is rendered obsolete.

So, this fragment charts some of the continued difficulties for object-focused interaction, even after we have included additional resources to address some of the initial problems observed in Furniture World. However, although it is too early to assess whether peripheral lenses and extendable actions can aid object-focused interaction in CVEs, there is enough evidence to warrant further investigation and refinement (see Fraser *et al.*, 1999). Therefore, what can we learn from this experiment and how can we develop the system and interface further?

One noted issue was that distortion could render representations of others' action unavailable within a peripheral lens. So we might contemplate reducing the distortion in the peripheral lenses to alleviate these misconceptions, either through a reduced fixed value, or through allowing a user to vary the lens angle (cf.

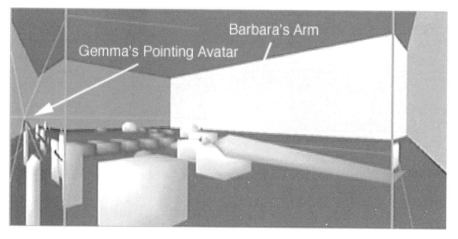

Figure 7.7 Barbara's view, in which Gemma's avatar and its gesture are barely perceptible in the left-hand peripheral lens.

Robertson *et al.*, 1997). However, as the horizontal space on the desktop display is limited, this would require a similar reduction in the participant's field of view, and thus contrast with our initial aim of providing a wider field of view. It may be, however, that for specific applications a lower distortion to field of view ratio may become relevant.

Another possibility is to address the ways in which representations of action are viewed in distorted conditions. This might allow participants to maintain know-ledge of the actions being performed with and around artefacts, even when they appear in distorted lenses. We might achieve this through rendering only certain features of the world within peripheral lenses, such as avatars, movements and/or objects relevant to the task at hand. Another possibility would be to use visual cues, such as high contrast or flashing, to make particular actions more clearly visible rather than simply charting their movement in the distorted lens.

Following our comments on the "jerky" movements of the extendable arm, the representation of an extended action could be designed to show the incompleteness of the action. For example an avatar's arm might be wire-framed while being extended or retracted, although we recognize that this particular suggestion might have the unwanted effect of making action even harder to perceive in a distorted lens.

A technique that we might consider as an "alternative" to peripheral lenses is the use of "virtual cameras" – in other words, the ability to alter one's viewpoint with respect to the avatar or to adopt the view of a third party with a comprehensive frame of current activity. These techniques have been used in the past in the MASSIVE systems, for example for broadcasting television from within virtual environments (Greenhalgh *et al.*, 1999b,c). Additionally, multi-user games and other CVE systems (e.g. AlphaWorlds) allow participants to change their point of view with respect to the avatar, thus getting a better sense of the action with respect to the environment. However, to note one issue that is likely to emerge in such a situation, we discovered problems in Furniture World where participants incor-rectly attributed a certain field of view to the other (Hindmarsh *et al.*, 1998). Imagine a situation where even the *location* from which a participant is looking is unavailable to the other. In some ways, then, the most critical benefits of using an avatar may be undermined; that is, if the position of the avatar completely belies the nature of the other's view of the world, the problem of establishing (for all practical purposes) what another is seeing would be exacerbated. As with all our proposals, this is very much a matter for future experimentation and development, and there-fore we are continuing to explore the different ways of displaying actions more clearly in CVEs.

7.6 Discussion

The studies that are reported within this chapter are the first steps towards our goal of developing more robust environments to support synchronous remote working in VR. In particular, we are interested in exploring the potential to support a range of activities that underpin a great majority of communicative encounters in the workplace, namely object-focused discussions and debates. Although workplace studies have charted the subtle and delicate ways in which texts, tools and technologies feature in everyday work, our observations (and the fragments reported in this chapter are two of many – see Hindmarsh *et al.*, 1998; Fraser *et al.*, 1999) reveal that VR systems currently fail even to support simple referential practice.

One key observation in VR is the major difficulty for participants in establishing what their co-participant is able to see at a particular moment within a sequence of events. Indeed, Buscher *et al.* in Chapter 5 observe a similar problem for participants using the various VR exhibits on show at ZKM. In the ZKM applications, the avatars in use were very simple representations (e.g. spheres) in large virtual spaces. In our experiments, however, the problems are equally evident even though the avatars provide opportunities for participants to gesture towards objects and spaces, and the virtual rooms in which they are situated are relatively simple and small (compared with the ZKM worlds). Therefore, if this is a problem in Furniture World and Duplication World, it points to a more widespread problem for collaborative VR systems.

Although we have adopted peripheral lenses to address this issue, we believe that by reflecting on everyday interaction, we can point towards some more radical solutions to this problem for virtual worlds. Schutz (1970) suggested that, in everyday interaction, common-sense thinking overcomes the differences in individual perspectives through what he has termed the *general thesis of reciprocal perspectives*. In particular, he notes how certain assumptions underpin our abilities to achieve intersubjective understandings and to know-in-common a world of objects[2]. A critical component of this is the "idealization of the interchangeability of the standpoints', where he suggests that (Schutz, 1970, pp. 183–4):

> I take it for granted – and assume that my fellow man does the same – that if I change places with him so that his "here" becomes mine, I would be at the same distance from things and see them in the same typicality as he actually does; moreover, the same things would be in my reach which are actually in his. (All this vice versa.).

However, when our basis for these assumptions is somehow fractured or disrupted, it can lead to the kinds of problems noted in our studies. That is to say, assuming the availability to the other of our actions, and indeed particular objects, can lead to difficulties in collaborative VR.

One possible design solution would be to provide a feedback monitor displaying the view available to the other person, thereby potentially removing such confusions. However, previous experiments with feedback monitors have proved problematic. In Heath *et al.*'s study of the MTVI system, participants did not use the monitor intuitively (Heath *et al.*, 1997). Moreover, in our own Furniture World experiment we provided a plan view which depicted the orientation of different avatars, and this was rarely used by participants either.

---

[2] Schutz uses the term "object" in a broader sense than adopted here. For Schutz, this term includes not only physical objects, but also features of the social environment (cultural artefacts, language etc.).

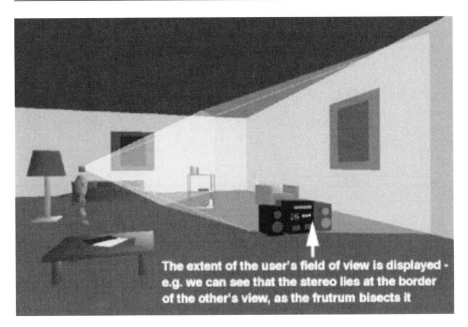

The extent of the user's field of view is displayed - e.g. we can see that the stereo lies at the border of the other's view, as the frutrum bisects it

Figure 7.8 Rendering visible the other's field of view (in Furniture World).

One possible reason for this is that participants face difficulties in juxtaposing and comparing two differing views on a scene (their own and their co-participant's) in order to render it, and the action of another, intelligible. In everyday interaction, we encounter a coherent scene – we note how a colleague glances at a document, or an event, as a single intelligible scene. Indeed, splitting up our view on a world from another's view so clearly may well raise more problems and difficulties than it solves.

Therefore we are attempting to integrate relevant information about others' orientations and field of view into the single available view on the world. Figure 7.8 provides an example of the kind of presentation that we envisage, where the actual field of view available to the other is mapped onto, and directly "radiates" out of, the avatar.

Our experimentation with such presentations is at an early stage, and there is the potential for additional difficulties to emerge (with regard to scalability and the like[3]). However, this kind of solution also points to more general concerns about the traditional reliance upon pseudo-humanoid embodiments in virtual worlds.

Generally within CVE design, there is an aim to use "realistic" or "humanoid" embodiments (e.g. Capin *et al.*, 1997; Guye-Vuillème *et al.*, 1999). Indeed, some may argue that the embodiments used in these experiments were not "realistic" enough and that this was the source of users' problems. However, the findings from our experiments would suggest that the straightforward translation of human physical embodiments into CVEs (however detailed) are likely to be unsuccessful, and indeed misleading, unless participants can also be provided with the

---

[3] Note, however, that incorporating feedback monitors would exacerbate the problems of scalability.

perceptual capabilities of physical human bodies, including a very wide field of view and rapid gaze and body movement. Indeed, to compensate for the constrained views and actions possible within virtual environments, more exaggerated embodiments may be required. Actions may best be represented across disparate features of the environment to enhance access to the sense and significance of an action in the CVE. So, for example, the added benefit of our presentation of the field of view (Fig. 7.8) is that even when the other's avatar is not visible, their field of view, and the objects and spaces they can see, could be.

Our concerns about the general aim of providing strictly "realistic" presentations of embodiments may also have relevance for the design of "gestures" in collaborative VR. Guye-Vuillème *et al.* (1999) and others have started to examine possible ways of presenting higly stylized gestures that accurately mimic the production of human gestures. So, rather than trying to manipulate an avatar's arm moment-by-moment, the user simply presses a button and a standard "type" of gesture is initiated to convey a particular meaning (e.g. display of mockery, joy or incomprehension). Indeed, the additional bandwidth benefits of such an approach are noted in Chapter 6. However, there are three key problems associated with such an approach, especially when designed to support referential gestures, that we aim to take into account when developing our use of "extendable arms" for pointing.

Firstly, the significant ability to shape and mould a gesture in, over and through the space would be constrained, as moment-to-moment control of the gesture would be replaced by a stylized or stereotypical alternative. Thus the opportunities to produce more inventive or evocative gestures around objects would be lost (c.f. Streeck, 1996; Hindmarsh and Heath, 2000).

Secondly, in work that attempts to furnish VR users with "realistic" representations of particular gestures, explicit interface actions are required to initiate those gestures, and specific choices must be made out of multiple possible gestures. However, the impact and import of those gestures is often tied to the interactional or temporal position in which they are produced. For example, by the time an appropriate button is selected and depressed and the avatar is animated on another's display, the gesture may be seen as a comment on a totally different turn at talk or activity, thereby disrupting the flow of interaction. Such problems would, of course, be heightened when subject to the additional problems of latency predicted by others (see Chapter 3 and Vaghi *et al.*, 1999). So the very intelligibility of the gesture could be distorted or transformed if, through the system and production lag, the sequential context in which the gesture is "initiated" is dislocated from the sequential context in which the gesture is encountered or seen by the other.

Finally, and maybe most importantly, participants could be "alienated" from their involvement in the interaction and the activity at hand. A critical feature of tacit practices (such as gestural communication) is that they are taken for granted and "glossed" by participants; that is, in doing what we do, we rarely attend to the ways in which we do it. When we explicitly attend to such practices, it changes the nature of our involvement, and can undermine our very participation in complex, and even mundane, activities (see Garfinkel, 1967; Goffman, 1967). To illustrate, Goffman describes the difficulties of hearing what another has to say, while simultaneously (and self-consciously) trying to be *seen* as a good listener. To be caught up in the latter makes it harder to accomplish the former (Goffman, 1967). So, if individuals overly concern themselves with how they are seen within an encounter, it can alienate them from their participation or involvement in the conversation itself. This has consequences for the idea of providing various options of stylized gestures to users of a collaborative VR system. If they are given the option of various buttons from which to select an appropriate gesture, then there is a danger that they will be encouraged to overly (and overtly) concern themselves with how their avatar will be viewed and seen. In such a way, participants may end up concentrating on "working their avatar", rather than on their collaboration with others. So, such a design direction may turn out to "alienate" participants from their involvement in the very tasks and activities that the system is designed to support.

The particular limitations and idiosyncrasies of these virtual (as compared with co-present) environments, and the ways in which participants experience them have led us to propose altering the (aimed for) "realism" of the space. Revealing the constraints in such limited (and limiting) environments through the presentation of field of view, for example, may give participants a sense of these deficiencies. For example, providing the ability to extend a pointing gesture may indicate or imply that the visibility of that gesture may become problematic in this environment. Moreover, we aim to consider the limits of the metaphor of "interaction in physical space" for designing collaborative VR and explore where the constraints of the technology render this metaphor problematic. Of course, a critical next step is to continue the evaluation of our changes to the "pseudo-humanoid" embodiment designs. Indeed, it is to be hoped that the unanticipated consequences (both positive and negative) of the redesigns are as interesting as the consequences of the original design of Furniture World.

A further development would be to provide an application robust enough to be used to engage in everyday work activities. One benefit of such an aim is that it would provide access to a body of naturalistic materials that would allow our understanding of object-focused tasks in collaborative VR to expand to include the additional demands of everyday work. With regard to our concern with pseudo-realism, we could begin to consider how the competence and familiarity of the participants is relevant to how, and indeed whether, particular system characteristics are displayed. It is likely, through use of the system, that individuals will become increasingly familiar with its limitations and will also develop a body of finely tuned practices and procedures with others in order to address those limitations and accomplish particular tasks (cf. Dourish *et al.*, 1996). As familiarity develops, therefore, the presentation of the system's limitations may become frustrating, or worse, threaten activities themselves. Alternatively changing the appearance of the CVE and removing resources that have been relied upon could be equally disruptive. Moreover, when participants of different degrees of competence and familiarity with the system are collaborating, further issues arise with regard to which resources should be provided, to whom, and when. Therefore the ways in which participants may usefully and easily configure information concerning the system for themselves (and others) could be explored.

Despite our interest in collecting naturalistic materials, the use of experiments has provided unanticipated benefits for understanding collaborative practices.

Although in some ways these data are problematic in contrast to naturally occurring data, they do contrast in interesting ways to our videos of object-focused interaction in everyday workplaces. Indeed, they place into stark relief the problems that individuals face when they are denied the resources which co-participants in co-present interaction routinely draw on to accomplish seemingly mundane activities such as referencing. For example, if we return to our introductory discussion of workplace studies, we can see how these analyses are enriched when compared with the problems faced by participants in collaborative VR. The seemingly mundane practice of referring to objects in the course of the working day is given more resonance and import when compared with the problems that arise within virtual environments. For example, they highlight the problems and difficulties that can arise when our assumptions about what another can see are corrupted and distorted. Even those traditionally concerned with the minutiae of interaction often overlook the ways in which interaction is dependent upon how it is embedded – produced and understood – in a common environment. Thus these experiments reveal in a spectacular way how seeing action in, and tied to, the "environment" is a critical resource for participants. In such a way, it can be seen how the studies of the everyday and the studies of collaborative VR can be mutually enriching.

Indeed, there is longstanding discussion in fields such as CSCW as to the ways in which social science, and in particular naturalistic studies of work, can inform the design and deployment of complex systems. Less attention is paid to the contribution of systems design to social science. The materials discussed here raise some potentially interesting issues for studies of work and interaction. So, whatever our sensitivities about using "quasi–experimental" data, they provide, as Garfinkel (1967) suggests, "aids to a sluggish imagination". They dramatically reveal presuppositions and resources that often remain unexplicated in more conventional studies of the workplace.

While we believe these presuppositions and resources are of some importance to sociology and cognate disciplines, it can also be envisaged how they may well influence the success or failure of technologies designed to enhance physically distributed collaborative work. However, our use of studies of everyday interaction does not lead us to argue that the "real world" must be replicated in all its complexity for collaborative VR to work. Indeed, if anything, these experiments reveal the enormous difficulties for participants in engaging in even simple tasks like pointing things out to another or discussing objects. Thus they highlight the immense difficulties associated with such a grand aim and lead us to consider more radical alternatives. We wish to focus on the benefits of looking at mundane activities in order to gain purchase on the kinds of resources that will be critical to the success of collaborative VR for work, and even for the emerging entertainment applications.

Acknowledgements

We would like to thank members of WIT (King's) and CRG (Nottingham), especially Chris Greenhalgh, Paul Luff, Dirk vom Lehn and Jolanda Tromp, who have discussed these issues and data with us. We are also grateful to Alan Munro, Elizabeth Churchill and Dave Snowdon for their comments on an earlier draft on the chapter. This research has been supported by ESRC Grant No. R000237136.

Part 4
Sharing Context in CVEs – Or "I Know What I See, But What Do You See?"

Chapter 8
How Not To Be Objective

Kai-Mikael Jää-Aro and Dave Snowdon

8.1 Introduction

There is today a spate of Collaborative Virtual Environments (CVEs) on the net (http://www.digitalspace.com/avatars/ indexes them), similar to the Metaverse in Neal Stephenson's *Snow Crash* (Stephenson, 1992). Some of these allow the users to construct buildings in the world, though in the majority the environment is fixed. These buildings serve as meeting points and atmosphere creators, but do not have any other meaning. *Information* can be presented in these spaces as imported objects or as placards with text and images placed in the environment.

Spaces such as these are being evaluated by various organizations as meeting places to increase social cohesion among geographically distributed colleagues. But while these environments lead to increased awareness and spontaneous communication, they do not give a good feeling for what one's co-workers are *doing* (Lenman, 1999). This is fairly obvious, as the actual work activity is not supported in, and therefore takes place outside, these virtual environments.

We will here outline a way in which a certain type of work can be brought into a virtual environment and the concomitant requirements that this places on the environment. To be more specific, we are concerned with 3D visualizations of abstract data, such as the contents of databases or other discrete data. We further make the case that in order to afford useful work such an environment must allow *subjective* representations of data.

Finally, we will describe a prototype implementation we have done of such a 3D data visualization with subjective presentation.

8.2 Populated Information Terrains

Consider a relational database. The data contained in it have no intrinsic geometric shape, so in order to be able to represent them in 3D virtual environment, a *mapping* from data to 3D space and 3D geometry has to be done. Since we also represent the users of these data in the environment, this type of data visualization has been termed *Populated Information Terrains* (PITs) (Benford *et al.*, 1995b; Mariani, 1998). As indicated in the introduction, the aim is that this type of shared data space will enable the important features of *peripheral awareness*, *informal meetings* and *learning by watching*.

8.2.1 Peripheral Awareness

It is well documented (e.g. Bentley *et al.*, 1992; Bowers *et al.*, 1995; Heath and Luff, 1991) how physically co-located workers, in a control room or an open plan office, for example, keep track of each other's work progress in order to take into account the effects of this on their own tasks. Workers also often use body language and tone of voice to indicate to others that they *should* monitor some unfolding event in that worker's task.

In a PIT, workers within an organization are visible to each other, even if not physically co-present, as is increasingly more common in contemporary white-collar work where employees may be geographically distributed, telecommuting or just in an office of their own. It has been shown that even fairly simple avatars allow the expression of important human interactions (Bowers *et al.*, 1996b). Furthermore, if the users' interactions with data are visualized in an effective manner, they will be apparent to other users, displaying what user X is doing with datum B.

Thus a PIT user will be able to gain a feel for what work is currently being done within her organization. Likewise, needed help can easily be raised among those present by gesturing, speaking louder or other such relatively unobtrusive means.

Now, while we would not promote computer-mediated communication in preference to everyday face-to-face contact, we still note that having to work in the same space as many others has drawbacks, both in terms of lost privacy and a noisy environment. A PIT could give the best of both worlds, in that workers can have an awareness of each other, but that their actions are *filtered* through the computer system and that they therefore need not give up more of their privacy than they choose to.

8.2.2 Informal Meetings

Unplanned and informal meetings are essential in order to coordinate work and disseminate information in an organization (Kraut *et al.*, 1990; Whittaker *et al.*, 1994) and since even being on separate floors drastically decreases the chances for informal encounters (Kraut *et al.*, 1988), there has been some development of CSCW tools that are intended to increase the frequency of chance encounters in distributed work groups (Huxor, 1998; Isaacs *et al.*, 1996).

8.2.3 Learning by Watching

Another process that is missed by dispersed members of a workgroup is the mutual transfer of practical knowledge of, in this case, the computer system. Informal studies have shown that users of a CVE observe the actions of other users, and pick up knowledge of previously unknown functions in the system.

8.2.4 Ease of Use

An underlying assumption of the previous statements is that the CVEs are in more or less continuous use, as the described benefits require awareness of the environment over some time. Few current CVEs are designed to remain in the background of a desktop environment for long periods of time, if for no other reason, then due to the lack of screen space. It may be that useful utilization of this kind of environments will require multiple monitor screens on or around one's desk (Lenman, 1999; Stevens and Papka, 1999).

8.3 Subjectivity

One could imagine several techniques for visualizing the same data set. If a data set has no "natural" representation (unlike a 3D CAD model for example), the choice of a particular technique will depend on the task at hand or on the preferences of the user. It is therefore natural for visualization systems to present the users with a number of choices which govern the nature of the visualization presented to them.

However, in most current systems all users are forced to use the same representation of the information and thereby trade flexibility for the ability to collaborate in the use of the information.

An alternative to this is to allow all users to have their private view of the data, even though it be a collaborative application. We refer to this as a *subjective* environment (Snowdon *et al.*, 1995).

We define subjectivity as the ability to add viewer-dependent features to a system (where a *viewer* may be a "real" user or a software agent). In other words the information presented to a viewer may depend on the nature of the viewer. This viewer dependence could either be on the basis of individual viewers or on the class or role that the view belongs to.

8.3.1 2D Subjective User Interfaces

The strictly objective WYSIWIS (What You See Is What I See) paradigm for CSCW implies that co-workers participate in a tight loop of interaction where everyone has to see the object(s) of discourse and comment on each other's changes to it/them. This is based on a conception of work as being in front of a whiteboard or by a draughting table where a group of co-workers jointly develop a design. However, even in these non-computerized cases work is not tied to a single representation – co-workers may leave and enter the room to retrieve additional material, may do alternative sketches on private notepads, or simply be thinking of other things; furthermore, the work may be organized in such a way as to not always entail concurrent, synchronous work with identical data. This has been acknowledged in several CSCW systems that may be nominally synchronous, yet allow different representations and/or perspectives of data, a "Relaxed WYSIWIS" (Greif and Sarin, 1987; Shu and Flowers, 1994; Stefik *et al.*, 1987a).

A number of groupware systems support configurable user interfaces, for example Mead (Bentley *et al.*, 1992) and Rendezvous (Patterson *et al.*, 1990). These systems allow users to view the shared data in radically different ways. For example, the air traffic control application Mead is capable of representing aircraft either as a flight strip or as a "radar blip", and allows individual users to select the representation most appropriate for their needs.

Bowers *et al.* (1998) have argued that customized displays are detrimental for the above-mentioned peripheral awareness. If all co-workers have personalized information displays, it will be difficult for others to grasp the situation at a glance. We claim that this is irrelevant for the case at hand, since we don't expect the members of the workgroup to be in the same physical room; the view they get of the environment is *through* the computer system, and thus the stable, familiar view of one's own customized environment. However, we readily acknowledge that a computer-mediated presence and situational awareness might not be the best for all situations and that a display layout in physical space may well be the best way to create a working environment. The decision of when one or the other is better is beyond the scope of the current discussion.

8.3.2 Subjective Programming Environments

Subjectivity is not only applicable to user interfaces. Smith and Ungar (1994) argue that subjectivity could be a valuable addition to a programming environment and give two examples where subjectivity might be useful in a programming environment:

1. Supporting group programming. A group of programmers may independently make changes to a system without conflict if each person's changes are only apparent when used by that person. By explicitly using someone else's view another person could elect to use that person's version of the system without having to merge different versions of the program source code.
2. Supporting *capabilities*. Many systems provide different users with different capabilities. For example only certain people may be allowed to read certain files, while other files may be read by all users but only modified by the system administrator. In a strictly objective environment these mechanisms must be provided by dedicated software. The use of subjectivity would allow such capabilities to be implemented without the need for special purpose software.

Smith and Ungar also describe a subjective object-oriented language called "US" (an extension to the Self language (Ungar and Smith, 1987)) in which the effect of a message sent to an object depends on the *perspective* through which the message is sent. In US, perspectives are extra levels of indirection between the sender and the receiver of a message which allow a message to be processed differently depending on which perspectives it passes through.

8.3.3 The Need for Subjective Virtual Environments

Most current multi-user virtual reality systems provide a highly objective virtual environment. That is, all users see the environment in the same way, albeit from different viewpoints, and all users see the same objects in the same places with the same appearances. This is partly due to the fact that multi-user VR systems evolved from single-user systems which have been extended to support a number of users. This aspect of the evolution of VR systems is similar to the way that groupware systems evolved from systems such as Shared X (Gust, 1988), which simply replicated an application's user interface to multiple users. We argue that, just as strict objectivity proved too constraining in other groupware systems, a degree of subjectivity is necessary to support collaboration in virtual environments. Smith (1996) shows how an existing 2D groupware toolkit, SOL, can be extended to provide customizable subjective virtual environments.

Compared with WYSIWIS, even an objective VE could be considered to support some degree of subjectivity. We shall first indicate some "subjective" features found in standard VEs and then give some examples of situations in which it might be useful to allow more radically different subjective views.

- Each user will typically have an independently controlled viewpoint from which the virtual environment can be inspected. This is our experience of the real world, and as such we expect people to be skilled at relating to viewpoints and reasoning about these kinds of subjective effects (though admittedly current virtual environments tend to confound this ability by, *inter alia*, the limited field of view (Hindmarsh *et al.*, 1998, Chapter 7).)

- Level-of-detail (LOD) effects. A common technique in interactive computer graphics is to provide several different representations of a given artefact, each with a different level of complexity. When viewing the object from a distance the user is shown a simple version of the artefact which is replaced by more detailed representations as the user approaches. It should be noted that the purpose of level-of-detail effects is to improve the interactive performance of the display software rather than to support subjective effects – in fact the normal aim is for users not to notice when one representation of an artefact is substituted for another. Also, since these alternative representations of an artefact can be packaged as a single data item for the purposes of distribution (or generated automatically by the renderer), adding LOD effects requires only that the renderer need be modified and the rest of the VR system can remain strictly objective.

Unfortunately, independently controlled viewpoints and LOD effects are special cases and support for these features does not allow more radically different subjective views to be created. It is therefore necessary to modify an existing VR system if truly subjective effects are desired. We shall now give some examples to justify why this additional implementation effort is worthwhile.

A 3D chat space benefits from an agreed-on layout as it simplifies navigation for its inhabitants: they can learn landmarks in the environment, agree on meeting points etc. Apart from the design of landmarks in order to make the landscape easier to navigate, the landscape may be shaped in order to increase the probability of particular types of encounters (Bowers, 1995).

However, a database visualization has quite different requirements. By its very nature it will not be amenable to landscaping. While the underlying relations (assuming a relational database for the sake of argument) may be fairly stable, their use is not – information is continually dynamically combined in new ways and the mappings from data to 3D space cannot be known beforehand.

It then seems reasonable that users may have different preferences for how particular views of data should be displayed; it may even be that different users need to experiment independently with alternative displays, even if their ultimate goal is to have the same common view of data.

On a more prosaic level, different users may have different levels of access to particular pieces of data, wherefore not all users can be allowed to see all data items. Moreover, users may carry around displays and tools in the virtual environment which are entirely private to themselves and therefore should not be displayed to others.[1]

If the virtual environment does not support subjective views then the users are denied the ability to work in parallel with different representations of the same data, and forced to work with those subsets of data that all users are allowed to see – or those subsets of users that are allowed to see all data. If, on the other hand, the virtual environment is capable of supporting subjective views, then users are free to choose their own preferred visualization style.

Leaving business databases aside, another use for subjective views is in computer-aided design. Consider an architectural review of a building. While the people taking part in the review would need a overview of the building, they might only want to see features relating to their speciality in detail – for example, an electrician might only want to see wiring plans in detail and not see the plans for the plumbing except in cases where there was a potential conflict (Leigh *et al.*, 1996).

A final example would be the use of subjectivity to enable multilingual text display in a virtual environment (Smith, 1996). In a subjective environment users would be able to explore the same basic environment, but see all textual annotations in their preferred language.

8.3.4 Degrees of Subjectivity

Figure 8.1 shows various classes of systems according to how much subjectivity they support. At the entirely objective end of the scale we have WYSIWIS user interfaces and normal objective programming environments (typified by the Self language in this example). Relaxed WYSIWIS is not entirely objective and 3D virtual environments (assuming they support independent viewpoints and LOD)

---

[1] An illustrative historical note: In the first versions of the DIVE system all graphics were indeed visible to all users, so that one could see the navigational icons of a user floating immediately in front of the face of that user's avatar. In later versions such displays have been "privatized" and are no longer visible to others.

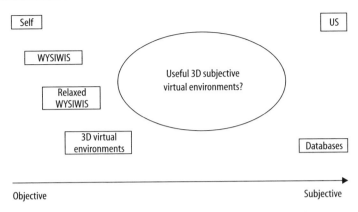

Figure 8.1 Scale showing degrees of subjectivity of several classes of system.

are slightly less so. At the entirely subjective end of the scale we have relational databases (since any number of views of the same data can be constructed to show different combinations and subsets of the database's field and contents) and subjective programming environments (typified by US in this example).

We have already argued that some degree of subjectivity is useful in collaborative virtual environments – however, it seems obvious that if we take subjectivity to extremes users will effectively be inhabiting different environments and will no longer be able to collaborate effectively (assuming they are still even aware of each other). We therefore hypothesize that *useful* subjective virtual environments span a range that is slightly more subjective than existing VEs but less subjective than databases and subjective programming environments (such as US).

Even so, in a shared subjective environment with a visual representation (be it 2D or 3D), where users wish to indicate objects to each other, a user may not see any object or, worse, see a completely different object at a spot indicated by another user with a different object layout. Smith has solved this problem by two methods: first, by letting a transparent version of the other user's world view become visible if two users seem to be interested in related items; and second, by highlighting indicated objects directly, rather than using pointers in space (Smith and O'Brien, 1998).

8.4 Creating a Subjective Environment

In this section we describe some of the ideas and concepts behind our prototype environment which allows us to maintain some awareness between users who may have different views of the environment. We shall describe *artefact-centred coordinates*, which allow us to represent users to other users with different subjective views, followed by *body-centred configuration*, a technique to allow users to specify their preferences for the display and behaviour of applications in a subjective virtual environment.

8.4.1 Artefact-Centred Coordinates

It is our experience that *embodiments* or *avatars*, visual representations of the users, are necessary in collaborative virtual environments. The embodiments indicate the presence and activities of a particular user to other users and also serve as the focus for communication – allowing "virtual face-to-face conversations" (Benford *et al.*, 1994c; Bowers *et al.*, 1996b). Since the artefacts in one user's view may be in very different locations in another user's view we cannot place user embodiments at the same world coordinates in each view, but must come up with some other mechanism for positioning user embodiments in subjective views. An empty space conveys no useful information; it is the artefacts, other users in the space and their actions in relation to one another that provide us with information. We therefore consider the position and orientation of a user in relation to the artefacts or other users in the environment rather than in terms of the user's location in world coordinates. We do this using a technique which we term *artefact-centred coordinates*, which uses the artefacts the user is aware of to determine the position and orientation of that user in other subjective views.

The basic concept behind artefact-centred coordinates is to compute a user's *awareness* of a set of artefacts, find which of these artefacts exist in the subjective view we want to represent the user in (the *target* view) and place the representation of the user (the *pseudobody*) in a position and orientation determined by the location of the artefacts that the user is aware of in the target view, as shown in Fig. 8.2.

The concept of awareness has been introduced in the Spatial Interaction Model (Benford *et al.*, 1995a). Briefly, all active objects in a CVE have, for each communication modality, a *focus*, a *nimbus* and, optionally, an *aura*. Conceptually, the

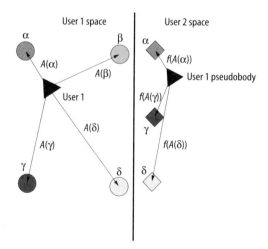

Figure 8.2 User 1, in her subjective view, is aware of the objects α, β, γ and δ, in that decreasing order. To make this information available to User 2, the pseudobody representing User 1 is, in the subjective view of User 2, placed proportionately closer to the objects User 1 is more aware of. As object β is not present in User 2 space, it is ignored in the computation.

nimbus is the representation of an object's *presence* in space, whereas the focus is the object's *attention* in space. An object's focus intersecting another object's nimbus makes the first object *aware* of the other, enabling subsequent interaction.

The standard formulation of the Spatial Interaction Model defines the focus, nimbus and aura in terms of volumes, but, following the argument in (Bowers *et al.*, 1999), we choose a formulation that is similar, though not identical, to the one by Greenhalgh (1997a). We define the focus and nimbus as functions that take on a value in the interval [0, 1] for any point in 3-space. The awareness computation then becomes

$$awareness(a, b) = focus(a, b) \cdot nimbus(b, a).$$

The aura is most suitably interpreted as some simple bounding volume (sphere or box) that completely encloses the points for which the *focus* and *nimbus* functions of an object have values > 0, so for example, if an object has the focus and nimbus functions

$$focus(a, b) = \begin{cases} 1 \; if \; |position(a) - position(b)| < 4 \\ 0 \; otherwise \end{cases}$$

$$nimbus(a, b) = \begin{cases} 1 \; if \; |position(a) - position(b)| < 6 \\ 0 \; otherwise \end{cases}$$

then the aura could be a sphere with a radius of > 6. In this way one can do a simple collision test for the auræ of two objects before doing a potentially complex focus and nimbus computation. In the given example focus and nimbus are extremely simple, but presumably an "intelligent" awareness function that approximates how a real human apportions interest in the environment would be considerably more complex and depend on a number of factors; however, this does not affect our basic argument.

In our implementation we have considered *focus* and *nimbus* to be purely geometrical functions, i.e. $f(position(a) - position(b))$.

The Aether extension to the Spatial Interaction Model (Şandor *et al.*, 1997), introduces *time* as an additional coordinate, we could thus allow the number of interactions with an object over a period of time to affect the awareness computation, for example. We will, however, not pursue this issue further here.

For each of the subjective views in which we intend to represent the user we must then find the subset of artefacts for which we have calculated the user's awareness that are present in the target view (if this subset is the empty set we can choose a suitable default location or not represent the user at all in that particular view). Our current method for placing the representation of the user in other users' views is simply to use a weighted sum of the artefacts' positions with the awareness of each artefact acting as the weight. This has the result that users are displayed close to the artefacts of which they are most aware. Likewise, we compute the direction of the avatar's gaze – using quaternions to represent angles lets us do averaging over directions – and display the user's pseudobody turned towards those artefacts to which she is mostly turned towards in her own subjective view.

If interaction with objects is represented in some particular manner, this interaction should be visualized in the target view as well. If this interaction is represented by high-level events, they can be translated to the appropriate visualization in the target view.

8.4.2 Body-Centred Configuration

In an application of interesting complexity there will be set of adjustable features, such as the default data set, entry point in the world, or enabled user interface features (available interaction hardware, window size etc.). However, in a distributed environment, the application that would need to receive these preference settings may not be allowed to do so, since the application may be running at a node which does not have read access to the file store of that particular user. We might of course simply require all users to place their preference settings at a "well-known place" or even store them at the node where the application runs, if this is constant over time.

However, we propose an alternative approach. Since the users' embodiments are projected into the environment to represent them to themselves and other users, we suggest considering users' preferences as properties of their embodiments that "represent" them to applications and allow these to inspect and store non-geometric information in the users' embodiments. We refer to this technique as *body-centred configuration*. This is conceptually similar to the resource database provided by the X Window System (Scheifler and Gettys, 1986) which (possibly remote) applications can inspect to retrieve information about user configuration options. Using body-centred configuration, an application is capable of configuring itself to adapt to the user's default preferences as soon as the user enters the world in which the application is resident, with no explicit intervention on the part of the user.

8.5 A Subjective Application

To test our ideas for subjective data representation we elected to use a modified version of VR-VIBE. VR-VIBE is a multi-user 3D visualization of a collection of documents or document references (Benford *et al.*, 1995c). Figure 8.3 shows several different visualizations of the same data set. Selecting a document icon causes some summary information to be displayed. If a document is available via the World Wide Web then VR-VIBE can invoke a Web browser to display the entire document contents.

We chose VR-VIBE as our test application because we had access to the source code and therefore could adapt it for subjective operation and because it already supports a number of visualization styles allowing the creation of subjective views that may differ substantially. VR-VIBE is implemented in DIVE.

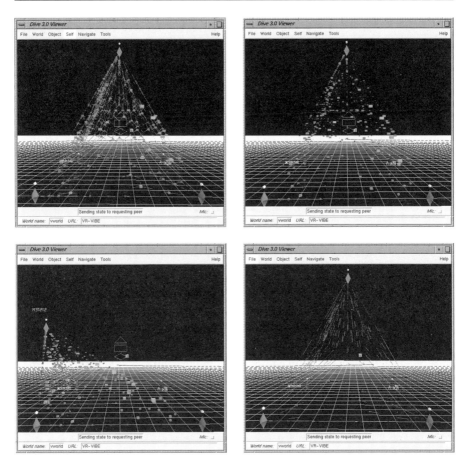

Figure 8.3 Different visualizations of a bibliography database. User-provided keywords (represented as green octahedra) are used to provide a spatial framework for the visualization. The documents are positioned in the space according to how well they match each of the keywords. Additional information can be given by lines, the lengths of which indicate the strength of relevance to the keywords.

8.5.1 DIVE

DIVE is a distributed virtual environment platform developed by the Swedish Institute of Computer Science (available at http://www.sics.se/dive/). DIVE is based on a notional shared database of objects, which are in fact replicated to all members of the process group that defines a world. Updates to an object at one node are distributed to all other nodes using IP multicast. DIVE also supports partial replication such that not all objects are automatically distributed to all nodes but are kept in a process subgroup that has to be explicitly joined. DIVE provides other useful features that greatly simplified our implementation:

- Support for partitioning a world between several multicast groups. Associating a lightweight group with each user provides an efficient mechanism for implementing subjective (viewer-dependent) views of parts of a DIVE world.

- All objects, including bodies, may contain Tcl code (Ousterhout, 1994) that gives the objects behaviour, so that they can react to user interaction or events in the environment, or perform application computation. In this manner, computation can be distributed over the objects (even though the actual computation normally will take place at a single node and then be distributed to all other member nodes). Objects/processes can send Tcl/Tk code to other objects/ processes, providing a mechanism for application-level interprocess communication.

- All objects may in addition use *properties* to hold information about the object which is publicly accessible to other objects and applications. Properties consist of tuples specifying the name, type and value of each property. Applications can augment objects with additional properties as a means of storing application specific information. The property mechanism provides a very powerful way for applications and objects to exchange arbitrary information via the DIVE database.

In addition to this list, DIVE has some other features which are generally useful:

- Human participants have an embodiment in the environment. This body can be shaped in any manner, but the DIVE visualizer supports the notion of body parts, such as eyes, feet and head, and if parts of the body are labelled accordingly they will be used for viewpoints, ground reference etc.

- DIVE can import VRML files.

- DIVE object files are passed through a macro-expanding pre-processor before parsing, which allows very rapid and efficient construction of complex objects.

We found the combination of Tcl/Tk and properties to be very powerful when developing applications. In our prototype the entire user interface is written using Tcl/Tk, which calls the various application processes to invoke specific operations. Each application process exports globally visible data as DIVE properties which can then be inspected by other objects or processes. This allows each application process to perform only a small number of well-defined functions, with Tcl code providing the "glue" required to create a complete system. This modular organization allows components to be modified or replaced without needing to update the other system components.

8.5.2 Subjective VR-VIBE

In order to support subjective visualizations, VR-VIBE needs to be capable of generating a different visualization for each user. It does this by explicitly separating objective and subjective state information. The objective state contains the content of the document store and other information that is not dependent on the nature of the generated visualization. There is exactly one copy of the objective state information. The subjective state contains the objects used to create a specific visualization and any other parameters that are dependent on the nature of the visualization (configuration options etc.). There is an instance of the subjective state for each subjective view generated by VR-VIBE.

DIVE does not by itself support data protection, but that can be simulated by adding an access list property to each restricted object and let the translator only distribute it to views owned by members of that access list.

8.5.3 Subjective Embodiments Using Artefact-Centred Coordinates

As noted above, all processes are members of the world multicast group, but in addition may be in a group of their own that we use to contain their subjective view of the world. We cannot place the user embodiments in the world multicast group because, as objects are (can be) placed differently in the subjective views, a user's coordinates are meaningless in any other view than her own. The solution, as described above, is to have different representations of each user in each subjective view. In her own view the user is represented by the normal embodiment mechanism provided by the DIVE visualizer process, while in other views the representation of the user is handled by the subjective translator process which displays a pseudobody[2] at a position and orientation which attempts to convey maximal information about the user's activities to the other users.

Figures 8.4 and 8.5 show the relationship between the standard user embodiments provided by DIVE, the subjective translator and the subjective embodiments created by the subjective translator. The DIVE visualizer process manages the representation of a user in her own view, and the translator process manages the user representation in all other users' views. Figure 8.6 demonstrates what it actually looks like.

8.5.4 Translation Functions

Our experiences with different functions for computing awareness and translating position to other spaces have indicated the following:

- The definition set of the *focus* function should not be too large. We first tried using $\mathbb{R}^3$ as the definition set, defining

$$focus(o_1, o_2) = nimbus(o_1, o_2) = \frac{1}{|position(o_1) - position(o_2)|}.$$

---

[2] At the moment each user gets to define her own representation in the views of others, but we are exploring ways in which to allow users to choose their view of other users as well.

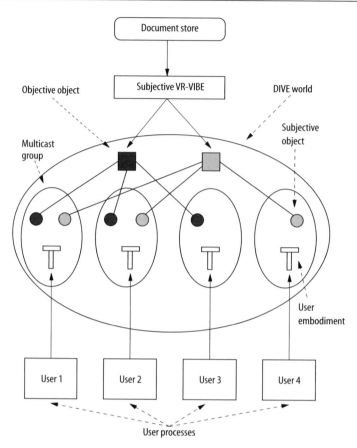

Figure 8.4 The structure of a subjective environment constructed by VR-VIBE. The main DIVE world (which also has a multicast group associated with it) contains only DIVE objects containing objective state information. Each subjective view has its own dedicated multicast group which contains the embodiment of the user "owning" that view and the subjective state information for that view. For simplicity we do not show the subjective representations of other users which must be present in order for users to be aware of one another. User representation is handled by another process, as described in Section 8.5.3.

This had the undesirable consequence that objects very far away had an inappropriately large effect on the positioning of the pseudobody – the awareness of them might be low, but if they were relatively far away in the target view, they could still pull away the pseudobody from the position that "looks right". Therefore the *focus* and *nimbus* functions should assume the value 0 at not too large a distance from the object origin, the exact distance depending on the application.

In general, the use of an awareness function which does not decrease (or at least stay constant) with increasing distance, will lead to unexpected behaviour in our current implementation.

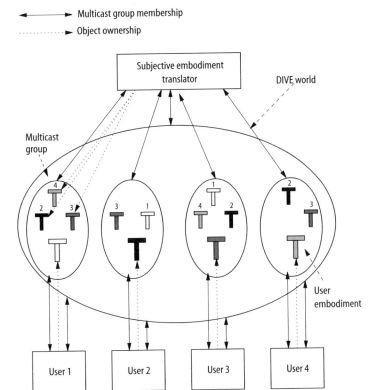

Figure 8.5 Solid lines indicate multicast group membership and dashed lines indicate the process responsible for an object. Object ownership by the subjective translator is only shown for the view owned by User 1.

- If a user moves from one artefact to another, which is nearby in her view, these may be far apart in a target view. The pseudobody may thus suddenly jump from one place to another. As this makes it difficult to follow a pseudobody around we have felt the need to limit the maximum speed of a pseudobody and animate its motion between distant points.

8.6 Discussion

It seems obvious that if users' subjective views diverge beyond a certain point then meaningful collaboration will become difficult or impossible. On the other hand we believe that if users are forced to share the same objective view then collaboration may occasionally become awkward if users have to continually negotiate an agreed common view – this was found to be the case for strictly WYSIWIS 2D shared editors and led to the development of the Relaxed WYSIWIS concept. This has lead

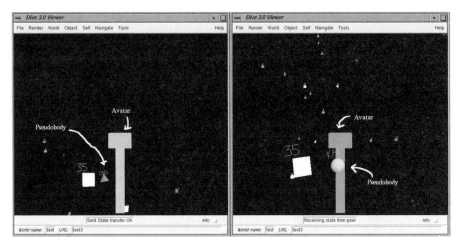

Figure 8.6 A screenshot from a test run with subjective translation. Several hundred objects have been randomly (and differently) placed by two users in their respective subjective views. In the left window we see the T-shaped "blockie" avatar of user KAI approaching object #35. The tetrahedral pseudobody of user DNS hovers nearby. In the right window we see the converse, the spherical pseudobody of user KAI in the subjective view of user DNS. We have chosen to have very different shapes for avatars and pseudobodies to make the difference clear, but this is of course not enforced by the system.

us to believe that a subjective environment that allows users to adjust their subjective views to suit individual needs, but still retain awareness of others and the ability to communicate, may be a useful tool.

We would imagine that over the course of a session users' views might converge and diverge, depending on the situation. We will therefore need to develop techniques that allow users to switch to a common view or to find information on how divergent their view has become from other users. It may also be useful for the system to monitor the parameters for each user's subjective view and allow users to switch to the currently most popular view.

It is worth noting that our current implementation allows objective applications to run in the same world without modification. If an objective application belongs to the world's multicast group then it will be available to all users in the world. Alternatively, objective applications might belong to a given user's multicast group and thereby be completely private to that user. This would allow users to still use tools such as the DIVE whiteboard while also using a subjective visualization.

8.7 Summary

In this chapter we have argued that in some situations providing subjective or viewer-dependent features in an environment may actually aid collaborative information visualization by allowing individual users to tailor their views while still maintaining contact with other users. We have described a prototype information visualization based on this idea. Since our implementation is based on a collection of applications it would be relatively easy to replace some components to provide a different set of features (e.g. to visualize other sorts of abstract information).

Acknowledgements

Many thanks to Lennart Fahlén and the Swedish Institute of Computer Science (SICS) for funding Dave Snowdon as a guest researcher at SICS while subjective VR-VIBE was implemented. We also thank Chris Greenhalgh and John Bowers for enlightening discussions, Olof Hagsand, Mårten Stenius and Emmanuel Frécon for DIVE help and the editors for encouraging and insightful comments.

Chapter 9

Supporting Flexible Roles in a Shared Space[1]

Randall B. Smith, Ronald Hixon and Bernard Horan

9.1 Introduction

People in a group play various roles. Manager, intern, department chair, guest speaker, the woman who knows how the fax machine works, the guy who got the pizza, the person speaking now, the person capturing this on the whiteboard; roles can be formal or informal, long-lived or ephemeral. They can be bestowed by ceremony, or assumed with the invisibility of the taken-for-granted. But it is the interaction of minds that creates and sustains a role: a role is a human construct. Even roles like "mother" or "father", which would seem to demand certain biological characteristics, cannot be defined at any depth without appeal to social convention. The largely hands-off approach taken by nature seems to work fairly well for groups of humans: when there is confusion or concern about who is playing what role, it is generally good for a group to work it out as a social issue. If roles were encoded solely in human biology or in physical law, life might be simpler but certainly more stultifying.

However, roles can be at least partly supported by physical reality. For example, a speaker benefits from adopting a special position (centre stage) with a particular spatial orientation (facing the audience). The note-taker benefits from physical proximity to pen and paper, the piano player by proximity to the piano. These spatial positions and orientations are available to all; they are simply used at certain times by certain individuals as part of their role.

When it comes to computer-supported cooperative work, it is perhaps natural to try to be helpful by supplying roles directly (Edwards, 1996; Neuwirth *et al.*, 1990; Brothers *et al.*, 1990; Kaplan *et al.*, 1992). Group dynamics can be difficult to proscribe, and individual activities can vary from group to group and from one context to the next. Consequently, most workers in this area realize that a system that prevents a group from modifying their roles can hinder rather than help. But roles can evolve in unexpected ways, even in the midst of a collaboration. More recently there has emerged a recognition for the importance of lightness and flexibility in the midst of a session. For example, Shen and Dewan (1992), Dourish and Bellotti (1992), and Edwards (1996), all argue the importance of having a flexible

---

[1] This chapter is based on the paper *Supporting Flexible Roles in a Shared Space*, by Smith, Horan and Hixon, published in the *Proceedings of the 1998 ACM Conference on Computer Supported Cooperative Work (CSCW '98)*, pp. 197–206. It is reprinted by kind permission of ACM © 1998 (http://www.acm.org/).

system that can support dynamically changing ways of working. We suggest taking a lesson from reality and supplying a virtual physics that may partly support roles, but does not define them. Real-world physicality was the model underlying the design of the Kansas system: a large, two-dimensional world in which multiple users can slide about, coming together in groups, dispersing as individuals, moving between various display objects to build and/or use applications.

A collaborative system takes input from each user and creates output to each user. The way the system handles these various inputs and outputs determines how it supports roles. Focus for the moment on the system's output to users. Different users will need to see and hear different things, based on the tasks associated with their role. In Kansas, we already have a mechanism in which different users see and hear different things based on their window size and placement in the larger Kansas world. As part of the need to support awareness (mutual comprehension of each other's position and activity in the world), we designed Kansas according to a principle we call WYSIWITYS (What You See Is What I Think You See), so that it is easy and natural to know who is seeing and hearing whom. We find we are able to support roles without violating the WYSIWITYS principle.

Focus now on the system's treatment of user inputs. We found that by giving novice users all the user input functionality available to developers, we had unintentionally booby-trapped the world. (Kansas differs from reality in that it is more flexible: the "laws of physics" and even of arithmetic can be changed from within Kansas while it runs.) What is responsive and empowering for a developer can cause confusion and rude surprises for a novice. We somehow had to introduce something new, a system to filter various user inputs for the various kinds of users. But we wanted the system to be flexible and lightweight, disturbing the underlying democracy of our reality as little as possible.

The system we added is based on "capabilities". A capability governs one object's access to another. In our case, a capability governs a user's access to an object on the screen. We take minimalist approach in our design: the capability system can in principle operate anywhere in the Kansas universe, with output as well as input, or with abstract data structures far from the user interface. However, we found it sufficient to use capabilities as filters on the inputs to the user interface. Furthermore, we employ a simple form of inheritance in the capability system: it mirrors that of the underlying language and we believe it gives expressive power without undue complication.

A capability is itself a display object, and so can be manipulated directly within the world. Because we normally use capabilities to govern access to user interface objects, the physical world metaphor is at play in this part of the system. A capability is loosely analogous to a key or tool that enables access to some tangible object or set of objects. (Unlike a tool, however, we do not require that a capability be visibly "held" by the user in order to be effective.)

We will show how a user's capabilities can be changed with a few gestures, and we will present several user interface mechanisms that we have created for that purpose. Because one can move through space quite simply and easily change one's capabilities, we are pleased that the resulting system is lightweight and flexible.

We are also happy that the physics of Kansas supports but does not delineate roles. Though a Kansas user may have a distinct location and unique input capabilities, any notion of role resides at the human, social level.

Two final comments: we are illustrating a system we feel is simple and limited, and the fact that it has worked in several real-world settings gives us hope that supporting roles need not mire one in confusion, nor muck up an entire architecture. Secondly, we are using Kansas mainly for synchronous small group interaction. Our support for roles in general, and our capability system in particular is not about providing security against malicious attack. Rather, we hope to show how these facilities alleviate user frustration and facilitate group work: we support roles to enhance usability.

9.2 Kansas

Kansas is so named because it is a large flat space containing multiple people. Users see only their window's worth of Kansas, a foot or so wide: the entire Kansas space is actually larger than its real-world counterpart, measuring millions of square miles, though it currently only supports small groups of a dozen or so users. A portion of the space is shown in Fig. 9.1, where we can see three users. For each user, there is a view bounds rectangle, indicating within the larger world the limits of the user's viewport. Each user's mouse pointer is present as an object in the world, normally showing the user's name as a label. Kansas also supports audio and video among users. Some of the objects in the world can be video images from desktop cameras.

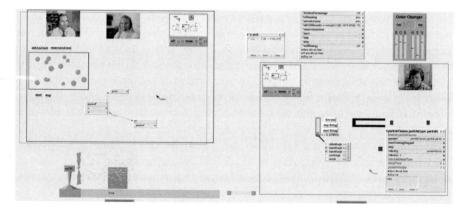

Figure 9.1 An overview of a portion of the Kansas space: each user's window into the Kansas world is limited, and here we see the view bounds for three users. The two on the left are working together on an ideal gas simulation, while the user at the right has moved off on his own where he is programming another simulation. Each user has an image from a desktop video camera, and, as with any object in Kansas, it can be moved, directly embedded into other objects, or even reprogrammed as it runs. Also shown here are two radar views, objects that display a miniature overview of a larger portion of Kansas. Radar views have buttons for sliding the user over the Kansas surface.

Users can slide their viewport across the Kansas surface, moving apart to work in isolation, or moving together for real-time collaboration. When left running for extended periods, a user can check into Kansas for a brief period of asynchronous work, or can rendezvous to meet others for synchronous group work. One might call an environment that is both synchronous and asynchronous "fully chronous".

9.2.1 Kansas Among CVEs

Compared with other environments described in this book, Kansas occupies an interesting kind of middle ground between systems that more literally emulate reality, and those that go after a collaborative environment only loosely modelled on reality. Kansas does have a fairly tangible feel of space, but it is only two-dimensional. A display object does represent each user's agency of action within the world, but it is merely a labelled mouse cursor, not the virtual body "avatar" typical of 3D CVEs. Furthermore, with video links added to Kansas, a new and disjoint sense of space is imposed upon the virtual surface: Each video image floats in the world as a first class object in Kansas with a location generally selected to be out of the way and graphically unrelated to the corresponding cursor. Users can peer into this video window past the heads of their collaborators to view the office or classroom space beyond. Elements of the embedding reality thus leak in to Kansas. When viewed by a strict measure of metaphorical purity, Kansas, with its video patches embedded onto a 2D plane, is some kind of hybrid composite of simplified or reduced analogs of physical reality.

Consequently, certain useful properties of everyday reality are likely to be disturbed under this peculiar mapping. Particularly problematic for group work is providing users with "awareness" of their collaborators' activities. In physical reality, it is fairly easy to for each of us to see what is visible to another. That is, if I can see you at all, I can generally tell what objects in our shared space are visible to us both. Even 3D virtual worlds can struggle to provide this awareness if they break the mapping to reality by providing a narrow field of view. Indeed, the field of view in most 3D CVEs is so narrow that other avatars are normally off screen. And interpreting the direction of gaze for an on-screen avatar is difficult.

In Kansas, we project rectangular screen bounds into the world so that the realm of visibility is realized in the world. We found that this is crucial for smooth discourse among collaborators with partially overlapping screens. Thus what is provided for free in reality had to be explicitly addressed by an additional mechanism in Kansas. The problem of awareness is further discussed later in this chapter (Section 9.4) and in Chapters 5 and 7.

Everyday life also seems to exhibit a variety of user roles, as discussed in the introduction. But such roles exist at the social level – the underlying laws of physics crank away blissfully unaware of such complications. Consequently, in its default mode (with no capabilities) Kansas was built to exhibit a kind of open, naive physics: any user can grab any object, press any button, or inspect and reprogram any object. Our reasoning was simply that social protocols are sufficient in most real-world situations, and we expect the intuitions that one has about object ownership to carry over into the virtual world of Kansas. These expectations proved correct in some ways; however, we did see problems arising from unintentional user actions, some of which had consequences that were hard to undo. Again, explicit mechanisms had to be added, especially when the objects in Kansas enabled functionality more far-reaching than available to any real-world counterpart (e.g. a single character typed in the wrong window can reprogram the way the system does display: this is analogous to reinventing parts of the laws of physics, and the consequences of error can be dire).

9.2.2 Self: Kansas as Programming Language

Kansas is unusually malleable. Kansas is essentially the programming environment for the dynamic object-oriented language Self (Smith *et al.*, 1995; Smith and Ungar, 1995). Objects can easily be reprogrammed even as the system is running. Kansas is itself written in Self, so its implementation can be changed while it is running.

Self is a quite pure and uniform object-oriented language. Everything is an object in Self, including collections, closures, and numbers. Furthermore, all computation happens by message passing. A Self object consists only of named slots containing references to other objects. A slot in an object can be activated by sending to that object a message matching the slot name. When a slot is activated, code found in the slot will be run, or an object stored directly in the slot will be returned. Consequently, all code in the system is unaware of whether a value is computed or stored. Edwards (1996) emphasizes the utility of dynamic computability by providing role-related information with functions rather than with constants. With Self, one can change representations (from stored to computed) without having to change anything else in the system.

Self provides object-based inheritance. If a message does not match any slot in the object to which the message was sent, the lookup continues through any "parents" of the object. Parents are themselves simply Self objects. In Self, any object can be a parent. Though there are no classes in the conventional sense, objects that are used as parents tend to be the repository for shared state and behaviour for use by their inheritance children.

We emphasize then that this is a very flexible world, and might be best thought of as a collaboration kit or a programming environment, as many different systems can and have been created from within Kansas.

9.2.3 Benefits and Dangers of a Dynamic Environment

A fully chronous environment can benefit from being programmable as things are running. Because a fully chronous system needs to run nearly continuously, changes can be made while the system is in use. Also, a long-running system accumulates important state: with dynamic programming it is not necessary to stop the world, recompile, start over and somehow restore the state of the world.

Because a change to Kansas itself, or to something critical (like integer addition), can crash the world, we have devised a robust architecture involving monitoring processes and dynamic creation of a parallel reality called "Oz", as described by Smith *et al.* (1997). If Kansas can no longer run, the system creates Oz, and Kansans are transported into this world where they can visit an (emerald) debugger to collaboratively solve their problems with life in Kansas.

9.3 Two Examples

9.3.1 Remote Physics Lab

This experience led us to introduce capabilities, and it illustrates the utility of their flexibility. Groups of three or four remote high school students were each given their own piece of Kansas in which to operate a simulation. The "instructor" (one of the authors) first explained how to use the environment, then "wandered about" to visit each student, clarifying the various phases of the simulated lab, answering questions, and occasionally adding a feature as requested by a student.

In our first trials, the students immediately started playing with buttons, popping up menus and flying around the Kansas space. Some default menu items can have unfortunate side effects in the world (such as deleting an object), so that, through simple curiosity as opposed to malicious intent, students would make a mess of things fairly quickly.

After introducing the capability system, we started the sessions with the students all in one place but with their mouse buttons essentially disabled. As the instructor explained each feature of the environment, he would incrementally enable a new capability so the students could try out and use the feature. The sessions became much more orderly. By the end of each session, the students had all the capabilities of the instructor, and, on one occasion, students came together on their own to combine their simulations, even inspecting objects at the Self language level to change some of the parameters.

Note again that though we talk about roles, the system does not explicitly reify any such notion. There are only users, their mouse cursors, view bounds and capabilities. Any kind of role object would seem to be more problematic than useful. Whereas initially the student role is very different from that of the instructor, by the end of the session, as far as the system is concerned, there is no difference.

9.3.2 DTVI

Kansas is being used in an experiment at California State University at Chico to test a learning paradigm called Distributed Tutored Video Instruction (or DTVI). In this usage, Kansas runs nearly continuously for months on end, and various student groups drop in for study sessions in which they view videotapes of lectures.

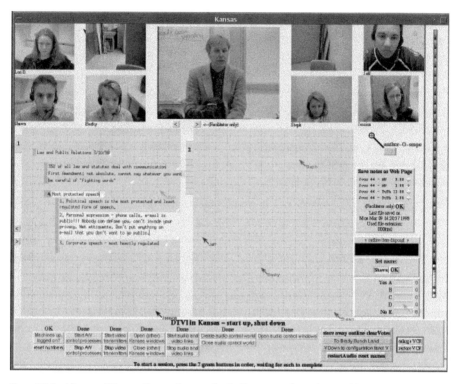

Figure 9.2 In this use of Kansas, five students and a facilitator watch a videotaped lecture (centre) while taking collaborative notes. Because this is a persistent world it is critical that students are prevented from (and need not worry about) making accidental modifications. The facilitator's window (shown here) is slightly larger than that of each student, giving the facilitator access to some more widgets.

This is part of a large multi-year study to compare the course grade performance of the DTVI groups with their co-present counterparts (Sepusic *et al.*, 1999).

The DTVI students see each other through desktop video links, and (in our current version of the system) can take notes collaboratively by typing into an outliner tool (see Fig. 9.2). Any student can type at any time, so note-taking task division is worked out through informal verbal discourse. A facilitator is present to start and stop the videotape, keep the discussion on track, save the notes to a Web page, and perform similar tasks having to do with administrative or system support.

The DTVI system is set up to support four different roles: student, facilitator, coordinator and developer. The Kansas world as experienced by each role differs in the input and/or output in subtle ways. DTVI students are the most restricted, in that they can operate the fewest user interface widgets, and have slightly smaller viewports onto the Kansas surface. The facilitator needs to perform certain administrative and support tasks, while coordinators are able to do anything. The developer is similar to the coordinator, except that in practice the developer is typically at a large geographical distance across the Internet, and so has no audio and video support.

Interestingly, we found it useful to let the facilitators manage some of their own capabilities, selectively enabling and disabling their own mouse buttons. We also prevent students from picking up and moving many of the objects on the main screen. With full capabilities, a student's accidental mouse click and release could move an object from a carefully placed location, wasting group time and generating frustration.

9.4 Awareness and WYSIWITYS

To support multiple users adequately in synchronous environments, one must provide some form of mutual "awareness" of each other's presence, current activities and potential actions (Gutwin and Greenberg, 1996). Ideally, this awareness should be easily attained (e.g., through a shift of gaze) rather than through some slower, complex action requiring a conscious distraction, such as finding and pulling down a menu (Dourish and Bellotti, 1992; Gutwin and Greenberg, 1998a).

An obvious way to take care of much of the need for mutual awareness is to build a WYSIWIS environment (What You See Is What I See). Because all participants in a WYSIWIS world see the same thing (the same widgets, the same telepointing mouse cursors), the presence and actions of participants are pretty obvious. However, WYSIWIS environments are rather limiting, in that, for example, they prevent customized or private views (Stefik *et al.*, 1987a). Consequently, there has been an interest in how to provide awareness in "relaxed WYSIWIS" or even "non-WYSIWIS" environments. A good example can be found in Chapter 8. In the CVE described there, the various users occupy slightly different realities. Specifically, each user's world represents objects in a different way so as to enhance awareness among users.

We have designed Kansas to support a property called WYSIWITYS (What You See Is What I Think You See) (Smith, 1992). WYSIWITYS can hold in a completely non-WYSIWIS environment. WYSIWITYS is a property of most everyday physical world settings. While together in an office conversation, you and I see largely different things: what is important is that I know what you are seeing, even though I do not directly experience your view myself. For example, I can tell from your position and direction of gaze whether or not my hand gestures are obstructed from your view. Such awareness greatly facilitates our conversation.

WYSIWITYS was a key discovery in earlier work of one author in the SharedARK world (Smith *et al.*, 1992; Gaver *et al.*, 1991), and WYSIWITYS was the motivation behind the design of the "Video Tunnel", a camera and monitor with half-silvered mirror (Smith *et al.*, 1990). (Using a video tunnel, A can read the apparent gaze direction of B to know about A's own visibility to B, much as A and B would interpret each other's gaze in the real world.) What has become called "gaze awareness" is a special case of WYSIWITYS.

Because it is a deeply ingrained property of physical reality, WYSIWITYS tends to emerge naturally in virtual realities: In a multi-user VR, user A's avatar's direction of "gaze" essentially depicts to other users that part of the space that is visible to A. In shared worlds that support audio, one's voice can be made to drop off with virtual distance, helping clarify who you are hearing and who can hear you.

But Kansas is not a conventional virtual reality because of its two-dimensional character and the lack of avatars. We therefore use the view bounds rectangle to designate that part of the space visible to each user. The telepointers further support mutual awareness: I know that if I highlight text in some text field that lies outside of your view bounds, you will not be able to see it. Finally, the radar view objects provide a miniature overview of a much larger portion of Kansas: users can discern the presence of quite distant collaborators in the small overview display. A miniature view bounds rectangle denotes their position, and the motion of tiny telepointers reveals their activity. (Gutwin and Greenberg (1998a) demonstrate the effectiveness of radar views.)

Audio volume level can be set to drop off with distance in Kansas, thereby supporting a natural intuition about mutual audibility, and the video images help make users aware of each other's presence and level of attention. Because the video windows are within the Kansas world, the view bounds make clear which image can be seen by whom.

9.4.1 Awareness and Roles

It is interesting to note how awareness and roles are intertwined. You might want others to be aware of your role. Conversely, as part of your role, you need to be aware of certain things. It is this latter category where we have found the spatial metaphor of Kansas to be particularly useful.

As an example, our DTVI users actually have two windows on the screen: the main window, as depicted in Fig. 9.2, and a small window containing an audio control widget, as shown at the top of Fig. 9.3. The audio control lets each user adjust the stereo placement and volume of the sound sources and the audio level of their own microphone. Naturally we want all users to be able to see and operate their own audio controls, whereas depicting the controls of others is a waste of screen real estate. However, it is hard to balance one's own voice in the audio mix, so each microphone level can also be adjusted by the facilitator. Furthermore, if the facilitator can access your control, he or she can teach you how to operate the various buttons and sliders or help you debug some audio problem. Thus the facilitator's role is supported by being able to adjust any audio control, while the students' role is supported by not having to worry about any controls but their own.

To support these goals, we laid out the audio controls in a rectangle isomorphic to the layout of video images in the main screen. The facilitator can see all of these controls in a single window. Each student, however, has a window exactly large enough to show only their personal control (see Fig. 9.3). The audio control appears as a more-or-less conventional application, except that occasionally the facilitator's mouse cursor may sweep past. If the facilitator wishes, he or she can move a troublesome audio control aside, to replace it with another or to give it to another user, perhaps to enlist their help in working with the control.

We utilize the main screen (featuring all the video windows) in a similar way: by giving the facilitator a slightly larger view, certain objects in the surrounding space can be accessed only by the facilitator. Because the students can neither resize nor

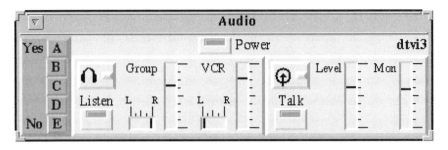

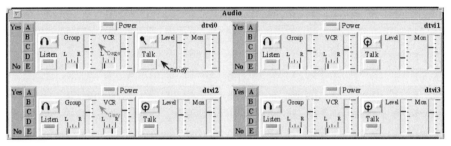

Figure 9.3 A large shared space can afford different views for different roles. The set of audio control panels for four users lies in a single shared world, though each participant sees only their own control panel: their view of the shared audio world is wrapped tightly about their own control. The facilitator, however, sees all four controls, and can help any one participant learn to use the widgets or make adjustments.

move their viewport, these objects remain accessible only to the facilitator. (These objects are primarily controls that start and stop a session.)

Awareness is in a way only half of the story, dealing with the graphical or auditory output of the system. What about the other half, the users' inputs?

9.5 Capabilities in the User Interface

9.5.1 Capabilities, Capability Tables and Capability Sets

Capabilities were first conceived in the 1960s for use in operating systems (for a review see Denning, 1976). A more modern exposition of capabilities can be found in Electric Communities (1997), which emphasizes the elegance and expressive power of capability-based security. Capabilities, because they can be passed from one object to another, allow for "delegation of authority", and can therefore solve problems that cannot easily be solved using an access control list mechanism.

A "capability" is an object representing the right to access some protected object. There are three objects in the story: some "protected object", some generalized "user" object wishing to access the protected object, and the capability object itself. In general, the user object maintains a collection of capabilities (the user's capability set). In normal capability usage, the capability not only stores the kind of access it represents, but retains a reference to the protected object: ideally the capability is the only access the user has to the protected object. In object-oriented programming, the capability would be called a kind of "transparent forwarder", "encapsulator" or "facade" object.

But we are adding this capability system onto an existing user interface programming environment, so references to the objects we wish to protect are already being passed about in many different ways. Furthermore, we wish to use inheritance to allow a single capability to represent access to an entire (and possibly changing) family of objects. Finally, we are supporting a situation in which we are less concerned with protecting against security attacks at the language level, and more concerned with facilitating interaction within a group of humans. In our implementation, we reverse part of the above story so that the protected object retains a reference to capability C: when the user wishes some sort of access, the object can test to see if the user's capability set includes C. Objects may in general issue many different capabilities for different purposes, hence each object maintains a capability table, logically a dictionary (a collection of key–value pairs) in which each key is a descriptive string name ("edit text") and each value is a capability (see Fig. 9.4).

While the system we describe could be used by any of the Self objects in Kansas, we have found it sufficient to use capabilities within the user interface. It is only the displayable objects that have a capability table, and only "user objects" that have a capability set. Thus, if one wants to protect, say, some text file from being over-written, one must do so through the user interface, installing capabilities in the widgets that enable such writing (such as a text editor). This might seem awkward, since all current and future text editors will need to maintain a capability table. However, as discussed below, user interface objects can inherit entries in their capability tables, and thus one capability placed sufficiently high up in the inheritance hierarchy can provide access protection for many objects.

A capability is itself a user interface object, so it can appear on the screen and can be more literally passed around among users.

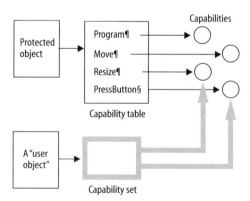

Figure 9.4 Relations among the key objects in the Kansas implementation of capabilities. Each user's access to an object is governed by the capabilities in the user's capability set and by the capabilities in the protected object's capability table.

In practice we cache the key (the string under which the capability is stored in the capability table) within the capability itself. This key is useful as a label in the user interface to describe the kind of access the capability governs. However, when a protected object looks to see if a given capability is in its capability table, the comparison is made based on identity, not based on name.

9.5.2 Programming and Lexical Access

As a programmer, how does one access a capability? Normally one is writing code for a method in a user interface object, such as a button, playing the role of the protected object. The programmer typically has a reference to some user interface event, provided as an argument to the method call. The programmer can access the entries in the button's capability table by sending to itself the message capabilityAt(keyName). The other half of the problem is finding whether this capability is in the user's capability set. In Kansas, every UI event (such as mouse move) has a reference to the user object from which the event originated, and hence its associated capability set can be queried to determine whether it contains a certain capability. Furthermore, every thread retains a reference to the user interface event from which it originated, and one can always obtain a reference to the currently active thread in which one is running. Hence if some event is not passed down the stack as an argument, the user who created the thread can be ascertained through the thread's originating event. These cases have proven adequate for our needs to date, although theoretically there are cases in which access to the appropriate event would have to be made available by construction of some new mechanism. Constructing new mechanisms is no problem if everything in the underlying language is accessible for reprogramming, but of course it is not a realistic option in general.

9.5.3 Inheritance

Every Self object can inherit from one or more other Self objects. References to these "parents", as they are called, are from specially marked slots known to the virtual machine. As previously mentioned, when a message is sent to some Self object, the object's slot names are searched to find one that matches the message name. If there is none, the object's parents slots are searched, and so on, until a match is found.

We have implemented the capability tables to mirror these semantics of message lookup. If a capability of a certain name (e.g. "pressButton") is not found in an object's capability table, then the search continues in the capability table of the object's parent, and so on. In Fig. 9.5 the object B3 inherits the "move" capability C1. Note, however, that the "pressButton" capability C4 overrides the "pressButton" capability C3 in B3's parent. (Capabilities are matched based on identity, so C3 and C4 are different even though they are stored under the same name.)

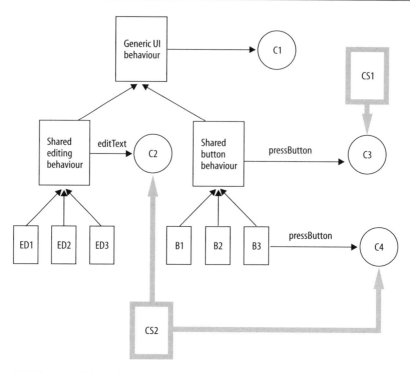

Figure 9.5 Objects may inherit their capabilities, which they use as access filters for various user interactions. Here are shown four capabilities (C1...C4) and two capability sets (CS1, CS2). For graphical simplicity, we just show labelled references to stand for capability table entries, so that, for example, C1 is stored under the string "move". The object within the user interface are in an inheritance hierarchy: depicted here is a simple case of three text editors (ED1...ED3) and three buttons (B1...B3). A user with capability set CS2 can edit text in any of the editors, but can press only one button, B3. A user with capability set CS1 can press only buttons B1 and B2. Notice that capability C4 has overridden C3, because it is stored under the same name in an inheritance parent of B3.

Why must the "pressButton" capability of B3 override that of its parent? One could imagine a system in which both "pressButton" capabilities are present in B3. Such an "additive" inheritance would evoke the method combination rules enabled by "super" or "call-next-method" invocations in object-oriented programming languages. The override semantics we use seemed to us simplest, and allow us to easily express the notion of a "specially protected object" in an inheritance hierarchy. That is, if you want a user to be able to press all buttons except B3, give the user the widely inherited capability C3, and store a special "pressButton" capability in B3's capability table. Thus with this use of inheritance we are able to get some of the benefits of "negative rights" as explained in Shen and Dewan (1992). (In a system with negative rights, giving a user a negative right on B3 would prevent the user from accessing B3.)

With the uniform object-oriented nature of the Self language that makes up the Kansas environment, we are in an ideal position to make use of inheritance for the other players in the capability story. Recall that there are three objects at play: the protected object, the user object and the capability itself. The capability table inheritance mechanism is associated with the protected object. Adding significant roles for the user object and/or for the capability would create a triple dimensional inheritance scheme. The implications of such a mechanism are discussed by Shen and Dewan (1992). However, we find the complexity of three simultaneous inheritance dimensions hard to comprehend, and are thankful we have so far not found it necessary to go down that path.

9.6 User Interfaces to Dynamic Capability Acquisition

Here are some of the ways we have made capabilities accessible from the user interface. Recall that capabilities are themselves displayable user interface objects, and so can be incorporated into various applications as the world is running.

9.6.1 Capability Set Transfer Button

This has proven useful for our own use in giving demonstrations. We can start with the DTVI world (as illustrated in Fig. 9.2) with some of us playing the role of students, and at least one playing the role of coordinator, with full capabilities in his capability table. In order to demonstrate collaborative programming, the coordinator carries this "copy my capabilities" button into a mutually shared region of Kansas. The "students" then hover their mouse over the special white square while the facilitator presses the button (see Fig. 9.6). The students are given a copy of all the coordinator's capabilities, and are thus transformed into coordinators themselves. This button was graphically assembled while the world was running. It contains a single though lengthy expression, so it was fairly easy for a Kansas/Self programmer to create.

9.6.2 Capability Tray

This was the interface we devised for the remote physics lab simulations. Because in this case we only used a small number of capabilities – enabled one at a time – an interface showing all the capabilities for each user seemed reasonable. The trays can be placed in a region of the world visible to the instructor but not to the students (by giving the instructor slightly larger view bounds, or a view bound offset by a small

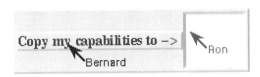

Figure 9.6 User Bernard is about to give user Ron a copy of his capabilities.

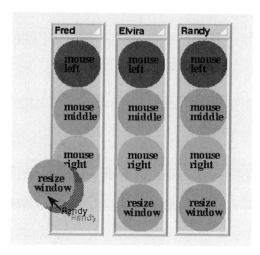

Figure 9.7 A capability tray reifies a user's capability set within the world. Dropping a capability into a tray adds it to the user's capability set.

amount). Dropping a capability in the tray causes it to be added to that student's capability set (see Fig. 9.7). Because each capability can be owned by only one tray, this may not be suitable for applications in which several users share a particular capability.

9.6.3 Small Computers

This is a session start-up mechanism through which the initial capability set can be established for each participant. The small computer represents a participant's host, including the capabilities that will be given to that participant if and when they are brought into Kansas (see Fig. 9.8). The functionality of the small computer is available in a pop-up menu. In this case the capabilities, though they are displayable objects, are held by language-level references only, references reachable from the small computer objects.

9.6.4 Drop/Acquire a Capability

Kansas currently assumes that each user has a three-button mouse, and the facilitators in the DTVI system are sometimes required to use pop-up menus that are triggered by the middle (or in rare cases, the right-most) mouse button. Accidentally pressing and releasing these buttons when the mouse is over the wrong object can have unpleasant side effects (for instance it could create large new objects or resize the object, or it might delete the object from the Kansas world). Consequently we found our facilitators were nervous about accidentally sending the system off into some state from which it would be tedious and time-consuming to recover. We

Figure 9.8 A small computer object is another way to establish a user's capabilities. Each participating host is represented within the world by such a small computer object. A user who joins the session through some host will be given a set of capabilities associated with that host. The user can be given more (or fewer) capabilities during the session.

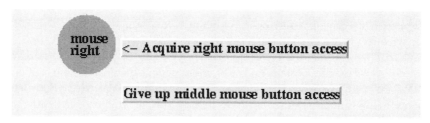

Figure 9.9 Buttons can enable a user to acquire or relinquish a particular capability. This can be used to provide a kind of safety mechanism, especially for, say, a novice user who is unfamiliar with functionality that may cause a sudden dramatic, or even destructive change to the environment. The user who needs the particular functionality can explicitly acquire the necessary capability and then relinquish the capability as soon as it is no longer needed.

therefore introduced a button which alternately enables or disables a user's mouse buttons (see Fig. 9.9). Press it once to acquire a capability, press it again to deposit the capability back in the world. We put two of these buttons in a part of the world reachable by the facilitator, one for the middle mouse button, one for the right. This is an example of a Kansas user intentionally modifying their own capabilities for the sake of usability.

9.6.5 The Infinite Tower of Gloves Metaphor

In Kansas, a mouse cursor is a regular display object, and we call it a "hand" since it is used for pressing buttons and carrying virtual objects about. Each hand has a capability set – a hand plays the role of the "user object" in the capability story. Each hand also has a "meta hand" which is normally invisible. By pressing the meta-escape key combination, a user's hand falls off, and their meta hand appears, coming to life. The original hand remains stationary and lifeless on the screen, though it can be manipulated as an ordinary Kansas object. By hovering over this discarded hand and pressing the shift-meta-escape key combination, a user can reabsorb the original hand, or any inanimate hand, for that matter.

Because each hand has its own capability set, different hands can represent different bundles of functionality. Users can run from one hand to the next, dropping this one to pick up that, much as one does with tools on a workbench. Or, one might come to think of these hands as gloves, each glove specialized for a different role.

Users can shed as many "gloves" as they wish, as there are always more, so the illusion is that one is wearing an infinite number of gloves. This is perhaps the authors' favourite interface to changing capabilities, though interestingly it is probably the least used. It requires those specially reserved key-presses, and it usually takes several gestures to affect a change (drop one glove, move to the other, pick it up). The other mechanisms we describe are more efficient.

9.7 Conclusions

The physics underlying reality does not define roles, though it supports them. We have tried to mirror this kind of support in the multi-user world of Kansas. We found that we can use the basic spatiality of Kansas to provide the necessary different views for different users. We have devised a capability system that operates on the user inputs to the interface. The capability tables used by protected objects follow an inheritance scheme that is simple, mirrors the underlying language Self, and has proven useful in providing the kinds of input filtering we need. The capability system is fairly simple to comprehend, allows for dynamic flexibility, and yet has proven sufficiently expressive to meet our needs.

If necessary we could extend the capability system to apply to graphical and auditory outputs as well as to user inputs, but our concern would be the resulting violation of the WYSIWITYS principle, which allows users to maintain an awareness of who sees what. It is interesting that, so far, we have been able to support roles without violating this principle.

Physical reality has provided some interesting metaphors for human–computer interaction. Direct manipulation, the desktop metaphor, virtual reality: all have been at least moderately successful in providing users with a model that is quickly comprehended. We have again benefited by turning to physical reality, this time to find an understandable and flexible way to support roles within a group.

Part 5
So, Now We're In A CVE, What Do We Do?

Chapter 10
Designing Interactive Collaborative Environments

Adrian Bullock, Kristian T. Simsarian, Mårten Stenius, Pär Hansson,
Anders Wallberg, Karl-Petter Åkesson, Emmanuel Frécon, Olov Ståhl, Bino
Nord and Lennart E. Fahlén

10.1 Introduction

We describe our experiences of creating and using a wide variety of techniques and applications to support collaboration in virtual environments for different activities and user groups. Our aim is to offer plentiful and rich possibilities for interaction across and between both real and virtual environments. This is informed through ongoing activities and projects, starting in the early 1990s, that have provided initial discoveries that point toward what is necessary to support interaction in a CVE. In the early stages, the focus of the work was on creating a programmable CVE, and the DIVE system (Frécon and Stenius, 1998) was born. Starting off as a simple, collaborative 3D graphical environment, the sophistication and functionality of DIVE have progressed, and so have the scenarios in which it is used.

In this chapter we report findings that have come from the day-to-day use of this environment as well as particular focused studies of supporting activities and interactions across a number of projects. A common theme throughout the work of the lab, and exemplified in the content of this chapter, is a strong evaluative and iterative approach. To begin with an idea is prototyped or developed into an application or demonstrator. This application is then used in a number of different settings, often with different criteria and goals. Our experiences then feed back into the further development of applications, which in turn are demonstrated and used in new settings and scenarios. The Web Planetarium, which will be discussed in the next section, is a good example of this "refine and reuse" approach. Starting life as a 3D Web browser, it evolved into the desktop-based Web Planetarium application, which was subsequently installed in a large projection dome and experienced by users as a real-life planetarium.

Further, we discuss issues concerning the interconnection and presentation of different virtual worlds, the use of CVE technology in participatory design, boundaries between the real world and virtual world visualization, and control of real world devices such as robots and novel interaction mechanisms to the virtual world.

We begin by introducing the concept of an electronic landscape, a merging of both physical and digital worlds in the same environment. Then we look at user-centred design of collaborative storytelling tools, where a unique and different experience is offered to the users (children) in a way not easily supported by traditional 3D worlds. Following this we examine a number of techniques and methods that can be used to build a bridge between the experience of the virtual environment and our experiences in the real world. In particular, we consider mixed reality environments, where representations of the real world appear in the virtual world (for example as video streams), and representations of the virtual world also appear in the real world coupled with tele-control of a remote robot. We also discuss interface techniques for large screen displays, where a user is able to interact with the virtual world using different interaction devices to the traditional mouse and keyboard.

In particular we discuss the following applications:

- The *Web Planetarium*: an application for collaborative 3D browsing of the World Wide Web with a focus on the visual presentation of information. The Web Planetarium incorporates a broad range of media in the visualization, in particular 3D models, and enables flexibility and enhancement potential in the presentation of information. The Web Planetarium has been presented in a dome-shaped projection space for the general public at the Centre for Arts and Media in Karlsruhe (ZKM).

- *The Klump* and *The StorySphere*: the Klump began life as an artistically inspired deformable object known as the Blob, an art installation that responded to physical touch-screen interactions from users with changes in shape, colour and sound. The Blob evolved within the context of participatory design with young children into the Klump, a co-located collaborative storytelling tool. The StorySphere is a storage device and permits children to manage and work on collections of stories.

- *Robot supervisory interaction and mixed reality*: a CVE has been used to enable a remote robot and human supervisor to collaborate on a particular task. This work has raised new questions about the remote environment visualization involving different methods of mixing real and virtual imagery, presentation of and interaction with the collaborative environment, and representation of user avatars.

- *Multi-screen interaction space*: work in the SICS Grotto, a multi-screen environment, has raised new questions about interaction and presentation that offer alternatives to standard monitor presentation and mouse and keyboard interaction.

We examine each of these in turn.

10.2 Electronic Landscapes – The Web Planetarium

There are many CVE systems in use today dedicated to supporting specific tasks. Each system will have been developed with a particular activity in mind and will no doubt do this well. The end result is a series of tools that, although they work well individually, have no way of offering any collaboration or interoperability between each other. From a larger perspective this can cause confusion, as many different interfaces and systems may need to be learnt to be able to fully access the required information or perform the necessary tasks.

By exploring the formation of "electronic landscapes" that promote cooperation across and between different applications and virtual environments, we examine techniques to overcome the problems of isolation and interoperability associated with the insular classes of applications discussed above. Through the development of certain techniques we allow a wide variety of different approaches and spaces to coexist. The resulting electronic landscapes help provide a coherent experience and offer better navigability of the resulting heterogeneous information space.

One popular, rich and large source of information today is the World Wide Web (WWW). There is access to plain text, images, sound and three-dimensional models, as well as to the people who are accessing the information themselves. We are all too often unaware that we are collaboratively browsing the Web, together with the rest of the Internet inhabitants. We use many different tools in a complementary manner when we normally surf the Net, these being common applications on our desktop for us. However, we do not know whether other people share the same common set of applications, and so whether they have access to the information we are seeing to the same level of richness. One application that attempts to address this integration is the Web Planetarium. This is an abstract electronic landscape, building up a 3D representation of the Web as the user navigates it, offering a common shared view onto a large information space (see Fig. 10.1).

10.2.1 Navigating the Web in Three Dimensions

The roots of the Web Planetarium (Stenius, 1998) lie in the WWW3D browser (Snowdon *et al.*, 1996b), an application that made a direct three-dimensional interpretation of the hyperlinked structures that make up the World Wide Web. A sphere represents a single document (or page), and arrows between the spheres represent hypertext links. WWW3D was initially developed in DIVE and, during a later port to MASSIVE-2 (Greenhalgh and Benford 1999), several issues relating to visual abstraction and scalability for large sets of Web sites were investigated.

When the user enters a sphere, the contents of the corresponding HTML page are retrieved over the network, and mapped on the inside of the sphere, rendering a rough overview of the information. Images are shown directly, text and link elements are represented as separate icons. When the user decides to follow a link, by selecting a link icon, a new sphere representation is created, a link arrow is displayed between the current and the new page, and the new page is fetched and mapped inside its sphere. Over time, when this pattern repeats, a three-dimensional graph is created as the user explores the Web. The layout of the graph can either be decided explicitly by letting the user freely move around the spheres to suit a personal preference, or by applying a force-directed placement (FDP) algorithm (Fruchterman and Reingold, 1991). This algorithm assigns mass to each node

Figure 10.1 The Web Planetarium.

(document) in the graph, depending on how many links enter or leave the page, and spring forces to each edge (link), and thus continuously calculates new positions for the nodes.

To cope with inherent scalability problems in the FDP algorithm, and to increase the legibility of the visualization, WWW3D supports a mechanism in which several closely related page representations can join to form *clusters*. Such a cluster provides a single abstract external view of these objects, and likewise the links between objects within different clusters would form *aggregate links* between these clusters. A simple example is partitioning the view depending on the server, thus rendering one cluster abstraction for each Web host, which the individual pages rendered inside the abstraction boundaries.

The visual representations of the clusters were used to hint at the popularity of a group of documents, or the size of a site, by changing the colour and shape. Using the possibility of creating clusters of clusters, the abstraction method could theoretically be used repeatedly, in many layers. With such a "meta-abstraction" technique it could be possible to handle a potentially large number of documents and address some issues of scalability.

10.2.2 The Web Planetarium

The Web Planetarium takes some of the concepts developed in WWW3D further, by elaborating on the visual representations of the Web sites and by putting the application to use in different display settings. The general aim has been to promote the "exploratory" nature of electronic landscapes. More precisely, some insights have been gained in how to encourage the user (or users) to navigate the information space of the Web through visual hints in the virtual landscape.

While the development of WWW3D took the path of mainly examining scalability issues (through clustering), the Web Planetarium has put focus on how the site representations can be extended. This has been done both by building "thumbnails" containing a visual abstraction of the information on the site (such as the largest image of a page), and as "visual attractors", where the direct information content is partly replaced by a pleasing visual appearance to promote navigation to a particular site. Previously, colour was used to give information on how recently a particular site had been visited by the user. This suited the primary role of a "history list view" well, but is less suited when regarding the visualization as an electronic landscape. In an electronic landscape, one would want to "scan the view" for interesting features, often for sites you have never been to. In the current Web Planetarium prototype such thumbnails are obtained by taking the first image or texture found on each site, and using it to texture the outside abstract view (assuming that every page or 3D environment contains at least one image or texture). This method gives remarkably good results for HTML pages: usually the first image is a logotype, or a picture of the owner of that page (see Fig. 10.2).

Figure 10.2 The use of thumbnails in the Web Planetarium.

Furthermore, the Web Planetarium enables the inclusion of 3D virtual models in the visualization. This means that whenever the user chooses to follow a link to a 3D model on the network, that model will be retrieved, enclosed by a suitable visual abstraction, and brought into the Web Planetarium space along with the usual link visualizations, and so on. The external sphere representation is shown as an abstract "outside" view of the model, to reduce the visual complexity of the plane-tarium landscape.

Incorporating arbitrary three-dimensional models from the network gives us "a space of spaces" that is built *in an opportunistic manner*, from bits and pieces found on the network, as the user navigates it.

The texture-based abstract site representations are useful to a certain extent – with a simple technique they manage to extract a quick overview of many HTML pages. However, the limitations are significant: it works well only for HTML pages of a certain structure, that is, pages that actually contain a "key" picture that can function as an icon, and placed at the beginning of the page. Most importantly, the methods may be less suited for 3D models, since it is harder to use a simple texture to convey information about the spatial structure of VRML, DIVE or other types of three-dimensional data.

Thus, it becomes interesting to develop and evaluate schemes of extracting high-level structural information from a 3D model to use as an abstract external view of a site. A related approach can be to cut out certain interesting parts of models to use as 3D thumbnails, such as outlined in Elvins *et al.*, (1997). Such 3D thumbnails could be automatically generated as they are needed, or pre-gener-ated and stored at the actual Web site. By further exploring the benefits of the clustering techniques of WWW3D, it could also be possible to perform such abstractions in several levels, allowing for a richer and deeper level of hidden complexity in the landscape.

10.2.3 From the Desktop to Multi-Screen Surround Displays

The Web Planetarium has been used in several different interactive settings. These have varied in many parameters, in terms of display techniques, hardware perfor-mance, interaction methods and so on. To make it applicable to a broader range of settings the application itself has been reconfigured to use different layout schemes, visualization complexity, and so on. Among these different interactive settings are floor projections, where the user stands over the visualization, touch-sensitive back-projected desktops, and immersive CAVE-like displays, such as described in Johnson and Leigh (Chapter 12).

The original WWW3D application used force-directed placement algorithms to position the nodes in three dimensions. In the Web Planetarium it is possible to restrict the positioning to a single plane, and to move the spheres around at free will. The two-dimensional layout creates a scene reminiscent of a road network, which can be further developed and compared with other demonstrators such as the virtual cityscape (Hidalgo-Panes *et al.*, 1999). The "classic" three-dimensional

Figure 10.3 The EVE Dome (a computer-generated simulation: Detlev Schwabe, © ZKM Institute for Visual Media).

layout is more in line with the "planetarium" idea, in that it is not restricted to some particular ground reference level (even though up and down naturally have meanings here too).

The Web Planetarium has been shown in a large domed inflatable environment called EVE (see Fig. 10.3) at the ZKM Surrogate show in Karlruhe (Surrogate, 1998). This alternative display showcased and emphasized the planetarium metaphor. Here the web nodes appeared as planets orbiting overhead steered by one of the visitors. The environment afforded approximately 20 users comfortably spaced out inside EVE. An essential part of the EVE experience was the sound environment. A special score was composed consisting of several layers of effect and environment sounds (e.g. when going from a node to another). The sounds were spatially rendered in three dimensions creating a rich and organic auditory tapestry. A more "musical" soundtrack for the Web Planetarium has also been composed, but this was not used in the EVE dome installation. This demonstration of the Web Planetarium showed new aspects of both the application itself and of the display environment. In this situation the Web Planetarium became an interactionally and visually engaging CVE demonstration, indicating that the right display environment can make a strong difference. Some of the observations from this public event are given below.

10.2.4 Navigability and Orientation in an Abstract Electronic Landscape

Experiences within public showings (Surrogate, 1998) have shown a low tendency among the users to use the link representations to fetch new sites into the visualization even though they are clearly available from inside each site. One possible reason for this is that new sites snapping into view would break the "landscape metaphor". There is accordingly a high tendency to explore what is seen at the moment, to wander around in the three-dimensional graph and look inside the different nodes to examine sites that seem interesting.

If there is a general conclusion to draw from these formative observations, it would be that to encourage navigation (exploration) of an electronic landscape, the landscape itself must provide the triggers, motivators and leads for the user (wanderer), it must itself *be* those properties. In other words, the landscape serves as *its own map*, as a navigational aid to find the underlying information, which in the case of the Web Planetarium are the interconnected Web sites.

In the next section we look at new displays and application of CVEs to support co-located collaboration.

10.3 A 3D Collaborative Storytelling Tool: From Blob to Klump

As part of the work in the lab we are investigating the use of three-dimensional collaborative environments as storytelling tools for children, looking at user-centred design and deliberately trying to move beyond traditional 3D CVE worlds and offer an experience that is unique and different. To do this we are using an application called the Klump, which started life as another similar application called the Blob. We detail their history and the work to date below.

10.3.1 The Blob

The Blob (Wallberg *et al.*, 1998) was originally created as a prototype for a deformable potato-like object that could be shaped through tangible interaction (see Fig. 10.4). It was created to be something that broke from polygonal shapes and stiff mechanical movement common in many virtual environments. It is a virtual plaything that can be manipulated by many people at the same time, with sounds produced as a direct result of the manipulations. In that way it tried to address a desire for organic behaviour in electronic landscapes.

The Blob can also be seen as a step towards experiments with organic massively interconnected displays. In addition, the Blob combines the development of animation and interaction techniques with the effects of ambient sound. In the KidStory project (Benford *et al.*, 2000b), the Blob was transformed into the Klump, a deformable storytelling tool intended to be used by children in a manner similar to the storytelling practice of "cloud gazing" ("I see a spaceship", "My dinosaur over there is going to eat your spaceship", etc.). In this way the transformation from

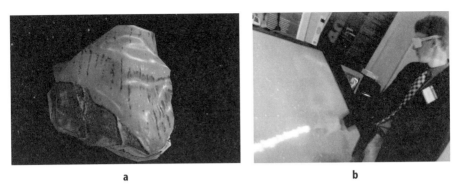

a   b

Figure 10.4 The Blob.

Blob to Klump is both a story about creating an engaging virtual artefact and about repurposement. When something is truly engaging, it can take on a life of its own and be appropriated for applications beyond its original intended application. This section first describes the technical aspects of the Blob and how it was used and then how and what became the Klump.

The Blob Way of Modelling a Fluid

The dynamic motion of the Blob object is generated from a physical model. Given the initial geometry of the object a data structure is generated with masses at each vertex and springs between vertices. Parameters such as mass, spring constant and damping factor are varied to produce a more "life-like" behaviour. When a user interacts with the object by pulling one vertex, forces are applied to that vertex. This causes the springs attached to that vertex to expand and in turn initiate forces acting upon the neighbouring vertices. Forces and movements then ripple through the object. If not controlled by a person, the object goes through different states of random activity. The texture library mapped onto the blob is divided into three sets depending on the brightness and saturation of the colours. More vivid textures are used when the blob is in a more active state, less vivid textures are mapped when the Blob is in a less active state (changes in vertex positions). State changes occur at random points in time and cause the textures to change. The random activity is stopped as soon as user interaction takes place.

The simple modelling of springs between the vertices on the surface of the object was not enough to get good dynamic properties. Internal springs were added to the Blob to model the interior volume. The internal springs also reduced the number of undesirable stable states that the Blob, as a dynamic model, could get into (one undesirable stable state is one where the Blob is wrung inside out). In addition to adding more springs to get better model deformations and reduction in incorrect states, there is another parameter that increases the accuracy: the update rate. Less time between updates means that each update moves the vertices by a smaller amount, better mimicking a continuous process. However, more springs imply more calculations, resulting in a trade-off in the update rate and interactivity.

Physical modelling is traditionally computationally expensive. Although the Blob physical model is simplified as much as possible and does not have "true" deformation properties, it has one big advantage: using the algorithms outlined above it runs in real time with quick interaction response. A fast response with interactive visual and audio feedback is important for the Blob as an interactive CVE object.

The Blob Screams

Along with the Blob's interactive organic behaviour, the Blob generates sounds that complement the Blob's behaviour. These sounds are based on MIDI (Musical Instrument Digital Interface) communication to control the playback of sampled sound files stored in a sampler. The MIDI data is generated mainly in two different ways, by Blob movement and by user interaction, to create the different sonic expressions. These sounds could be aptly described as "screams".

The Blob's screams are controlled by the user interaction. In its present configuration the vertices are grouped into 20 groups, each of which generates a different "screaming" sound (processed and complex gurgles, screams, murmurs and "blobby" sounds). When a user pulls on a vertex the associated sound is started. As the user keeps pulling the vertex the pitch of the sound is changed. The screaming sound stops when the user ceases vertex interaction. This yields a musical instrument of sorts that the user can "play" by pulling on different areas.

The collective movement of the vertices within the different groups triggers more distinct musical phrases. There are presently five different phrases, of which a maximum of three can be activated at the same time. When a vertex group's collective movement exceeds a threshold value, and not more than two of the five samples are playing, the group number is mapped to one of the musical phrases, which will then be started. The collective movement of all the groups triggers dull murmuring sounds. The sound is easily triggered because it is meant to be playing most of the time, and therefore the sample is looped in the sampler. When no interaction occurs for some time, the Blob changes to a random movement state (as described above). When in this mode, the "wildness" of the movements is changed at random points in time. There are three different levels of wildness in the current implementation. The least wild mode doesn't trigger the musical "screams", and the wildest triggers them almost all the time. In the background, murmuring sounds are playing most of the time as well.

The modelling behind the Blob can be generalized and used to breathe life into virtual environments. In addition to dynamics generated by tracking equipment, animation and simple scripts, more organic motions can be added by applying these simplified dynamic modelling techniques to, for example, clothes, skin and plants with swaying branches.

The Blob has been shown in a number of public demonstrations, from conference venues to public technology fairs and conventions, often attracting relatively large crowds and comments related to its surprising organic and dynamic behaviour and abstractness. The Blob became something different, something "fun" to interact with.

10.3.2 Klump – a 3D Collaborative Storytelling Tool

Starting life as the Blob, the Klump is an application for conjuring up stories and collaboratively developing creative ideas (see Fig. 10.5a). The Klump follows the metaphor of modelling, for example, clay, and enables users to simultaneously shape the Klump, mainly by stretching and pushing, to generate story elements and tell stories "in the moment". To provide a greater story structure, the concept of a StorySphere has been developed as a placeholder for Klump shapes (see Fig. 10.5b). Modelled Klumps can be frozen and placed into a sphere for storage and later retrieval for storytelling. The mechanisms of the Klump together with the StorySphere offer multimedia means of collaboratively creating, storing and retelling stories.

The Klump and the StorySphere are being used to investigate methods and mechanisms that promote collaborative exploration and creative play and the creation of novel methods for novel story structuring within the 3D environment. The Klump supports multiple, simultaneous users by providing mechanisms for multiple input devices (e.g. mice and other tangibles) working with a shared output display. In this way, the work follows the Single Display Groupware (SDG) philosophy (see Fig. 10.6; this is discussed further in the next section).

The enthusiasm and involvement the users expressed when interacting with the Blob is what was desirable to capture and use in the context of creating story characters and free-form improvisational story telling. The Klump uses the same physics as the Blob, runs under the Windows NT platform, and has support for multiple simultaneous child users and more controlled modelling (i.e. fewer autonomous behaviours). The development of the Klump benefits from "cross-pollination" and iterative development with our child and teacher partners in the schools. Development has proceeded through frequent participatory design sessions in schools with children.

The Klump has retained many of the Blob's qualities as a 3D graphical object with a physically based spring model that gives it organic dynamic properties. The Klump also generates sounds that are directly related to its movements and user

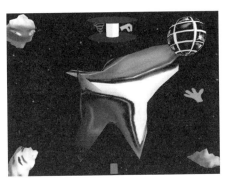

a   b

Figure 10.5 a The Klump and **b** the StorySphere.

Figure 10.6 Children using The Klump in a classroom.

interaction. Like the Blob, this combination of sound, movement and textures works to create the Klump into an engaging electronic artefact.

The most salient human–computer interaction aspects of the interaction with the Klump are the following:

- *Gestural modelling*: In interaction with the Klump, there is a strong notion of using "mouse gestures" to model both the shape of the Klump object and the colour of the textures, as well as the sound that is produced. What are generally meant by gestures are the movements of the mouse. These movements are beyond "pointing and clicking", and include "stroking", "pulling" and "poking". In this way, users can pull out parts of the Klump surface as well as shape the sounds emitted from the Klump.

- *Subjective interaction*: Input device interaction among simultaneous co-located users can differ. For example, while one user is moving or colouring the textured surface, another user can be modelling the Klump's shape. Interaction is then subjective and users need to be made aware of the mode of their input device when using it. This concept relates to the user's input, and is not to be confused with the concept of subjective views found elsewhere within this book (Chapter 8).

- *Multimodal output and interaction*: The Klump employs different modal outputs. These are visual, including shape and texture, as well as aural, including modulated MIDI sounds. It is believed that it is partly this coupling of interaction modalities with the dynamic behaviours that make the Klump an engaging focus of attention. For many children the Klump seems to grab collaborative focus when working in groups of two or more.

- *Storytelling 3D shapes and structures*: The Klump provides mechanisms for shaping and forming shapes that can be used for storytelling. The Klump's organic movements, abstract textures and sound tend to create an environment where child users are given ideas for stories. Interaction with the Klump tends to be engaging for many users. Through this interaction, ideas for stories tend to spring out. We call these "unintentional offers" that can be picked up by collaborating users and built upon. In this way the Klump provides a mechanism for facilitating an improvisational storytelling between the children working with it.

- *Local Tools*: Following the experience with KidPad, the Klump application has adopted the "Local Tools" approach (Bederson *et al.*, 1996) over a menu and palette approach common in many GUIs. Local Tools are tools that can be picked up and that retain their state when left again. In this way, the cursors are 3D objects as well as mechanisms for selecting the 3D cursors.

- *Single Display Groupware*: The Klump follows the Single Display Groupware philosophy of collaboration. This sharing of the display provides a platform for encouraging collaborative activities. These are partly done by the focus of activity being interaction with the Klump.

- *Children as design partners*: The Klump has been developed together with children and it is through this process, together with researchers, that the concepts, metaphors and new functionalities have evolved.

Single Display Groupware

The scenario we wish to support sees co-present collaboration where a display is shared. One reason for using this scenario with children is a desire not to replace "person-to-person" communication with an artificial separation enforced by computer separation. Instead we think of supporting "shoulder-to-shoulder" collaboration where the computer offers support for dirt-world activities. With storytelling tools we are interested in supporting forms of play in which children naturally instigate and partake (e.g. make-believe). Here we see improvisational storytelling as a partial formalization of that practice. Co-present groupware is then seen as a collaborative framework for this work. In the extreme one might see a CVE as being co-present with a real space, e.g. a model of that space, and interaction happening as much in the real world as in the virtual world. As starting points this work requires support for multiple input devices and mechanisms for interacting with and viewing a shared display (or displays).

The current version of the Klump supports simultaneous input from two separate mice. This allows two children to interact with the Klump at the same time. To investigate how multiple input devices affect cooperation, we have implemented a few tools that enforced working together. For instance, when selecting textures, both users are required to click on the icon at approximately the same time. The Klump yields a natural focus, and this practice generates discussion and negotiation. From that point we recognized a need for tools that "encourage" (rather than enforce) collaboration, where a better effect was achieved through coordinated interactions (this is partly a pedagogic interest; see Benford *et al.* (2000b) for more information). When the possibility of combining textures is used, there will be a possibility for one user to change textures, and for two users to combine textures.

StorySphere

The StorySphere is based on the idea of a "story quilt", drawing from traditional American and the African-American cultural practice of building a family quilt over generations where each pane tells a story about an episode in family history. Further, it is based on the idea of juxtaposed images forming a greater story. Story quilts are in a similar artistic storytelling genre to triptychs and Renaissance multi-panelled paintings. The StorySphere adapts this notion of a panelled quilt to a virtual 3D object. It then becomes a shared 3D manipulable storytelling device, a container for events, characters, settings etc. As a sphere it affords multiple entry points with no particular beginnings or endings.

The StorySphere is a way of organizing scenes into a greater story, a set of panels each of which tells a small part of a story and together forms a greater narrative. The StorySphere is a 3D object with panels covering its face. Each "panel" is a small scene containing story elements. The sphere can be manipulated to display different panels, which can then be zoomed in on and worked on or presented individually each panel representing a session with the Klump. A story structure can be laid out onto the sphere and then later be used to play back collaborative story constructions. Using this structure, stories that are built can be played back for the audience. So in addition to being a method to store the story elements, the StorySphere is a way to organize the greater structure of the scenes that are created.

The sphere can be rotated, spun, enlarged, augmented etc. It can become a (nearly) infinite container for story scene elements. Together, the storytellers can rotate the sphere to select a scene to be worked on, bring this scene to the foreground (by zooming into the sphere) and work on it. They can then zoom out, rotate to another place and work on that area, and so on. In addition, the StorySphere provides a placeholder for storytellers to incorporate the stories of previous storytellers becoming part of a greater social narrative. The StorySphere, upon startup, can be loaded with scenes containing settings, characters and events from previous story creating sessions.

The StorySphere also has natural affordances for tangible interaction: for instance a ball that is rotated in real space. This ball could be the same object that is used for manipulating the Klump object for modelling. Thus the same interface can be designed to support the capture of Klump modelling gestures and for manipulating the StorySphere and selecting scenes to be worked on.

10.3.3 Coming Together

In this way, work with the potato-like object became the Blob which became the Klump, finding new life and purpose. One pedagogic observer commented "this is the most different thing I have ever seen on a computer". Given the intentions of the work with the Blob this is taken as one of the strongest compliments that could be given. In addition we have been asked by teachers and children to install the Klump application in schools for day-to-day use.

In the next section we describe a project that explored the mixture of real and virtual imagery and the control of a real world robot through a CVE interface and how this makes new demands on CVE work.

10.4 Supervisory Robot Control and Mixed Reality

We will now describe a CVE that has been used to create a medium for human–robot collaboration. The situation where a robot and human user collaborate over distant raises new challenges on how to share deictic references for task objects. Such deictic references (e.g. "that object there", "this table here"), often pose difficulties in collaborative work over distance. In the particular situation where work is to be performed in one partner's environment (e.g. the robot's), some medium of interaction with that environment, or some representation of that environment, needs to be constructed. In the situation of remote robot supervisory control, the choice was made to use a CVE to represent the robot's remote environment to enable a common environmental framework for interaction. A project and study were undertaken to look at these issues in depth (Simsarian, 2000).

The robot is a semi-autonomous entity, so it is not strictly under direct control; rather, it is viewed as a collaborative partner. Through a user-centred design, a number of traditional CVE practices were re-evaluated regarding the role of model fidelity, interaction and user-representation (e.g. avatars). We then present a methodology and some issues of mixing real and virtual imagery with models to make the CVE as useful as possible.

10.4.1 Human–Robot Interaction

In building a collaborative relationship between a human user and a robot it is important to take into account the nature of collaboration. For example, the division of work into tasks with the robot may not neatly divide *a priori*. Such situations are when the task is such that decisions need to be taken while the work is in progress. The next step of the process, or the next action, may depend on the results obtained by the previous one. For such tasks it would be difficult to make a division of the work beforehand. Another such situation is in dynamic environments, where the constraints and perhaps locations of the task are changing frequently. There are also sure to be tasks where the ability to perform an action is impeded. This might be caused by an impediment such as lack of competence, lack of information or lack of dexterity. In these situations, although it might be possible to divide the work of the task beforehand, the conditions upon which that division was made might have changed. This category of situations indicates a need for a *collaborative* mode where the division of labour between the robot and the human is not set, but can be fluid.

It could be claimed that any complex task in unstructured environments would involve this sort of fluidity between modes. This mode of work will be referred to as *human–robot collaboration*. This fluidity of the division of labour is referred to as a *working division of labour* (this follows from the CSCW work of Hughes (Bentley *et al.*, 1992)). With such a working division, elements of the task might then run the gamut of modes: extending, relieving, backing up and replacing human efforts. This swapping of modes may be entirely tacit, i.e. happen without conscious attention. There then needs to be "working space" for human and robot to attend to the moment-by-moment contingencies that emerge in the doing of work. CSCW research makes the case that this is so in the use of computer systems: this has been observed and carried through as a situation of collaboration with the use of robots.

As regards the interface, to allocate roles and resources (e.g. between human and robot) on the basis of some formalized notion of a plan-in-advance, ignores the practical realities of situated action and therefore risks "designing out" support for the realities of effective collaborative work. For the practical design of the interface this implies a construction that enables the sharing of tasks where this facility is part of the base structure of the interface. An interface can provide for this not by just one supported method for direct manipulation, but by providing several options available, at any time, enabling the human and robot to collaborate.

For the robot project this has meant installing a structure that enables control interactions to interrupt previous interactions, producing a working collaborative coupling between robot and supervisor. Because of the distance and interaction with a physical object, which involved issues of lag, inertia and control, direct coupling of interaction is not always possible. The structure for collaboration involves the ability for the human user to issue commands at any time, as seems appropriate. Feedback from the robot involves responding to these commands in a sensible manner. Such feedback involves acknowledgement of the commands and simply executing the task and displaying these robot activities to the human user.

The issue of not having direct control of an "object" in a CVE raises new control issues. Often worlds are contained and hermetic, and do not involve outside events. This situation is bound to change with increased interaction between real and virtual environments and with it the traditional modes of control. In such situations new demands will be placed on CVE interaction that are beyond the control of application designers. Designers of CVEs that involve physical spaces and devices, need to take into account contingencies that are the result of interaction with a complex environment outside the world model.

10.4.2 Model Fidelity and Environment Visualization

One finding of the robot user study is that the appropriate detail, functionality or display of a number of features depends on the task at hand. That which is appropriate for one setting may not be for another. For this style of control of a mobile robot, it may mean there is no general interface and instead that the controls available change depending on the exact circumstance. This seems to depart from other efforts in CVE work, where a general interface is often sought. The features that have been initially shown to be task-dependent are, for example:

- *The fidelity of the CVE model*: A sparse model can be a benefit. The desired amount of detail displayed, or fidelity, will most likely be linked to the task at hand. While in many CVE applications detail, like pictorial or model realism, is seen as a goal, and lack of detail is a failing, in some search tasks there may be a desire to have less detail. In the robot control situation one of the tasks was a visual search in the real world employing the robot in the physical environment and a CVE that represented that space. In such a space, it can be an asset to have less detail and instead have display detail focused around the search task at hand.

- *The views on the CVE*: The view that a user has on the CVE will depend highly on the task. For this task a top map-like view and a behind-the-robot view were the most useful, while the more traditional avatar side views were not employed. This is to say that the benefits of a particular view will depend on the task at hand. In the traditional use of a CVE it is often assumed that an avatar-based side view of the CVE is the most appropriate. However, through the study with the robot this was seen as not the case. For the control and interaction with the robot, and with the physical environment via the robot, a view from the top looking down and a view from the robot's perspective were the most frequently used. For another task, with different structure, it may be that side views are critical. However, it is clear that this is dependent of the situated use and more investigations are in needed to demonstrate utility of various views.

- *Reality Portals displayed*: The Reality Portals, as described in the next section, are features in a CVE that display real-world video stills in the virtual model. The desired number and quality of these was found to be linked to the task at hand. Reality Portals that displayed images related to the task at hand were necessary, whereas others that might have contributed to "pictorial realism" were not seen as necessary. Thus the value of displaying a particular Reality Portal may change for a particular task. Before performing the study this issue had not been considered in depth. Pictorial reality may not be a goal in and of itself, and methods for the control and categorization of Reality Portals from the user interface should be researched. The above finding suggests an interface that is flexible with respect to the dimensions given above and that enables a user to control these features with respect to a given task.

In general, much effort has been expended creating detailed virtual worlds, down to such things as furniture and other mundane objects. The robot example is one such application where, instead of this process of replicating the real world within the virtual world, we now wish to explore the possibilities for boundaries between the real and the virtual and discover what is necessary to display.

In order to be able to offer smooth interactions between people and objects in the real and virtual worlds, we have to consider new interface possibilities and new and novel interaction devices. However, before we move on to describe a number of potential interaction methods for large screen display technology (such as that described in Johnson and Leigh (Chapter 12), we reflect on mixed reality environments and exemplify this through some work on remote interaction using an augmented virtual environment. In this next section we describe the system for inserting these Reality Portals into the CVE to create mixed realities: environments that mix elements of virtual and real spaces.

10.4.3 Reality Portals and Remote Interaction

The visualization and manipulation of remote environments, particularly where tasks concerning security, monitoring and exploration in distant or hazardous locations are undertaken, is an area that is particularly suited to mixed reality or Augmented Reality techniques. An augmented virtual world is created that contains real-world images as automatically created object textures, called *Reality Portals*. These allow a user to interactively explore a virtual representation of video from a real space. To capture the video in a remote setting we use an active mobile robot with a video camera that explores the remote physical environment. We also use a 3D graphical model of the remote environment. Segments of video are taken from the robot's video stream and "smartly" placed in the 3D environment as textures on virtual objects. This constructed multi-user 3D environment can be explored interactively concurrent with the texturing and exploration process.

The CVE is used as a control interface for manipulating objects in the real world. An advantage of the virtual world is that it is not dependent on physical location and can be manipulated in a way not subject to the temporal, spatial and physical constraints of the real world. It also has the advantage that irrelevant parts of the real world can be left out. Thus the "interesting" parts of the world are extracted and made salient. In this way a custom view of the world is created, forming an instantiation of selective vision. This combination of real and virtual environments is called Augmented Virtuality, which is the converse of the better known technique of Augmented Reality. The goals of using video images in the virtual world are plenty. The first is the same as the goal of using textures in a virtual environment: to give a richness of "reality details" in the virtual world. Such photographic elements contain information and afford immediate access through user-visual memory for object identification and understanding. Another purpose is to furnish a 3D means of viewing visual information taken from the real world, for example to visually monitor physical spaces in near real time via the CVE.

10.5 Potential Techniques for Spatial Interaction in Multi-User Surround Display Environments

We have been exploring the notion of tangible spatial interaction in multi-scene displays as it relates to interfaces. We use the term interface in a restricted way, covering the gap between the user and the CVE, i.e. instantiations of different techniques of interaction within a virtual world. The goal is to create interfaces that are compelling while at the same time more effective and less encumbering than merely extending the standard 2D GUI tools (Hansson and Wallberg, 1997). This work has been carried out using large projection environments (CAVE-like environments such as those described in Johnson and Leigh in Chapter 12 intended for multi-user applications). Designing such interfaces presents a series of design choices, centred on granting user control, the number of degrees of freedom to be presented and how large to make the human–computer "language". We are far from final conclusions, but are instead presenting a number of our experiments (see Fig. 10.7).

The first experiments involved using a 6D mouse, a tethered mouse with three buttons and magnetic coils determining the three orientation angles and three position values yielding six degrees of freedom. Navigating with the full six degrees of freedom has been shown to be difficult for people not accustomed to this type of

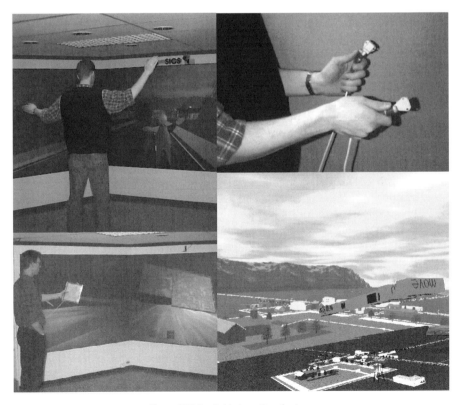

Figure 10.7 Spatial interaction devices.

mouse. When using what we have called "scrolling viewpoint", navigation is restricted to a horizontal plane (often used with gravity). The avatar, and thus the viewpoint, is moved forward or backward when the cursor, controlled by pointing with the 6D mouse, is moved above or below the three screens ("active borders", as often seen in graphical Unix environments). The travel velocity is related to the distance the user points outside the screen borders. In a similar way, the user rotates by pointing off the screen to the side.

An informal test showed that people found the scrolling quite intuitive, and it seemed to have a short learning process. We have made other experiments where we try not to use the hands for navigation, leaving them free to do other tasks, such as selection. We had thought it better to decrease the manipulative load this way. However, our test subjects preferred using the 6D mouse for all interactions.

Perhaps the most powerful and least encumbering of all the devices was a setup using unencumbered video tracking. Having mostly used magnetic trackers, we realize that it would be an improvement to rid the user of cabling and sensors. Toward this end we have implemented a navigation technique that uses the Pfinder system developed at MIT Media Lab (Wren *et al.*, 1995). Pfinder extracts information from video images of a person in a scene, and gives 2D+ data about the location of the hands, head and centre of the person's body. This information can be used to navigate and manipulate objects in a CVE. We have implemented a way of navigating using a simple body gesture command language. Raising your arms increases the speed; lowering one of your arms makes you turn in that direction. This navigation is based on the metaphor of "gliding", in much the same way as a gull might turn and bank in the air.

This test system proved sensitive to changes in lighting conditions and had a low frame rate. However, the fact that it is completely unencumbered still makes it an interesting tracking technique if used in a controlled environment.

In a virtual environment, one way to let the user gain a larger context of the environment is by using the WIM (Stoakley *et al.*, 1995) metaphor, which in our implementation is called a Path Planning Map (PPM). This provides the user with a handheld miniature representation of the world, somewhat like a map in the real world. The virtual map metaphor benefits from the notion of everyday maps, something most people are familiar with, and thus a concept that can be grasped quickly. The PPM can be used for locating and orienting the user, searching for other users and for moving directly to a point on the map.

One mode lets the user draw a path on the map, which will be replicated in the virtual environment and displayed to those that choose to see it. A user can follow the path freely or be taken on the path automatically. A tracker can also be attached to a physical plate directly linked to the virtual map, allowing the user to hold a real representation of the map at the same time as controlling the virtual PPM. Actually holding the "physical map" resulted in positive feedback from informal users indicating that it was engaging. We have used this setup in a virtual maze, with good results. We believe that it might be useful in complex environments where a 2D map is not sufficient.

When constructing a "tank navigation" interface we looked at how a tank driver steers a tank. Two wands control the speed of the virtual tracks. Magnetic trackers are attached to two sticks to simulate tank navigation. Rotating both sticks forward will give you a forward velocity. Rotating the left stick back makes you turn left. The directional velocity is determined by averaging the sticks' rotation, and the angular velocity is computed by looking at their rotational difference. An advantage of this interface, apart from being intuitive, is that it uses only one degree of freedom (pitch), which prevents a beginner from producing unexpected movements. The fewer degrees of freedom an interface uses, the shorter the learning period needed, since the "vocabulary" is limited. However, a limited "vocabulary" prevents use of the interface in a general sense. The "tank" interface is most appropriate for navigational purposes. Using the base mechanism of the angular control sticks, the tank vehicle is extendable to other vehicles, such as a virtual forklift. The shifting of mode would depend on the application.

This setup generated positive responses, the general feeling being that it was quite intuitive, which was also proved by the short learning process. Some users thought it was more precise than the other interfaces, and we got suggestions that it might be suitable for precision walkthrough applications. However, we also feel that there is a drawback in occupying both hands.

To achieve more direct manipulation and more natural environments (in the sense of manifest affordances), we are working on novel projection displays in connection with touch-screens as a method of achieving alternatives to "fish-bowl" interfaces. An example setup has a horizontal "desktop" with a touch-screen interface and a vertical "communication wall" that we can use for conferencing. Both surfaces provide an interface into the virtual environment/workspace. The horizontal projection surface also provides an elegant mechanism for local groupwork. The desktop can also be used in conjunction with a multi-screen display to provide a view of the virtual desktop, which is located in the CVE, and objects on the desktop can be manipulated by direct touch.

10.6 Summary and Conclusions

In this chapter we have discussed various aspects of interfaces to CVEs and design approaches for presenting information and supporting collaboration within virtual environments. In particular we have discussed how the Web Planetarium application as a 3D depiction of a WWW exploration can change and become an engaging experience in different contexts of use. We have also presented long-term experiments in using CVEs to support co-located collaboration for a creative storytelling application for children. We explored how a number of traditional CVE notions are challenged when controlling a robot over distance. We have also shown a systemic method for displaying real-world elements inside a virtual world to create a mixed reality. We concluded by presenting a number of interaction experiments that offer alternatives to standard mouse and keyboard for navigating and browsing CVE environments in multi-user, multi-screen environments.

Overriding these presentations is the idea that setting, presentation and task influence the overall success of the application. Here we have concentrated on the interface between the virtual environment and the real world, on applications that present alternatives for displaying and accessing information, and on methods of building applications through collaborative participatory design. When mixing the real and the virtual in the same environment it has become clear from trials and ongoing use of various applications (e.g. the robot studies and the Reality Portals) that a user has a more complete experience than with just one of these media. Without the mixture of real and virtual (be it the real world augmenting the virtual world or the other way around), and the interaction insights gained from its use, our applications would be poorer and less engaging.

Our discussions have been informed by our experiences of developing a general CVE platform and using this to investigate design and interaction themes through project work. Common to much of the work presented here has been something we will call "refine and reuse", which has enabled us to produce engaging and rich environments. By making use of different media and different interaction styles we have been able to create appealing applications. To some extent it is the richness of the applications that makes them appealing, and it is only through the reuse of components across projects and applications in an iterative prototyping manner that we have been able to create these rich environments in the first place. The Klump is an excellent example, where a potato-like object evolved, through the artistic Blob, into an engaging collaborative storytelling tool due to its use and the reactions of people to it. User experiences guided the direction in which its development went. By confronting users with our concepts and applications, we have been able to observe how they react and whether they accept what we are proposing, and even gain insights that otherwise would never have been apparent. Using these observations we can build up an understanding of how well our applications are used, understood and accepted, and use this to guide future development plans. We are able to refine our applications designs, and by using inputs across a number of application areas new ways of thinking about solutions present themselves. On a more pragmatic level, the reuse of components not only helps in generating inviting environments, but also increases the speed of prototyping, something that is important in an iterative design process.

Another conclusion to be made is that the display and interaction mechanisms can have a large influence on collaboration in an application. In both the work with children and the Web Planetarium we have seen different reactions to the same applications presented to end users on different displays and using an array of input devices. So not only do we need to concern ourselves with the design of the application, but we also need to consider how the application is to be viewed and shared by people.

If we consider the work of the group as a path through time and space, the origins of our work lie in the concepts of virtual reality systems and applications that support distributed meetings. As we move forward along this trajectory, we observe the introduction of richer and more engaging environments, exemplified by the work on electronic landscapes. As the future beckons we see our work turning to incorporate tangible objects and interactions and the growing importance of mobility and mobile communication to CVEs.

Acknowledgements

The musical accompaniments to the Blob and the Web Planetarium were composed by Jonas Söderberg, and the graphic design work for the Blob and Web Planetarium was done by Bino Nord. The installation of the Web Planetarium in the EVE dome would not have been possible without the help of Detlev Schwabe from ZKM. We would like to thank the support of the EU-funded projects eSCAPE and KidStory and the EU Esprit funded COVEN project, which have supported parts of the work described here.

Chapter 11
Designing to Support Collaborative Scientific Research Across Distances: The nanoManipulator Environment

Diane H. Sonnenwald, Ronald E. Bergquist, Kelly L. Maglaughlin, Eileen Kupstas-Soo and Mary C. Whitton

11.1 Introduction

Collaboration, and increasingly multidisciplinary collaboration across distances, is a fundamental and strategic component of the scientific research process. The importance of collaboration in the scientific research process has long been recognized by the National Institutes of Health (NIH) in the USA. Its current policy is to fund the development or purchase of specialized scientific instruments in (not-for-profit) research labs across the USA and to help fund scientists to travel to those labs to collaborate and conduct scientific experiments using these specialized scientific instruments.

Many scientific instruments employ time-critical control systems, and frequently the user depends on large quantities of data, e.g. images, from the device to make control decisions. Collaborative access to machines with real-time control systems and high data IO rates is only now becoming possible with the emergence of high-quality, high-speed Internet 2 network communications. NIH is questioning whether its current policy should change; should it fund work to provide access to scientific instruments across distances?

Collaborating scientists often work face-to-face, sitting side-by-side in a real laboratory and sharing the use and control of instruments and tools. Can scientists in different locations collaborate effectively when virtually sitting side-by-side in a shared virtual laboratory with distributed access to shared instruments and tools? Our research addresses this question, focusing on collaborative, multi-disciplinary scientific research across distances that utilizes a specialized scientific instrument called a nanoManipulator (nM) (Finch *et al.*, 1995; Taylor and Superfine, 1999). There are five nanoManipulators worldwide. Our research goals are to design and evaluate a distributed, collaborative environment to support scientific research using an nM. We will refer to the entire environment as the nM collaborative virtual environment (nM CVE); we will refer to the nM instrument, an element of the nM CVE, simply as an nM, an nM tool or an nM instrument. The term "scientists" is used throughout this chapter to include faculty members, research scientists, graduate science students and postdoctoral fellows, i.e. anyone who does scientific research and development.

We began this research by conducting an ethnographic study to develop an understanding of the scientific research process, current collaborative work practices, the role of an nM as a scientific instrument, scientists' motivation for multidisciplinary collaboration across distances, and scientists' expectations regarding technology to support scientific collaborations across distances. This understanding suggests that collaborative scientific research in an nM context is cognitive work that is supported by social and physical activities, and our collaborative environment should support the cognitive work and its supporting, or enabling, social and physical activities. This is in comparison with other CVE approaches that primarily support social interaction with the expectation that the social interaction will support cognitive work. The design was further guided by a synthesis of social awareness literature. Control, sensory and distraction factors that appear to contribute to social awareness in virtual environments were analysed to discover implications and improvements to our design. Our design brings geographically distributed scientists together into a shared virtual laboratory that is modelled on a real laboratory environment as faithfully as possible.

The nM CVE system we designed required enhancements to the nanoManipulator instrument and new components. The nM CVE includes consistent shared and private work modes, or spaces; the ability to customize an individual view of a shared workspace; the ability to dynamically switch between shared and private work modes; and multiple pointers or cursors that show each collaborator's focus of attention, interaction mode and actions simultaneously when in shared mode. Additional elements include telephones for audio communication; video conferencing to provide views of hand gestures and other physical objects that scientists use during experiments in addition to facial views of collaborators; and shared access to data analysis tools and other applications that are used during the scientific process. We are currently evaluating the usability of the nM CVE, its impact on scientific experiments and its impact on the process of science over time.

The chapter begins by describing the scientific research context, and our design to support collaborative cognitive work across distances in this context. We then discuss the refinement of the design using social awareness theory. We conclude with a description of the new system and a discussion of our ongoing evaluation and implications of this work.

11.2 The Scientific Research Context

To design a system to support collaborative multidisciplinary scientific research that utilizes specialized scientific instrumentation we began by developing a deep understanding of scientific research in this context. We used ethnographic techniques (Bloomberg *et al.*, 1993, 1996; Hughes *et al.*, 1992; Suchman, 1995), including semi-structured interviews, critical incident interviews and participant observation. In particular we conducted 27 interviews with scientists who are experts in using a (non-collaborative) nM and scientists from several disciplines who want to use an nM to collaborate across distances. We also observed scientists on nine occasions as they conducted experiments using an nM. The interviews and observations were iterative, thereby illuminating discrepancies between perceived and actual work practices (Bloomberg *et al.*, 1993; Murray, 1993; Kensing *et al.*, 1998).

Analysis of these data informed our understanding of the role of an nM as a scientific instrument, the scientific research process, current collaborative work practices, scientists' motivation for multidisciplinary collaboration across distances, and scientists' expectations regarding technology to support scientific collaborations across distances.

11.2.1 The nM Scientific Instrument

An important component of the scientific process for scientists is the instrumentation that allows them to investigate physical samples. High-powered microscopes and probes, and their associated methods of use, provide scientists with a means to conduct experiments. The nanoManipulator (nM) instrument provides a natural scientist with the ability to interact directly with physical samples ranging in size from DNA to cells (Guthold *et al.*, 1999, in press). An nM, incorporating visualization and haptic technology, allows scientists to see, feel and modify biological samples being studied with an atomic force microscope.

As illustrated in Fig. 11.1, components of the existing nM instrument include: (a) a connection to an atomic force microscope (AFM) that scans samples on the nanometre scale; (b) personal computer (PC) based AFM controls and data analysis tools; (c) video display of the sample in the microscope taken by a camera in the AFM; (d) 3D graphics display of a virtual model of the data collected by the AFM; (e) software controls for the virtual environment system, including the 3D graphics display, AFM and haptic feedback device; (f) the haptic feedback device that allows users to feel a sample; and (g) PC-based data analysis software tools.

An AFM works by moving a tip across the surface of a sample, measuring its height at locations on a regular grid. The AFM software provides only a greyscale image of the sample as viewed from above (element (b) in Fig. 11.1). An nM instrument augments this greyscale display by using a graphics computer to render the

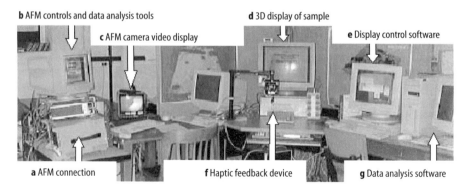

Figure 11.1 Today's non-collaborative nanoManipulator (nM) system.

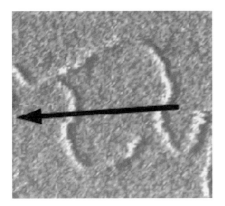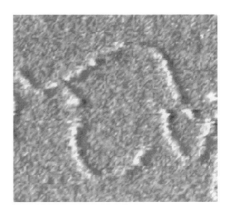

Figure 11.2 Visualization and manipulation of DNA.

height data as a 3D coloured surface (see Fig. 11.2). An nM greatly expands the scientist's data visualization options; scientists can change the way the data is displayed by rotating and scaling the data, varying the mapping of colours to height data, and changing the position of the light in the scene. These capabilities help scientists to find and identify features that can be missed in the greyscale image.

An nM can be used in two modes: live and replay. In live mode, an nM is used to control, display and record measurement data from the AFM. When in live mode, the stream of data produced by the microscope is saved in a "stream file" so that it can be replayed for later analysis. In replay mode, a stream file supplies the data input to an nM, allowing the scientist to review an entire experiment, moving forward and backward through the data with the ability to stop at critical points to perform additional visualization and analysis. Replay mode allows the decoupling of detailed data collection and analysis.

In addition to a visual display of the AFM data, an nM provides a haptic interface to the data. A haptic feedback, or force-feedback, device (element (f) in Fig. 11.1) lets scientists feel the surface of the model of the sample. In addition the haptic feedback device can be linked directly to the AFM tip, allowing the scientists to directly feel and manipulate their samples by physically moving the tip against the sample. Figure 11.2 illustrates how DNA was modified by moving an AFM tip through the sample. Although samples can be modified by programming the motion of the AFM tip, this is imprecise because samples are often moved by the act of scanning and may not actually be where they appear in the visualization which is used to plan the tip movement. The haptic feedback device allows the user to precisely locate the feature of interest and directly control tip motion during modification, feeling the changes as they occur. The haptic device provides fine control over modification and enables innovative types of experiments.

The nM is a virtual reality interface to an AFM in the sense that telepresence, feeling as if you are somewhere else, is virtual reality. In this case the teleportation is over scale, not distance or time. The sample is scaled up (or the user is scaled down) by a factor of about a million to one, making the visualization of the sample under study a comfortable table-top size relative to the user. In an nM, the user is real and maintains a bird's eye view of the scaled-up sample, changing that view by repositioning the sample. The effect is that of holding the sample in your hands, turning it to change your view, and moving it closer to see more detail and further away for a better overview. Because the sample is virtual and viewed on a PC screen, scientists can point passively, but not effect changes using their real hands. Instead, they use the PC mouse and the force-feedback device (used as a 3D tracker) to control a cursor through which they control and interact with a sample. In this manner, an nM provides new ways of interacting with samples at the nanometre scale.

11.2.2 Scientific Research Using a nanoManipulator

Multidisciplinary collaborative research is being done with an nM which could not be done without the combined scientific expertise of the collaborators and could not be done without an nM. Physicists, chemists and gene therapy researchers are investigating the mechanical properties of fibrin (Guthold *et al.*, in press). Understanding these properties will advance our knowledge of the wound healing process, heart attacks and strokes. Another team is investigating the mechanical properties of DNA, the central molecule in numerous cellular processes. Understanding the mechanical properties of DNA may provide new insights into these processes. We observed these collaborations to understand how the scientists work together to do science with an nM.

When conducting research using an nM instrument, scientists typically engage in five major tasks: experimental design, sample preparation, data collection, data analysis and dissemination. Each of these tasks contains multiple subtasks that are often interwoven. For example, data analysis often begins during data collection and will continue after data collection ends, and the results of data analysis may indicate that additional data collection and/or a new experimental design is needed.

To design an experiment or set of experiments scientists plan ways to investigate a topic or question under consideration. The topic or question may develop from discussions with a colleague(s), outcomes of previous experiments, suggestions from funding agencies or organizations, and personal interests. Often questions are refined and new ones developed as an experiment or sets of experiment progress.

The goal of sample preparation is just what it says: put a small amount of the material under investigation on a substrate, e.g. a small piece of mica or graphite, so it can then be loaded into an AFM attached to an nM and examined. The materials studied with an nM are extremely small, measuring in tens of nanometres (10^{-9} m). Because of their size and because many of these materials have not been studied with an nM before, preparing them properly without damage or contamination often requires developing new sample preparation techniques.

The goal of data collection is to examine the samples, collecting data that will help characterize the material's physical properties. Types of data typically collected include measurements of particles' height, width and length; the distances between particle components; and the forces needed to move, bend or flatten particles. Other types of data collected include images that reveal structural features of the material or how features change during different stages of a process, such as DNA replication. These data are collected during an experiment by recording measurements and observations in a lab notebook (electronic or paper-based), saving (electronic) output from data analysis programs, and saving output, such as stream files, from an nM. Live data collection may take 3–24 hours.

The data are analysed and interpreted using quantitative methods found in a variety of statistical software applications and through qualitative observations and discussions with colleagues. Data analysis can be a time-consuming task that takes days, weeks or months.

Typically, many experiments are performed before the results of the analyses are disseminated. Scientists collect multiple sets of data over multiple experiments to illustrate the validity and reliability of their research. Dissemination may occur through publication of journal articles and conference papers, presentations at conferences, workshops and other research labs, and publication of patents.

11.2.3 Scenarios of Face-to-Face Scientific Collaboration

In this setting, faculty members, postdoctoral researchers and graduate students work individually and/or collaboratively on research projects. There are several AFMs, nMs and general-purpose personal computers (PCs) in their labs and they schedule access to these tools by reserving time slots on calendars posted on lab doors. The labs are typically "open" environments; more than one tool is located in a lab and any number of people can be in a lab using tools or observing others using tools. In addition, computer scientists may also be in and out of the lab implementing new versions of an nM or troubleshooting a problem with the system. New students or collaborators are taught how to use an nM through hands-on training by more experienced students, postdoctoral researchers and faculty.

All experiments are done in these labs although sample preparation and data analysis may be done in a different lab or in offices near by. An experiment may take 3-24 hours and may consist of preparing a sample(s) and loading it into an AFM; searching for samples of particular types of molecules within the sample; investigating the examples by taking height and width measurements; applying multiple data visualization techniques to illuminate different features of the sample; "feeling" the sample by controlling the movement of the AFM tip and taking force measurements; and capturing and analysing the resultant data. In addition, an experiment may include replaying a previous experiment or looking at pictures or data from a previous experiment to examine them further.

Two types of collaborative interaction were observed: two or more local scientists working together, and a local scientist working with a visiting scientist. Collaboration with visiting scientists is formalized in this setting. Part of one scientist's job is to work with visiting scientists who come to use an nM in their research. Supporting such visitors is part of the mission of the laboratory. We observed two collaborations involving visiting scientists.

In the first situation the scientist (a postdoctoral researcher) and visiting scientist (a PhD student) had previously met at a conference but had not worked together. In another situation the scientist and visiting scientist (professional scientist on sabbatical at a university) had not previously met; their supervisors arranged the collaboration. In both situations, the scientists were using an nM to investigate the physical properties of biological and polymer molecules. (This research is proprietary; thus, additional details concerning the research are omitted.) The visiting scientists had not used an nM before, and the local scientist had not worked with the visitors' molecules before. Interviews before these visits were conducted with the local scientist, and interviews after the visits were conducted with all participating scientists.

Through the observations and interviews we learned about scientists' work practices that appear to support collaboration. In particular, scientists spent time coordinating complex tasks, establishing confidence in each other's scientific skill and knowledge, focusing attention on scientific details, developing a working understanding, and creating new knowledge.

Coordinating Complex Tasks

When working in the same lab, scientists were continually looking around to see who else was in the lab, and to see what others were doing. While working together during a four-day series of experiments, two scientists routinely worked simultaneously on related tasks. As one scientist inserted a sample into an AFM, the second scientist prepared the nM for the visualization process. Both kept an eye on each other as they coordinated the steps of their joint endeavours so that they could see when each step had been completed and when it was time for each to take the next sequential action. During this period, the two scientists continually used their eyes to check what the other was doing in the lab. During a three-day series of experiments involving a different set of collaborating scientists, the local scientist watched the visiting scientist from across the room as she prepared samples for him to insert into an AFM. He timed his actions based on when he could see her coming to the termination of her task.

Building Mutual Confidence

Observations of collaborative work using the non-collaborative version of an nM appear to indicate that the process of building mutual confidence in each other's skills and abilities is one of the foundations of building a strong working collaborative relationship. Scientists reported that *watching each other work* was an integral part of developing confidence in the skills of their collaborator. For example, a scientist had not had any previous experience working with a particular collaborator. While working together in the lab, the scientist often chose to stand close to the visiting scientist during the sample preparation process so he could see exactly what her hands were doing. (This was observed by us and explained by the scientist during a subsequent interview.) What he saw told him that she was not only skilled at the task, but that she knew more than he did about the techniques required to prepare this type of sample. He was able to feel confident in the quality of the samples she prepared and also to learn additional sample preparation skills that he would need in subsequent experiments. By standing with her in the sample preparation area, he could watch her technique and develop a trust in her skills, a trust that could not have been as easily developed had he not been able to watch her work.

The reverse situation also occurred. Visiting scientists were able to watch a resident scientist adjust parameters in the AFM and nM software and watch him conduct an nM visualization. While both these activities theoretically could have been done at a distance, the close physical proximity of scientists permitted the visitor to be in total control of his focus of attention, to have total control of what he observed. Physical proximity permitted the visitor to rapidly alter his focus of attention without having to bother or inconvenience the collaborator who was performing an operation. Both visiting scientists reported that they grew progressively more confident in the collaboration by being able to see how skilled their collaborator was with scientific techniques and equipment.

Focusing Attention

In both sets of experiments mentioned above, two collaborators worked in very close physical proximity to each other, often speaking in such low tones that an observer less than a metre away could only hear that words were being exchanged, but could not distinguish the words. Much of the time, the two collaborators concentrated on a single image on a single computer monitor, with their heads on the same plane and not more than 50 cm apart. In this atmosphere of close proximity, they were able to focus each other's attention on particular things with little more than a glance, a slight movement of the head, a quick point with a finger, or a murmur. The ability to turn their heads to immediately gain a close, face-to-face view of the collaborator appeared particularly important for communication, especially since all verbal exchanges between the participants were in English, a second language for both scientists. Sentences that may have been difficult to understand in written form (a chatroom, for example) had meaning for the partner who received them aurally, because they arrived with an accompaniment of facial and hand gestures.

Developing a Working Understanding

Artefacts were also used to gain a detailed understanding of scientific concepts and processes. In two different sets of experiments, the visiting scientist continually used a lab notebook to instruct his collaborator about the possible sample shapes that should be observable in the nM. The resident scientist thus had an image to use as a reference when he was looking at the visualization of the samples during the experiment. In these experiments, which occurred over three to four days, the visiting scientists routinely used images and text they had brought with them to help navigate their collaborator through uncharted areas. Another scientist who uses an nM routinely uses physical models of the molecules being investigated to illustrate shapes for collaborators who have never previously thought about the molecule's physical attributes. The model, when passed around and felt with hands and studied with eyes, provided a tactile and visual embodiment of the molecule for people who might only have considered it in intellectual or conceptual terms.

Creating New Knowledge

We observed collaborators, sitting side-by-side or working together in the lab, continually pull out sheets of paper to sketch out their ideas or suggestions. They also used existing artefacts such as posters and diagrams on the walls of the lab to explain their ideas. Using the poster to provide background information and their hands to describe a new situation, their hand gestures seemed to construct a new artefact, which the observer was able to see and comprehend. Again, the close proximity of the collaborators enabled the exchange of ideas, since both could see each other closely and recognize when a thought was registering or confusion was occurring.

11.2.4 Motivation for New Ways of Working

Scientists have expressed an interest in collaborating with colleagues in other disciplines using an nM. For example, scientists from chemistry, physics, gene therapy and biology have expressed a desire to collaborate using an nM to explore particles such as DNA, fibrin and adenovirus. One scientist explained:

> [an nM is] really a tool of collaboration... you don't want to spend all your time trying to do the whole thing... that's why both my big projects are collaborations with other labs. They do a lot of the biochemistry, we do a little bit of it... it's just too much to try to cover all of those bases.... There's two kinds of science – and of course there's everything in between – but there's kind of project-oriented science and instrument-oriented science or technique-oriented science.... I have a technique that I can do very cool things with and so I don't want to apply it to a single system. I'll apply it to multiple systems. And so there's usually more collaboration involved in technique-oriented science.

Benefits of such collaboration include the discovery of new knowledge, e.g. the discovery of physical properties of biological organisms and systems. One collaboration between physicists and gene therapy researchers already shows promise of such a discovery. A scientist explained:

> ...he's showed us some stuff [i.e. data from an nM] that I never imagined and that was the plasticity of the virus when they could push on it and show that it's like a marshmallow.... We had some prehistoric notion that viruses are like acorns, very tough, rigid type of particles.... A lot of viruses go through the gut, a very acid pH or

a caustic-like environment and they survive those settings. So we inherently think that if you're going to go through that kind of an environment, it [the virus] has to be [a] stainless steel resistant-like material. [The plasticity of the virus] was totally unexpected. [I] don't know if I understand it well enough, but it just makes you stop one way of thinking about things and start to consider others.

A difficulty with the existing nM instrument is that scientists must physically travel to the instrument to use it, or wait until a collaborator visits and brings still pictures and graphs of data from experiments. This introduces delays into the process of doing science and reduces spontaneity and possibilities for serendipity. It means the "plan experiment–conduct experiment–analyse data" research cycle is sequential from start to finish, with no quick iterations or backtracking between steps.

For example, Joe, Sam (Joe's graduate student) and Bill typically meet to plan an experiment or set of experiments. Bill is a gene therapy researcher who does not have an nM in his lab; Joe and Sam are physicists who have an nM in their lab. After planning the experiments collaboratively, Sam typically conducts the experiments, collects data and does preliminary data analysis. The experiment may need to be repeated several times to collect data that he believes are valid and significant. Next Sam, Bill and, perhaps, Joe meet to analyse the data together. Because Bill is from another discipline, he may question the data because it is difficult to analyse from pictures and graphs and/or because he has limited knowledge about the constraints and possibilities of an nM. Or he wants to see data that Sam did not bring or perhaps thought to collect because such data may not be meaningful or interesting from Sam's and Joe's disciplinary perspective. This cycle can take months and may need to be repeated because data of interest to one partner was not captured or because original planning decisions based on limited experience with an nM need to be revised.

As shown in other studies, even with short distances (e.g. a 15-minute walk), distance is an impediment to collaboration. For example, when discussing collaborating with colleagues whose labs and offices are 15-minute walks away, two scientists report:

> The interactions so far has been almost... almost [as if we're in] separate camps in the sense that we supply the sample and they do the analysis and then we get together and try to make sense of it. What we would like is something a little more interactive where we can manipulate the samples to some extent and then get a new set of observations and see what our manipulations have done.

> When I find something unexpected, then I tromp over there and tell them what I'm seeing. And, really it should happen more often because whenever I do, I pick up a lot of other things that I was overlooking.... I just for some reason don't get down there, one reason or another.

Thus, developing an environment that allows scientists, even when physically separated, to plan experiments, conduct experiments and analyse data at the same time, as if they were face-to-face, holds great promise for facilitating collaborative science across distances.

11.2.5 Collaborative Cognitive Work

Our empirical data suggest that scientific research is cognitive work supported by social and physical skills and activities. Throughout all steps of the scientific research process, including the collaborative research process, cognitive work emerges and plays a significant role. The major scientific research tasks – experimental design, sample preparation, data collection, data analysis and dissemination – all require cognitive skills and activities.

Physical skills and activities, such as placing particles on a surface, appear to emerge to facilitate cognitive work. That is, these skills appear to be driven or motivated by the cognitive demands of doing science. For example, placing particles on a surface is done to fulfil requirements in an experimental design, which is primarily cognitive in nature.

Social skills and activities play a role in facilitating cognitive work, especially collaborative cognitive work. Our empirical data illustrates the importance of discussions of experimental designs, interaction during data collection, and discussion of intermediate results from the scientists' perspectives. Again, many of the social skills and activities are explicitly linked to cognitive work. Of course, other social activities, such as a group going to lunch, emerged in our empirical data. These activities and associated skills appear to be implicitly linked to the cognitive work. Because of project constraints these are not explicitly addressed in our work.

Our analysis of the empirical data suggests that scientific research in this context is primarily cognitive in nature, and social and physical skills and activities are used to support the cognitive activities. We propose that it is important to discover ways in which technology can support the cognitive nature of the work explicitly, and ways in which technology can support social and physical activities that support the cognitive nature of the work. This is in comparison with other approaches, such as email, threaded discussion tools, fully immersive virtual environments with avatars and MUDs/MOOs (Multi-User Domain/MUD Object-Oriented), that primarily support social interaction in the hopes that the social interaction will support cognitive work.

11.3 Design to Support Collaborative Cognitive Work Across Distances

We designed the nM collaborative virtual environment to support collaborative cognitive work, including social and physical activities that appear to support collaborative cognitive work (see Table 11.1). That is, the majority of its features are intended to explicitly support the cognitive work. Other features support social interaction as a means to support cognitive work. Several features support multiple activities. For example, audio communication supports social interaction, cognitive work and physical activities. Each feature is described below according to the activity that we propose it primarily supports.

Table 11.1. Features to support collaborative cognitive work

Social interaction	Cognitive work	Physical activities
Scheduler	(also supports)	–
–	Shared visualization and modification of sample	–
–	Individual touching of sample	–
–	Pointer	(also supports)
–	Individual, customized visualization	–
(also supports)	Switch between private and shared modes	–
–	(also supports)	New interface design
–	–	Data tablet
Audio	(also supports)	(also supports)
(also supports)	Video (1)	(also supports)
Video (2)	–	Video (2)
–	Shared applications	–
–	Distributed, shared file system	(also supports)

11.3.1 Supporting Cognitive Work

To support collaborative cognitive work the nM CVE provides all the functionality of the non-collaborative version of an nM instrument as well as new features that allow scientists to visualize and modify samples collaboratively. These are core features of the new system that allow two scientists to conduct an experiment across distances synchronously. In particular, they enable two scientists to visually and haptically explore the surface of the sample simultaneously. Currently, passing of control between users is transparent for all parameters except microscope tip movement, where there is potential for damage to the AFM. (As technology evolves and evaluations of the system are completed, additional synchronous collaborators may be supported.)

The nM CVE can be used in shared or private mode. When a user is in private mode, all system parameters are set locally and changes are visible only to that user. In shared mode, one set of system parameters is shared by both users. Both users see the same image of the same data; when either user changes a setting, both see the results immediately. In future versions of the nM CVE we expect to be able to share only designated subsets of parameters. Then, when two scientists are in shared mode, each may individually customize their visualization. This can be useful when a scientist is colour blind or wants to independently try different colour mappings to help highlight various features of the sample.

In shared mode collaborators using the nM CVE can always see each other's pointers or cursors. The pointer plays two roles in supporting cognitive work and physical activities. First it is a pointer that indicates a scientist's focus of attention. This allows both scientists to independently and simultaneously point to different aspects of the visualization, mimicking two scientists working face-to-face and

Figure 11.3 Collaboratively placing lines to measure the density of fibrin molecules.

both pointing with their hands to the screen to draw attention to different aspects of the visualization. Second, the pointer indicates which operation mode is enabled (grab, measure, scale up, scale down). For the local scientist, the nM CVE uses the same set of operation-specific icons as in the non-collaborative system. This reduces the burden of learning a new system and negative transfer between the interface of the nM CVE and the nM instrument. The distant collaborator's cursor is always displayed as a red cone and is labelled with the name of the enabled interaction mode.

Figure 11.3 illustrates two pointers in a shared visualization. In this illustration scientists are working together to investigate and measure the density of crossings in fibrin. Density of crossings is an important structural feature that plays a role in catching red blood cells.

Data from the shared mode or space may be moved into a user's private mode or space and vice versa. The ability to dynamically switch, or toggle, between private and shared modes may prove particularly valuable to scientists with replaying an experiment (i.e. a stream file). This capability allows scientists to explore different sections of a stream file independently. In future versions of the system we will provide the capability to switch between live experiments and different stream files. This dynamic switching allows scientists to collect and analyse data in parallel, possibly reducing the overall time required to conduct experiments. In addition it gives each scientist the capability of following an independent line of reasoning or investigation periodically, and then sharing results when they believe it is appropriate.

A video camera was included and positioned to display a scientist's hands, a physical model or a paper document. As noted previously, we observed scientists using hand gestures and/or using physical artefacts such as modelling clay and paper models to explain scientific concepts and processes. To facilitate this behaviour, a flexible gooseneck camera that scientists can use to show hand gestures and physical models was selected.

An additional feature to support cognitive work in the nM CVE is a shared application capability. In addition to investigating a sample through its visualization, scientists need to document what they see and analyse the data using a variety of statistical methods. To support these activities, shared application software will allow scientists to share control of data analysis software and text editing software. The nM CVE also makes use of the computer system's distributed shared file capability to allow scientists to save their output for later use either individually or collaboratively. The distributed shared file system eliminates the need to electronically or physically transfer files or data among collaborators.

11.3.2 Supporting Social Interaction

Several components of the nM CVE were designed to support social interaction. A scheduler, or scheduling tool, supports social interaction including coordination or scheduling of cognitive work by enabling scientists to reserve access to nM CVEs across distances and to communicate with others about the experiments they have scheduled. Previously scientists typically did this via a "sign-up sheet" posted on the lab door. Even without distributive access, scientists reported that this system was problematic because if they want to change their plans or have questions about the schedule while away from the lab, they have to contact someone physically at the lab who is willing to modify or check the sign-up sheet for them. When working from different locations these problems will be exacerbated. Thus we designed a Web-based scheduler that allows scientists to reserve and check the usage of nM CVEs.

Audio communication was selected to support social interaction among scientists, including coordination of tasks, discussion of data and data analysis, and interpersonal interaction. Verbal interpersonal interaction can be the "oil that keeps the motor running smoothly" when people work together. When using an nM, scientists' hands are usually busy at the PC keyboards, mouse or haptic device; a chat room or MUD/MOO that requires scientists to type to communicate does not appear feasible. Thus a speakerphone with optional untethered headsets was selected to facilitate audio communication. We chose the standard telephone over network-based audio solutions for reasons of quality and simplicity.

To further support social interaction (and coordination of physical activities) a second video camera that provides a facial and/or view of a partner's workspace was selected. We chose to provide a live video image of the remote collaborator rather than an avatar or graphical icon so that the nM CVE would, as realistically as possible with commercial PC-based products, mimic collaborators sitting side-by-side in a real laboratory. The details (expressions, hand movements) are important and, today, video images communicate those details faster and more faithfully than any other state of the art solution, including avatars. The video is displayed on a separate PC monitor.

11.3.3 Supporting Physical Activities

Physical activities such as manipulating the human–computer interface were addressed by a complete redesign of the software controls for the virtual environment (i.e. (e) in Fig. 11.1). The redesign will, ideally, support cognitive work by reducing the cognitive skills and attention required to set parameters in the system. A graphics tablet was added to reduce the physical skills needed when drawing a diagram electronically. Often individuals find using a mouse to draw figures difficult; a pen and touch-sensitive tablet can be easier to use than a mouse. However, we will not eliminate the option of drawing with a mouse or on paper and subsequently displaying the diagram via video. Other physical activities such as those occurring in sample preparation were not addressed due to resource constraints.

11.3.4 nanoManipulator Collaborative Virtual Environment Implementation

Figure 11.4 illustrates the new nM CVE system that has been implemented based on the design recommendations discussed above. The system includes (a) enhanced nM, as described earlier, with a new user interface that supports single investigator and collaborative experiments; (b) a haptic feedback device that allows both collaborators to feel and modify a sample whether the sample is in a remote or local AFM; (c) two cameras that can be adjusted to capture local documents, facial expressions, gestures or wider views of the environment – scientists can select which camera is

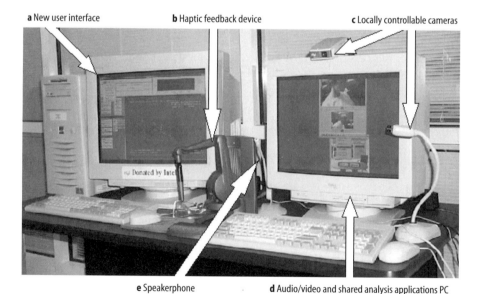

Figure 11.4 The collaborative nM environment.

Table 11.2. Representation of collaborators and samples in the collaborative nM

Collaborator	Sample
Pointer	Visualization of sample
Video (1)	Touch of sample
Video (2)	Modification of sample
Audio	–

active; (d) a PC that provides videoconferencing and shared application capabilities; and (e) a speakerphone with optional non-tethered headsets. A graphics tablet to support drawing and labelling captured images is also included in the system but is slightly out of the camera view in Fig. 11.4.

Collaborative virtual environments typically incorporate a sense of inhabiting a shared space. In the nM CVE, the shared space is a shared virtual laboratory space that includes a specialized scientific instrument and other tools used to do science. If the nM CVE successfully creates a shared space, the scientists will have a sense of working face-to-face.

The system uses a combination of pointers, video and audio to bring virtual representations of the collaborators into the shared virtual laboratory space (see Table 11.2) An important component of the virtual lab space is the 3D rendering of the surface of the sample via an nM instrument. Collaborating scientists can simultaneously "inhabit" or view and control this shared virtual space. In this space the size of the sample has been scaled up by a factor of one million, and scientists are accustomed to looking at the sample as if it were big enough to hold in their hands. When scientists collaborate face-to-face, they use the pointer or their fingers to indicate their focus of attention. We mimicked this in our collaborative system by representing the other person as a readily identifiable pointer, about the scale of a finger, rather than as a more complex avatar. The pointer displays the location or focus of the scientist, perhaps with more precision than an avatar can. It also provides additional information, i.e. information about the current function that the other person is executing. This information helps increase a scientist's awareness and knowledge about pending and perhaps current modifications to the shared space. The pointer's graphical representation of the remote collaborator ("pointer as avatar") is augmented by audio and video communications that support social interaction and provide a view of physical activities.

We also provide a mechanism by which scientists may individually customize their point of view and/or individually explore other spaces (e.g. a previously recorded experiment). At any point scientists can select their partner's point of view and location in space and begin to work or act in that space.

An open issue is whether the representation of a collaborator via a combination of pointers, shared actions and audio and voice communication is sufficient to support collaboration during scientific experiments across distances.

11.4 Design Verification and Refinement: Guidance from Social Awareness Literature

To perform an initial *gedanken* verification of our design and to refine and add details to our initial design we utilized social awareness research. Tollmar *et al.*, (1996) define social awareness as the awareness of the social situation of the collaborator. Repeated observations of scientists at work, coupled with the articulated experience of scientists as revealed through interviews, demonstrate that they rely strongly on social awareness when conducting scientific experiments. It is an integral component of collaboration, including coordinating complex tasks, establishing mutual confidence, focusing attention on scientific details, developing a working understanding and creating new knowledge. When people work together in a single locale, they are quite readily aware of the social situation, including their collaborators. When collaborating across distances, the physical nature of many of the social cues (sense of movement, catching sight of collaborators in peripheral vision, sense of smell, feelings of physical co-presence) may be absent and social awareness is heavily dependent on the ability of communicative collaborative tools to convey a sense of social awareness across distance. Thus we used previous research in social awareness to help guide the detailed design of the nM CVE.

When collaborators separated by distance experience high degrees of social awareness across that distance, they appear to approach a level of presence akin to that experienced in virtual reality situations. Witmer and Singer (1998) claimed that a number of factors contribute to a sense of presence in virtual reality. These factors include *control factors* (degree of control, immediacy of control, anticipation, mode of control and physical environment modifiability); *sensory factors* (modality, environmental richness, multimodal presentation, consistency of multimodal presentation, degree of movement and active search); and *distraction factors* (isolation and selective attention). We propose that these factors also contribute to enhancing levels of social awareness in collaborative virtual environments, and examined these factors in the context of our design.

In analysing these factors and their implications for our design context we found that several factors reinforced some initial design decisions and others suggested new features. For example, control factors, such as degree of control and anticipation, suggest that the more control collaborators have over their local and remote environments, the greater their awareness. These factors reinforced our design decision to support local and remote control of the AFM and visualization of the sample in the AFM. They also suggest that providing a wide-angle or bird's-eye view of a remote environment may help collaborators anticipate actions in a remote environment. This feature has not been implemented due to resource constraints.

Sensory factors, such as environmental richness and modality, suggest that providing greater amounts of detail about the remote environment using multiple modalities will increase awareness. These factors re-enforced the design decision to provide desktop audio and video capabilities that show facial expressions, gestures and local objects to enrich each collaborator's awareness of the remote environment. They also suggest that a "picture in a picture" feature that allows a scientist to view a collaborator's remote screen while still viewing their local screen may enhance awareness of the remote environment. This capability is currently difficult to implement because it requires very large amounts of data to be transmitted and processed with minimal lag time; it is left as a possible future enhancement.

Analysis of the distraction factors, selective attention and isolation, also reinforced design decisions and suggested new features. Selective attention proposes that a collaborator's willingness to ignore stimuli from the local environment should enhance his or her awareness of the remote environment. A method to focus attention is through pointing. We observed scientists pointing to computer screens with their pointer, mouse, finger, pens etc. to call a collaborator's attention to specific data. This reinforced the decision to make a scientist's pointer viewable by the remote collaborator and to indicate what function the scientist is currently performing. This enables each individual to point to data displayed in a visualization and visually indicate what function they are performing. The distraction factor, isolation, suggests that devices that isolate collaborators from their local environment would enhance their awareness of the remote environment. An example is the use of headphones to reduce ambient noise in the local environment so that concentration may be focused on shared interactions between collaborators. Based on this, we decided to provide collaborators with the option of using telephone headsets to communicate.

Surprisingly, the control, sensory and distraction factors do not suggest that avatars would increase a collaborator's sense of awareness in the shared environment. For example, avatars of one or both collaborators will not in themselves increase either collaborator's control of the remote environment. However, in the nM CVE the video and audio presentation of a collaborator, which may be thought of as an avatar, increases the sensory modality of the information presented when compared with no avatar or other graphical representations. The audio–video avatar was chosen primarily because it is computationally difficult to provide a virtual avatar that adequately mimics a collaborator's dynamic facial expression or even a collaborator's pointing finger. An avatar which is unrealistic in either appearance or behaviour may be a distraction, failing to provide useful information and pulling a collaborator's focus of attention away from their work or task.

The results of analysing the implications of control, sensory and distraction factors were discussed with scientists in participatory design meeting formats (as discussed in Kensing *et al.* (1998) and Mumford (1995)) and revised to incorporate their perspective and suggestions. In every design there are trade-offs between costs, time and benefits. The features that will not initially be supported may be reconsidered as technology needed to support these features decreases in price and increases in functionality or when data clearly indicates the importance of these features.

11.5 Evaluation

Three types of evaluation for the nM CVE are under way: usability, experimental and longitudinal studies. These studies strive to evaluate multiple aspects of an nM collaboration system including the usability of its features in task performance, its impact on scientific experiments and its impact on the process of science over time. These evaluations were developed to improve the design of our collaborative system, and to provide data to help inform NIH policy regarding distributive collaborative access to scientific instruments.

Usability evaluation includes asking users and representative users to perform tasks using the system, observing the human–computer interaction to see what appears to work and what needs to be improved, and soliciting feedback from the study participants concerning their perspective about what works and what needs to be improved. Even when performed by a small number of users, this method can help to identify strengths and weaknesses in a design (Easton and Olphert, 1996; Neilsen, 1989). Working with scientists we developed two sets of tasks that reflect the tasks that scientists perform during experiments. We recruited scientists and university students in a variety of departments to perform the tasks and evaluate the system. During these sessions we discovered several "bugs" in the system and the study participants made specific recommendations concerning the interface, user manuals and system in general. For example, study participants commented on the names of menu items, inconsistencies between the user manual and the interface, inconsistencies in the way menu boxes worked etc. We incorporated their feedback to improve the system.

In the *experimental evaluation* we will compare and contrast the process of conducting scientific experiments across distances and face-to-face using a repeated measures factorial experiment design. In the evaluation study partici- pants will work together on two different experiments that investigate physical properties of fibrin (the protein involved in the wound healing process, heart attacks and strokes). In groups of two they will work face-to-face to do an experi- ment and they will work in separate locations to do another experiment. Both times they will have access to an nM CVE as described above. The two experiments were developed in collaboration with scientists who are experts in using an nM and the relevant science. Each experiment takes two to three hours to perform and consists of a variety of tasks typical of natural science experiments using an nM, including generating lab notes that contain pictures and graphs of the data and explanations of the data.

We plan to collect multiple types of evaluation data, including a pre-survey that asks participants about their previous science and computer experience and their preferences for collaborative work (Owens and Straton, 1980); video and audio tapes of participants and the computer screens during the natural science experi- ments; computer logs; lab notes created by the participants; post-experiment surveys; and post-experiment interviews (one after each experiment). The post- experiment survey is based on Rogers' diffusion of innovation theory (Rogers, 1995). Rogers proposes five attributes that influence the adoption of innovations by individuals. These attributes are relative advantage, observability, trailability, complexity and compatibility. Numerous studies have validated the importance of these attributes (e.g. Tornatzky and Klein, 1982; Mackie and Wylie, 1988) and survey questions that measure these attributes have been developed (Ghani *et al.*, 1991; Chidambarram and Jones, 1993; Dennis, 1996; Dennis and Kinney, 1998;

Green and Taber, 1980; Gowan and Downs, 1994). Our post-experiment survey is a synthesis of these questions with the goal of better understanding the potential (or lack thereof) for adoption of the technology by scientists. The post-experiment interview asks about critical incidents (Flanagan, 1954) during the experiment from each participant's perspective and participants' perceptions of the technology and the role it plays. The goal of the interviews is to increase our understanding of participants' perceptions, including their explanation of things that occur during the natural science experiments.

Using multiple types of data, and data collection instruments and techniques that have been documented as reliable, will, ideally, increase the validity and reliability of our results. In pilot tests of the evaluation experiment, several participants who had not worked together previously reported they preferred working in separate locations because they did not have to focus on interpersonal interactions to the same extent as when working face-to-face. We look forward to further data collection and analysis.

The *longitudinal evaluation* will investigate the impact that an nM CVE has on the collaborative scientific process as it occurs across distances and over time in field settings. We plan to interview and observe scientists, including physicists, chemists, biologists and gene therapy researchers, as they collaborate over several months to a year. We conducted interviews last year as some scientists were just beginning to collaborate across distances or think about collaborating across distances. During these interviews we learned about scientists' previous experiences with collaboration, their current work and expectations with respect to an nM CVE. We will compare these expectations to activities and perceptions as an nM CVE is installed in the scientists' labs.

11.6 Conclusion

Using technology to support collaborative scientific research that utilizes specialized scientific instrumentation such as an nM across distances is an emerging area of research. The results may influence funding policies and the process of scientific research in the years to come.

We began this research with an ethnographic study to develop an understanding of the scientific research process, current collaborative work practices, the role of an nM as a scientific instrument, scientists' motivation for multidisciplinary collaboration across distances, and scientists' expectations regarding technology to support scientific collaborations across distances.

This understanding suggests that collaborative scientific research in the nM context is cognitive work that is supported by social interaction and physical skills and tasks. That is, it is collaborative cognitive work that is enhanced by social interaction and specialized physical skills and tasks in addition to cognitive skills and tasks. Thus our design focuses on supporting cognitive work and the social and physical activities that support the cognitive work. This is in comparison with other approaches, such as email, threaded discussion tools, fully immersive virtual environments with avatars and MUDs/MOOs (Churchill and Bly, 1999), that primarily support social interaction in the hopes that the social interaction will support cognitive work. Our approach is specific to the nM scientific research context, while these other approaches are more general and applicable broadly. However, we hope results from the evaluation of the nM CVE will be generally applicable in other contexts.

The design was further guided by a synthesis of social awareness literature. Control, sensory and distraction factors that appear to contribute to social awareness in virtual environments were analysed to discover improvements to our design and confirmation of initial design decisions.

Collaborative virtual environments should evoke in the collaborators a sense of being in a shared space. Our nM CVE brings geographically distributed scientists together into a shared virtual laboratory that is modelled on a real laboratory environment. The shared virtual laboratory includes shared control of an nM instrument, the ability to dynamically switch between shared and private mode or spaces, audio communications, videoconferencing that provides views of hand gestures and other physical objects that scientists use during experiments in addition to facial views of collaborators; and shared access to data analysis tools and other applications that are used during the scientific process.

In the strictest sense, the shared space in an nM CVE is the surface of the sample as rendered in a 3D visualization and the ability of both collaborators to touch and modify this surface. Collaborating scientists can simultaneously "inhabit" or view and control that surface. Each scientist is uniquely represented as a pointer, about the size and shape of a scientist's finger. This pointer displays the location or focus of the scientist and their current action. It mimics scientists working side-by-side and physically pointing to a visualization. It further provides informational cues regarding a collaborator's actions and changes to the surface. Scientists easily obtain this type of information in face-to-face situations when they sit together in front of an nM instrument and observe the shape of the single pointer. We propose that the pointers in the collaborative virtual environment need to provide these same informational cues in a way that is integrated with the visualization of the surface and does not distract a scientist's focus and concentration on details about the surface that they are investigating.

To evaluate the nM CVE, including its impact on scientific experiments and its impact on the process of science over time, three types of evaluation study are under way. These studies include usability, experimental and longitudinal field studies. Usability testing has been completed, the experimental study is under way, and the system is currently being installed in scientists' labs. While our experimental and longitudinal evaluation studies are only beginning, initial data indicate that the system may affect the process of conducting experiments using the nM and the process of science.

Participants in the experimental study demonstrate several different work strategies while collaborating across distances. Sometimes participants take advantage of the ability to switch between private and shared modes and follow a "divide and conquer" work strategy. That is, participants divide tasks into subtasks and then distribute responsibility for those subtasks that can be done in parallel. They perform the subtasks working in a private mode and then share the results. This mirrors how participants work in other environments. As a participant explained:

> I'm a coordinator for... a program in [a dorm on campus] and I'm in a lot of leadership positions. Usually the best way to get things done if there's multiple tasks that work best with only a few people doing it.... So the best way... [is] to divide and conquer – divide it up and say "I'll do this part and you do that part".... That way it takes us half the time.

At other times, participants explicitly go into a shared mode to learn from their partner how to perform a task or to copy results from their partner. One participant told us:

> I went into the shared view and I watched him [manipulate and tilt the surface.] And then I couldn't quite get that angle [myself] so I copied [his results] back into my personal [private state] to work on it there.

Initial data appear to indicate that the system supports participants' work style preferences and allows them to creatively build on each other's strengths and knowledge. For example, the divide and conquer strategy is not as easily implemented when working face-to-face. As more data is collected, additional work strategies that affect the process of conducting scientific experiments may emerge.

For example, scientists indicated that they expected that the system might change the way they collaborate and the nature of distributive, collaborative research. Scientists reported that currently when collaborating across distances, there are many peaks and valleys during the process, and unfortunately often more valleys than peaks. That is, there are long periods of inactivity (valleys) and then shorter periods of high activity (peaks.) Collaborators often wait to share data and research outcomes until they are certain of the results. This limits the spontaneity of the research process, including a partner's ability to understand what happened during an experiment, make suggestions and ask questions. Scientists envision that the new system will help facilitate frequent, persistent interaction, which may be a more effective and efficient way of conducting science. Scientists explained:

> the way I envision this working... is that we [will be able to] see what is going on [during experiments] and we could participate. This means that for us it will be a minimum effort to divert from doing something in my office or in the lab to going over to the screen and basically seeing what they were doing or asking a question or something like that.... If you're actually experiencing or have the opportunity to participate [during an experiment], you clearly add different types of insight versus when it's communicated to you [later] and you're trying to decide how was it done and what were they doing and things like that.

> I see it as a vehicle for promoting interaction.... I think that giving our investigators a way to do things in collaboration... [across distances] will just make it easier to get our people engaged and to keep them engaged.... My view is [that it will be] a facilitating device as opposed to a primary data collection device.

> I would say the project will probably take on a new life when [the system is] in place... [our work] will probably go at a faster pace.

Thus the nM collaborative virtual environment may affect the process of science. We anticipate collaborating scientists will have new ways of dynamically conducting and participating in scientific experiments using the nM collaborative virtual environment. Ideally, the scientific process will be no longer strictly limited to a "batch mode" where collaborators share results and conduct discussions in batches when they feel the results are significant enough to merit the burden of travelling to see each other or opportunistically when they happen to be in the same place at the same time.

Perhaps, in an ideal CVE, collaborating scientists would be able to interact with 3D holographic images, simulating the size, shape and location of their distant partner and the remote environment. In such an environment, local and distant collaborators would seem to be located directly in the same room with each other although they may be continents apart physically. Until such environments are available, we believe scientists can benefit from technology that supports the discovery, sharing, use, creation and dissemination of information in the scientific research context by providing distributed access to a scientific instrument, and features that support the collaborative cognitive work process and the social and physical activities that support the cognitive work process.

Acknowledgements

Our thanks to the participating scientists who currently use or plan to use the nanoManipulator; to the team who have and continue to build the nanoManipulator, including Frederick P. Brooks, Jr, Martin Guthold, Aron Helser, Tom Hudson, Kevin Jeffay, Don Smith, Richard Superfine and Russell M. Taylor II; and to Bob Losee and the anonymous reviewers who provided comments on previous versions.

The development of the nM has been funded by the NIH National Center for Research Resources, NCRR 5-P41-RR02170. The nanoManipulator project is part of the GRIP Research Resource at the University of North Carolina at Chapel Hill.

Chapter 12

Tele-Immersive Collaboration in the CAVE Research Network

Andrew Johnson and Jason Leigh

In this chapter we will discuss our work to enable effective collaboration between remote participants within immersive virtual reality environments. We will discuss several of the environments we have created, the lessons we have learned and the issues that are driving our current research. Our focus is on high-quality collaboration among a handful of participants connected by high-speed, high-bandwidth national and international networks in areas such as scientific visualization, education, and design. Sharing these virtual environments with your remote collaborators as well as the topic of your collaboration may be better than collaborating with them in person, as you can now collaborate while standing inside your data, sharing the context of your discussions.

12.1 Introduction

In 1992 the Electronic Visualization Laboratory (EVL) developed the CAVE. Now, in 2000, with more than 200 CAVE and related projection-based VR environments around the world, there is a community that is eager to collaborate. The CAVE™ Research Network (CAVERN) is an international alliance of research and industrial institutions equipped with CAVEs, ImmersaDesks™, and high-performance computing resources, interconnected by high-speed networks. This high-end visualization hardware, combined with high-bandwidth networks allows us to explore new research problems and applications of this collaborative technology without being hindered by the limits of the existing Internet.

The CAVE (Cruz-Neira *et al.*, 1993) is a virtual reality (VR) system where the display is a 10 foot cubic room that is rear-projected with stereoscopic images, creating the illusion that 3D objects appear to coexist with the user in the room. A user dons a pair of lightweight liquid crystal shutter glasses to resolve the stereoscopic imagery, and holds a three-button "wand" for three-dimensional interaction with the virtual environment. An electromagnetic tracking system attached to the shutter glasses and the wand allows the CAVE to determine the location and orientation of the user's head and hand at any given moment in time. This information is used to instruct the Silicon Graphics Onyx that drives the CAVE to render the imagery from the point of view of the viewer. This way, the user can physically walk around an object that appears to exist in 3D in the middle of the CAVE. Viewers who want to look behind a virtual object walk around to the back. If they want to look under an object in the CAVE, they crouch down and physically look under the virtual object. The wand contains three buttons and a joystick that can be programmed for different features depending on the application. Typically the joystick is used to navigate through environments that are larger than the CAVE itself, such as architectural walk-throughs. The buttons can be used to change modes, or bring up menus in the CAVE, or to "grab" a virtual object. Speakers are mounted at the top corners of the CAVE structure to provide environmental sounds from the virtual environment and audio from the remote participants. CAVEs and CAVE-like devices are currently in use in universities, research labs, design centres such as General Motors and Caterpillar, and museums such as Ars Electronica in Austria and the Foundation for the Hellenic World in Greece.

In 1994, EVL developed the ImmersaDesk (Czernuszenko *et al.*, 1997) – a smaller, drafting-table-like system with a 6" × 4" angled screen that is also capable of displaying rear-projected stereoscopic images. Originally designed as development and testing stations for CAVE applications, the ImmersaDesk, and its successor the ImmersaDesk2, quickly found a place as immersive display devices in research laboratories and as a convenient way to "take VR on the road" to conventions for presentations. Whereas the CAVE is very well suited for providing panoramic views of a scene (particularly useful for walking through architectural spaces), the ImmersaDesk is better suited for displaying images that fit on a desktop (for example, CAD models).

The CAVE and the ImmersaDesk can run the same VR applications, providing their users with different views of the same virtual worlds. These applications are typically written in C or C++ using OpenGL or SGI Performer to render the computer graphics and the CAVE library to deal with interfacing with the VR hardware. The CAVE library has traditionally been run on SGI computers, but a Linux version is now available and a Windows NT version is under development that will take advantage of the new generation of fast personal computers and broaden the accessibility to these virtual worlds. The CAVE and ImmersaDesk are shown in Fig. 12.1.

Figure 12.1 The CAVE and ImmersaDesk. The left image shows three people in the CAVE. All three wear shutter glasses to see the virtual world in stereo, but only one has a tracked pair of glasses and carries the wand. The right image shows a single user sitting in front of the ImmersaDesk wearing the same tracked glasses and carrying the same wand as in the CAVE. The CAVE and ImmersaDesk users can interact with the same virtual worlds from different perspectives.

It is common to have several people standing in the CAVE or in front of the ImmersaDesk at the same time. While only one person has the correct stereo viewpoint and the ability to interact with the environment, the other viewers can still see the virtual world in 3D. We have found that the ability to talk with co-workers who are standing next to you is very important, and since the CAVE and the ImmersaDesk do not isolate the user from the real world, it is convenient to have these interactions. Our current work focuses on tele-immersion – making remote collaboration just as easy, and in fact *better* than standing next to your collaborator, because now each user can stand within the shared virtual environment seeing a view of that environment that is customized to their interests and experience.

12.2 Tele-Immersion

Tele-immersion connects users of high-end VR equipment, such as CAVEs and ImmersaDesks, together over high-speed, high-bandwidth networks. The focus of tele-immersion is supporting high-quality interaction between small groups of participants involved in design, training, education, scientific visualization or computational steering. The ultimate goal of tele-immersion is not to reproduce a face-to-face meeting in every detail, but to provide the "next generation" interface for collaborators, worldwide, to work together in a virtual environment that is seamlessly enhanced by computation and access to large databases. While the goal of audio and video teleconferencing is to allow distributed participants to interact as though they are in the same physical location, tele-immersion allows them to interact as though they are the same immersive virtual environment. In this way they can interact with each other and the objects in their shared environment.

This shared environment may be the design of a new car, a visualization of climatological data, or other three-dimensional environments that do not physically exist, or cannot be physically visited. The participants are not talking about a thunderstorm, they are standing inside it; they are not looking at a scale model of a new car design, they are standing inside the full-size engine block. We believe that by transmitting gestures as well as audio and video between the collaborators, these shared virtual environments give their users a greater sense of presence in the shared space than other collaborative mediums. By encouraging collaboration and conversation within the data, these environments may become the preferred place to work and interact even if more traditional face-to-face meetings are possible. However, tele-immersion is not going to replace email, phone calls or existing teleconferencing systems. They each have their strengths and uses. Just as word processing documents, spreadsheets and whiteboards are shared across the Internet to put discussions into their appropriate context, sharing a virtual space with your collaborators, as well as the 3D design being considered or the simulation being visualized, puts these discussions into their appropriate context.

A typical tele-immersive space will be a persistent virtual environment maintained by a computer simulation that is constantly left running. The space exists and evolves over time. Users enter the space to check on the state of the simulated world, discuss the current situation with other collaborators in the space, make adjustments to the simulation, or leave messages for collaborators who are currently asleep on the far side of the planet. For example, in a computational steering application, a supercomputer may be running a very large simulation that takes several days to complete. At regular intervals the supercomputer produces a 3D snapshot of the current data, perhaps a visualization of cosmic strings. A scientist can then step into the CAVE and look at the 3D data that has been produced to see if the simulation is progressing correctly, or whether the simulation needs to be tuned to focus on particular details, rather than waiting for the simulation to complete.

Presence in the virtual world is typically maintained using an avatar, or a computer-generated representation of a person. These avatars may be as simple as a pointer that depicts the position and orientation of the wand in the virtual world. However, having representations of the physical bodies of the collaborators can be very helpful in aiding conversation and understanding in the virtual space, as you can see where your collaborators are and what they are looking at or pointing at. Tracking the user's head and hand position and orientation allows the computer to draw computer-generated characters representing each of the remote collaborators. These articulated characters move along with the remote user, and are able to transmit a certain amount of body language such as pointing at objects in the scene, and the nodding or tilting of the head. They are very useful in task-oriented situations, but do not work as well for negotiation. Seeing high-quality live video of a person's face can improve negotiation. Video avatars – full-motion, full-body video of each user – allow very realistic looking collaborators in the space, which improves recognition but requires much higher network bandwidth and careful setup to achieve high quality. Figure 12.2 shows a user interacting with an articulated avatar in the CAVE and a user interacting with a video avatar at the ImmersaDesk2.

In light of the complex interaction of computer graphics, networking, databases and human factors involved in tele-immersion, developing these applications can be a daunting task. To address this issue, EVL has been developing CAVERNsoft – a

Figure 12.2 Remote participants in tele-immersive sessions can be seen in the shared virtual space in several ways. The user on the left is interacting with the articulated computer-generated avatar of a remote participant in the CAVE. The user on the right is interacting with the live video avatar of a remote participant on the ImmersaDesk2.

Figure 12.3 CALVIN and NICE. The left image shows the CALVIN design space with the mortal working within the scene and the deity towering overhead. The right image shows Eddie interacting with Jim, depicted as an avatar, in the NICE garden.

software infrastructure that supports the rapid creation of new tele-immersive applications and eases the retrofitting of previously non-collaborative VR applications with tele-immersive capabilities. Software frameworks for collaborative virtual environments have been under development for some time by several research groups (Kessler *et al.*, 1998). Their focus, however, has been largely based on supporting existing low-bandwidth Internet infrastructures or massive connectivity involving thousands of participants at the same time (as in military simulations or Internet-based computer games). Our focus on the use of VR for manufacturing, scientific and information visualization has had a different set of requirements. We are building systems for small working groups (typically no more than seven collaborators at a time) but with large data distribution requirements. This is motivated by the need for high-fidelity audio and video communications, and the sharing of large engineering and scientific data stores that are connected over high-speed nationwide (vBNS – very high-speed Backbone Network Service – and MREN – Metropolitan Research and Education Network) and worldwide (STAR TAP, TransPAC, EUROLINK) networks.

The CAVERNsoft framework was developed based primarily on our experiences in creating two tele-immersive applications, CALVIN and NICE, in 1995 and 1996 respectively, which are shown in Fig. 12.3 and described next.

12.2.1 CALVIN

CALVIN (Collaborative Architectural Layout Via Immersive Navigation) (Leigh *et al.*, 1996) was a collaborative virtual environment that allowed multiple users to synchronously and asynchronously experiment with architectural room layout designs in the CAVE. Participants were able to move, rotate and scale architectural design pieces such as walls and furniture. Participants could work as either "mortals" who see the world life-sized (classically known as an "inside-out" view), or as "deities" ("outside-in" view), who see the world as if it were a miniature model. Deities, by virtue of their enlarged size relative to the environment, towered above the scene and were better at performing gross manipulations on objects. Mortals, on the other hand, were at the same scale as the environment, and were hence better able to perform fine manipulations and see how the layout felt from the perspective of someone walking through it. The roles of "mortal" and "deity" were not fixed. Users could decide to change their role, and their size, at any time.

The avatars for the mortals and deities in CALVIN were human-shaped, but with minimal detail and exaggerated features. Our main inspiration for them was the Muppets. Kermit the Frog is not very detailed or realistic looking, but he seems quite alive through his motions and his actions and reactions. We wanted to try emphasizing realistic motion over realistic appearance and use the exaggerated features of these articulated avatars to make those motions easier to see. For verbal communication, ambient microphones at each participating site were connected through a telephone conference call. At the time (late 1995), the networks were not fast enough to stream multi-participant high-quality audio reliably, and the conference calls gave us high-quality audio with multiple participants at very high reliability. If only two sites were collaborating, the participants could also connect over an ATM network, enabling them to bring up a window in the virtual space to see live video of the other participant. This allowed the collaborators to see each other face-to-face and aided in negotiation.

Asynchronous access to the current design allowed users to enter the space whenever inspiration struck them, rather than requiring them to wait to schedule formal meetings with their collaborators. Participants were able to work on their own, and save different versions of the design as the collaboration progressed. They could then hold a collaborative session and discuss either the current design or any of the previous designs in a collaborative session.

12.2.2 NICE

When the CALVIN project ended, we were still very intrigued by this idea of asynchronous collaboration and heterogeneous views, and wanted to investigate them further in other application areas. The NICE (Narrative Immersive Constructionist/Collaborative Environments) project was a collaborative environment in the form of a virtual island for young children (Roussos *et al.*, 1999). In the centre of this island the children could tend a virtual garden. The children, represented by articulated avatars, could collaboratively plant, grow and pick vegetables and flowers. They needed to ensure that the plants had sufficient water, sunlight and space to grow, and kept a look out for hungry animals which might sneak in and eat the plants. The idea was to help teach children simple concepts about plant growth, though the application turned out to be much more successful as a social space and a testbed for tele-immersion than as an educational space.

With a new generation of graphics computers available, the avatars in NICE became more sophisticated than those in CALVIN, though our emphasis was still on realistic motion more than realistic features. In NICE we also included avatars that were clearly non-human. Participants could be birds or bunny-rabbits or bees. Since the world is virtual, it can be rather limiting always to be represented as a humanoid avatar, and there may be advantages to looking like something else. In NICE we allowed adults to share the virtual space with the children without appearing as obvious adult authority figures. Instead of having the avatar of a man or a woman, the adult could appear as a friendly owl. Continuing with our interest in heterogeneous perspectives, the children in NICE could shrink down to the size of a mouse and walk under the garden to see the root system. This also allowed a full-size child to pick up one of the shrunken kids and carry them around. Using the same audio connection as CALVIN, the children could talk to each other using ambient microphones connected through a conference call.

In CALVIN the virtual world only changed when one of the users made a change. In NICE we wanted a more sophisticated world that could evolve on its own, even when all the participants had left the environment and the virtual display devices had been switched off. Unlike CALVIN, where the server that maintained the state of the virtual world was started before each session, NICE's virtual environment was, and still is, persistent; the server remains running. The plants in the garden on the island keep growing, and the autonomous creatures that inhabit the island remain active. The current garden has been growing since spring of 1996. Taking the VR equipment and these worlds to various conferences like SIGGRAPH and Supercomputing made us acutely aware of the issues involved in connecting to these shared worlds conveniently. Leaving a server running at a constant location made it easy to go on the road and connect back to the server at home. This also made it easier to add new collaborators, since we could send the NICE client software to a remote site and they could just run it, knowing that the server would always be available.

Because of this flexibility, we could take NICE with us to more places and watch more people experience it. At SIGGRAPH '96, the visitors found they wanted a friendly way to greet new visitors to the space, and began using the flowers in the garden. When a new person appeared on the island, one of the older visitors would offer the new visitor a flower. At Supercomputing '97 we had 17 visitors from three continents on the island and we used the avatars to look at the speed of the network connections. We had everyone stand in a circle and we did the hokey-poky. Watching all of the users "put their right arm in, take their right arm out" etc. gave us a simple but very effective method of seeing which users had fast connections, and we still use this method today as a quick initial check of the networks.

It was not uncommon for members of the NICE team to meet each other in the virtual world before meeting in the real world on a given day, since the Electronic Visualization Laboratory is spread out over several floors. Sometimes it was easier to find members of the team in the virtual world than in the physical laboratory. Allowing easy access to the island from several remote sites meant that we would occasionally encounter other people on the island and not know who they were or where they were from. We quickly implemented avatar "nametags" to make identification easier.

Beyond, this, we also needed a convenient way to see who was currently in the virtual world without having to start up a CAVE or an ImmersaDesk. Since the

WWW is pretty ubiquitous, it was natural to monitor the NICE garden with a Web page. So just as people would set up a "Web cam" in their office, we set up a virtual Web cam to monitor our virtual world. Now that we could monitor the NICE garden from the Web, we also wanted to look at interacting with it from the Web as another form of heterogeneous perspectives. We created a 2D Java applet where the desktop user's mouse position was used to position an avatar in the 3D virtual world, and the locations of the bodies of the VR users were used to position 2D icons on the desktop. At the time Java was still too slow to make this work effectively, but we continue to work on CAVE-to-desktop collaboration.

Whereas in CALVIN we wanted to see what was possible, in NICE we wanted to see how we could improve the quality of the collaboration and expand access to the shared world.

12.3 Current Applications

Scientists, engineers and educators are interested in using tools that help them do their work more conveniently and efficiently. When we first introduce scientists to the CAVE, their typical reaction is low-key. It is often hard for them to make the intellectual jump from whatever virtual world they are experiencing to seeing how they could apply this technology in their own field. But when these same people see their own data visualized in the CAVE, then the ideas for how this can be applied come pouring out.

Current tele-immersive work is priming the pump with collaborative projects with interested domain scientists to create these tools, deploy them, evaluate them and then generalize their effectiveness. Candidate problems for tele-immersion are those that, firstly, can benefit from visualization in an immersive environment, and secondly can benefit from a collaborative solution. Several of these projects are described below and shown in Fig. 12.4. These are compelling applications, because not only do they enhance problem solving in their respective domains, but they provide real-world test cases for observing how collaborators work in these high-end visualization environments.

12.3.1 General Motors Tele-Immersive VisualEyes

General Motors has developed VisualEyes (Smith *et al.*, 2000) – an application that allows designers to import 3D CAD models into the CAVE for quick visual inspection and design reviews at 1:1 scale. This initial use of CAVE-based technology has generated considerable interest in other General Motors sites around the world, some of which are planning their own CAVE installations. This prompted General Motors to work with EVL to further extend VisualEyes to allow General Motors' trans-globally situated design and manufacturing teams to collaborate in remote design reviews. The goal is to allow designers to both synchronously and asynchronously access a design that persists and evolves over time. A typical working scenario involves a team evaluating the current design in the CAVE and then asking the designer to make

Figure 12.4 Several current tele-immersive worlds. Clockwise from top left: GM's Randy Smith sits in the driver's seat and a remote participant sits in the passenger seat evaluating a new panel layout using GM's VisualEyes; two users investigate the compression of a sponge lattice in TIDE – the Tele-Immersive Data Explorer; three remote users, represented as avatars, join the local user in exploring the mouth of the Chesapeake Bay using CAVE6D; a doctor conducts a tele-immersive training session on the structure of the inner ear using the Virtual Temporal Bone; three users explore one of the cave shrines in the Mogoa Grottos in China within the CAVE; a pair of children collaborate in the Round Earth Project – one child explores the surface of a small spherical asteroid while a second child guides the first from an orbital view – the children must integrate their two views to complete their mission. © General Motors Research and Development Center. Reproduced with permission.

modifications on a workstation using a three-dimensional modeller such as Alias. Changes in lighting and materials are then propagated automatically to the networked virtual environment, allowing all collaborating participants to see the changes simultaneously. They are then able to critique the design and suggest changes to the designer who can do so immediately at the CAD workstation.

12.3.2 CAVE6D – a Tool for Tele-Immersive Visualization of Environmental Data

CAVE5D (Wheless *et al.*, 1996) from Old Dominion University, is a configurable VR application framework supported by Vis5D, a very powerful graphics library that provides visualization techniques to display multidimensional numerical data from atmospheric, oceanographic and other similar models. In collaboration with EVL, CAVE6D emerges as an integration of CAVE5D with CAVERNsoft to produce a tele-immersive environment that allows multiple users of CAVE5D to jointly visualize, discuss and interact with data sets in the environment. Avatars possess long pointing-rays that can be used to point at features of interest in the data set while they converse. Visualization parameters, such as salinity, circulation vectors, temperature and wind velocity slices, which can be visualized by CAVE5D, have been extended in CAVE6D to allow participants to manipulate them collectively. As collaborators are able to operate these visualization tools independently they are able to effectively reduce the individual load of interpreting the data by distributing the multiple observable dimensions between them. We are currently in the process of studying the conditions under which collaborative independent or coordinated view customizations can accelerate or hinder the data interpretation process.

12.3.3 The Virtual Temporal Bone

The Virtual Temporal Bone (Mason *et al.*, 1998) is a tele-immersive educational application from the VR in Medicine Lab and EVL allowing a remotely located physician to teach medical students about the three-dimensional structure and function of the inner ear. In this environment the students and instructor may point at and rotate the ear to view it from various perspectives. They may also strip away the surrounding outer ear and the temporal bone to view the inner anatomy more clearly. Audio from their voice conference is used to modify the flapping of the eardrum to illustrate its function. This application is effective because it leverages the stereoscopic capabilities of the CAVE and ImmersaDesk system to disambiguate the spatial layout of the various structures in the inner ear – something ordinarily difficult to do on standard flat images in medical textbooks.

12.3.4 Silk Road Cave Shrines

The cave shrine project is an ongoing collaboration between historians, artists and computer scientists at Northwestern University and EVL to create a virtual cultural and artistic exhibit of the Mogoa Grottoes of Dunhuang, China. The grottoes, one of western China's ancient cultural sites, are considered the gateway to the well-known Silk Road – the East–West trade route between Asia and Europe. They consist of 492 caves with murals covering 25 000 square metres, wall fresco paintings, and more than 3000 painted sculptures. These caves were built over a period of 1000 years, from the 4th century to the 14th century. VR is important here because physical access to these caves is limited, and photographs do not accurately convey the relationships between the murals that surround the visitor. Tele-immersion will allow historians to take remote visitors on tours of the caves.

12.3.5 Tele-Immersive Learning Environments

The successor to the NICE project was the Round Earth project. While NICE was successful as a tele-immersion testbed, it was not as successful as an educational space because it did not have a focused educational goal. The Round Earth project has a very focused educational goal – using tele-immersion to help teach young children the concept of a spherical Earth (Johnson *et al.*, 1999). Two children collaborate in exploring a small spherical asteroid. One child, acting as an astronaut, explores the surface of the asteroid. The other child, acting as mission control, guides the astronaut from an orbital view that shows the spherical asteroid and the astronaut's position on its surface. VR helps situate the astronaut on the surface of the asteroid, where he or she can experience circling the globe and coming back to the same place, not falling off of the "bottom" of the asteroid, and seeing objects appear over the horizon top-first. VR gives mission control an obviously spherical world to monitor. The two children share the same virtual environment, but see it in different ways. The children experience both roles, and must integrate these two different views to complete their mission – searching for enough fuel cells on the surface to allow their stranded spaceship to leave. Through integrating these two views they learn to map from the "flat" surface of the sphere to its true spherical shape.

We typically run this application using heterogeneous VR devices, emphasizing the heterogeneous roles. In the lab, the astronaut explores the asteroid in the CAVE while mission control monitors from an ImmersaDesk. In a local elementary school, where we have set up an ImmersaDesk, the astronaut uses the ImmersaDesk while mission control uses a 19" stereo monitor.

12.4 Lessons Learned

We have learned many lessons from building, using and watching others use these virtual worlds. Several of the more interesting lessons are described below.

In all these applications a single hand (wand) and head were tracked; hence each avatar possessed a movable head, one movable hand and a body. For the most part this was sufficient, as it allows a user to see where another user is standing, looking or pointing with their tracked hand. The tracked head also conveys a certain amount of body language, from nodding yes or no to a confused tilt. These motions are also recognizable. We frequently record our tele-immersive sessions on video for later review. One day ,while reviewing one of these tapes without the audio, one of the students in the lab walked by the monitor, looked at the avatar gesturing on the screen, and said "Oh, that's Andy". While the body was different, the body language was the same.

However, having only one hand made it difficult to express concepts of size, such as "it is this big", which usually requires the use of two hands. The correspondence between the wand and the hand was not always clear to new users. Hence when users waved at each other or pointed, they often used the non-tracked hand, forgetting that the position and orientation of their other hand were not being seen by the remote users. We are currently moving towards a standard set of four trackers to allow both hands to be tracked. Ideally each of the hand trackers should be worn on the back of the palm as an obvious affordance to their function.

The avatars are also useful in alerting other users about a person's next actions. For example, the declaration: "I'm going to move this chair" combined with the visual cue of your avatar standing next to a chair and pointing at it, alerts other users that you are about to grab that chair. As in real life, we know that if we also try to grab that chair that it will be awkward. We have tended to rely on these social cues rather than a computer-based locking scheme to discourage users from trying to jointly modify a shared object.

Different avatar forms are useful in different virtual worlds. In certain situations, such as pointing at an object on the ImmersaDesk, pointers can be better than full avatar bodies, because a remote user's avatar body may block your view if you are standing close together – like in real life. For small objects, short pointers work well, but in larger spaces it helps to have a long beam allowing the users to point accurately at objects 100 feet (30 m) away. When articulated avatar bodies represent the users, each user can see what the other participants look like and often want to know what they themselves look like. In NICE we solved this problem by allowing the children to look into the sea to see their reflection.

Avatars with highly stylized bodies are much easier to differentiate within the environment but may not be appropriate for all types of user. First-time users tend to laugh the first time they meet one of the articulated avatars, as they are greeted by what appears to be a living cartoon character, but they quickly adapt once this character begins interacting with them and have no trouble treating that character as a living person. Other users desire a more "serious" representation of themselves in the virtual world. Using photographs to generate avatar heads that look like the actual user is a way to help bridge between recognition in the virtual world and the real world. However, as in educational environments such as NICE, having avatars that do not look like the actual user may be beneficial. The avatars can help to "equalize" people in the virtual world. In one session with NICE, Eddie, who was 6 years old, was collaborating with Jim, a 6' tall graduate student. Within the virtual world they were roughly the same size and had identical powers. When the virtual session was over, Jim came over to Eddie and introduced himself again, this time in person. Eddie craned his neck to look up at Jim, and it was clear that their relationship changed at that point.

For international collaborations, when English has been used as the default language, foreign speakers whose first language is not English may find it difficult to converse naturally, and hence these participants tend to be less vocal. While the tracker is able to transmit gross gestures, it is harder to spot more subtle gestures.

What is normally considered a clear nod in the real world usually amounts to a suggestion of a nod in the virtual world. Cultural differences also affect the degree to which a participant gestures. For example, Americans tend to gesture considerably while speaking, whereas the Japanese tend to gesture very little. In these situations it may be useful to include video to help mediate discussions so that the faces of the participants can be clearly seen.

Audio is the most important communication channel to maintain the shared collaborative space. If the audio deteriorates then the collaboration quickly falls apart. When multiple people are in the space it can often be difficult to tell who is speaking if the audio does not come from a particular point in space. Adding mouth movements, even with crude lip synching to the avatars, is useful to give cues about who is speaking. We previously used telephone conference calls to maintain the audio link since they are of high quality and highly scalable, and we still use this path when we collaborate over the standard Internet. When more high-bandwidth networks are available, we stream the audio over the network as well as the avatar data, giving us more control over the volume levels and position of each audio stream in the virtual space.

Collision detection is useful to maintain social comfort. People feel very uncomfortable if they accidentally walk through another person, and apologize profusely. In general, people tend to maintain an appropriate distance from other users and try to avoid violating their personal space. However, this same collision detection can be a hindrance if several people are trying to manoeuvre down a narrow hallway in the virtual world. In certain situations it is good to have real-world constraints such as gravity and collision detection, and at other times it is good to be able to turn that reality off and be able to do more than you could if this was a real space.

Some of our clients in the CAVE Research Network are familiar users of VR, and others are not. Even for those that are, their initial steps into a collaborative virtual world require a tour guide. Initially this tour guide was a person who would stand next to the new user in the CAVE or in front of the desk and show them the controls and point out the features in the virtual space. Since then we have found that it is very useful to have this tour guide give that initial tour remotely as an avatar. This draws the user into the shared virtual space and immediately starts up a dialogue between the new user and one of the users already in the space. This dialogue often deals with how to navigate around and interact with the shared environment, with the remote tour guide showing the new user around their shared space. This way the new user's attention stays focused on the virtual world, rather than their physical world.

Through a combination of actual trans-oceanic tele-immersive sessions between Chicago and Japan, Singapore, Australia and the Netherlands and controlled experiments conducted within EVL we are looking at the affect of network latency and jitter on the ability to collaborate (Park and Kenyon, 1999). Network jitter (the variability in the time it takes packets of data to arrive at their destination) has a greater effect on the quality of the collaboration than the overall latency (the time it takes packets of data to arrive at their destination.) The collaborators are able to adapt when the latency is high, as people are able to adapt to international phone calls with long delays, but find it hard to adapt when the jitter is high, as the behaviour of the system is unpredictable. These experiments suggest that latencies as high as 200 ms do not adversely affect performance. Our international collaborative sessions have typically been undertaken with latencies of less than 150 ms and acceptable jitter – so trans-oceanic tele-immersion is workable, although the speed of light is becoming a barrier when the data needs to be routed through a satellite in geosynchronous orbit.

12.5 New Challenges

Our current research is focusing on two areas of collaboration in these shared virtual worlds: asynchronous collaboration and heterogeneous views – topics that we first explored with CALVIN and NICE.

12.5.1 Asynchronous Collaboration

When the collaborators are distributed around the world, tele-immersion becomes more challenging, as this involves multiple networks, multiple time zones and multiple cultures. Because of time zone issues it may be inconvenient to schedule synchronous meetings, so asynchronous work may be the most appropriate mode for trans-oceanic tele-immersion. Asynchronous work also has the advantage that geographically distributed teams can work on the same problem around the clock, by passing the work off at the end of the day to another team who is just arriving at work in their morning. Lessons can be learned from the sharing of more traditional text and image information on remote computers through such tools as Lotus Notes, Microsoft Netmeeting, and MUDs/MOOs (Schiano and White, 1998; Bruckman and Resnick, 1995), and from the sharing graphical, audio and video data through media spaces (Bly *et al.*, 1993).

Email is a very successful tool supporting asynchronous work. However, in international collaborations there is typically a one-day turnaround time to get responses, so collaborators can easily waste days clarifying the work to be done and making instructions clear. When working in a virtual environment this is even more difficult, as it is hard to use text, speech or even 2D images alone to describe work to be done, or discoveries that have been made in a dynamic 3D environment. It is important that the messages between the distributed team members be clear, to reduce misunderstandings. In a virtual environment it is important to be able to put these messages into their appropriate context – the context of the virtual world itself.

One of the advantages of doing design or scientific visualization in an immersive environment is the ability to have geographically distributed participants sharing space with each other and the objects under discussion. This allows the participants to point at specific objects in the scene or set the parameters of the simulation to specific values to clarify what they are saying. It gives the users a common context for their discussions. Especially in international collaborations, where the language barrier can be a large hurdle, being able to gesture relative to the environment (pointing at the red box, turning your head to look at the green sphere) helps to clarify the discussion. The ability to hand off work quickly and accurately is also of great importance. A user stepping into the virtual environment needs to know what work has been done since he or she was last there, and what new work may need to be done. We are currently investigating several approaches: v-mail, virtual sticky notes and the VR-VCR.

When asynchronously working in a virtual space, email and telephone conversations are not enough to describe changes that need to be made or observations that need to be verified because the email and the telephone conversation are not in the context of the virtual space. V-mail allows a user to record themselves as an avatar talking and gesturing within the virtual space. Thus the user in the recorded v-mail appears just as they would if they were in a synchronous collaborative session. In fact, during our initial studies of the system we found that the user retrieving the v-mail would often talk back to the pre-recorded avatar (Imai *et al.*, 1999) as though they were conversing. These recordings preserve the important head and hand gestures, should help clarify the process that went into creating the artefacts in the world, and should help support orientation in the space.

Like v-mail, virtual sticky notes will help explain changes that were made or need to be made in a collaborative design environment, specify where interesting phenomena were discovered in scientific visualization environments, and give researchers an easy way of creating meta-data recordings from within the virtual space. Most computational scientists agree that a crucial part of the knowledge crystallization process (Card *et al.*, 1999) includes the creation of snapshots and annotations to track the progress of the exploration and to record discoveries (Springmeyer *et al.*, 1996). In desktop environments these annotations (meta-data – data about the data) are typically entered in text windows; however, this common mode of data entry is problematic as well as limiting in an immersive environment. Current VR displays lack the resolution to display text clearly in a virtual window. Recording and replaying audio messages has been used to try and circumvent these problems. Adding in the avatar of the person recording the message complete with their gestures allows those audio messages to be put in the proper context. We have also used the sticky notes to create pre-recorded tour guide avatars for visitors to our virtual worlds, such as the Silk Road Shrines. If there is no live expert tour guide available, the world can still introduce itself and take a user on a tour, giving information at various points of interest.

The VR-VCR allows users to record the entire VR experience for playback and analysis. Since all of the state changes to the collaborative virtual world come through the application's networking layer, we can store the time-stamped sequence of changes and play back the virtual experience as an immersive movie and experience it from with the virtual environment, watching the action unfold around us. This allows a person to see everything that they would have seen if they had been present in the immersive space at the time the recording was made. With a video recording of the collaboration, the user is limited to seeing the action from the position of the camera; here the user can walk (fly) through the space while the collaboration is under way, watching the action from whatever location seems most interesting. These recordings could also be shared tele-immersively during playback, allowing geographically distributed participants to collaboratively watch the recording of a previous collaborative session. We first recorded these VR movies while several groups of children were interacting with the NICE environment. During their sessions, we could watch their interactions with the VR hardware; later, we could replay their interactions within the virtual world. Currently we have been using simple VCR-like controls for playing back this data, but more sophisticated querying of this data is also possible, dealing with spatial relations between the users and the world and temporal relations between actions, and phonetically searching the collaborator's dialogue.

12.5.2 Heterogeneous Representations

Environments such as CALVIN, CAVE6D and the Round Earth allow and in fact *emphasize* giving each user a different view of the shared space. These heterogeneous views allow us to leverage the capabilities of a shared virtual space to allow each user to customize their view to their needs.

Collaboration can improve the overall efficiency of the data analysis process. One aspect that we are particularly interested in developing is the concept of Multiple Collaborative Representations (MCR). Individuals who are trying to solve a common problem gather (in workshops, for example) in the hope that their combined experience and expertise will contribute new perspectives and solutions to the problem. In many existing collaborative VR applications, participants typically all view and modify the same representation of the data they are viewing. It is our belief that a greater benefit will be derived if the participants are given the power to create and modify their own representations, based on their particular areas of interest and expertise (Leigh *et al.*, 1996; Smith and Mariani, 1997; Gutwin and Greenberg, 1998b; and Chapter 8 of this volume).

Recent work in providing multiple representations to enhance learning have implied that this is a non-trivial problem (Bibby and Payne, 1993; Larkin and Simon, 1987). It has been shown that students perform better in tests when they learn a concept given more than one representation than students given only a single representation do (Salzman *et al.*, 1998). However, it has also been shown that this is not necessarily always the case; another study has found that multiple representations increased the cognitive load on a learner at the expense of learning (Ainsworth *et al.*, 1997). These contradictory findings would suggest that multiple representations help rather than hinder when the benefit of the multiple representations is offset by the increase in the cognitive load incurred in interpreting these representations. This cognitive load may be lessened if the proper tools are provided to coordinate the correspondences between the representations.

We envision a potential application of multiple collaborative representations in the visualization of multidimensional datasets. Here a large number of dimensions may be partitioned across multiple users to assist in reducing the overall complexity of the content being visualized. The goal of this research is to develop tools to allow participants to coordinate their interpretations of each representation to enable a more efficient collective understanding of the data being explored.

Our testbed for this work is TIDE – the Tele-Immersive Data Explorer. TIDE is a tele-immersive application for the exploration of massive tera-scale datasets. TIDE is designed to enable the following scenario: three (or more) users – one in a CAVE, another on an ImmersaDesk and a third on a desktop workstation – are engaged in a routine data exploration enterprise within a virtual laboratory. The users are separated by hundreds of miles but appear co-located. Avatars convey position and gesture information while digital audio is streamed between the sites to allow them to speak to each other. The desktop workstation displays a data-flow model that can be used to construct the visualization that is shared between all three display devices. The participants in CAVE and ImmersaDesk can use three-dimensional tools to directly manipulate the visualization: for example a user in the CAVE may change an isosurface value in the dataset. These changes are automatically propagated to all the other visualization displays. In the meantime the ImmersaDesk user, noticing an anomaly, inserts an annotation in the dataset as a reminder to return to more closely examine the region. Closer examination of the region is achieved by instructing a remote rendering server, consisting of multiple gigabytes of memory and terabytes of disk space, to render the images in full detail as a stereoscopic animation sequence. These animations will take some time to generate, so the users continue to examine other aspects of the dataset. Eventually the rendering is complete and the remote server streams the animation to each of the visualization clients for viewing.

TIDE's current focus is on visualizing massive datasets from the Department of Energy and weather data from the National Oceanic and Atmospheric Administration. TIDE's main research foci are: to develop techniques for managing and mining massive datasets for visualization and navigation; to develop collaboration and network-aware visualization tools which can adapt to changing network conditions; to develop tools for creating three-dimensional annotations and recordings of discoveries during collaborative sessions; and to perform user studies of collaborative data exploration to evaluate the effectiveness of these tools

We are currently in the process of performing user studies to observe how users take advantage of multiple collaborative representations, and in what situations they are effective or a hindrance. These studies should also allow us to form ideas on the kinds of tools that will be needed to help participants coordinate the representations. What we have seen so far reaffirms that previous CSCW findings are applicable to tele-immersion:

- There is a need for individual pointers to allow collaborators to point at shared data items. However, these pointers can become a source of distraction and users should have the ability to toggle them on/off (Lauwers and Lantz, 1990; Tang, 1991; Stefik *et al.*, 1987b).

- It is useful to have some cue of which region of space a user is manipulating (Patterson *et al.*, 1990; Roseman and Greenberg, 1996).

- Even in a fully shared environment, participants found the need to work with localized views (Roseman and Greenberg, 1996).

- There is a frequent transition between parallel/independent and coordinated activities (Stefik *et al.*, 1987b).

- In a fully shared WYSIWIS system, frequent usage collisions will occur (Stefik *et al.*, 1987b).

- The user interface should be considered part of the visualization so that collaborators can gain greater awareness of their collective actions as they manipulate the visualization (Gutwin and Greenberg, 1998b).

In fact our work most mirrors the work of Gutwin and Greenberg (1998b), except that we are exploring these issues in the context of a fully immersive environment in which co-presence as well as computer-mediated and augmented interaction is simultaneously possible.

12.5.3 New Devices

Even with mirrors, a CAVE takes up a 30' by 20' by 15' space and requires a couple of days to set up and align. The ImmersaDesks were designed for laboratories, and take up a large amount of space in a typical office. The ImmersaDesk screen is large to present a wide field of view, but the desk structure itself is large because the rear-projection distances are significant and the desk uses a large and heavy projector. EVL's current work is focusing on desktop systems that are more suited to an office environment. Fish-tank VR using CRT monitor technology has been used for several years, but these systems typically have very small fields of view. Increasing the field of view without filling the office with equipment means an increased reliance on flat-panel display technology. Instead of leaving your office to walk over to a CAVE or an ImmersaDesk to enter a tele-immersive space, the goal is that the surface of your desk becomes a display device, the walls become display devices, and perhaps even the floor and the ceiling. In effect, your office becomes a CAVE on demand.

The CAVE, ImmersaDesk and ImmersaDesk2 are commercial products. Several companies offer well-designed, non-tracked displays for the office and showroom. Others have products similar to the CAVE and ImmersaDesk. The goal of EVL's research is not to compete with the commercial sector, but to investigate and inspire new display and tracker technologies for tele-immersion. Given that affordable, bright, wall-sized, high-resolution, borderless displays with high refresh rates and fast decay rates do not yet exist, we are prototyping these systems using available components: existing flat panel technologies, or simulating flat panel systems with rear-projection hardware. These more office-friendly systems may change the way that people interact with virtual environments, and perhaps more importantly may change the way people think about interacting with virtual environments.

12.6 Summary

Our goal is not simply to make tele-immersive work possible, but to make it convenient: convenient access to the VR hardware, convenient access to the virtual world, convenient synchronous or asynchronous access to collaborators, and tools which make it convenient to share your data tele-immersively. We believe the best way to reach this goal is to build tele-immersive environments for a variety of domains and evaluate their effectiveness, thinking not in terms of how to recreate reality, but how to leverage virtual reality to make the collaboration better than being there in person.

Acknowledgements

The virtual reality research, collaborations, and outreach programs at the Electronic Visualization Laboratory (EVL) at the University of Illinois at Chicago are made possible by major funding from the National Science Foundation (NSF), awards EIA-9802090, EIA-9871058, ANI-9980480, ANI-9730202 and ACI-9418068, and by NSF Partnerships for Advanced Computational Infrastructure (PACI) cooperative agreement ACI-9619019 to the National Computational Science Alliance. EVL also receives major funding from the US Department of Energy (DOE), awards 99ER25388 and 99ER25405, as well as support from the DOE's Accelerated Strategic Computing Initiative (ASCI) Data and Visualization Corridor program. In addition, EVL receives funding from Pacific Interface on behalf of NTT Optical Network Systems Laboratory in Japan.

The CAVE and ImmersaDesk are registered trademarks of the Board of Trustees of the University of Illinois. ImmersaDesk2 is a trademark of the Board of Trustees of the University of Illinois.

Part 6
The Emerging and Existing Cultures of CVE Communities

Chapter 13
Designing an Emergent Culture of Negotiation in Collaborative Virtual Communities: The DomeCityMOO Simulation

Elaine M. Raybourn

Virtuality need not be a prison. It can be the raft, the ladder, the transitional space, the moratorium that eventually is discarded in order to reach greater freedom. We don't have to reject life on the screen, but we don't have to treat it as an alternative life either. Like the anthropologist returning home from a foreign culture, the voyager in virtuality can return to a real world better equipped to understand its artifices. (Turkle, 1998, p. xvii)

13.1 Introduction

It is provocative, but no longer unrealistic to consider that virtuality may serve as a transitional space that allows us to explore both the rewards and consequences of communicative freedom. Explore. Experience. Learn. Reset. Repeat. To some, virtuality may be an opportunity to communicate more freely, and/or more safely explore interpersonal relationships. Collaborative Virtual Environments (CVEs) can be pro-social multi-user worlds that provide friendships, intimate relationships or business partnerships as a result of synchronous, pseudo-anonymous computer-mediated communication. Virtual environments may also foster vibrant communities that are home to a host of interesting characters. For example, many social CVEs support playful exploration of one's online identity or public persona. Today, a growing number of individuals who communicate in electronic environments experiment with gender swapping, disinhibition and role-playing a romanticized version of the self, via multi-user dimensions object-oriented (MOO). In the midst of all of this identity play, however, inhabiting a MOO or 3D CVE is still a very *real* experience. Inhabitants communicate in real time, have meaningful communication transactions, and exhibit normative behaviours or feelings that they might exhibit in real-world face-to-face settings.

Collaborative virtual environments are used in business settings (Jeffrey and McGrath, 2000; McGrath, 1998), for scientific collaboration (Van Buren *et al.*, 1995), education (Galin, 1998), entertainment (Murray, 1997), and procedural training (Mateas and Lewis, 1996). Nevertheless, an unexplored potential of CVEs remains the area of intercultural communication training. Intercultural communication is the exchange, and co-creation, of information and meanings by individuals or groups when at least one party perceives itself to be different from others. Most intercultural training today employs the use of face-to-face simulations as an experiential learning tool. Social-process simulations, or learning environments (usually role-plays) that involve human interaction and communication in pursuit of social goals, are often successful vehicles to facilitate learning about different cultures and diverse communication styles. Participants of intercultural social-process simulations practice real-world behaviours associated with competition, empathy and communication. Nevertheless, few real-time, multi-participant, computer-based social-process simulations are available today, even though synchronous computer-based environments such as text-based MOOs or 3D CVEs are capable of authentically replicating real-life (RL) experiences (Raybourn, 1997b) as well as providing non-threatening workspaces that are participant-controlled (Raybourn, 1998b).

The present chapter discusses the design of the DomeCityMOO (Raybourn, 1998a). The DomeCityMOO is an experimental intercultural social-process simulation created to allow participants to safely explore feelings of power and powerlessness while interacting with each other in a computer-based environment to co-create a better virtual world. I introduce the notion that virtuality and anonymity can be important design criteria for creating experimental simulations in CVEs that support intercultural understanding. I suggest that the act of communication is the means by which both physical and social spaces are created in a MOO. I also briefly discuss the role of culture and perception in communication, and provide the motivation for creating the DomeCityMOO.

In reviewing the design of the DomeCityMOO, I describe how negotiation, awareness of intercultural dynamics (power and identity) and collaborative behaviours can result from non-threatening interactions occurring in a "dystopian" virtual environment. On some levels, it is counter-intuitive to consider a less than utopian environment as facilitating collaboration and the negotiation of power. Nevertheless, an emergent culture of negotiation can be achieved through communication interactions that introduce role and power interdependencies and encourage participants of the simulation to co-create their virtual space together. Finally, I offer lessons learned for designers of text-based and 3D CVEs.

13.2 Communication in Virtual Spaces

13.2.1 MOO Communication as a Physical Space

Computers have become comfortable *interaction* spaces for many individuals. I believe that the communication transactions, or interactions in a text-based CVE, constitute both the physical space that is inhabited as well as the social space that is co-created. This may sound paradoxical at first, but consider the example of persistent communication in the Waterfall Glen MOO (see Chapter 14). Kolko (1996) asserts that in a MOO one negotiates the norms, values and social dimensions of the space while inhabiting the database and using the programming language to create artefacts and interact with others. Even as an inhabitant navigates through the MOO and manipulates objects or solves puzzles created by other inhabitants, s/he is communicating with others via the artefacts (objects) left in the MOO database (e.g. see Norman, 1988). Every person, place or thing in the MOO is a string of code that occupies physical space in the database. Thus the size of the database increases as more objects are created for the MOO environment or the number of inhabitants grows. Inhabitants communicate with each other by existing in, and interacting with, the objects in the database (artefacts and avatars). Establishing an individual's presence in the MOO, then, becomes a matter of occupying database space and participating in the social interaction space through one's communication.

13.2.2 Text as a Metaphor and Visual Marker for Embodied Identity

Communication in a text-based virtual reality lacks the body or a physical manifestation of the self. The importance of appearance and other non-verbal communication aspects in everyday conversation is greatly diminished. In order for a self to have spatial presence in online communication, the interlocutor must construct his or her identity and spatial presence in terms of a history of communication events and the visible electronic text. Cushman and Cahn (1985) described the self-concept as a construct that is negotiated, or co-created, *in interaction* with others. In this sense, self-concepts are not determined by *who* others think we are, but rather by *how* the presentation of the self is co-constructed and maintained by both parties in interaction. This notion of self-concept and its relationship to communication is particularly useful in describing how the text serves as an agent for the body in text-based CVEs.

For example, in the absence of physical markers such as biological sex, race, physiological and involuntary non-verbal reactions, and other general state characteristics, the individual has an extraordinary degree of control in presenting any self s/he wishes. For many participants of electronic communities, including IRCs, MOOs and 3D CVEs, communicating becomes a heightened, directed, goal-oriented activity – instead of a cursory, everyday activity that may involve unconsciously *reacting* to another's utterances. Inhabitants of CVEs use text as the *primary* medium to co-create and negotiate meaning, construct multiple selves through interaction, and achieve spatial presence.

In order for an inhabitant to have presence in the MOO, the individual *must* construct her or his persona in terms of the communication events. In addition to establishing presence by occupying space in the database, presence in the MOO is accomplished by the production of text for the purpose of social interaction. An inhabitant's spatial representation is achieved through the quality (and quantity) of her/his communication, and the frequency of the communication. Imagine yourself sitting in front of your computer communicating in real time in a text-based MOO. Your computer screen serves as a window to a world that you and your friends inhabit. As you interact with others, you see the text that you and others generate scroll before you. You become aware that the text you generate is a representation of you and your personality. You can present yourself to be funny, light-hearted, serious, enigmatic etc. However, your persona is ultimately sustained, or negotiated, *through your interaction* with others.

Now imagine that there are several people in the room – which makes the text scroll even faster. As you struggle to read the conversation threads and participate in at least one conversation, you realize that the amount of text you have generated is considerably less than some of the other inhabitants. You begin to see certain people dominating the conversation and therefore the screen real estate, or space. Since the text serves as an agent for the body in a MOO, the more text you generate – the more space you occupy in the database and on other users' screens – and the more memorable you become.

The text is the only visual representation of the self in a MOO or IRC. Therefore, recognizing that communication is represented physically in a MOO is integral to understanding how MOOers attempt to embody their virtual identities. MOOers learn to maximize the creative potential of the electronic text medium. For instance, MOOers may send large pictures generated by patterns of text that fill the entire screen or execute subroutines of code that perform actions on other characters. They occupy valuable screen real estate by "spoofing" or "spamming". MOOers communicate nonverbally through the use of articons (for example, @-->-->---- looks like a rose when you view it sideways) and emoticons (for example, ;-) looks like a winking face and smile if you look at it sideways), and by adding paralinguistic features to their text (for example, "eek!" becomes "EEEEeeeeekkkkk!"). The text, which generates the emergent identity, serves as an agent, or replacement, for the body in online communication. In a MOO, *who* you are is literally determined by what you say and what you do with the text. In a textual environment such as a MOO, the text not only represents one's verbal communication, but also one's *actions*. In a text-based virtual reality, one's communication *is* one's identity.

13.3 Culture and Collaborative Virtual Community Design

13.3.1 Culture and Perception

In one sense, virtuality is a "living laboratory" or unique simulated environment within which one's communication can profoundly affect inhabitants' social interactions and the co-creation of a virtual space. I refer to virtuality as a simulated environment, not because the events and actors in CVE aren't real, but precisely because they *are* real as long as we perceive them to be. Perception and interpretation largely dictate the manner in which we process information. Culture is a perceptual filter that impacts how we make sense of our world.

Communication is the dynamic process in which two or more interlocutors strive for, or engage in, shared meaning. Meaning in communication is co-created by interlocutors through the use of a system of mutually agreed upon symbols that are interpreted by each interlocutor in a particular context, or situation. The system of mutually agreed upon symbols I speak of may be characterized as the interlocutor's culture. In *Beyond Culture*, anthropologist Edward T. Hall (1976) indicated that "culture is the total communication framework" comprised of words, actions, non-verbal behaviours, the handling of time, space, and materials, world view, beliefs, and attitudes passed over time from generation to generation. Culture serves as a perceptual filter with which we determine that which is important to us and that which is not. That is to say, we understand each other best when the interpretations of the receiver line up with the meaning desired by the source of the communication event. Further, we best understand our socio-cultural world when our interpretations have accurately simulated the collective cultural meaning attributed to events over time[1]. Sometimes, however, our interpretations fail us. Communication is a dynamic, complex, social process. Meaning can be ephemeral and fleeting, especially when compounded by the variability of interlocutors' cultures and communication styles.

Recall the definition of intercultural communication as the exchange, and co-creation, of information and meanings by individuals or groups when at least one party perceives itself to be different from others. Often, in intercultural encounters, culture is the primary perceptual filter that is used to make sense of interactions. Each of us makes sense of incoming stimuli by interpreting their meaning and subsequently categorizing the information in accordance with the cognitive schema we have developed to better understand our world (Varner and Beaner, 1995). Culture often provides an initial framework for grouping information either by ignoring cues that are not meaningful to an existing category, matching information to a existing category schema, newly creating a category schema for unfamiliar information, or by erroneously forcing unfamiliar information into familiar, but inappropriate, reference frames.

Our cultural references may fail us from time to time, especially when we perceive a cue to be unfamiliar or unexpected. In many ways, it is necessary to *unlearn* the lessons of culture so that we may effectively communicate with others whom we perceive to be different from ourselves. Recall that culture acts as a perceptual filter in which we are predisposed to value some information over other. When striving for shared meaning in cross-cultural contexts, strict adherence to cultural values may actually impede the process of negotiating intercultural relations. For example, some readers might recall the "golden rule" which suggests – do unto others as you yourself would have done unto you. In fact, when engaging in an intercultural interaction, this rule is precisely what we should avoid! It is more useful to consider the following as a rule of thumb – *do unto others as they themselves would have done unto them* (Bennett, 1998). To this end, effective intercultural communication cannot successfully occur without awareness, negotiation, collaboration, and the co-creation of meaning.

---

[1] This point prompts the question "What is real?". Since perceptions count, events are real as long as they seem to be real, a point which supports the real feelings generated in virtual environments.

13.3.2 Toward Designing for Equitable Communication

Collaborative virtual environments offer unique opportunities to begin anew in a rich communication medium – and experiment with unlearning the lessons, or biases, of culture in order to ultimately foster more equitable communication practices and interactions. Designers of virtual places can facilitate this process. Therefore, like the anthropologist returning from a foreign culture, inhabitants of virtual places may bring back a newly found self-awareness necessary to achieve intercultural communication competence in both face-to-face and virtual environments.

Designers of collaborative virtual communities have both the responsibility and the opportunity to consider the impact of underlying dynamics of culture and intercultural interactions such as identity, negotiation, conflict, power, equity and trust on virtual spaces and collaborative communities. Although we may strive to create equitable virtual environments, the differing cultures of the creators, owners, developers and users of such spaces make for complex and largely misunderstood cultural dynamics. Using intercultural communication principles as a guide, can we achieve equity and negotiation across culturally diverse community members? When designing virtual spaces, what are we to do when one person's utopia is another's dystopia?

13.4 The DomeCityMOO

13.4.1 Why Design the DomeCityMOO Simulation?

Most simulations are designed to encourage the participant to undergo a certain degree of stress. Social-process simulations designed for face-to-face environments and focusing on intercultural relations have historically involved participants in experiencing a frustrating or traumatic event in order to learn to function in a negative condition (Gredler, 1992). For example, certain early stages of culture shock are often cited as a "negative condition." Unfortunately, placing face-to-face participants in even a *simulated* negative condition (such as culture shock) often produces negative unintended effects.

Social-process simulations are usually conducted face-to-face, although tactical decision, data management or crisis management simulations are often used in a computerized context. Gredler (1992) argued that the focus of social-process simulations is human interaction, reflection on one's actions and the post-simulation discussion. To date, most if not all, intercultural social-process simulations are designed for the face-to-face setting. This fact reflects several biases and assumptions that are made with regard to intercultural simulation design. First, a face-to-face context is widely regarded by simulation designers as the best, if not the only, setting suitable for a multiple person simulation that supports synchronous communication. Second, instantaneous verbal and non-verbal feedback is preferred. Third, supporting participant anonymity is not usually possible, since many social-process simulations hinge on nuances in non-verbal communication. Last, the possibility to easily design cost-effective multi-user intercultural computer-based simulations may not have existed until a few years ago.

Unfortunately, the face-to-face context is largely taken for granted as the optimal setting in which to conduct a social-process simulation, especially in intercultural communication training and education. Scores of simulations, role-plays, and other learning tools have been developed to explore intercultural communication dynamics *without ever having tested whether a face-to-face environment is the best medium in which to explore these issues.*

A potential problem with face-to-face social-process simulations that has been largely overlooked by simulation and game designers, educators and trainers (Bruschke *et al.*, 1993) is that some respondents perceive face-to-face to be a threatening setting in which to discuss certain topics. In the case of the intercultural simulation *Ecotonos*, which addresses power imbalances, respondents perceived face-to-face to be a threatening setting in which to discuss topics such as identity and power (Raybourn, 1998b). In the age of improved communication technologies, interlocutors now choose their preferred communication channels. As electronic communication proliferates into the mainstream, a growing number of individuals are becoming more comfortable with computer-mediated communication.

I argue that one of the unique attributes of computer-mediated communication is its potential for anonymity. What effect does anonymity have on synchronous communication and the interlocutors? Could anonymity facilitate certain communication outcomes? Until recently, designing a social-process simulation for a computer-mediated context did not make design sense. However, CVEs can be multi-user environments that provide several new opportunities for social-process simulations (Raybourn, 1997b).

13.4.2 The Purpose of the DomeCityMOO Simulation

The purpose of the DomeCityMOO was to explore the medium of electronic communication as an arena for generating social-process simulation experiences that are engaging, non-threatening, participant controlled and authentic. In this case, the simulated reality, albeit in many ways a *real* experience, is a safer arena for many people in which to confront cultural differences. In designing the DomeCityMOO I had the following questions in mind that reflect certain principles of computer game design: is it possible to design a simulation that does not introduce the facilitator's biases? Will the simulation be perceived to be non-threatening? Is it engaging without the elaborate construction of rules and roles? Can it be played individually and with groups? Can it be played more than once with different learning outcomes and not get boring over time? Does it support different degrees of communication competence? In order to answer these questions and successfully design the *DomeCity*MOO simulation, I exploited certain characteristics of MOO communication that I had identified in an ethnographic study I conducted in LambdaMOO which were also supported in part by the literature (Raybourn, 1997a).

First, MOOers are not required to ever present their RL identities. MOOers may therefore perform actions they might not in a face-to-face encounter (Reid, 1995; Dibbell, 1993; Curtis, 1992). Computer-mediated communication is often more intimate, but also more aggressive than real-life, as illustrated by Huxor's memory of an accidental encounter with two avatars who were engaged in a private session of cybersex (see Chapter 15). *Anonymity* produces a lower perceived risk to interlocutors that allows them to express themselves more freely (Raybourn, 1998b). As individuals feel more comfortable expressing themselves, they may monitor their communication less, and consequently concentrate more on their interactions with others.

Anonymity also supports individual agency. That is, interlocutors decide for themselves the degree to which they wish to reveal facets of their identities and are not limited to enacting their RL roles. MOOers are more aware of the presentation of the self and have more control over whom others perceive them to be. For example, a very shy individual may "clam up" in RL interactions, but may be warm, friendly and popular in the MOO. MOOers can experiment with new modes of being, and learn skills that they might use in RL as well. The anonymity of computer-mediated communication in MOOs supports playful experimentation with one's identity, and ultimately *mastery* over presenting the self to others in a virtual environment. Thus, computer-mediated communication supports reinvention of the self. According to Csikszentmihalyi (1991), achieving mastery in an activity leads to personal growth, and a more in-depth understanding of the self.

Next, community is built on common interests, not proximity. Community building in cyberspace reflects the common interests that bring people together, without the stress sometimes associated with the social groups one must belong to because of RL expectations, physical attributes or geographical locations. The absence of the physical body focuses the interlocutor striving for on communication competence. The disembodied self offers online interlocutors the opportunity to develop new interpersonal communication skills and represent themselves in new ways, including text (Raybourn, 1997b). Text-based communication affords greater control of unintended nonverbal feedback. The potential for contradictory non-verbal messages is thus lessened, since online interlocutors have more agency over the kind of signals they send to others. For example, MOO communication features the potential to edit a message, or regulate the kind of feedback given in an exchange. In other words, feedback need not be given immediately. Many MOOs are plagued with a communication "lag" in which messages are delayed for several seconds. This "lag" can offer interlocutors (especially those communicating in a non-native language) the opportunity to think carefully about the message one is sending.

Last, there is enhanced potential for developing better reading, writing, and imaginations. Communicating in a different medium presents the interlocutors with opportunities to develop more sophisticated skills in certain areas. Online, conciseness, directness and imagination are important communication skills. Interlocutors also learn to read and generate messages at the same time. MOOers may print a record of all of their online interactions, creating instances of persistent communication with a traceable history. Some MOOers have kept logs of their inti-mate relationships that have developed online. Looking over interaction history is like reliving the experience or revisiting memories (Turkle, 1995; Bruckman, 1992).

13.4.3 DomeCityMOO: a Detailed Description of the Simulation

I designed the DomeCityMOO simulation over a period of approximately two years (the design process included an extensive literature review, a quantitative study of a face-to-face simulation, an ethnographic study of MOOs, visiting RL places and observing how people interacted in them, and finally prototyping the DomeCityMOO simulation in a face-to-face setting to work out design bugs before I started programming). I conducted the three 90-minute simulations over three nights. Seventeen participants logged in to the DomeCityMOO from across the USA in New Mexico, Michigan, Florida, California, Oregon and Maryland. Participants were recruited by word of mouth (announcing simulation participation in univer-sity classes), and through posting solicitations for participation on several listservers.

Of the study participants, 5% were freshmen, 5% sophomores, 14% juniors, 5% seniors, 38% graduate students and 14% were out of school with Masters degrees. The median age was 27; the mean age was 29. Sixty-seven per cent of the students were male; 14% were female. Eighty-one per cent of the participants had experi-enced educational face-to-face simulations in classes at least once, but no more than 10 times. Almost half of the participants (48%) had never MOOed before, or had MOOed less than three times. Three of the participants were more experienced and had MOOed several times over a few months in a 2 to 5-year period. No one considered her/himself to be of "MOO wizard" ability. None of the respondents had participated in the DomeCityMOO simulation before. Nearly half of the partici-pants identified as European American (48%). Fewer respondents identified as Latino (24%), African American (5%), and Asian Indian (5%).

Designing Negotiation by Way of Dystopia

The DomeCityMOO simulation design supported the goals of taking participants on a personal journey to self-awareness through the vicarious exploration of iden-tity and power. In order for the experience to be as *real* as possible, it was important that the simulation be *engaging* as well. In order for computer-based games and simulations to actively engage players, three conditions must exist – curiosity, chal-lenge and fantasy (Malone, 1980). These conditions were built into the MOO envi-ronment and the simulation design.

The simulation was named DomeCityMOO because a domed city is theoretically a closed system that has limited resources and therefore inherent problems that may be logically built into the simulation. Participants entering the DomeCityMOO dystopian environment were given a predetermined, albeit loosely defined, role, and asked to create an identity that reflected racial/ethnic, religious background,

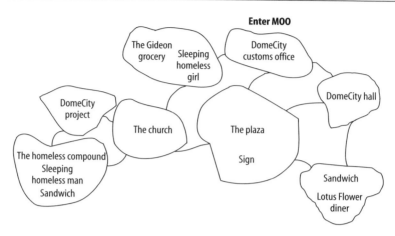

Figure 13.1

age, gender or sexual orientation. Power dynamics were introduced into the simulation by providing some roles with programming privileges and the ability to change (enhance and destroy) aspects of the DomeCityMOO architecture or social structure. Other roles reflected varying degrees of social (perceived influence) power. Some roles had both programming and social power. Role interdependencies were designed to facilitate collaboration and communication. For example, some roles with programming privileges were able to award programming capabilities to others at their own discretion. However, awarding programming capability to another resulted in a proportional loss of one's own. In addition to role interdependencies and imbalances of power, the "physical" environment of the MOO also reflected dystopian ideals (see Fig. 13.1).

Upon entering the Plaza, participants saw the following description on their screen:

> **The Plaza** "You step into a concrete courtyard strategically littered with a few trees and shrubs. Small benches seem randomly scattered about. You note how difficult it must be for children to play here. Too bad, the Plaza has so much potential."

Notice that I have incorporated both order and chaos (a conflict), and introduced a value-laden evaluation (a bias) to the participant as part of my design as in "too bad, The Plaza has so much potential". In fact, later you will see how the descriptions prompted users to create objects that predictably followed the design of the dystopian environment. In the next example

> **The DomeCity Project** "You push the black knobless door of the first floor entrance. Although inhabited, the damp foyer smells distinctly of mothballs and stale beer. Discarded beer bottles are strewn along the hallways. The red carpet is dingy and old."

Note that I engage the participant's haptic and olfactory senses with my description, as well as use language that is "loaded" to conjure images and stereotypes in the minds of the participants. According to the research in *A Pattern Language*

(1997), discarded bottles are a sign of a community that does not care about its environment – something I wanted to depict in the DomeCityMOO so that participants would feel more urgency about improving the area. Next,

> **The Lotus Flower Diner** "You are greeted by the smell of pinon coffee brewing and the soft melodies coming from the jukebox. Cozy booths hug the walls of the diner and a spacious lunch counter encircles the soda fountain in the middle of the room."

A diner was chosen as the metaphor for "real world" space because people from all walks of life go into diners. It was important, in this case, to choose a "real world" representation that does not exclude any participants based on the perceived power dynamic attached to the representation. Additionally, a diner is a shared space that can be easily designed to support interpersonal, small group and public communication. I designed at least one space that might facilitate collaborative activities and serve as a "safe space" for inhabitants and a sanctuary from the dystopia. Last,

> **The Homeless Compound** "Upon first glance, you decide you probably shouldn't have come here. Rows of cardboard boxes and garbage cans litter the grounds. You dare to look inside one of the makeshift homes and see... a sandwich. You see a sleeping homeless man here."

Finally, in this example I suggest how one might feel as one see the compound. I "dare" the participant to interact with the objects in this space – increasing curiosity, but suggesting an unpleasant experience. In fact, during the simulations participants never stayed in the homeless area to converse with others.

Since the participants' objective in the MOO was to improve the domed city, the initial environment was designed to reflect a rather depressed city, rife with problems. For example, the sterile environment clearly delineated an affluent and an impoverished area of the MOO. The combination of the role interdependencies and the environmental power imbalances of the DomeCityMOO design contributed to conflict that encouraged each participant's exploration of identity and power. As participants rebuilt their environment, they negotiated expressions of power and powerlessness through their communication with others, in a simulation that a statistically significant number of participants later reported was perceived to be a non-threatening environment (Raybourn, 1998b).

Designing Negotiation by Way of Power Imbalances

Participants entering the DomeCityMOO were given a title such as "inner city youth, grassroots leader, mayor, building commissioner, etc." and asked to create a character representing multiple levels of identity in racial/ethnic, religious background, gender or sexual orientation. By randomly assigning participants culturally biased titles – some of perceived importance, and not others, an instant power struggle is incorporated into the simulation. In other words, some participants were given perceived social privilege while others were not. Participants were told to create an identity for a role in the absence of detailed simulation instructions. Participants chose the gender they wished to present in the virtual environment. In

Table 13.1. DomeCityMOO simulation roles and perceived interdependencies

Mayor	Building and social power
Homeless	No building or social power
Senior Citizen	Social power, no building power
Grassroots Leader	No building power, but social power with disadvantaged
Inner DomeCity Teenager	No building or social power, lives in projects
Landlord	Building power, owner of projects
Church Official	No building power
Self-Employed	No building or social power, lives in projects
Unemployed	No building power, owner of diner and grocery
Building Commissioner	Most building and social power

addition, participants were encouraged to re-create their identities (or add further detail) at any time during play. For example, a person may have been asked to generate a character who was the mayor of the city. There were certain programming privileges associated with this character that enabled her/him to change (enhance or destroy) parts of the DomeCityMOO architecture or social structure. Another person may have been given the character of a homeless person, who had no perceived social power or programming privilege. If the participant had played in the simulation prior to her/his assignment as a homeless person, s/he may have somewhat resented the lack of flexibility in her/his present role by not being able to exercise the same privileges of the previous character. Nevertheless, the participant would have had to continue as a homeless person if s/he wished to continue to participate in the simulation. In each case, participants remained anonymous, that is, their characters were given names and could not be identified by the participants' passwords or email addresses. Character roles and descriptions are provided in Table 13.1.

Powerful characters were determined by the amount of building quota, or number of bytes they could use to create objects in the database. Powerful characters usually possessed both social power (perceived by other members in the simulation) and building privileges (quota). Powerless characters, on the other hand, ranged from possessing no building privileges nor social power, to being awarded some building quota from the more powerful characters and possessing perceived social power among the less powerful. A stratified microcosm of society was created by introducing into the simulation the option to award characters building quota. However, awarding building privilege to another character resulted in a loss of one's own quota. An example of a powerful character is the DomeCity Building Commissioner, who possessed both building privileges and perceived social power. A less powerful character is the Grassroots Leader, who possesses no building power, but has perceived social power for some characters. The least powerful character in the simulation is the Homeless character, who possesses no building privileges and no perceived social power.

Building in a MOO is largely a collaborative effort. Therefore, a natural objective of the simulation is for participants to "better their world" by investing in their community and building, or making changes to it. However, some changes to the DomeCityMOO must be agreed on by a team of characters. For instance, if the mayor wanted to make some changes, s/he might have to solicit consensus from the homeless person, or others. This "problem" in the simulation encourages participants to interact with one another, especially across boundaries of social status.

The problem is further compounded when participants engage in the simulation more than once. Each time an individual participated in the simulation, s/he played a different character. Therefore the participant was never sure which character s/he would play – so any changes s/he wished to make while in a position of power had to be made as long as s/he *was playing that character*. Additionally, imagine that prior to one's assignment as the homeless person the participant had been the mayor – but had not been able to make all of the changes s/he wished. As a homeless person, s/he would not have the programming power to institute the change, but that does not mean that s/he could not persuade someone in a position of power to do it.

13.5 Power Negotiation and Collaboration in DomeCityMOO

After three 90-minute simulations, three different groups of users totalling 17 in all had reconstructed the DomeCityMOO. Interestingly, the simulation participants behaved in ways that reinforced the dystopian environment, even though, all things considered, the simulation had successfully allowed participants to collaboratively come to agreements about their world, and individually experience the negotiation of power imbalances. Figure 13.2 provides a graphical representation of the "improved" DomeCity.

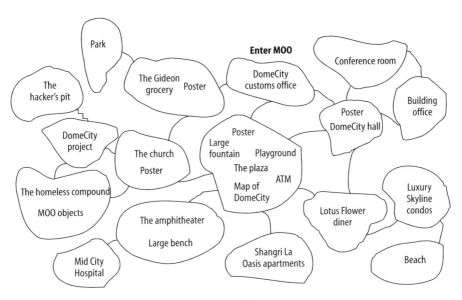

Figure 13.2

Participants worked together to build their virtual world. Note that in the Plaza, where it had been suggested that "children could not play", the participants built a playground, fountain, provided posters, an automatic teller machine and a map of the DomeCityMOO. The map was actually one of the first items constructed collaboratively by sending "scouts" out to various parts of the MOO so they could report back what they saw to the Building Commissioner. Next, notice that the Hacker's Pit was built "above" the Projects, in accordance with the suggestion that one "entered the first floor" therefore insinuating that there could be a second. Additionally, most of the participants collaborated with others on building the MOO in one form or another, except for the homeless individual in the case of the last simulation trial. The homeless man tried at first, but after no success he decided to go around the MOO and collect the objects in the other rooms that could be carried out (sandwich, sign and sleeping homeless girl) and take them back to the homeless compound to keep for himself. Therefore, even though he did not collaborate with others on the task of improving the DomeCity, he did participate in his brand of "building" or rather, "nesting".

Finally, examine the entire MOO plan in Figs. 13.1 and 13.2. Do you see how the participants built up the city by providing a park, amphitheatre, hospital, new apartments, condominiums, building office and a beach – but did not alter the overall affluence vs. poverty imbalance in the MOO? I have a tentative explanation for this behaviour. Based on my personal experience in MOOs, both building objects and observing others build objects, I believe that when MOOers construct their worlds they engage in storytelling. Perhaps the participants of the DomeCityMOO simulation were unconsciously following the storyline I had set up for them, and perhaps they did not have enough time to notice the power imbalance inherent in the design and then reinvent a new story. Nevertheless, throughout the simulation trials I was fascinated with what appeared to be a cohesive world view among the collaborators. The DomeCityMOO participants were on the road to forming their own culture – a phenomenon that has been noticed in CVEs such as MOOs, newsgroups, listservers and more.

Qualitative open-response data collected from the participants suggests what the participants may have learned from the simulation. In response to the question, "What did you notice about the way others interacted with you in the MOO?", some participants wrote:

- "I was the Building Commissioner and, as one of the "powerful" ones, I felt my self challenged to constantly us my power to benefit others. For example, the Landlord kept pressing me to build for her/him when I was still trying to figure out the extent of my power. In the MOO, I felt torn between my own need to build and other's needs to take my quota or have me build for them. However, it was only the power the other characters responded to. No one commented on my assumed identity (a white male, seemingly traditional) or used that identity as a means of assessing my control. Identity, in fact seemed less of an issue. As Building Commish I interacted freely with the character identified as Inner City Teen, a situation that seems less likely in RL."

- "I played as a Guest, so some who thought they were powerful (mayor, building commish) at first didn't really listen to me because they perceived me to be unimportant because I had no power. Others would listen to me (landlord, grassroots_leader) and I felt somewhat important and had some power by influencing them with ideas about construction plans."

- "I found that if I said something funny or wacky that everyone would pay attention to you and talk to you like if you were some interesting person, because you said something totally off the wall. I felt powerful, because I could be whoever I wanted to be and say whatever I wanted to say. After a while of telling lies I just felt like I needed somebody real to talk to, but knew it was pretty much impossible because everyone else seemed to be pretending also. So after a while I felt powerless, because I was searching for someone who would be honest with me, but was unsuccessful."

Several responses given by those participants who role-played characters with little or no perceived power ranged from "I was utterly invisible", to "I felt more powerful in the beginning than in the end – I thought I would accomplish more". Participants were able to articulate their experiences with power imbalances in the simulation. These comments are examples of how personal the relationship between identity and power is for each individual. Respondents experienced power and/or powerlessness for a variety of reasons. The variability embedded into the MOO experience enhances the intimate exploration of the relationship among identity and power dynamics. Whether respondents react to the imbalances in power created by the social hierarchy, system constraints or quality of communication – they still learn in a safe, player-controlled manner.

13.6 Conclusions

Previous research (Raybourn, 1998b) established that a text-based networked virtual reality, or MOO, is a real-world setting which provides an individual the opportunity to express feelings or practice normative behaviours while being anonymous. In other words, MOOs are virtual environments where real things happen. MOOs are collaborative virtual environments built in a hierarchical programming language, and built on a history of rewarding the most skilful participants with social and programming privileges. Therefore, designing a computer-based multi-user social-process simulation in a MOO that addresses participant exploration of identity and power imbalances is a natural exploitation of a system that supports such activities. Measuring the effects of participation in an anonymous, computer-based, multi-user simulation on the perception of threatening subjects such as identity and power is a worthy research endeavour.

Additionally, Raybourn (1998b) investigated the degree to which identity and power were perceived by users to be threatening subjects to address in an anonymous, computer-based, multi-user simulation. Since identity and power were among the themes explored in many intercultural simulations, and since more intercultural trainers are faced with the problem of designing training in computer-supported environments, it was beneficial to determine the effect on users of designing simulations around these concepts in multi-user collaborative virtual environments.

The results of the quantitative study mentioned above indicated that for the subject of power, respondents who participated in the computer-based multi-user DomeCityMOO simulation perceived its environment to be less threatening compared with respondents who participated in a face-to-face simulation (*Ecotonos*) following participation in their respective simulations. Moreover, the DomeCityMOO participants indicated that the DomeCityMOO simulation had met its goal of creating an environment in which they could explore power. Additionally, it should be noted that respondents who participated in the DomeCityMOO simulation also indicated that they did not perceive the virtual environment to be a threatening setting in which to address the subject of identity. In fact, they believed the simulation had met its goal of creating an environment in which to explore identity. Perhaps the anonymity of the computer-based DomeCityMOO simulation created a buffer because of which participants felt less threatened in general, and also believed the simulation allowed them to experience how the character's role and perceived power shaped how they were treated by others in the MOO.

13.7 Lessons Learned for CVE Designers About Emergent Culture and Negotiation

Negotiation, awareness of intercultural dynamics (power and identity), and collaborative behaviours can result from non-threatening interactions occurring in a "dystopian" virtual environment. On some levels, it is counter-intuitive to consider a less than utopian environment as facilitating collaboration and the negotiation of power and identity. Nevertheless, this emergent culture was achieved through interactions that introduced role interdependencies and by encouraging participants to co-create their virtual space together. Several lessons were learned from observing interactions in the DomeCityMOO. For example, both individual creativity and predictable behaviours resulted from the perceived constraints of the simulation. The dystopian environment and role interdependencies created a "need" for MOO participants to collaborate and negotiate their power imbalances in order to co-create a more "utopian" environment. Second, when designing the CVE, often the mere suggestion of a cultural cue (in the descriptions of the rooms) was more appropriate than actually providing the cue itself. That is, a "parenting approach to design" (as suggested by Andrew McGrath) was taken that facilitated the means by which participants contributed to their interaction environment. As the designer, I did not own the outcome of the participants' collaboration – *they did*. Last, the role of storytelling proved to be very important in identifying roles and their subsequent behaviours. By enabling participants to co-create their own story in the DomeCityMOO, more equitable intercultural communication behaviours ensued from the interactions.

A CVE may be a particularly rich context to explore learning and the goals of social-process simulations as the interactions are co-constructed by the participants, outcomes left open-ended, and the rules of collaboration are very subtle. CVEs may also provide simulation designers the medium to develop simulations with less confining rules or tasks and more organic places that users co-create. In the case of the DomeCityMOO, I used computer game design and intercultural communication principles to create a dystopian environment that fostered an emergent culture of power negotiation and collaborative behaviours.

In the DomeCityMOO, participants experimented with intercultural relations in a shared space in which they created an identity for themselves that was played out in the co-created virtual world. As they interacted with others in the MOO they may have noted how their own identity was negotiated through their communication with others. In other words, information about oneself and others is gathered through relationships, conflict, intimacy, negotiation and self-disclosure. DomeCityMOO is an open-ended, non-scripted environment, like real life, in which participants construct their own rules and pursue narrative possibilities they create together through communication with each other, and the shared meaning assigned to the programmed and virtual objects in the MOO (Rheingold, 1993).

13.8 Next Steps for Culture and Collaborative Virtual Community Design

I have already begun working with colleagues from BT Labs on introducing organizational and cultural cues in the 3D CVE called The Forum (see Chapter 6 for a description of The Forum). While I was a short-term Fellow at BT Labs Advanced Communication Centre, we completed the first, difficult steps towards designing CVEs that support cultural understanding. I conducted a cross-organizational study of work practices among with BT researchers and Sandia National Laboratories scientists. Based on ethnographic research and design of the DomeCityMOO, I developed two distinct scenarios of how groups with different cultures and needs might use CVEs that provided cultural or organizational cues. I identified three major questions that drive the notion of introducing cultural and organizational cues into CVEs:

- How does knowledge of tacit culture support organizational trust and community within virtual environments? Across different organizations?

- How can we design environments that facilitate communication interactions that engender feelings of trust, or curiosity that are associated with learning more about the people you work with etc.? That is to say, is it possible to design environments that increase users' curiosity about the other members of the shared space?

- How can we create virtual environments that approach intercultural understanding in a non-threatening way?

My prior experience with designing and evaluating the DomeCityMOO provided the framework for preliminary design ideas for introducing cultural cues in virtual environments. This research indicates that CVE designers can support effective intercultural communication by employing lessons learned from intercultural interaction design to increase the users' intrinsic motivation for participation, and investigating how we can create more equitable communication spaces that enable enhanced information sharing, interdependency and the negotiation of power.

In summary, the present chapter argued that a computer-based social-process simulation offers unique opportunities to explore issues of identity and power, because its environment is less threatening than face-to-face under certain conditions. The motivation for the DomeCityMOO was to *create* a computer-based social-process simulation that allowed participants to explore a potentially threatening subject in a safe, participant-controlled, communication-rich environment and *evaluate* its effects. I believe that a computer-simulated environment is a richer medium in some specific cases for facilitating communication regarding issues of identity, and power than is face-to-face communication. Discovering that a computer-mediated multi-user social-process simulation can be successfully designed to foster intercultural awareness may have interesting implications for future directions in CVE design, training, education and human–computer interaction.

Acknowledgements

I thank Elizabeth Churchill, Dave Snowdon, Alan Munro and Andrew McGrath for their valuable suggestions on the first draft of this chapter. I also send a very heartfelt "thank you" to the newbies and MOOers who participated in the DomeCityMOO simulation despite their busy schedules.

Chapter 14

Waterfall Glen: Social Virtual Reality at Work

Rémy Evard, Elizabeth F. Churchill and Sara Bly

14.1 Introduction

Waterfall Glen is a MOO, a form of MUD or "multi-user domain". MUDs are immersive virtual environments – one enters the MUD environment and conversations take place within it. Traditionally MUDs have been used for multi-player Internet gaming and for social chat, and have not been used extensively to support work-related activities. However, MUDs have been gaining attention as potential environments for supporting collaborative learning and cooperative work. Recent publications describe the use of MUDs for supporting teaching and learning (e.g. Penn MOO; Diversity MOO; see also discussions by Hand and Skipper, 1996; Bruckman, 1998; O'Day *et al.*, 1998), for building social and vocational communities (e.g. Curtis, 1996; Mynatt *et al.*, 1998; Schank *et al.*, 1999), for virtual conferencing (e.g. Towell and Towell, 1997), for exploring issues of culture (Chapter 13) and for supporting collaborative work activities (e.g. Doppke at al, 1998; Evard, 1993; Churchill and Bly 1999a,b,c; Tomek and Giles, 1999).

MUDs are multi-user, end-user extensible, low-bandwidth, distributed, network-accessible environments. In comparison to media spaces, video-conferencing tools and distributed 3D graphical environments, MUDs are technologically lightweight. MUDs have a client–server architecture with most of the computational work within text-based MUDs being done on the server. The server holds the MUD "core", a persistent database containing information about the virtual world, about objects and their properties within the virtual world and about "player" or user information. MUDs are therefore experienced as persistent virtual worlds; objects, people and places do not disappear when one leaves the MUD. The server also houses the MUD "engine" which is responsible for run-time activity, parsing input from clients, interacting with the databases to update the world, object and user states and sending output to clients.

Unlike Internet-based text chat, MUDs utilize a spatial metaphor in their design. MUDs usually consist of multiple interconnected communication spaces or "rooms". MUDders can move easily from one room to the other (by issuing a move command). This spatial metaphor is intended to exploit our knowledge of the way in which physical spaces structure interaction. The MUD has different rooms for different actions and interactions. MUD users experience the "ambience" of these interconnected, virtual rooms through text descriptions. A textual room description contains information about the room itself (e.g. a room could be described as an office, a lounge, a field etc.), who else is "present" in the room and the objects that are currently located in the room. People in the MUD are also represented in text; they usually appear as names with associated descriptions.

The spatial metaphor is central to MUDs, and is a natural way of organizing information and of framing activities and behaviours. Virtual rooms can be dedicated to different projects, and to different social groupings and different conversations. Because it is so easy to move from one communication space or room to another, and because MUDs are end-user extensible (new rooms can be created), the MUD environment easily accommodates changing group interactions. Research indicates that most people maintain multiple intersecting "constellations" of collaborators who may be widely distributed (Salvador and Bly, 1997). MUDs afford support of multiple groupings on an as-needed basis – within a single environment and with a single technology. It is also possible to have multiple windows onto a MUD at any time and also to have multiple personae in a MUD environment. Therefore MUDs enable one to be in more than one virtual place (and in more than one conversation) at a time – it is possible to be chatting in several different rooms simultaneously.

As noted above, objects are persistent and maintain their identity due to the core database structure, but they can be moved from room to room. Objects may be dynamic, having certain properties that are only apparent when a user interacts with them, and objects and players can have properties that may only be visible when a command like "look" is issued. This offers a kind of hypertext quality to rooms, objects and characters, reducing descriptive (textual) clutter. It is also possible to program events that occur when some "trigger" or cue takes place in a room.

Typically, conversations in MUD rooms consist of typing text strings (which may be pure "chat" or command strings) to the server. The server then distributes these text strings to other people who are currently in the same virtual room. Logs of these conversations can be retained so that playback is possible. Thus a continuing dialogue can exist over time without requiring the constant attention of participants. Although many MUDs only support text-based conversations of this kind, many recent systems include simple graphics (e.g. The Palace offers 2D graphical background, avatars and props; Tapped_In offers visual room layouts and images of users) and multimedia technologies (e.g. The Jupiter system supplements a text MOO with audio, video and interactive artefacts; Curtis et al., 1995). These systems also have a client–server structure although more computation tends to take place on the client-side than within the purely text-based MUDs.

In this chapter we describe the evolution of a particular MOO, Waterfall Glen, which has been developed and is in use in the Mathematics and Computer Science division of Argonne National Laboratory in the USA. Waterfall Glen represents one of the most successful work-related MOOs. We describe the evolution of Waterfall Glen and offer observations of its past and current use. We end the chapter with speculations drawn from our observations about the success and failure of such text-based environments for the support of ongoing collaborative work.

14.2 The Waterfall Glen Project

The Mathematics and Computer Science division (MCS) of Argonne National Laboratory is an organization devoted to mathematics and computer science research, with a focus on parallel and high-performance scientific computing. Since 1993, MCS has been running Waterfall Glen – a MOO named after the forest preserve which surrounds Argonne – as an informal experiment. Not only has the experiment been successful, in that MCS has learned much about how a MOO can and cannot be used in their setting, but also more generally Waterfall Glen can be considered to be a successful example of computer-based collaboration technology in use by an active community.

Waterfall Glen may be used by any member of the MCS community, with no specific restrictions or directions on what it may be used for. Thus the user community of Waterfall Glen is a self-selected set of scientists, programmers, administrators and associates of MCS. Users are not all co-located – some work within the building at the main Argonne site, others are at other sister sites in the USA or within other organizations, and some are abroad. Not everyone is working in the same time zone. The main activities are software research, development and deployment. Not everyone in the division uses it; of the 100 people in the division, 50 of them used their Waterfall Glen characters in April of 2000. Including other participants, the average number of active users on Waterfall Glen is around 125 people, nearly all of whom work at MCS or are active collaborators in MCS projects.

As one would expect, most of the activities in Waterfall Glen revolve around work at MCS. It would not be fair, however, to say that most of the activity is focused on work or is centred on some task – conversations are more akin to what one would find in a real-world hallway. Discussions range from programming questions to the weather, from coordination of lunch to coordination of a cross-country demo. The format is inherently social, creating an atmosphere of what we have termed "café-style interaction", where one converses about whatever is on one's mind, including, but not limited to, work.

Because Waterfall Glen is a conventional MOO with no special extensions, all of these interactions take place in a text-based format. Indeed, from a technical standpoint, Waterfall Glen is a typical MOO – it is running on the current version of the MOO server from Xerox PARC, based on the latest release of the JHcore database from the Jay's House MOO (JHM) community (`ftp://ftp.ccs.neu.edu/pub/mud/sites/jhm/database/`). The entire set of related files takes 20 Mbyte of disk space, and the MOO server process itself runs on whatever spare server happens to be available. In the past, this has been a Sun4 and a SPARCstation 20; at present it is a Pentium 500 running Linux.

14.2.1 The History of Waterfall Glen: InfoPark

Waterfall Glen was created after the success of InfoPark, one of the first documented work-related MOOs (Evard, 1993). InfoPark has been in use at the College of Computer Science of Northeastern University since early 1993 by a group of system administrators to discuss issues associated with building and maintaining the computing environment at Northeastern. Initial observations revealed that the MOO was useful for supporting synchronous and asynchronous networked interactions (Evard, 1993). Successful online meetings were held regularly. InfoPark's existence created a nexus of systems administrators, many of whom were located in other institutions, and enabled the development of new communication patterns for the group. In particular, InfoPark provided a forum for discussion of (very) current problems, known as the "problem of the moment". Previously such immediate problem solving support would not have been possible. Central to the success of InfoPark were the informal synchronous interactions that allowed collaborative work to occur while fostering a social atmosphere and the development of social relationships that may not otherwise have developed. This was particularly useful for newcomers to the team.

A year into the use of InfoPark, the interactions in the room used by the administration team were observed in detail (Evard, 1994). It was noted that at this time the average user made 50 comments a day ranging from 5 to 200 for an individual's comments. Social and work-related comments were interleaved; informal communications have long been noted as being central to the maintenance of social fabric of the workplace. This, in turn, fosters the sharing of work-related information and the development of collaborations (for example see Whittaker, Frolich and Daly-Jones, 1994). The topics of conversation could be categorized as follows:

5% greetings

15% miscellaneous

13% synchronization: idling, coordination comments

22% work content: technical discussions, questions

45% social discussion: lunch, movies, weather, and moods

It was clear from the pattern of interactions that the social interactions provided the foundations of the community that in turn supported the development of effective collaborative problem-solving about specifically work-related problems. The most important aspect of InfoPark was that it was not aurally disruptive – all interactions took place by text. This cast doubt that audio and video would add qualitatively to the experience, or that multimedia conferencing systems would be suitable for this context.

14.2.2 From InfoPark to Waterfall Glen

Two of the people who frequented InfoPark were staff in MCS – Bob Olson and Bill Nickless. They brought up a MOO at MCS in August of 1993 in order to experiment with the technology. Along with Evard and several others, they built Waterfall Glen. The MOO was small and was used by a very small number of people, and served primarily to introduce people to the concept of a MOO rather than as a collaboration mechanism. At this point in its existence, it felt much like many other early MOOs. In

December of 1993, Evard presented his findings about InfoPark to the MCS division, which caused some amount of interest among the division. He and Olson created characters for all of the members of the division and sent them each an introductory message explaining how to use the MOO. There was a flurry of activity on Waterfall Glen, during which most of the users logged in at least once to satisfy their curiosity. Most of these didn't reconnect, but a small core started to use it regularly. While there were plenty of virtual rooms on Waterfall Glen, most of the users clustered into one room and chatted. Slowly, Waterfall Glen stabilized into a regular set of users.

We speculate that there were three reasons that encouraged people to interact in Waterfall Glen:

- Interest in the potential uses of the MOO. These early adopters of the technology were clearly interested in the technology itself and in investigating its potential as a communication medium.

- Access to key personnel, particularly to Olson, who frequently answered technical questions, and to Stevens, the division director of MCS, who was typically too busy to be accessible in person but who could occasionally be found online.

- The social atmosphere. Aside from access to key people, the informal, quick interactions created a sense of camaraderie and of "co-presence" with colleagues even when people were not co-located. These interactions provided a lightweight means of keeping in touch with each other and a means of having quick, informal information exchange – such interactions are crucial for maintenance of ongoing collaborative working relationships.

Once a small core of users had stabilized, the MOO's population began to grow slowly. The division's systems administration group created a one-page handout on using the MOO, and people continued to try it out. For the most part, it was still used as a one-room MOO, but small groups began to use other rooms to discuss project-related material. This gradual growth of new users and focus around one central room with outlying rooms for specific uses has continued to the present time, with the occasional punctuating event. For example, in late 1994, one member of the Waterfall Glen community decided to create a new "hangout room", a place that was separate from the primary group, but not specifically intended to discuss a project or work-related topic. Over the next several weeks, the primary social hangout space slowly migrated from the original room to this new hangout room. This was the first time that the community as a whole dealt with the spatial metaphor and the potential social implications of it – if there are two places to hang out, where does one go?

In the autumn of 1994, MCS started the LabSpace project in order to investigate the potential of mixing other collaboration formats such as audio, video and remote instrumentation in the context of a shared space. In November of 1994, MCS created SchMOOze'94, a demonstration of a MOO integrated with Mosaic at the Supercomputing '94 conference in Washington DC. This created additional interest in the division in the MOO, and brought in a few external users.

In January of 1995, Waterfall Glen moved from the LambdaCore database to JHcore. Much like upgrading an operating system on a computer, this involved an almost complete reconstruction of the MOO. Shortly after this, the basic topology of Waterfall Glen was completely reconstructed. The original topology had grown rather haphazardly, and the new topology, which included buildings for "homes" and project spaces, was designed to create a more organized construction mechanism. People, particularly new users, experimented with room construction, but rarely with any lasting effect on the larger community. During the next several years, usage of the MOO settled into constant activity in four to five rooms, each inhabited by distinctly different groups of people. The active user community of Waterfall Glen was around 50 people, many of whom actually used multiple characters in order to inhabit multiple rooms.

In the following years, use of the MOO continued to grow slowly. The purpose of some rooms changed to match the changing projects in the division. For example, one group decided that the room they used was simply too busy for everyone to follow the work-related train of conversation. After several discussions about this, they decided to split into two rooms – one for work topics, and one for non-work topics. Many of the members of the group now inhabit both rooms, although a few only hang out in the workroom. Also during this time, the existence of Waterfall Glen became a supported and standard service in the division. Some users would frequently use the MOO as a way to report problems to the systems administration team. One development group used the MOO as a critical piece of supporting technology to support activities that span the country. As a result, many of the newer users of Waterfall Glen are collaborators of this group who are all working together to deploy new technology.

Some experiments have been carried out which have had varying success. One experiment was the development of a Java-based MOO client in order to experiment with mixing the World Wide Web and Waterfall Glen. A more significant second experiment was the development of a proxy server that allowed users to maintain a permanent connection to the MOO. The effect of this was to allow virtual characters to always be present in rooms, even when their human counterparts were not actively logged on. The effect of this is to make logs of activities and conversations available for later review. This had a profound effect on people's sense of being available at all times to each other and to the group. To aid in reviewing of logs for salient comments (that is, comments directed at oneself), various summarization commands have been developed. In a third experiment, a primitive "poke client" was developed. This allows someone in the MOO to pop up a window on someone else's computer screen in order to get his or her attention.

Through all of these events, transitions and modifications, Waterfall Glen has somehow moved from being an experiment and curiosity to being part of the basic infrastructure of the division. Although the MOO is not an "official" division communication tool, all new members of the division learn about the MOO when they learn about other resources for communicating with colleagues.

14.2.3 A Typical Day on Waterfall Glen

In order to fully understand the observations and discussions presented later in this chapter, one must understand how Waterfall Glen is used in a typical working scenario. We have found through experience that the easiest way to explain to a new user how to use the MOO is to sit down with them and show them an example of its use while explaining the technical issues involved – thus we present a sample Waterfall Glen interaction. For privacy reasons the following scenario is entirely fictional – none of the users described actually exists, nor did these interactions take place. However, the mechanisms and interactions described are completely typical of a day on Waterfall Glen, and every user will find some portion of this scenario to be familiar to their own experiences in spirit, if not in detail.

A Scenario

In the morning, before going in to work, Cathy sits at her home PC to check her email. The PC is connected to the lab over her home Internet dial-up. She launches the MOO client on her PC (a standard MUD client that she picked up from one of the freeware Web sites), and tells it to connect to Waterfall Glen. She has previously configured the client to know the hostname and port number of the Waterfall Glen MOO server.

Because she is using a PC MOO client, she connects to the Waterfall Glen "proxy server", a system developed by Bob Olson of Argonne to support persistent connections to the MOO. The proxy server maintains a permanent connection to the MOO for Cathy, keeping her character logged in at all times. Whenever Cathy changes locations, she establishes a new connection between her MOO client and the proxy server. The proxy server then refreshes her MOO client with any recent activity. The effect for Cathy is that she is able to see anything that happened in her room on the MOO while her MOO client was disconnected, which creates the feeling of permanently existing on the MOO.

Cathy is in a room on Waterfall Glen called the Quantum Computing Lab, which is currently occupied by three other people. These are her closest colleagues on her main project. One of them has an office in the same building, another is in a different building on the Argonne site and the other collaborator is in France. They are currently working collaboratively on the development of scientific visualization software. Since the proxy server has allowed her to reconnect to the session that she left running on her workstation the evening before, she is able to "scrollback" and view the events of the evening that took place in this room since she was last active. All comments and activities of the previous night, including comments from her colleague in France who has been working on a current problem, are still available. She doesn't see anything of interest, so she looks to see who is active by typing:

```
look
```

The MOO responds with this as output:

```
A small laboratory with bright paintings on the wall. Manuel is
here. Jen is here. Albert is idling. Becki is staring off into
space.
```

The names Cathy sees are people's MOO "avatars" or characters – their representatives in the virtual place. The text tells her that Manuel and Jen (in France) are present in the MOO and have been active recently, Albert is here but isn't paying attention to his MOO screen, and Becki hasn't been active for quite a long time. Cathy can see more information about someone by typing:

```
:look becki
```

The Moo prints:

```
Becki, a researcher who works too hard. Carrying: a cup of tea,
a sketchpad and a pencil.
```

Of course, MOO character descriptions vary considerably. Some contain further contact information such as telephone numbers and email addresses. Cathy decides to indicate that she is active and types the command:

```
:blinks
```

The MOO prints:

```
Cathy blinks
```

Conventions like "blink" (indicating one's presence) have developed over time (and interestingly, many have also migrated into Waterfall Glen from other MOOs.) Everyone in the room (Manuel, Jen, Albert and Becki, as well as Cathy herself) receive this message on their screen. Cathy is reasonably sure that only Manuel and Jen will notice it right now, but she has no real way of knowing. Having now discovered who is around at the moment and having checked for any evening activities, she switches to her mail program and reads her email. After about 10 minutes, she switches back to her Waterfall Glen window and sees this output:

```
Manuel waves.
Manuel says, "how's it going this morning?"
```

She responds and they both interact:

```
Cathy says, "just starting the day, still at home. I'll be
heading in to the lab in a few minutes."
Manuel nods. "See you in a few. Drop by when you get in?"
Cathy nods.
```

She then types a command to indicate that she's doing something other than using the MOO:

```
idle driving in to the lab
```

The MOO responds to Cathy with:

```
[Idling at 8:22 A.M. on Wednesday: driving in to the lab]
```

Everyone else in the room sees:

```
Cathy idles: driving in to the lab
```

At this point, she shuts off her PC, gathers her things, and drives in to work. When she gets in to work she drops by Manuel's physical office and takes care of other business around the division, then sits down at her workstation. She logs in, brings up her various windows, including the MOO client session with the Waterfall Glen window. Once again, she reads the recent past history in her MOO window. She sees that since she left home, Becki has "woken up" on the MOO, Becky and Manuel have had a short discussion over who was working on a particular section of programming code, and then the room has been quiet. As is customary, she "emotes" a blink:

```
:blinks
```

Jen has noticed that Cathy is here now and responds, beginning an interaction. Note that in terms of time zone, Jen is several hours ahead of her Argonne colleagues:

```
Jen blinks from France
Cathy waves
Cathy [to Jen]: Hi there, thanks your comments.
Jen nods.
Jen [to Cathy]: I have a meeting soon and then will be heading
home. Let me know what else you want me to do. I will be in
early tomorrow morning so can get it done before you get in.
Cathy nods.
```

Cathy then informs the others she's starting to concentrate:

```
Cathy starts to work on her paper again.
Becki is glad she's not working on a paper.
Manuel laughs.
Becki says, "but you might be interested in some of the results
of last night's computer computations for your paper."
Cathy says, "oh really? Where should I look?"
Becki says, "check out /www/proj/quantum/current.html"
```

And so the morning goes. The participants work on their projects, with occasional informal discussion. Most of the conversation, which Cathy ignores, consists of Becki and Manual coordinating on a library interface. Around lunchtime, Cathy sees:

```
Thomas pages, "Hey, a bunch of us in the room here are planning
on lunch. Interested?"
```

This is a message from Thomas, who is in another room on Waterfall Glen. He's in the Hangout Room, which she usually avoids because it has a larger number of users and is too loud for her. He has sent her a message from another location (referred to as "paging"). She agrees that lunch would be good:

```
page thomas sure, meet you out front in 5 minutes
(from the Hangout room) Thomas grins
```

She idles on Waterfall Glen, saves her document, grabs her coat, and heads out. Following lunch, she starts working on her paper again. She realizes that she needs some information from Albert (who is still idle) so asks him a question by typing:

```
Albert, Do you have a reference for the Dyson quote?
```

She sees on her screen:

```
Cathy [to Albert]: Do you have a reference for the Dyson quote?
Manuel [to Cathy]: Al's still in travel in California.
Cathy says, "oh yeah."
Cathy shrugs, he'll see the question anyway.
Manuel nods.
```

Later in the afternoon, Manuel decides to get some coffee, announces this fact on the MOO and the others join him for an impromptu meeting around his whiteboard. Eventually the working day is over, and everyone heads out for the evening. In the evening, Cathy sits down at her home PC to work on her paper a bit more, and checks Waterfall Glen to see what's happening. Albert has de-idled while she was out and answered her question.

```
[5:45 pm]
Albert blinks from California while checking his email
Manuel waves
Albert reads scrollback.
Albert [to Cathy]: Sure, that quote was from the latest ACM.
Albert thinks for a moment.
Albert [to Cathy]: If you can't find it there, let me know and
I'll double-check for it.
Albert [to Manuel]: Hellohello. Gotta run. See you later.
Manuel grins.
Albert idles: back to the conference
[9:15 pm]
Cathy blinks, but missed Albert. "Oh well."
Cathy logs out for the night.
Cathy idles: offline
```

The scenario above exemplified one of the simplest uses of Waterfall Glen: a small research group using a project room in the MOO to coordinate their day-to-day activities. In it, we presented examples of the use of a persistent communication channel, synchronous and asynchronous interactions, basic MOO commands, social and work communication (and how they're inextricably intertwined), cross-room communication and the ability to access the MOO remotely.

While this captures the essence of MOO interaction, many users of Waterfall Glen have more complicated scenarios – they may have multiple characters, move around the MOO, or take advantage of MOO programming features to enrich the environment. Some scientists use Emacs and the Unix "screen" command to maintain persistence rather than using a PC MOO client and the proxy server – but the effect is nearly the same. Also, some days on Waterfall Glen may be substantially less productive than the above example. For the most part, however, people do have useful interactions that benefit their professional and social interactions; this is the type of environment envisioned when the Waterfall Glen Project began.

In the next section we offer some more general observations about the successes and problems with using a MOO environment for the support of collaborative work. These observations are derived from our own use of the environment, from a questionnaire study carried out in 1998 (with 23 respondents), and from two field studies carried out in 1996 and 1998. The field studies included interviews with active users (for more information see Churchill and Bly 1999a,b,c). We frame our observations in the context of other computer-based collaborative environments for supporting ongoing working relationships.

14.3 Observations

Waterfall Glen has been, and continues to be, an extremely effective and successful collaborative virtual environment. It has been in operation for over seven years and has been the underlying support for many collaborations – in a recent week, over 16 000 interactions were recorded.

So why is Waterfall Glen such a success? One reason is that Waterfall Glen is populated by people who wish to communicate with each other – it has long been acknowledged that getting a "critical" mass of people (the "right" people) to use any communication medium is crucial to its success (Ehrlich, 1987; Kraut *et al.*, 1994). From our usage of Waterfall Glen and from our interviews and observations we have derived a number of characteristics that we believe are fundamental to why those people are there. These characteristics centre on:

1. The technology itself and what it affords. There are a number of elements to this:
   - Waterfall Glen is a lightweight, modifiable, continuously available, persistent environment.
   - Waterfall Glen supports multiple groups to coexist within the same environment – and supports people moving freely between those multiple groups. Groups themselves can freely change and evolve.
   - Waterfall Glen allows people to have multiple personae, matched to multiple roles. It also supports multiple simultaneous interactions.
2. The social context of work. The people in Waterfall Glen collaborate on a regular basis and share a social work context and a culture of work. Further, there is a match between features of the technology and the working practices of the group.
3. The broader organizational context within which Waterfall Glen exists. There is ongoing administrative and infrastructure support for the use of Waterfall Glen.

We will consider each of these points in turn. Before doing so we would like to note, however, that Waterfall Glen has had its share of problems; there have been the occasional technical and social disasters (Churchill and Bly, 1999a). It does not satisfy *all* of the collaboration and interaction requirements of its users. Some people enjoy using the MOO; others don't. However, overall, it works exceedingly well for a subset of the division and as a more peripheral tool for the rest.

14.3.1 Technology Affordances

A Lightweight, Modifiable, Continuously Available, Persistent Environment

Waterfall Glen is computationally and cognitively lightweight. Relative to many collaborative virtual environments, it makes few demands on computers and on users. These low overheads in terms of computational requirements, screen real estate and technical training are critical to its success. Logging on to Waterfall Glen does not require a mass of technology and technological know-how. Furthermore, it is easy to get immediately involved in Waterfall Glen – one can begin traversing the virtual terrain and conversing almost immediately. While it is clear that a text-only world has its limitations, many more graphically rich collaborative virtual environments require considerably more technology, computing power and practice to achieve successful interactions. Furthermore, navigation and communication are not trivial for beginners. For example, Bowers *et al.* (1996b) have observed that puppeteering virtual bodies in graphical virtual environments requires considerable effort.

Waterfall Glen is also unobtrusive; there are few visual interruptions and little noise: Waterfall Glen interactions intrude only minimally on other work on the workstation screen and not at all on the room noise level. All these features mean that it is possible to access the Waterfall Glen environment from many more locations than many other virtual environments allow – one can log on from a hotel room or a cyber café with little fear that the technology will not be sufficient or that interactions in the virtual world will interfere with those ongoing in the physical world.

Although starting to interact in Waterfall Glen requires little technical skill and the basic environment is not very sophisticated, more in-depth learning of the capabilities of the technology can occur as the desire for use increases – it is possible to learn how to modify one's character, create and modify rooms and create objects in Waterfall Glen. This type of appropriation and adaptation of technologies has been shown to be central to their success; ease of modification allows technology to be moulded to the needs of the users as and when those needs change. This was noted by Harrison and Dourish (1996) in their reportage of the success and failure of different media space experiments – where people could not easily modify the location of cameras and the ways in which the media space connections were set up, technologies were rated as less successful. Notably, end-user modifications to Waterfall Glen are also usually local – they do not necessarily affect the entire environment. Rather, we observed that new features are developed (e.g. some of the text-log summarization tools) and are disseminated along conversation lines – a new feature is created and then shared among one's closest collaborators. In this way different groups establish very different practices around the use of the technology, and in turn the technology evolves with those practices. Waterfall Glen has the flexibility to support the existence of multiple micro-environments within it.

The fact that Waterfall Glen is continuously available and up and running whether people are there or not is central to it being viewed as a collaborative virtual environment rather than a chat application – Waterfall Glen goes on whether you are there or not. It does not go away when I go away, and life continues in other virtual rooms even when one's own main collaborators are not present.

Equally critical is the fact that the environment is always present and easily accessible through the addition of screen and proxy server support. Participants can move from office workstations to home computers to travel laptops without losing their place in the conversations. This ease of access gives people the ability to "catch up" after moments or hours of absence, and makes visiting places or rooms in the MOO viable and adds to the sense that this is a familiar place for interaction. This sense of continuity and knowing that others may be there means that there is little overhead in terms of social planning for meeting friends and strangers – it is possible to simply "bump into" people in the virtual rooms of the MOO and strike up opportunistic conversations.

The fact that Waterfall Glen is persistent is also crucial – conversations, rooms, objects and people all remain the same unless actively changed. They do not disappear or go away when one leaves the virtual environment. This kind of persistence underlies the development of a notion of place – and places can make people feel like they belong and want to go back – which in turn will determine the success or failure of a virtual environment. And, as noted, the continuous availability of the MOO rooms and the fact that others may be there mean that the virtual rooms have temporal properties – they evolve and develop through being lived in. The development of an idea of place requires the development of conventions of use which in turn require time and the unfolding of shared, lived experiences; it is the experience over time, the lived and observed patterns of use that make a space into a place (Harrison and Dourish, 1996). The persistence of MOO rooms means that these spaces can become places with ongoing patterns, patterns which continue without our active presence.

Multiple Groups, Changing and Evolving

Support for multiple groups is one of the key features of the success of Waterfall Glen. Although the spatial layout or geography of the MOO rooms is not used at all – people do not tend to wander through the virtual terrain, and in fact seldom change rooms – the fact that there are several rooms in the MOO is central to this support for multiple groups. If only one communication space (i.e. one room) existed, the "noise" level would be unbearable. Rooms are used as a communication scoping mechanism for different project specific or social groups. New groups are able to easily create new rooms for their own conversations and collaboration. Groups are free to make rooms either open or closed, although seldom are rooms closed explicitly by MOO (technological) enforcement. Rather, we have found that in the MOO, as in physical environments (Clement and Wagner, 1995) social conventions are invoked to keep people out of certain spaces. Any particular group may be idle for hours, sometimes days. But as noted above, the place or room remains accessible to all as long as the MOO is up and running – which, except for server crashes, it is.

Crucially, because these different groups, although in different rooms, cohabit the same MOO environment, it is possible to be active within more than one group at a time within requiring a change of technology. Further, MOO rooms have permeable boundaries – I can page from one room to another and, if necessary, I can easily go into another room. I can also look to see if particular people are in the MOO, and if so, where they are. Such easy movement and communication facilitates the active creation and maintenance of different networks or constellations – something that has been observed to be a crucial basis of collaboration (Salvador and Bly, 1997; Wellman *et al.*, 1996).

Multiple Characters, Multiple Interactions

Because conversations may be ongoing over a long period of time, and because people belong to multiple different groups, it is crucial that members be free to participate in multiple conversations simultaneously, and to be privy to activities within a number of different MOO rooms. To achieve this in Waterfall Glen, people have multiple MOO characters or avatars. This is unusual in MUDs and MOOs; most only allow one virtual environment character per person. It is worth noting that these characters do not represent different personae that the owner has, as might be the case in more gaming or fantasy oriented virtual environments. In Waterfall Glen most character descriptions are fairly straightforward and the emphasis is on representing oneself in accord with "real life" (Schiano and White (1998) observed the same practice in their observations of users of a text-based virtual environment). However, having multiple characters does allow people to "appear" or be present in more than one MOO room at a time. People can either be actively taking part in multiple conversations in different rooms, or simply having their character(s) "listen in" – that is, having a character in a room means one can record relevant conversations in the form of logs for asynchronous review. Of course, the relatively small technological, screen real estate and cognitive (attentional) demands the MOO places on its users makes active participation in multiple rooms far more possible. It is easier to be in more than one MOO place at a time then it is to be present in multiple 3D worlds or multiple video conferences at one time.

In general, people do not explicitly represent their characters differently to indicate whether they are actively attending or not. However, there are hints in the MOO that someone may not be attending directly although their character is in the room. If the owner of the character has not typed anything for a while, then the character will have a slightly different description tied to it. This was illustrated in the "typical day" scenario above. If the owner has typed something in the last minute, the description of that character is "alert". If nothing has been typed for less than 5 minutes, they are "daydreaming". If they are idle for more than an hour, they are "staring into space". There are also tools available for giving hints to character owners about the activities that have been going on in rooms whilst they have not been directly attending. One such tool was initially developed for InfoPark but has migrated to Waterfall Glen; when a character becomes active after some time idling, the owner gets a private message that summarizes some of the events that have taken place during their (attentional) absence. For example, the MOO might type:

```
** First event: 5.30pm 05/11 Last event: 6:39 05/11
** Becki entered and stayed in the room
** Manuel spoke directly to you
Cathy blinks
```

This text indicates that Cathy idled at 5.30pm, blinked at 6.39pm and during that time Becki entered the room and Manuel spoke to Cathy. These pieces of information give information about whether it is worth scrolling back to read the logs of conversations that have taken place.

14.3.2 Shared Social Work Context and Practices

A significant aspect of Waterfall Glen is that it is in use by people who already know one another and have working relationships with one another. In fact, the work itself, not Waterfall Glen, is the shared context in which participants come together. Social interactions imply work interactions. Thus, the MOO provides another means of carrying on conversations and collaborations that are already occurring.

Furthermore, the work itself is most often centred on computation. Members not only know one another, they also spend a great deal of their day sitting at or near their workstation(s). The user community is comfortable with being online and is willing to experiment. Waterfall Glen becomes a natural extension to their workspace and to their interactions.

In this way, there are interesting intersections between the physical and digital worlds. Waterfall Glen provides one way of getting in touch with others. It is by no means the only means available – it has its niche, but it fits in neatly with the other available technologies. People interact in Waterfall Glen to organize and coordinate phone conversations, face-to-face meetings, email exchanges and so on. We have observed explicit coordination of this kind and also more kinds of activity awareness. The activity may lead to the use of other technologies for communication (e.g. I saw you typing in the room so I knew I could phone you). This form of "waylaying" or opportunistic communication has been noted also by Erickson *et al.* (1999) and Bradner *et al.* (1999) in their use of a lightweight group chat system, "BABBLE".

However, it is notable that seeing someone in a virtual room is not an indication that they are in any particular physical place. While Waterfall Glen creates a communication link, people could be connected in from anywhere. Unlike media spaces which link physical locations and where the connection between two physical spaces is the virtual element, Waterfall Glen provides a completely virtual place for interactions to take place (Bly *et al.*, 1993; Harrison and Dourish, 1996).

As with most remote or mediated communication, social interactions are not without problems. In particular, the MOO tends to magnify aspects of interactions that might not occur in face-to-face encounters. For example, "whispering" (that is sending a private text message to an individual rather than to the whole room) promotes secretiveness even when that isn't the intention. There is always the potential for disastrous typing mistakes. And rooms make who is hanging out with whom more obvious.

Of course, the flexibility of Waterfall Glen does not presuppose any structure on the communications. Emoting is important; blinks and waves are frequent actions. Actions stated on the MOO generally reflect real life, not virtual-only interactions. The MOO is simply part of the working practices of the group.

14.3.3 Administrative and Infrastructure Support

Although life continues apace in the Waterfall Glen virtual environment, its success rests on factors in the culture of the material world in which Waterfall Glen is embedded – perhaps the most important aspect of Waterfall Glen's success is the support it receives from the division itself. There is both strong technical support and positive managerial participation. These make it possible to program new features as needed, to offer help to new users, and to ensure ongoing value in the MOO interactions.

Installing, maintaining and developing the MOO require considerable technical expertise. The staff in the division support the MOO server, MOO database, custom features and external processes. For example, two of the most useful additions to Waterfall Glen have been the "poke" client and the "idle summary" text that summarizes activities in a room since a character was last active (both of these were described above). Interestingly, more effort has gone into the creation and support of persistence mechanisms than any other type of development.

The technical staff, in particular, also provide much of the initiation and instruction for new users. Resources include email aliases, a clue sheet and mail instructions, as well as general instruction as people connect. Equally significant are the clues on how to act, offering a model of MOO culture.

Finally, both the technical and the managerial staff are actively involved in Waterfall Glen interactions daily. This participation encourages the use of Waterfall Glen by others in the division as well as providing an opportunity for members of the division to interact directly with staff members who might otherwise be inaccessible.

14.4 Summary

In this chapter we have described the development and use of Waterfall Glen, a text-based MOO that is used to maintain work and social relationships within a distributed working group.

Our observations suggest several factors that are important in making Waterfall Glen so useful: its lightweightness, modifiability, continuous availability and persistence; its flexibility in the ability to support multiple groups and for individuals to be in multiple conversations at the same time; the underlying shared culture of work that lends familiarity and that allows working rhythms to be collaboratively established; the organizational support for Waterfall Glen; and the nature of the work itself.

The success of Waterfall Glen suggests that there is a greater potential than is being realized for tools that fill a niche in conversational gaps for people who are not always co-located. Waterfall Glen supports and augments normal day-to-day interactions by giving group members a persistent virtual place, unrelated to physical location, in which to communicate. These interactions are the key to successful collaboration; Waterfall Glen's greatest strength is that it lets different groups of users interact with minimal overhead.

Waterfall Glen is primarily a basic interaction tool; it does not support documentation sharing or video conferencing. There is considerable evidence that people meaningfully collaborate with each other despite the simple representational nature of the MOO; rich interactions do not *require* rich interfaces. Quick responses, familiarity with each other and with each other's work practices, and the ongoing ubiquity all play a part in this. In addition, the seamless move between synchronous and asynchronous communication lets interactions and collaborations continue across time and space. The utility of the environment for these collaborators is created in the match of the technology to their working practices and communication needs.

Finally, we note that Waterfall Glen was not designed to be a success and its real success evolved over time – the interactions created the places. Too often technologies assume an arrangement of access to people and information, and often are focused within organizational boundaries. Often also the technical requirements are a limitation on who can use virtual environments. But people's relationships with collaborators seldom follow these boundaries. Waterfall Glen's availability beyond the organization in which it is housed and its low technical requirements mean that it can support broad networks and does not limit the people who can be talked to what the technology allows.

Acknowledgements

The authors would like to thank Bob Olson and Rick Stevens for their support of this work. We would also like to thank all those who took part in our interview studies, online questionnaire and email discussions for their insightful comments and suggestions about the use of Waterfall Glen. Last, but certainly not least, we would like to thank FX Palo Alto Laboratory and Argonne National Laboratory for their support of this work.

Chapter 15
The Role of the Personal in Social Workspaces: Reflections on Working in AlphaWorld

Avon Huxor

15.1 Introduction

Increasingly, many of us find our working life having to work not only in a main office, but also at home, at other institutions, from hotel rooms and so on. Such multiple sites, however, create problems in that all too often we find our documents and our colleagues unavailable at our current physical location. In a world where telecommuting is the norm, it seems plausible that a stable shared virtual office might be of benefit, creating a set of places that can be accessed to locate content and meet colleagues. This chapter will describe the issues that have arisen from three years of regular use of collaborative 3D virtual space built within AlphaWorld, a popular Internet-based shared 3D world. A small virtual "office" was constructed to try to understand the possibilities and the problems of this technology in actual use. It is these possibilities and concerns that will be discussed.

One issue that I hope to address is the nature of what 3D shared spaces can offer to distributed collaborations. Why is there an interest in 3D at all? There does seem to be a commonsense view that if, as seems the case, the 2D WIMP (windows, icons, mouse, pointer) interface, such as the standard Macintosh or Windows desktop, is such an improvement over the command line interface, then surely 3D must offer yet more advantages. But it is still somewhat unclear what these are, for although shared 3D environments have been freely available on the Internet for many years, they seem to have had little impact, except in the multi-user gaming community. Given that many of the problems and benefits of any innovation often take time to make themselves clear, I decided to use an easily available technology – AlphaWorld – to support regular ongoing collaborations. The motivation for investigating collaboration spaces arose from increasing requirements in both research and teaching at the Centre for Electronic Arts (CEA), which is a postgraduate centre within Middlesex University. Many of the research projects we work on have a collaborative aspect with other institutions, and many of the students now work from home or a workplace, rather than coming into the Centre itself.

I first came across AlphaWorld in autumn of 1995, soon after its official public release in June of that year, as part of a review of the various shared world technologies. However, I did not begin to use it fully until a year later, in late 1996. The main reason being that, having a background in design, the students, and myself felt that AlphaWorld offered limited scope for design, as the object types were selected from a limited range. Also, to be honest, we found the visual style one that was hard for us to feel comfortable with. So for the first year we experimented with Black Sun (now Blaxxun) technology, which allowed for shared spaces to be constructed in VRML. But these more designer-oriented technologies exhibited other important problems. At that time, it proved difficult to persuade my collaborators to download and run the browser, as it was so demanding on their machines, and the performance was unacceptable to those who did not have a specific interest, as we did, in 3D worlds. The Active Worlds browser (used to access AlphaWorld), however, is small, easy to download and install, and – unlike the more conventional VRML browsers – runs fast. These features proved crucial in drawing other users into my virtual office, creating a working environment in which issues stood some chance of arising.

The approach taken below in describing these issues has been partly inspired by published informal descriptions of online use. For example, Julian Dibbell (Dibbell, 1999) has written an interesting personal history of his experiences in LambdaMOO. This chapter, unlike his book however, takes only a few of the many events and problems that occurred in the functioning of the space, and uses them as a jumping off point to investigate the wider design issues: it is not a diary. But equally, these issues have not been derived from a study of the existing theoretical literature alone. I have, instead, used a readily available technology, and, as problems or benefits are identified, sought to investigate the reasons and themes that arise from these. What is interesting is that many of the problems and solutions that arose in the past few years were somewhat unexpected.

However, the research project overall employs a somewhat more formal view of this approach, one based on a participatory design (PD), as described by O'Day *et al.* (1998). They employed PD in the development of Pueblo: a text-based virtual environment built on MOO technology. The social aspects of design matter, as they note, for the following reasons, all of which apply to the AlphaWorld space:

1. The boundary between users and designers is blurred. My colleagues and I not only use the technology, we also design adaptations to make it work better. For example, we have recently added links to audio chat to overcome some of the problems of text-chat, which is the AlphaWorld standard communication format, as we found that we mainly use the system to create the first encounter and engage in lightweight social exchange. Often the next step, if an important issue needed to be discussed, would be to phone one another up. It seemed valuable to add voice-chat into the space directly. One benefit of so doing, for example, is that one could continue to work another task on the machine while talking. Text-chat required that the user switched frequently between windows. It was the negotiation of these requirements that made all users feel involved.

2. The social nature of the space permits immediate response to the space by users, including requests for changes and notes of problems. As the owner of the virtual office, I am the only user who can edit both its appearance and functions. One colleague in particular has frequently engaged in negotiation over the

content to be placed in its various rooms. But as we often met in the space, he could request changes as they arose in his mind and quickly respond to any changes made.

3. The flexibility and open nature of these systems allows for quick changes. Active Worlds has links to other Web resources and handles for small applications that make extensions to the browser and its worlds possible. For example, my co-worker Martin Kaltenbrunner has used the Active Worlds bot technology to allow for users to have multiple avatars simultaneously, allowing awareness of activity in a variety of different locations in any one world, or across different worlds. Such multiple representations are common in MUDs, and useful when used in a workplace environment (Churchill and Bly, 1999c), but are rarely found in 3D spaces.

Participatory design makes users subjects, investigators and designers. It allows for initial problems to be quickly overcome, and moving the use of the virtual environment into a more long-term productive phase. It is true that this created a distinction between those who were able to make the modifications and those who could not, and this is an important point for the future. Simple interfaces to allow for improvements by all users can only improve the acceptance and uptake of collaboration systems.

The possibility of extended use, more likely when users can have their concerns addressed, brings new possibilities for study, for as Dourish *et al.* (1996) note, the value of long-term studies, as the technology co-evolves with use, and throws up questions and solutions. And this was a feature of the PD approach that, as is described below, did occur. The greatest surprise was that I found myself slowly, but radically, changing my view on both the value of 3D as a navigation mechanism, and of the visual style underlying AlphaWorld.

15.2 The AlphaWorld Virtual Office

The virtual space that I have been using is within AlphaWorld, a large and established world that uses Active Worlds, an Internet-based shared 3D environment technology.[1] Active Worlds offers many advantages which led to its adoption by me in late 1996 over competing systems such as Black Sun (now Blaxxun[2]), and Onlive[3] Traveller. As stated above, early work concentrated on the Black Sun browser, due to the ability for us to design and build complex VRML worlds, before it was dropped in favour of Active Worlds, and its potential to reach a wider audience.

The early experiments with Black Sun's worlds did however, produce interesting lessons. The main Black Sun world – Cybergate – was used for both a number of

---

[1] The Active Worlds browser can be downloaded from http://www.activeworlds.com/. The building described is at 188S, 34E, and can be teleported to once the user has entered AlphaWorld,
[2] http://www.blaxxun.com/
[3] http://www.onlive.com/

committee meeting, and for online tutorials between myself and one of the CEA's students. On the whole these were not very successful. The issues that arose were:

1. After initial exploration, it was found that the spatial nature of the world was not used. Each user would find no reason to move their avatar, and would simply engage in text-chat from wherever they found themselves. The machine was rendering a 3D space for no real purpose, except tying up its resources. The objects in the world had not been designed or built by the users, and contained no objects relating to their discussions. Thus there was no reason to move in and interact with the world.

2. The lack of content: in both the committee meetings and the tutorials, one often needs to have access to personal materials, such as documents, emails and so on. The virtual world was like a open public space, rather than a workplace in which various "residents" have access to such resources. (Furthermore, the large 3D window took up valuable screen real estate that other tools, useful to the chatting, such as email readers and Web browsers, required.)

3. The lack of privacy: the space had a strange sense of belonging to only one person, its creator, but also belonging to all that chose to visit. We wanted to use a space that all interested users could access, but which would not be like a public bar.

4. The behaviour of many of the other users: many of the users who passed through the space during the meetings often used the text-chat to express various forms of verbal abuse, which was very upsetting for others. Similar results were found by Churchill and Bly (1999a) in their investigation of text-based MUD use. There seems something about the gaming roots of the technology that encourages a playful, but sometimes malevolent, approach, which affects its use for work.

Based on the experiences in these meetings, it was decided to continue the experiment in AlphaWorld, for the following reasons.

Firstly, the very size of AlphaWorld allows us to manage the privacy and behaviour issues, since by arranging to meet away from the central area (which is where all users appear by default) the chances of encountering users who have not been invited to the specified coordinates are low. This creates a sense of privacy, without there being one of exclusion, very much like the physical world. One feels part of a larger community but can also escape the crowds.

Secondly, unlike most shared 3D worlds, in AlphaWorld registered citizens can build their own spaces on any unclaimed land. The ability for each user to build a space within AlphaWorld allows the introduction of content, as each object can be easily linked to any external URL. Thus, they can hyperlink to user-specific content.

In the virtual office I use this content is primarily managed with a Web-based, document-centred, collaboration tool called BSCW[4]. Just as my physical office contains my personal work materials and resources, so I can link walls, floors and

---

[4] Basic Support for Collaborative Working is a publicly available shared file and collaboration management system. See `http://bscw.gmd.de/` for further details.

other objects in my virtual office to folders in BSCW that only my colleagues can access by password. These two features of AlphaWorld, its large size and the ease with which users can build their own spaces, means that we can have a gradation of spaces – from the very public, to that appropriate for colleagues, to the private.

One basic principle we have aims to ensure ease of use and, as far as possible, an openness. Tollmar *et al.* (1996) found that their experimental awareness system, named @Work, although initially used by the subjects, was soon dropped from use. One reason for this was that the system was closed: persons outside the trial could not use it. By using existing, open and useful tools, such as BSCW and Active Worlds, there remains the hope that users who enter the community for one reason will stay as they can co-opt the tools for their own uses. For this reason, the option of developing our own tool meeting our specific requirements was soon discarded, as few except my colleagues on the trial would be reachable through it. Using a stable public technology, such as AW, makes the project open.

Also, unlike other tools, AlphaWorld employs a "land claim" metaphor, in which users can stake out a part of the world, and using a library of objects, very quickly build a simple building. As we shall see below, this feature is central to the character of AlphaWorld, and explains many of its benefits over competing systems, and thus warrants some explanation. The building process in AlphaWorld is very simple. First one must find a plot of ground which is still "green grass", one on which no one else has built. One creates new objects from an existing one. A right click on the mouse brings up an "object properties" box, with various operations. Only the owner can edit the properties, but any user can copy an existing object to create their own. There is thus an individual ownership and control in AlphaWorld, a central feature in the text-based MOOs, but which seemed to be lost in the move to 3D, possibly as the designers thought that it took their skills to create a world.

To begin a new construction, one must find a nearby object in the world, which is copied and moved to your own plot. Doing so makes the user the owner of the object and the plot: only that user can edit the building in future. The seed object can be further copied and, by simply editing the name, it is possible to change it into one of many of the library objects, which include floor panels, walkways, walls, roofs etc. Once a user has placed objects on a plot the area is "claimed", and others cannot build in it. In addition, it is possible to script each object. For example, a wall can be scripted so that if a user avatar bumps into the wall, or the user clicks on it with the mouse, it will pull up a Web page on an associated Web browser. The very simple building tool, which is integrated with world viewing (it is not a separate application), facilitates very fast space creation and modification by users who do not need to have demanding 3D design skills. For example, in Fig. 15.1, the user is editing an object to add the "activate" command. This will initiate the download of a page to which the object is linked when the object is clicked by any user.

Using these tools, a simple virtual office was constructed. However, given that in Cybergate we found the 3D space little used, what else could the spatial nature of the world offer? The answer seemed to lie in the support of chance encounters, which is discussed next, although, as we shall see later, extensive use of the space showed other benefits emerging.

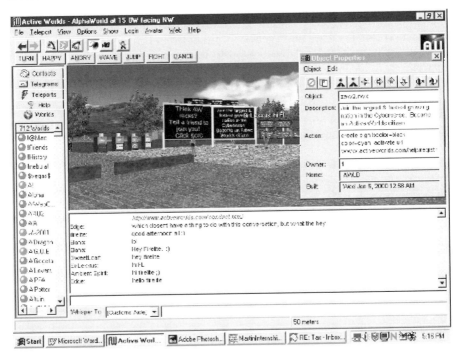

Figure 15.1 Editing an object in AlphaWorld.

15.2.1 Chance Encounters in Shared Space

The subject of chance encounters is one that often arises when discussing support for distributed working, for the new forms of working introduce new problems, especially in the maintenance of collaboration and team building. If members of a workgroup are not co-present, there is a lack of community feeling. There are many technologies to facilitate the formal meetings (such as Microsoft's NetMeeting) that make up much of the traditional workplace, but these seem to miss many of the informal aspects that are crucial to working life. An increase in the use of email, the telephone and other communication tools might appear to threaten the more unplanned and social aspects of work. Tom Erickson, a researcher at IBM who teleworks extensively, has observed of his own behaviour, that "In fact, I take part in 'planned spontaneity' – I wander the hallways on purpose so I can bump into people" (Scholtz *et al.*, 1998).

While at work, it is our colleagues that we can access most easily, and the relationships of offices and studios act to bring people of related interest within the same region of a building. But equally, we have chance encounters with others in the workplace that may not be directly working on one's own project, but on another that may be, in some way, related by the nature of the organization. These effects have been researched in some detail, and in a variety of building types, including offices, research laboratories, universities and prisons (Space Syntax Laboratory, 1997) and are more generally discussed in Hillier (1996).

After the failure of the Cybergate world to facilitate meetings, we decided to concentrate on dealing with the problem of informal encounter, of "awareness" – knowing who in the team are around and what they are involved in. Other, non-3D, awareness tools, such as ICQ[5] and Virtual Places, were used but all exhibited their own problems. For example, in ICQ, a user is only aware of other users that are on the contact list – and have agreed to be part of it. There is no support for "weak ties", those contacts who are not those we would immediately list as colleagues, but which have been shown to be crucial to the working of an organization (Feldman, 1987). There are other approaches: Virtual Places allows for co-presence and awareness on the same Web page. But the range of awareness is too small. How long does a user spend on a single Web page? In a physical office, we go about our business on a range of tasks but have a relatively stable location, which allows for encounters with those passing by.

The fact is that the "chance encounters" are not really totally chance. If that were the case we would have an equal chance of encountering anyone from the planet wherever we are. The chance encounters we experience are with people we half expect to meet, even if not at that time: colleagues, friends or whatever. We work in the same buildings, visit the same parts of town and go to the same bars. These social relations, which make chance encounters more valuable than the purely random ones, are both expressed and affected by the architecture (among other things). In other words, the spatial arrangement of places matters, and it was with this in mind that the virtual office was constructed. Its primary aim was to allow for the management of encounters between users who are come to the place in the virtual world for content (pointers to content), but may then meet others, both immediate colleagues and weak ties. These places draw on the idea of "locale": that space is a resource for interactions that suggests certain actions and prohibits others. For example, a shopping centre increases the chance of shopping occurring; although it does not force passers-by to purchase, it certainly encourages it.

The virtual office thus acts as a shared space in which content relevant to certain tasks is brought together, and the possibly of visual encounters is managed by the layout of the building. In Fig. 15.2, the left-hand window shows the virtual office and the right-hand window is the BSCW page invoked by clicking on one of the walls within the office, which contains shared content. It is this content that is intended to draw users to the space, knowing that they might encounter the owner of the space or others interested in the content.

As hoped, the virtual office did function as intended, and over the past few years chance encounters between my collaborators and myself, and with weak ties, did occur. It is this aspect of the space that has been previously most fully documented and explored (Huxor, 1999). The role it played in managing encounters became clear from the how the space came to be regularly used. Text-chat was the main communication mechanism in AlphaWorld, as in most of the virtual world

---

[5] http://www.icq.com/

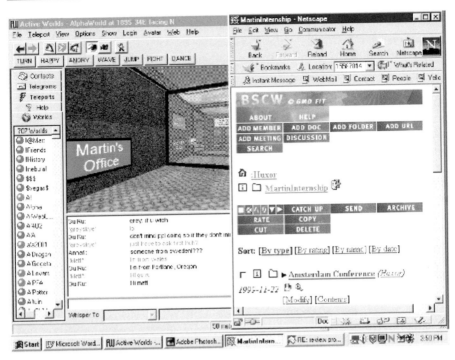

Figure 15.2 The virtual office and associated BSCW content.

technologies, due to hardware and network constraints which made voice and video communication difficult for many potential users. However, early experiences showed that this form of communication is rather limited for many. It takes time for a sentence to be written, and spelling is often a problem due to the need to type faster than usual. It was found that in most situations, where I was in conversation with one other user, we would normally resort to telephoning each other. That is, the text-chat was fine for the initial encounter and exchange of pleasantries, but if more was to be said, other existing communication tools performed better. It supported encounter rather than communication or other aspects of work. The valuable role that shared spaces can play in encounter management has also been observed in real settings by Churchill and Bly (1999a,b,c).

15.3 Beyond Encounters

Although aimed to facilitate encounters, extended use of the AlphaWorld space has lead to a reassessment of the possibilities of virtual spaces. It has been interesting how many of the problems and unexpected solutions that have arisen were unexpected. Early experiences with Cybergate, and even AlphaWorld, seemed to lead me to early conclusions that proved to be quite ill founded. In particular, as mentioned above, it appeared that the 3D nature of the spaces had little to offer for navigation over traditional means. Secondly, the visual style and metaphor of AlphaWorld appeared retrogressive, almost an offence to the designers' eye.

15.3.1 Virtual Space as an Art of Memory

It has often been observed that 3D should support navigation. That is, users can navigate around content, as they might a city. But experience appeared to question this, both my own, and that from published findings. For example, Henderson and Card (1986) found that a spatial metaphor was not readily used within their *BigScreen* system, in which (task-related) virtual desktops were laid out in a large single virtual workspace. Users would jump from one desktop to another, rather than navigating through the 2D space over the virtual workspace to get to the desktops. As they state, "task switching seemed to have a non-spatial representation in the user's mind: tasks were easy to name (read the mail), but hard to locate in space (Is mail north or south of here?)". They do, however, concede that there may be situations in which spatial proximity and analogies might be used to advantage. When I linked my BSCW content to the AlphaWorld virtual space, this view initially seemed to still apply. I would often use the BSCW Web interface to access content rather than the hyperlinks from the virtual building. The space, as far I as could determine, functioned only as a space for encounters with other users.

The real surprise came many months later. I found that as my use of BSCW expanded and the number of document files and folders grew, it became increasingly less easy to access through its standard Web interface. Instead, I found that I would go to the AlphaWorld window and navigate through it to where I knew links to specific folders were linked. Just as in a physical office, one can walk in blindfold and almost place one's hand on papers and books left on desks and cupboards. But like one's own office, this requires that the virtual space is often visited – is a home.

There is a precedent for such a technique of accessing information. In the past a trained memory was considered vitally important, and a widespread technique is one that has come to be known as "The Art of Memory", or the "method of loci". The best description of the technique, according to Yates (1966), comes from Quintilian. It is based on the use of places and images. A locus is a place easily grasped by the memory: a house, an arch etc. It can be either a real building or a totally imaginary one. An image represents the thing we wish to remember. The loci are like wax tablets for an inner writing; when not used further they fade away, leaving the loci for reuse. It is suggested that loci should not be too similar in appearance, or their resemblance will be confusing, and the best images are those that are striking or dramatic.

More recently, Spence (1984) has described a modern application of the technique, based on the mnemonics employed by contemporary medical students in an attempt to learn the vast amount required. In his example he imagines that a student, within memory, creates an image of a city. There are various parts of the city devoted to different subjects, one of which is a building, the "Physiology

House". In each room, images represent various aspects of medical knowledge. If asked to name the bones of the upper limbs, she goes, in her mind, to the upper body room, at the top of the building. There stands a Canadian Mountie in a bright scarlet jacket upon a horse, with a manacled figure tied to the horse's crupper. This gives the student a reminder of "Some Criminals Have Underestimated Royal Canadian Mounted Police", the first letters of which give the answer: scapula, clavicle, humerus, ulna, radius, carpals, metacarpals, and phalanges.

Experimental evidence suggests that the technique has cognitive validity (Zechmeister and Neiberg, 1982): that loci and images can be used as an aid to memory. The data also, however, suggest some modifications. Thus it is more important to form images in which items are interacting than necessarily being bizarre. It was found quite easy for subjects to learn 52 loci and repeat them back both forward and backward fluently. Crovitz (1971) also undertook an empirical study, which mainly aimed to test whether having more than one image at any one location would interfere with retrieval. Again the results showed that the system did indeed work.

The fact that the AlphaWorld office is a virtual one, seen through a monitor screen, seems not to hinder users in forming a complex spatial model, just as they might in a physical building where one walks around more actively, and upon which the method of loci relies. Gillner and Mallot (1997) have shown that people can learn a virtual space from a sequence of local views and movement decisions – other movement information (vestibular and proprioceptive, as found in physical navigation) were not crucial. It appears that desktop 3D virtual environments can support the method of loci, and this indeed was what I found from my own experience. It is an interesting research question to ask how 2D shared workspaces function in this regard. It seems likely that one needs the full 3D sense for the spatial memory to be effective, and would provide 3D virtual environments with a distinct advantage over the lighter weight 2D and textual shared spaces.

But what else is required for the mind to create a "theatre of memory" from the 3D space? What was crucial was that the creation of a memory of the space, one that allowed me to access links to content so easily, came from using the space daily. Equally important was the ease with which one could readily edit both the space and the links to adapt to the projects and collaborations that arose. I could add a new room to the virtual office, or change the name of a room, and its links to BSCW content, to match an important ongoing project very quickly. It was my space. It is this very personal nature of the space that, paradoxically, supported its social nature, for increasingly I entered the space to ease my own personal work practice, and that made me available for social contact through social encounters. The social space worked only in so far as it supported personal objectives.

And ironically, the social nature of shared environments adds a new twist to the method of loci. As Cicero notes (cited in Yates, 1966) "when we return to a place after a considerable absence, we not merely recognize the place itself, but remember things that we did there, and recall the persons whom we met and even the uttered thoughts which passed through our minds". In this manner we can integrate the personal and the social. The very support for memory that the space provides also supports memory of encounters with other users, in a way that cannot happen in the traditional method, for our memories of a place cannot have unexpected visitors. I can still remember, some four years later, an encounter I had in one of the Worlds Chat space station rooms. Two other avatars were there, but no chat appeared in the chat window, so I introduced myself. The tide of abusive language was both unexpected and also very hurtful. I certainly learned a lesson about how some users would retreat to a distant part of the world and use the whisper feature (private chat) for "cybersex". Spaces act as a trigger and repository for memories. Indeed, it has been observed that it is these memories that make a space become a place. The structure of space may guide and manage our actions and interactions, but place is space that has been invested with meanings, the classic example being that between a house and a home. One is full of memories of events. That is, space has up–down, left–right, but places have yesterday-tomorrow, good–bad (Harrison and Dourish, 1996). It is to this investment of meaning, possible in place, to which we now turn.

15.3.2 The Individual and the Community at the Frontier

A subtler example of the interplay between the individual and the social arose from a consideration as to the wider success of AlphaWorld. As suggested in Section 15.1, the first reaction of my colleagues and myself to AlphaWorld was not totally positive. The visual style seemed uninspired, owing more to the television series "Little House on the Prairie" than to the imagined "cyberspace" of William Gibson. Indeed, one of the first buildings to go up, as documented in the *New World Times*, the community's local newspaper, was "The Little Red Schoolhouse" (Fig. 15.3). Only later did it become apparent that this style may have had an important bearing on the subsequent success of the world.

The ability to claim land and build simple constructions has played a central role in the development of AlphaWorld. It can be argued that the metaphor of land claiming helps in understanding the history and success of the world, compared with other virtual worlds. The notion of staking out a piece of land in the wilderness and building a home on it is one that has roots deep in American culture, one central to the new technologies. The experiences of text-based shared environments, MUDs and MOOs, which have been available for much longer, has also shown the importance of building and ownership to their uptake and use. It is the ease with which users can add their own rooms to the textual environment that has been identified as crucial to their success (Schiano and White, 1998).

A look at the visual style of many of the first shared 3D worlds on the Internet showed a proliferation of frontier imagery. For example, a space station in outer space (as found in Worlds Chat), or the valley of the Western frontier (as found in AlphaWorld) – each waits to be occupied. This is significant, as no interpretation of American history has attracted as much attention (not all positive) as the "Frontier Hypothesis" put forward by Frederick Jackson Turner (Ellington, 1966). The hypothesis was originally presented in 1893 in a paper entitled "The significance of the frontier in American history" before a meeting of the American Historical

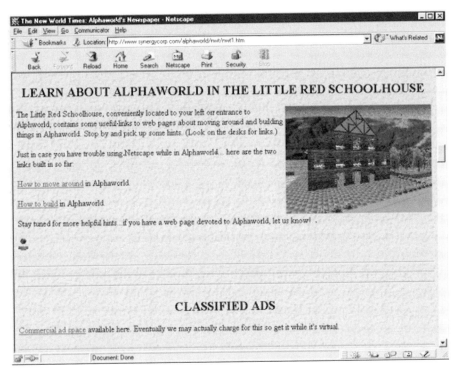

Figure 15.3 The Little Red Schoolhouse.

Association. In it Turner argued that what made Americans different from their forebears was the struggle to settle the new continent, leaving their homes to settle a series of successive Western frontiers. They had to discard many of the customs and institutions they had brought with them, from either the eastern seaboard, or even further – from their European roots – as no longer being appropriate to the new conditions. A number of factors were central to the change: most importantly that in the new lands people were few and land was plentiful. But conditions in these lands were very difficult. A second major factor was that people from different backgrounds met and intermingled, bringing together different customs and creating a new American identity.

The validity of the thesis is not at issue here. In fact, many historians have questioned not just its details, but also the idea as a whole as being less to do with historical fact than as being as much a part of the creation of the notion of American identity as the process it claims to describe. But what is beyond question is the impact that this notion has had on the public imagination, one that has led to its use to inform the understanding of many aspects of culture. Unsurprisingly, the idea of the frontier has been adopted to understand the Internet by Epperson (undated). In this model, the system administrators who began the Internet play the role of the "natives". The "early settlers" are the researchers and academics that used it as originally intended. Finally, the young hackers and bulletin board operators play the nomadic "trappers", who exploit the resources in a transitory manner. Recently, however, they have all been joined by

> the new crowd of business and commercial users play[ing] the role of "settlers", who have newly arrived from the East, have little respect for the frontier, its lore, its etiquette or it limitations. They have come to expect the Internet to service them as if it where a private business venture for their benefit. They have arrived with the advertising flyers still buzzing in their ears: 'Free resources, open frontier, plenty for all, new horizons, perfect communications, digital reliability.' What they have discovered, to their disappointment, is a lawless and strange place filled with bandits of various kinds and very little elbow room, except for the technically adept (Epperson, undated).

But there are also more specific reasons why the "frontier image" can be applied to shared 3D worlds, such as AlphaWorld; features that have close parallels with Turner's "Frontier Hypothesis". One of the characteristics of the frontier, as described by Turner, was that people were few but land was plentiful – however, the conditions in which the people had to live were very difficult. That is, the plenty that exists (in terms of space), in the physical and the virtual frontiers, comes at the cost of very demanding conditions. It is these demands that contribute to its nature. For the frontier is challenging, challenges that one must accept or else perish. Clearly the virtual is nowhere near as hazardous as the physical world; but the new virtual worlds offer their own challenges. Trying to log into AlphaWorld sometime fails, or the Internet can be so slow that you sit in frustration as the graphics wait to be downloaded. The Internet is itself unstable at times, as is the application software. AlphaWorld citizens even created a myth based on the problems that arise with very new technologies. In August 1995 there was a serious problem with the server, in which the existing buildings created by users just disappeared. This problem was grudgingly accepted by its users, who read in their local paper, the *New World Times* (a Web site run by some of its inhabitants) that their world had been hit by a natural disaster: an asteroid had struck the virtual world, destroying everything. Later, in the January 1996 edition of the *New World Times*, other problems with the server were attributed to an "Ice Age".

The second major feature of the frontier that Turner identified was that people from different backgrounds met and mingled, bringing together different customs and creating a new Americanized character. AlphaWorld provides an example: at various times of the day one can find Finns, Swedes, Spaniards and various other nationalities present – all trying to chat in either their own language or a variant of Internet English. Various forms of what constitutes acceptable behaviour collide in one space. To an outsider, this can look absurd, as various degrees of sexual innuendo and verbal abuse appear on screen. But the conditions of these new spaces allow for the creation of new social norms, calling on the strengths and weaknesses inherent in the technology. For example, who can be certain that all the characters are being "truthful" in their descriptions of themselves? The use of text-chat removes the chance of exploiting the quality of voice to make certain determinations of other people. Virtual communities are trying to create new forms of social formation, adopting what works from the physical world and abandoning those that are not appropriate.

AlphaWorld – as a visual interface of the Internet – makes this frontier metaphor more manifest. It has the appearance of a valley in the American West, and the look of many of its building elements has something of a Western town (or the image as projected through film and television). But AlphaWorld is more interesting – it goes further: not only its appearance, but also its functionality enhances the frontier myth. As described earlier, the technology implements a form of "land claiming", an imitation of the system which is so archetypal of the imagined history of the Western frontier. Indeed, land was such a central feature that its allocation, division and ownership occupied more legislative time in the Congress's first century than any other issue.

As found above, in the discussion of the "method of loci", the ability of users to have personal ownership, control and a relationship with the space has larger social implications. AlphaWorld is both a social space and personal space: their place and my place. This situation is unlike my early experiences in Cybergate, in which all were visitors except for the lone designer. The ability of AlphaWorld citizens to create and own their own personal spaces is central to its sense of community, one in which all are part of the "manifest destiny" to extend the frontier into the new virtual worlds.

15.4 Conclusions

After three years, I find that I have come to feel a genuine affinity to AlphaWorld, and my own space within it. I feel guilty if I do not have the browser running when I have the opportunity, be it at the CEA or while visiting colleagues. What has become clear over that time is that we cannot look at shared spaces or collaborative environments as separate places from the individual experience. It is the daily personal use of the space that allows for it to become a viable place for navigation and hence social encounter. Equally, the culture of AlphaWorld owes much to its ability for individuals to express themselves, and to become stakeholders. This ability to create a personal space within a wider social context is what, I believe, makes AlphaWorld work. We can get on with our work, but engage in a community while doing so. For surely this is also part of what makes a traditional "place" function.

Other lessons can also be drawn. My original beliefs about the role of 3D were challenged by the manner in which the virtual office slowly came to be a theatre of memory. Equally, initial criticisms of the visual style of AlphaWorld came to be tempered by an understanding of the need to address users' sense of narrative and community. Both lessons came from extended use of the virtual space, stretching over a period of years. To sustain this engagement with the virtual space for such a period has required that it become central to my everyday working practice.

Strangely, it is the very need for constant engagement that has recently created problems for the virtual office in AlphaWorld. As the years have passed, my working style has changed, meaning that I spend less time at a machine (be it at Middlesex University, at home or at a collaborating institution), and more time in meetings and travelling to meetings. The lack of my presence in the space has recently led to a reduction of encounters, as others feel I am less likely to be in the space. This too then reduces chance encounters between weak ties, creating a vicious circle. For this reason, the system is currently being extended to support mobile access. It is intended that encounter and communication activity within the space will allow desktop users to text-chat (using SMS) and voice-chat with users who, although away from a machine, have an Internet phone or PDA. To maintain critical mass, collaboration systems must be ubiquitous to support rapidly changing patterns of work. It is hoped that this new work will point to how the physical and the virtual workplaces can be brought together, creating a unified augmented information and social space.

Acknowledgements

I would like to thank Tim Regan of BT Laboratories, Adastral Park, who supported much of the work through a Short-term Fellowship to the author, and his colleague Andrew McGrath who provided many insights. A word of gratitude is also deserved for many of my colleagues, including Paul Rodgers of Napier University, Andy Smith of UCL, and Ralph Schroeder of Chalmers University who have used the ActiveWorlds space and provide content for this chapter. I would particularly like to thank Martin Kaltenbrunner of the FH Hagenburg in Austria, who recently undertook an internship at the CEA. His technical skills in extending Active Worlds and observations about the nature of virtual environments proved invaluable in my work.

References

Ackerman, M.S. (ed.) (1996) *CSCW '96: Cooperating Communities.* http://www.acm.org/pubs/contents/proceedings/cscw/240080/index.html.

Ainsworth, S., Wood, D. and Bibby, P. (1997) Evaluating principles for multi-representational learning environments. *7th EARLI Conference*, Athens.

Alexander, C., Ishikawa, S., Silverstein, M., Jacobson, M., Fiksdahl-King, I. and Angel, S.A. (1977) *A Pattern Language.* New York: Oxford University Press.

Anders, P. (1998) *Envisioning Cyberspace: Designing 3-D Electronic Spaces.* New York: McGraw-Hill.

Armstrong, G. (1998) *Football Hooligans: Knowing the Score.* Oxford: Berg.

Auramäki, E., Robinson, M., Aaltonen, A., Kovalainen, M., Liinamaa, A. and Tuuna-Väiskä, T. (1996) Paperwork at 78 k.p.h. *CSCW '96.* Boston: ACM.

Balsamo, A. (1995) Forms of technological embodiment: reading the body in contemporary culture. In: M. Featherstone (ed.) *Cyberspace, Cyberbodies, Cyberpunk.* London: Sage: 215–237.

Barnard, P., May, J. and Salber, D. (1996) Deixis and points of view in media spaces: an empirical gesture. *Behaviour and Information Technology* 15(1): 37–50.

Barrus, J.W., Waters, R.C. and Anderson, D.B. (1996a) Locales and beacons: efficient and precise support for large multi-user virtual environments. *IEEE Virtual Reality Annual International Symposium*, Santa Clara, CA.

Barrus, J.W., Waters, R.C. and Anderson, D.B. (1996b) Locales: supporting large multiuser virtual environment. *IEEE Computer Graphics and Applications* 16(6): 50–57.

Becker, B. and Mark, G. (1998) Social conventions in collaborative virtual environments. In *Proceedings of Collaborative Virtual Environments* (CVE 1998), Manchester, UK, 17–19 June.

Bederson, B., Hollan, J., Druin, A., Stewart, J., Rogers D. and Proft, D. (1996) Local tools: an alternative to tool palettes. *User Interface and Software Technology – UIST 96*, pp. 169–170 (TechNote).

Bellotti, V. and Rogers, Y. (1997) From Web press to Web pressure: multimedia representations and multimedia publishing. In *Proceedings CHI'97, ACM Conference on Human Factors in Computing*, Atlanta, GA, March.

Benford, S.D., Bowers, J.M., Fahlén, L.E., Mariani, J. and Rodden, T.R. (1994a) Supporting co-operative work in virtual environments. *The Computer Journal*, 37(8): 653–668.

Benford, S.D. and Fahlén, L.E. (1994b) Viewpoints, actionpoints and spatial frames for collaborative user interfaces. In *Proc. HCI'94*, Glasgow, August.

Benford, S., Greenhalgh, C., Fahlén, L.E. and Bowers, J. (1994c) Embodiment in collaborative virtual environments. In B. Pehrson and E. Skarbäck (eds.) *Proc. 6th ERCIM Workshops.* ERCIM.

Benford, S., Bowers, J., Fahlén, L.E., Greenhalgh, C., Mariani, J. and Rodden, T. (1995a) Networked virtual reality and cooperative work. *Presence: Teleoperators and Virtual Environments* 4(4): 364–386.

Benford, S., Snowdon, D. and Mariani, J. (1995b) Populated information terrains: first steps. In R.A. Earnshaw, J.A. Vince and H. Jones (eds.) *Virtual Reality Applications.* New York: Academic Press: 27–39.

Benford, S., Snowdon, D., Greenhalgh, C., Ingram, R., Knox, I. and Brown, C. (1995c) VR-VIBE: a virtual environment for co-operative information retrieval. In F. Post and M. Göbel (eds.) *Proc. Eurographics '95.* Eurographics Association/Oxford: Blackwell: 349–360.

Benford, S., Brown, C., Reynard, G. and Snowdon, D. (1996a) The Internet Foyer. *3rd Conference of the UK VRSIG*, De Montfort University, Leicester.

Benford, S., Brown, C., Reynard, G. and Greenhalgh, C. (1996b) Shared spaces: transportation, artificiality, and spatiality. In *Proc. CSCW '96.* Cambridge MA: ACM Press: 77–96.

Benford, S., Ingram, R. and Bowers. J. (1996c) Building virtual cities: applying urban planning principles to the design of virtual environments. In *Proc. ACM Conference on Virtual Reality Software and Technology (VRST'96)*. Cambridge, MA: ACM Press.

Benford, S.D., Greenhalgh, C.M. and Lloyd, D. (1997a) Crowded Collaborative Environments. In *Proc. CHI'97*. Cambridge, MA: ACM Press.

Benford, S., Greenhalgh, C., Snowdon D. and Bullock, A. (1997b) Staging a public poetry performance in a collaborative virtual environment. In J. Hughes *et al.* (eds.) *Proceedings of the Fifth European Conference on Computer Supported Cooperative Work - ECSCW'97*. Dordrecht: Kluwer Academic.

Benford, S., Greenhalgh, C., Reynard, G., Brown, C. and Koleva, B. (1998) Understanding and constructing shared spaces with mixed reality boundaries. *ACM Transactions on Computer–Human Interaction* 5(3): 185–223.

Benford, S., Greenhalgh, C., Craven, M. *et al.* (1999a) Evaluating Out Of This World: an experiment in inhabited television. In *Proc. ECSCW'99*. Dordrecht: Kluwer Academic: 179–198.

Benford, S., Greenhalgh, C., Craven, M., Walker, G., Regan, T., Morphett, J., Wyver, J. and Bowers, J. (1999b) Broadcasting on-line social interaction as inhabited television. In S. Bodker *et al.* (eds.) *Proceedings of the Sixth European Conference on Computer Supported Cooperative Work - ECSCW'99*. Dordrecht: Kluwer Academic: 129–198.

Benford, S., Reynard, G., Greenhalgh, C., Snowdon, D. and Bullock, A. (2000a) A poetry performance in a collaborative virtual environment. *IEEE Computer Graphics and Applications*, 20(3): 66–75.

Benford, S., Bederson, B., Åkesson, K., Banyon, V., Druin, A., Hansson, P. *et al.* (2000b) Designing storytelling technologies to encourage collaboration between young children. In *Proc. CHI 2000*, The Hague, pp. 556–563.

Bennett, M. (1998) Overcoming the golden rule: sympathy and empathy. In M. Bennett (ed.) *Basic Concepts of Intercultural Communication: Selected Readings*. Yarmouth, ME: Intercultural Press.

Bentley, R., Hughes, J.A., Randall, D., Rodden, T., Sawyer, P., Shapiro, D. and Sommerville, I. (1992) Ethnographically-informed systems design for air traffic control. In J. Turner and R. Kraut (eds.) *CSCW '92: Sharing perspectives*, pp. 123–129. http://www.acm.org/pubs/articles/proceedings/cscw/143457/p123-bentley/p123-bentley.pdf.

Bentley, R., Appelt, W., Busbach, U., Hinrichs, E., Kerr, D., Sikkel, K., Trevor, J. and Woetzel, G. (1997) Basic support for cooperative work on the World Wide Web. *International Journal of Human-Computer Studies: Special Issue on Innovative Applications of the World Wide Web* 46(6): 827–846.

Bentley, R., Rodden, T., Sawyer, P. and Sommerville, I. (1992) An architecture for tailoring cooperative multi-user displays. In J. Turner and R. Kraut (eds.) *CSCW '92: Sharing perspectives*, pp. 187–194. http://www.acm.org/pubs/articles/proceedings/cscw/143457/p187-bentley/p187-bentley.pdf.

Berlage, T. and Sohlenkamp, M. (1999) Visualizing common artefacts to support awareness in computer-mediated cooperation. *Computer Supported Cooperative Work: The Journal of Collaborative Computing* 8(3): 207–238.

Bibby, P. and Payne, S. (1993) Internalization and the use specificity of device knowledge. *Human-Computer Interaction* 8(1): 25–56.

Biocca, F. and Levy, M.R. (1995) Virtual reality as a communication system. In F. Biocca and M.R. Levy (eds.) *Communication in the Age of Virtual Reality*. Hillsdale, NJ: Lawrence Erlbaum Associates: 15–32.

Bloomberg, J., Giacomi, J., Mosher, A. and Swenton-Hall, P. (1993) Ethnographic field methods and their relation to design. In D. Schuler and A. Namioka (eds.) *Participatory Design: Principles and Practices*. Hillsdale, NJ: Lawrence Erlbaum Associates: 123–155.

Bloomberg, J., Suchman, L. and Trigg, R. (1996) Reflections on a work-oriented design project. *Human-Computer Interaction* 11: 237–265.

Bly, S.A., Harrison, S.R. and Irwin, S. (1993) Media spaces: bringing people together in a video, audio, and computing environment. *Communications of the ACM* 36: 28–47.

Bowers, J. (1995) The social logic of cyberspace, or, the interactional affordances of virtual brutalism. In A. Bullock and J. Mariani (eds.) *Esprit COMIC Project Deliverable 4.3: Assessment and Refinement of Models of Interaction*, pp. 89–145. ftp://ftp.comp.lancs.ac.uk/pub/comic/D4.3.ps.Z.

Bowers, J. and Martin, D. (1999) Informing collaborative information visualisation through an ethnography of ambulance control. In *Proc. ECSCW'99*, Copenhagen, 13 September, pp. 311–330.

Bowers, J., Button, G. and Sharrock, W. (1995) Workflow from within and without: technology and cooperative work on the print industry shopfloor. In H. Marmolin, Y. Sundblad and K. Schmidt (eds.) *Proceedings of the Fourth European Conference on Computer-Supported Cooperative Work*. Dordrecht: Kluwer Academic: 51–66.

Bowers, J., O'Brien, J. and Pycock, J. (1996a) Practically accomplishing immersion: co-operation in and for virtual environments. In *Proceedings of the ACM 1996 Conference on Computer Supported Cooperative Work*. New York: ACM Press: 380–389.

Bowers, J., Pycock, J. and O'Brien, J. (1996b) Talk and embodiment in collaborative virtual environments. In *Proc. CHI'96*, Vancouver, 13–18 April. New York: ACM Press: 58–65. http://www.acm.org/pubs/articles/proceedings/chi/238386/p58-bowers/p58-bowers.html.

Bowers, J., Martin, D. and Wastell, D. (1998) An ethnography of ambulance control to guide the development of information visualisations for electronic landscapes. In J. Mariani, M. Rouncefield, J. O'Brien and T. Rodden (eds.) *Esprit eSCAPE Project Deliverable D3.1: Visualisation of Structure and Population within Electronic Landscapes*, pp. 35–58. http://bscw.comp.lancs.ac.uk/pub/english.cgi/d64394/Escape-D31.pdf.

Bowers, J., Jää-Aro, K.-M., Hellström, S.-O. and Carlzon, M. (1999) Event management in electronic arenas by visualising participant activity and supporting virtual camera deployment. In S. Hirtes, M. Hoch, B. Lintermann, S.J. Norman, J. Bowers, K.-M. Jää-Aro, S.-O. Hellström and M. Carlzon (eds.) *Esprit eRENA Project Deliverable D4.3/D4.4: Production Tools for Electronic Arenas: Event Management and Content Production*, pp. 58–79. http://www.nada.kth.se/erena/pdf/D4_3-D4_4.pdf.

Bowker, G. and Star, L. (1999) *Sorting Things Out: Classification and its Consequences*. Cambridge, MA: MIT Press.

Bradner, E., Kellogg, W.A. and Erickson, T. (1999) The adoption and use of BABBLE: a field study in the workplace. In *Proc. ECSCW'99*, Copenhagen. Dordrecht: Kluwer Academic.

Broll, W. (1998) SmallTool – a toolkit for realizing shared virtual environments on the Internet. *Distributed Systems Engineering – Special Issue on Distributed Virtual Environments* 5: 118–128.

Brooks, P. (1999) What's real about virtual reality? Keynote address in *Proc. UKVRSIG'99*, University of Salford.

Brothers, L., Sembugamoorthy, V. and Muller, M. (1990) ICICLE: groupware for code inspection. In *Proc. CSCW '90*, Los Angeles, CA, October. New York: ACM Press: 169–181.

Bruckman, A. (1992) Identity workshop: emergent social and psychological phenomena in text-based virtual reality. Available via ftp://ftp.parc.xerox.com/pub/MOO/papers/identity-workshop/.

Bruckman, A. (1998) Community support for constructionist learning. *Computer Supported Cooperative Work: Special Issue on Interaction and Collaboration in MUDs* 7(1–2): 47–86.

Bruckman, A. and Resnick, M. (1995) The MediaMOO project: constructionism and professional community. *Convergence* 1(1): 94–109.

Bruschke, J., Gartner, C., and Seiter, J. (1993) Student ethnocentrism, dogmatism, and motivation: a study in BAFA. *Simulation & Gaming* 24(1): 9–20.

Button, G. and Harper, R.H.R. (1993) Taking the organisation into account. *Technology in Working Order: Studies of Work, Interaction, and Technology*. London and New York: Routledge.

Button, G. and Harper, R. (1996) The relevance of "workpractice" for design. *Computer Supported Cooperative Work* 4(4): 263–280.

Button, G. and Sharrock, W. (1997) The production of order and the order of production. In J. Hughes *et al.* (ed.) *Proc. Fifth European Conference on Computer Supported Cooperative Work – ECSCW'97*, Lancaster, 9–11 September. Dordrecht: Kluwer Academic.

Buxton, W. and Moran, T.P. (1990) The workaday world as a paradigm for CSCW design. In T.P. Moran and R.J. Anderson (eds.) *Proceedings of the Conference on Computer-Supported Cooperative Work*, pp. 381–393.

Capin, T.K., Pandzic, I.S., Noser, H., Thalmann, N.M. and Thalmann, D. (1997) Virtual human representation and communication in VLNet. *IEEE Computer Graphics and Applications* 17(2): 42–53.

Card, S., Mackinlay, J. and Schneiderman, B. (1999) Readings in Information Visualization, Using Vision to Think. San Francisco, CA: Morgan Kaufmann: 10–12.

Cassell, J., Sullivan, J.W., Prevost, S. and Churchill, E.F. (eds.) (2000) *Embodied Conversational Agents*. Cambridge, MA: MIT Press.

Cherny, L. (1999) *Conversation and Community. Chat in a Virtual World*. California: CSLI Publications.

Chesebro, J. and Bonsall, G. (1989) *Computer-mediated Communication: Human Relationships in a Computerized World*. Tuscaloosa, AL: University of Alabama Press.

Chidambarram, L. and Jones, B. (1993) Impact on communication medium and computer support on group perceptions and performance: a comparison of face-to-face and dispersed meetings. *MIS Quarterly* 17(3): 465–491.

Churchill, E.F. and Snowdon, D. (1998) Collaborative Virtual Environments: an introductory review of issues and systems. *Virtual Reality: Research, Development and Applications* 3: 3–15.

Churchill, E.F. and Bly, S. (1999a) It's all in the words: supporting work activities with lightweight tools. In *Proc. Group'99, ACM SIGGROUP conference on Supporting group work*, Phoenix, AZ. 14–17 November. New York: ACM Press.

Churchill, E.F. and Bly, S. (1999b) Ubiquitous access to others: maintaining co-presence through MUD locales. Workshop position paper, *Workshop on Ubiquitous Virtual Environments, ECSCW'99*, Copenhagen, 13 September. Also available as FX Palo Alto Lab. Technical Report FXPAL-TR-99-024.

Churchill, E.F. and Bly, S. (1999c) Virtual environments at work: ongoing use of MUDs in the workplace. *Proc. WACC'99*, San Francisco, CA. New York: ACM Press: 99–108.

Clement, A. and Wagner, I. (1995) Fragmented exchange: disarticulation and the need for regionalised communication spaces. In *Proc. ECSCW'95*, Stockholm.

Crandell, G. (1993) *Nature Pictorialised*. London: Johns Hopkins Press.

Crang, M., Crang, P. and May, J. (1999) *Virtual Geographies: Bodies, Space and Relations*. London: Routledge.

Crovitz, H.F. (1971) The capacity of memory loci in artifical memory. *Psychonomic Science* 24: 187–188.

Cruz-Neira, C., Sandin, D. and DeFanti, T. (1993) Surround-screen projection-based virtual reality: the design and implementation of the CAVE. In *Proc. ACM SIGGRAPH '93*, New York: ACM Press: 135–142.

CSC (1998) *Proc. ACM 1998 Conference on Computer Supported Cooperative Work*. http://www.acm.org/pubs/contents/proceedings/cscw/289444/.

Csikszentmihalyi, M. (1991) *Flow: the Psychology of Optimal Experience*. New York: HarperPerennial.

Curtis P. (1992) *Mudding: Social Phenomena in Text-Based Virtual Realities*. Available from ftp://parcftp.xerox.com/pub/MOO/papers/DIA'92.txt.

Curtis, P. (1996) Social phenomena in text-based virtual realities. In M. Stefik (ed.) *Internet Dreams: Archetypes, Myths and Metaphors*. Cambridge, MA: MIT Press: 265–292.

Curtis, P. and Nichols, D. (1992) MUDs grow up: social virtual reality in the real world. *Proc. Third International Conference on Cyberspace*, Austin, TX.

Curtis, P., Dixon, M., Frederick, R. and Nichols, D. (1995) The Jupiter audio/video architecture: secure multimedia in network places. *Proc. MultiMedia '95*, San Francisco, CA. New York: ACM Press: 79–90.

Cushman, D.P. and Cahn, Jr, D.D. (1985) *Communication in Interpersonal Relationships*. Albany, NY: State University of New York Press.

Czernuszenko, M., Pape, D., Sandin, D., DeFanti, T., Dawe, G. and Brown, (1997) M. The ImmersaDesk and Infinity Wall projection-based virtual reality displays. *Computer Graphics*, 31(2): 46–49.

Daly Jones, O., Monk, A. and Watts, L. (1998) Some advantages of video conferencing over high-quality audio conferencing: fluency and awareness of attentional focus. *International Journal of Human Computer Studies* 49: 21–58.

Das, T.K., Singh, G., Mitchell, A., Kumar, P.S. and McGee, K. (1997) NetEffect: a network architecture for large-scale multi-user virtual worlds. In *Proc. ACM Symposium on Virtual Reality Software and Technology 1997 (VRST'97)*. New York, ACM Press: 157–163.

de Certeau, M., Giard, L. and Mayol, P. (1998) *The Practice of Everyday Life*. Minneapolis, MI: University of Minnesota Press.

Deering, S.E. and Cheriton, D.R. (1990) Multicast routing in datagram internetworks and extended LANs. *ACM Transactions on Computer Systems* 8: 85–110.

Denning, P. (1976) Fault-tolerant operating systems. *Computing Surveys* 8(4): 359–389.

Dennis, A.R. (1996) Information exchange in group decision making: you can lead a group to information but you can't make it think. *MIS Quarterly* 20: 433–455.

Dennis, A. and Kinney, S. (1998) Testing media richness theory in the new media: the effects of cues, feedback, and task equivocality. *Information Systems Research* 9(3): 256–274.

Dervin, B. (1997) Given a context by any other name: methodological tools for taming the unruly beast. In P. Vakkari, R. Savolainen and B. Dervin (eds.) *Information Seeking in Context*. London: Taylor Graham: 13–38.

Deutsch, D. (1997) *The Fabric of Reality*. London: Penguin.

Dibbell, J. (1993) A rape in cyberspace or how an evil clown, a Haitian trickster spirit, two wizards, and a cast of dozens turned a database into a society. *Village Voice* 36–42.

Dibbell, J. (1999) *My Tiny Life*. London: Fourth Estate.

Dix, A. (1994) Computer supported cooperative work: a framework. In D. Rosenberg and C. Hutchinson (eds.) *Design Issues in CSCW*. Berlin: Springer-Verlag.

Dix, A. (1997) Challenges for cooperative work on the Web: an analytical approach. *CSCW: The Journal of Collaborative Computing* 6(2-3): 135-156.

Dodd, C. (1998) *Dynamics of Intercultural Communication*. Boston: McGraw-Hill.

Dongbo, X. and Hubbold, R. (1998) Navigation guided by artificial force fields. In *Proc. ACM CHI'98 Conference on Human Factors in Computing Systems* Vol. 1. ACM SIGCHI/ Reading, MA: Addison-Wesley: pp. 179–186.

Doppke, J.C., Heimbigner, D. and Wolf, A.L. (1998) Software process modelling and execution within virtual environments, *ACM Transactions on Software Engineering and Methodology* 7(1): 1-40.

Dourish, P. (1998) Introduction: the state of play. *Computer Supported Cooperative Work: Special Issue on Interaction and Collaboration in MUDs* 7(1-2): 1-7.

Dourish, P. and Bellotti, V. (1992) Awareness and collaboration in shared workspaces. In *Proc. ACM CSCW'92 Conference on Computer-Supported Cooperative Work*. New York: ACM Press: 107-114.

Dourish, P. and S. Bly (1992) Portholes: supporting awareness in a distributed work group. *Proc. ACM CHI'92*. New York: ACM Press.

Dourish, P., Adler, A., Bellotti, V. and Henderson, A. (1996) Your place or mine? Learning from the long-term use of video communication. *Computer-Supported Cooperative Work: The Journal of Collaborative Computing* 5(1): 33–62.

Easton, K. and Olphert, W. (1996) Early evaluation of the organizational implementations of CSCW. In P. Thomas (ed.) *CSCW Requirements and Analysis*. London: Springer-Veralg: 75–89.

Edwards, K. (1994) Session management for collaborative applications. In *Proc. CSCW'94*, Chapel Hill, NC, 22–26 October. New York: ACM Press: 323–330.

Edwards, K. (1996) Policies and roles in collaborative applications. In *Proc. CSCW'96*, Cambridge, MA. New York: ACM Press: 11–20.

Egido, C. (1988) Videoconferencing as a technology to support group work: a review of its failure. *Proc. Conference on Computer-Supported Cooperative Work (CSCW'88)*, Portland, OR, 26–28 September. New York: ACM Press.

Ehrlich, S.F. (1987) Strategies for encouraging successful adoption of office communication systems. *ACM TOOIS* 5: 340–357.

Electric Communities (1997) White paper on "Introduction to Capability based security". http://www.communities.com/company/papers/security/index.html.

Ellington, R.A. (ed.) (1966) *The Frontier Hypothesis, A Valid Interpretation of American History?* New York: Holt, Rinehart and Winston.

Ellis, S.R. (1996) Presence of mind. Presence: Teleoperators and Virtual Environments 5(2): 247–259.

Elvins, T.T., Nadeau, D.R. and Kirsh, D. (1997) Worldlets – 3D thumbnails for wayfinding in virtual environments. *Proc. ACM User Interface Software and Technology Symposium, UIST'97*, Banff, Canada.

Engeström, Y. and Middleton, D. (1996) *Cognition and Communication at Work*. New York: Cambridge University Press.

Epperson, K.L. (undated) Patterns of social behavior. In *Computer-Mediated Communications*. http://www.eff.org/pub/Net_culture/Misc/web_social_behavior.paper.

Erickson, T., Smith, D.N., Kellogg, W.A., Laff, M.R., Richards, J.T. and Bradner, E. (1999) Socially translucent systems: social proxies, persistent conversation, and the design of "BABBLE". *Proc. CHI'99*, Pittsburgh, PA. New York: ACM.

Evard, R. (1993) Collaborative networked communication: MUDs as system tools. *Proc. Seventh Administration Conference (LISA VII)*, Monterey, CA, 1–8 November.

Evard, R. (1994) A study of communication patterns in InfoPark. *DIAC '94*, Cambridge, MA, 23–24 March. http://www.cpsr.org/conferences/diac94/diac.html.

Feldman, M.S. (1987) Electronic mail and weak ties in organizations. *Office: Technology and People* 3(2): 83–101.

Finch, M., Chi, V., Taylor II, R.M., Falvo, M. *et al.* (1995) Surface modification tools in a virtual environment interface to a scanning probe microscope. In *Proc. ACM Symposium on Interactive 3D Graphics – Special Issue of Computer Graphics*. New York: ACM SIGGRAPH: 13–18.

Flanagan, J.C. (1954) The critical incidence technique. *Psychological Bulletin* **51**: 1–22.

Fraser, M. and Glover, T. (1998) Representation and control in collaborative virtual environments. In *Proc. UKVRSIG'98*.

Fraser, M., Benford, S., Hindmarsh, J. and Heath, C. (1999) Supporting awareness and interaction through collaborative virtual interfaces. In *Proc. UIST'99*. New York: ACM Press: 27–36.

Frécon, E. and Stenius, M. (1998) Dive: a scalable network architecture for distributed virtual environments. *Distributed Systems Engineering*. **5**: 91–100.

Frécon, E., Greenhalgh, C. and Stenius, M. (1999) The DiveBone - an application-level network architecture for Internet-based CVEs. In M. Slater (ed.) *Proc. ACM Symposium on Virtual Reality Software and Technology (VRST'99)*, University College, London, 20–22 December. New York: ACM: 58–65.

Fruchterman, T.M.J. and Reingold, E.M. (1991) Graph drawing by force directed placement. *Software Practice and Experience* **21**(11): 1129–1164.

Galegher, J., Kraut, R.E. and Egido, C. (eds.) (1990) *Intellectual Teamwork – Social and Technological Foundations of Cooperative Work*. Hillsdale, NJ: Lawrence Erlbaum.

Galin, J. (1998) MOO central: educational, professional, and experimental MOOs on the Internet. In C. Haynes and J.R. Holmevik (eds.) *High Wired: On the Design, Use, and Theory of Educational MOOs*. Ann Arbor, MI: University of Michigan Press: 325–338.

Garfinkel, H. (1967) *Studies in Ethnomethodology*. Cambridge: Polity Press.

Gaver, W.W. (1992) The affordances of media spaces for collaboration. In *Proc. CSCW'92*. New York: ACM Press.

Gaver, W., Smith, R.B. and O'Shea, T. (1991) Effective sounds in complex systems: the ARKola simulation. In *Proc. CHI'91*, New Orleans, LA, April. New York: ACM Press: 85–90.

Gaver, W.W., Sellen, A., Heath, C.C. and Luff, P. (1993) One is not enough: multiple views in a media space. In *Proc. INTERCHI'93*, pp. 335–341.

Ghani, J.A., Supnick, R. and Rooney, P. (1991) The experiences of flow in computer-mediated and face-to-face groups. In *Proc. Twelfth International Conference on Information Systems*, pp. 229–237.

Gibson, J.J. (1986) *The Ecological Approach to Visual Perception*. London: Lawrence Erlbaum.

Gibson, W. (1989) *Neuromancer*. New York: Grafton.

Giddens, A. (1984) *The Constitution of Society*. Cambridge: Polity Press.

Gillner, S. and Mallot, H.A. (1997) Navigation and acquisition of spatial knowledge in a virtual maze. *Technical Report 45*, Max-Planck-Institut fur biologische Kybernetik. Available online at http://www.kyb.tuebingen.mpg.de/bu/techr/abs45.html.

Goffman, E. (1967) *Interaction Ritual: Essays on Face-to-Face Behaviour*. New York: Pantheon Books.

Goodwin, C. and Goodwin, M.H. (1996) Seeing as situated activity: formulating planes. In Y. Engeström and D. Middleton (eds.) *Cognition and Communication at Work*. Cambridge: Cambridge University Press: 61–95.

Gowan, J.A. and Downs, J.M. (1994) Video conferencing human–machine interface: a field study. *Information and Management* **27**(6): 341–356.

Gredler, M. (1992) *Designing and Evaluating Games and Simulations: a Process Approach*. Houston, TX: Gulf.

Green, S.G. and Taber, T.D. (1980) The effects of three social decision support schemes on decision group process. *Organizational Behavior and Human Performance* **25**: 97–106.

Greenhalgh, C. (1997a) Large scale collaborative virtual environments, *PhD thesis*, University of Nottingham. ftp://ftp.crg.cs.nott.ac.uk/pub/cmg/cmg-thesis.ps.gz.

Greenhalgh, C. (1997b) Analysing movements and world transitions in virtual reality tele-conferencing. In *Fifth conference on Computer Supported Cooperative Work (ECSCW'97)*. Dordrecht: Kluwer Academic.

Greenhalgh, C. (1999) *Large Scale Collaborative Virtual Environments*. London: Springer-Verlag.

Greenhalgh, C. and Benford, S. (1995) MASSIVE: a virtual reality system for tele-conferencing. ACM Transactions on Computer Human Interfaces 2(3): 239–261.

Greenhalgh, C. *et al.* (1998a) *MASSIVE-3, a development of HIVEK*. http://www.crg.cs.nott.ac.uk/research/systems/MASSIVE-3/.

Greenhalgh, C., Benford, S., Bullock, A., Kuijpers, N. and Donkers, K. (1998b) Predicting network traffic for collaborative virtual environments. *Computer Networks and ISDN Systems* 30: 1677–1685.

Greenhalgh, C., Bullock, A., Tromp, J. and Benford, S. (1999a) Evaluating the network and usability characteristics of virtual reality tele-conferencing. In P.J. Sheppard and G.R. Walker (eds.) *Telepresence*. Dordrecht: Kluwer Academic: 170–207.

Greenhalgh, C., Benford, S., Taylor, I., Bowers, J., Walker, G. and Wyver, J. (1999b) Creating a live broadcast from a virtual environment. In *Proc. SIGGRAPH'99*. New York: ACM Press: 375–384.

Greenhalgh, C., Benford, S. and Craven, M. (1999c) Patterns of network and user activity in an inhabited television event. In M. Slater (ed.) *Proc. ACM Symposium on Virtual Reality Software and Technology (VRST'99)*, University College, London, 20–22 December. New York: ACM: 34–41.

Greif, I. and Sarin, S. (1987) Data sharing in group work. *ACM Transactions on Office Information Systems* 5(2): 187–211. http://www.acm.org/pubs/articles/journals/tois/1987-5-2/p187-greif/p187-greif.pdf.

Gronbaek, K., Kyng, M. and Mogensen, P. (1992) CSCW challenges in large-scale technical projects – a case study. *Proc. ACM CSCW'92 Conference on Computer-Supported Cooperative Work*. New York: ACM Press: 338–345.

Grudin, J. and Poltrock, S.E. (1996) CSCW, groupware and workflow: experiences, state-of-the art and future trends. *CHI 2000 One Day tutorial, CHI 2000*, The Hague, 1–6 April.

Gust, P. (1988) Shared X: X in a distributed group work environment. *2nd Annual X Conference*, Boston, MIT.

Guthold, M., Matthews, G., Negishi, A. *et al.* (1999) Quantitative manipulation of DNA and viruses with the nanoManipulator scanning force microscope. *Surface Interfacial Analysis* 27: 437–443.

Guthold, M., Falvo, M., Matthews, W.G. *et al.* (in press) Investigation of molecular structures using the nanoManipulator. *Journal of Graph. Model.*

Gutwin, C. and Greenberg, S. (1996) Workspace awareness for groupware. In *CHI'96 Conf. Companion*. New York: ACM Press: 208–209.

Gutwin, C. and Greenberg, S. (1998a) Effects of awareness support on groupware usability. In *Proc. CHI'98*. New York: ACM Press: 511–518.

Gutwin, C. and Greenberg, S. (1998b) Design for individuals, design for groups: tradeoffs between power and workspace awareness. *Proc. ACM CSCW'98 Conference on Computer Supported Cooperative Work*. New York: ACM Press: 207–216.

Guye-Vuillème, A., Capin, T.K., Pandzic, I.S., Thalmann, N.M. and Thalmann, D. (1999) Nonverbal communication interface for collaborative virtual environments. *Virtual Reality: Research, Devlopment and Applications* 4(1): 49–59.

Hagsand, O. (1996) Interactive multiuser VEs in the DIVE system. *IEEE Multimedia* 3(1): 30–39.

Hall, E. (1976) *Beyond Culture*. New York: Doubleday.

Hand, C. and Skipper, M. (1996) A Collaborative environment for role-playing in object space. In *Proc. CVE'96*, Nottingham, 19–20 September.

Hansson, P. and Wallberg, A. (1997) Techniques for "natural" interaction in multi–user CAVE–like environments. *Poster/Short paper ECSCW'97*, Lancaster.

Harper, R. (1997) Gatherers of information: the mission process at the International Monetary Fund. In *Proc. 5th European Conference on Computer Supported Cooperative Work (ECSCW'97)*. Dordrecht: Kluwer Academic.

Harper, R. (1998) *Inside the IMF: An Ethnography of Documents, Technology, and Organisational Action*. San Diego, CA: Academic Press.

Harrison, S. and Dourish, P. (1996) Re-place-ing space: the roles of place and space in collaborative systems. In *Proc. CSCW'96*. Cambridge, MA: ACM Press: 67–76.

Heath, C.C. (1997) The analysis of activities in face to face interaction using video. In D. Silverman (ed.) *Qualitative Research: Theory, Method and Practice*. London: Sage: 183–200.

Heath, C. and Hindmarsh, J. (2000) Configuring action in objects. *Mind, Culture and Activity* 7(182): 81–104.

Heath, C. and Luff, P. (1991) Collaborative activity and technological design: task coordination in London Underground control rooms. In L. Bannon, M. Robinson and K. Schmidt (eds.) *Proc. ECSCW'91*. Dordrecht: Kluwer Academic: 65–80.

Heath, C.C. and Luff, P. (1992) Collaboration and control: crisis management and multimedia technology in London Underground line control rooms. *Journal of Computer-Supported Cooperative Work* 1: 69–94.

Heath, C. and Luff, P. (1996) Convergent activities: line control and passenger information on the London Underground. In Y. Engestrom and D. Middleton (eds.) *Cognition and Communication at Work*. New York: Cambridge University Press: 96–129.

Heath, C. and Luff, P. (2000) *Technology in Action*. Cambridge: Cambridge University Press.

Heath, C., Luff, P. and Sellen, A. (1997) Reconsidering the virtual workplace. In K. Finn, A. Sellen and S. Wilbur (eds.) *Video-Mediated Communication*. Hillsdale, NJ: Lawrence Erlbaum.

Heim, M. (1993) *The Metaphysics of Virtual Reality*. Oxford: Oxford University Press.

Heim, M. (1995) The design of virtual reality. In M. Featherstone (ed.) *Cyberspace, Cyberbodies, Cyberpunk*. London: Sage: 65–95.

Henderson, D.A. and Card, S.K. (1986) Rooms: the use of multiple virtual workspaces to reduce space contention in a window-based graphical user interface. *ACM Transactions on Graphics* 5: 211–243.

Heritage, J. (1984) *Garfinkel and Ethnomethodology*. Cambridge: Polity Press.

Hewstone, M., Stroebe, W., Codol, J. and Stephenson, G.M. (1988) *Introduction to Social Psychology*. Oxford: Basil Blackwell.

Hidalgo–Panes, E., Pettifer, S. and West, A. (1999) Generating virtual cities with an algorithmic approximation. *eSCAPE Esprit project 25377*, Deliverable 5.1, Chapter 5.

Hillier, B. (1996) *Space is the Machine: a Configurational Theory of Architecture*. Cambridge: Cambridge University Press.

Hindmarsh, J. (1997) The interactional constitution of objects. *PhD thesis*, University of Surrey.

Hindmarsh, J. and Heath, C. (2000) Embodied reference: a study of deixis in workplace interaction. *Journal of Pragmatics* 31(12): 1855–78.

Hindmarsh, J., Fraser, M., Heath, C., Benford, S. and Greenhalgh, C. (1998) Fragmented interaction: establishing mutual orientation in virtual environments. In *Conference on Computer Supported Cooperative Work, CSCW'98*. New York: ACM Press: 217–226. http://www.acm.org/pubs/articles/proceedings/cscw/289444/p217-hindmarsh/p217-hindmarsh.pdf.

Hindmarsh, J., Fraser, M., Heath, C., Benford, S. and Greenhalgh, C. (in press) Object-focused interaction in collaborative virtual environments. *ACM Transactions on Computer–Human Interaction*.

Hollan, J. and Stornetta, S. (1992) Beyond being there. In *Human Factors in Computing Systems CHI'92*. New York: ACM Press: 119–125.

Hubbold, R., Cook, J., Keates, M., Gibson, S., Howard, T., Murta, A., West, A. and Pettifer, S. (1999) GNU/MAVERIK: A micro-kernel for large-scale virtual environments. in *Proc. ACM Symposium on Virtual Reality Software and Technology*.

Hughes, J.A., Randall, D. and Shapiro, D. (1992) Faltering from ethnography to design. *Proc. Conference on Computer Supported Cooperative Work*. New York: ACM Press: 115–122.

Hutchins, E. (1990) The technology of team navigation. In J. Galegher, R. Kraut and C. Egido (eds.) *Intellectual Teamwork: Social and Technical Bases of Collaborative Work*. Hillsdale, NJ: Lawrence Erlbaum.

Hutchins, E. and Klausen, T. (1996) Distributed cognition in an airline cockpit. In Y. Engestrom and D. Middleton (eds.) *Cognition and Communication at Work*. New York: Cambridge University Press.

Huxor, A. (1998) An Active Worlds interface to BSCW, to enhance chance encounters. In D. Snowdon and E. Churchill (eds) *Collaborative Virtual Environments '98*, pp. 87–93.

Huxor, A. (1999) An Active Worlds interface to Basic Support for Cooperative Working (BSCW) to enhance chance encounters. *Virtual Reality* 4(11): 4–14.

IEEE (1993) Institute of Electrical and Electronic Engineers, International Standard ANSI/IEEE Std 1278-1993, *Standard for Information Technology, Protocols for Distributed Interactive Simulation*. March.

Imai, T., Johnson, A., Leigh, J., Pape, D. and DeFanti, T. (1999) Supporting transoceanic collaborations in virtual environment. In *Proc. 5th Asia-Pacific Conference on Communications/4th Optoelectronics and Communications Conference - APCC/OECC '99*, Beijing, 19–21 October, pp. 1059–1062.

Isaacs, E.A., Tang, J.C. and Morris, T. (1996) Piazza: A desktop environment supporting impromptu and planned interactions, in M.S. Ackerman (ed.) *CSCW '96: Cooperating Communities*, pp. 315–324.

http://www.acm.org/pubs/articles/proceedings/cscw/240080/p315-isaacs/p315-isaacs.pdf.

Ives, H.E. (1930) Two-way television. *Bell Labs Record* (8).

Jeffay, K., Smith, D. and Parameswaran, R. (1999) *Deployment of the nanoManipulator on Internet 2.* Available at http://www.cs.unc.edu/Research/dirt/

Jeffrey, P. and McGrath, A. (in press) Sharing serendipity in the workplace. *CVE 2000 (Collaborative Virtual Environments)*, San Francisco, CA, 10–12 September.

JHcore: ftp://ftp.ccs.neu.edu/pub/mud/sites/jhm/database/

Johnson, A., Moher, T., Ohlsson, S. and Gillingham, M. (1999) The round Earth project: collaborative VR for conceptual learning. In *IEEE Computer Graphics and Applications* 19(6): 60–69.

Kaplan, S., Tolone, W., Bogio, D. and Bignoli, C. (1992) Flexible, active support for collaborative work with conversation builder. In *Proc. CSCW'92*. New York: ACM Press: 378–385.

Kasbi, C. and Montmollin, M. D. (1991) Activity without decision and responsibility: the case of nuclear power plants. In B.B.J. Rasmussen and J. Leplat (eds.) *Distributed Decision Making. Cognitive Models for Cooperative Work*. Chichester: John Wiley: 275–283.

Kendon, A. (1990) Behavioural foundations for the process of frame attunement in face-to-face interaction. In G.P. Ginsburg, M. Brennan and M. von Cranach (eds.) *Conducting Interaction*. Cambridge: Cambridge University Press.

Kensing, F., Simonsen, J. and Bodker, K. (1998) MUST: a method for participatory design. *Human–Computer Interaction* 13: 167–198.

Kessler, G., Hodges, L. and Ahamad, M. (1998) Ravel, a support system for the development of distributed multi-user VE applications. In *Proc. Virtual Reality Annual International Symposium (VRAIS)* '98, pp. 260–267.

Kolers, P. and von Grunau, M. (1976) Shape and color in apparent motion. *Vision Research* 16: 329–335.

Koleva, B., Schnädelbach, H., Benford, S. and Greenhalgh, C. (2000) Traversable interfaces between real and virtual worlds. In *Proc. CHI 2000 Conference on Human Factors in Computing Systems*, pp. 233–240.

Kolko, B. (1996) Building a world with words: the narrative reality of virtual communities. http://acorn.grove.iup.edu/en/workday/Kolko.html#anchor246244.

Kolko, B.E., Nakamura, L. and Rodman, G.B. (2000) *Race in Cyberspace*. London: Routledge.

Kraut, R., Egido, C. and Galegher, J. (1988) Patterns of contact and communication in scientific research collaboration. In *Proc. Conference on Computer-Supported Cooperative Work*, pp. 1–12. http://www.acm.org/pubs/contents/proceedings/cscw/62266/.

Kraut, R.E., Fish, R.S., Root, R.W. and Chalfonte, B.L. (1990) Informal communication in organizations: form, function and technology. In S. Oskamp and S. Spacapan (eds.) *People's Reactions to Technology In Factories, Offices, and Aerospace, The Claremont Symposium on Applied Social Psychology*. London: Sage: 145–199. Reprinted in J. Galegher, R.E. Kraut and C. Egido (eds.) (1990) *Intellectual Teamwork – Social and Technological Foundations of Cooperative Work*. Hillsdale, NJ: Lawrence Erlbaum: 287–314.

Kraut, R.E., Cool, C., Rice, R.E. and Fish, R.S. (1994) Life and death of new technology: task, utility and social influence in the use of a communication medium. *Proc. CSCW'94*. New York: ACM Press: 13–21.

Lambda MOO server: ftp://ftp.lambda.moo.mud.org/pub/MOO/LambdaMOO-latest.tar.Z.

Larkin, J. and Simon, H. (1987) Why a diagram is (sometimes) worth ten thousand words. *Cognitive Science* 11: 65–99.

Lauwers, J. and Lantz, K. (1990) Collaboration awareness in support of collaboration transparency: requirements for the next generation of shared window systems. In *Proc. ACM CHI'90 Conference on Human Factors in Computing Systems*. New York: ACM Press.

Lea, R., Honda, Y. and Matsuda, K. (1997) Virtual society: collaboration in 3D spaces on the Internet. *Computer Supported Cooperative Work: The Journal of Collaborative Computing* 6: 227–250. Dordrecht: Kluwer Academic.

Leigh, J., Johnson, A., Vasilakis, C. and DeFanti, T. (1996) Multi-perspective collaborative design in persistent networked virtual environments. *Proc. IEEE Virtual Reality Annual International Symposium '96*, Santa Clara, CA, 20 March-3 April, pp. 253–260, 271–272. http://evlweb.eecs.uic.edu/spiff/calvin/calvin.vrais/index.html.

Lenman, S. (1999) 3D digital environments for social contact in distance work. In *Proc. Webnet '99 World Conference on the WWW and Internet*.

Luff, P. and Heath, C. (2000) The collaborative production of computer commands in command and control. *International Journal of Human–Computer Studies* **52**: 669–699.

Luff, P., Hindmarsh, J. and Heath, C. (2000) *Workplace Studies: Recovering Work Practice and Informing System Design*. Cambridge: Cambridge University Press.

Macedonia, M. and Zyda, M. (1997) A taxonomy for networked virtual environments. *IEEE Multimedia* **4**(1): 48–56.

Mackie, R.R. and Wylie, C.D. (1988) Factors influencing acceptance of computer-based innovations. In Helander, M. (ed.) *Handbook of Human-Computer Interaction*. New York: Elsevier Science Publishers: 1081–1117.

Malone, T. (1980) What makes things fun to learn? A study of intrinsically motivating computer games. *Unpublished doctoral dissertation*, Stanford University.

Mandviwalla, M. and Khan, S. (1999) Collaborative Object Workspace (COWS): exploring the integration of collaboration technology. *Decision Support Systems* **27**: 241–254.

Mariani, J. (1998) Visualisation approaches and techniques. In J. Mariani, M. Rouncefield, J. O'Brien and T. Rodden (eds.) *Esprit eSCAPE Project Deliverable D3.1: Visualisation of Structure and Population within Electronic Landscapes*. Chapter 1, pp. 9–34. http://bscw.comp.lancs.ac.uk/pub/english.cgi/d64394/Escape-D31.pdf.

Mariani, J., Rouncefield, M., O'Brien, J. and Rodden, T. (eds.) (1998) *Esprit eSCAPE Project Deliverable D3.1: Visualisation of Structure and Population within Electronic Landscapes*. http://bscw.comp.lancs.ac.uk/pub/english.cgi/d64394/Escape-D31.pdf.

Marsh, J., Pettifer, S. and West, A. (1999) A technique for maintaining continuity of experience in networked virtual environments. In *Proc. UKVRSIG'99*, University of Salford.

Mason, T., Applebaum, E., Rasmussen, M., Millman, A., Evenhouse, R. and Panko, W. (1998) The virtual temporal bone. In *Proc. Medicine Meets Virtual Reality Conference*.

Mateas, M. and Lewis, S. (1996) A MOO-based virtual training environment. *Journal of Computer-Mediated Communication* **2**(3). Available at http://www.ascusc.org/jcmc/.

McGrath, A. (1998) The Forum. *Siggroup Bulletin* **19**(3): 21–25.

Middleton, D. (1996) Talking work: argument, common knowledge, and improvisation in teamwork. In Y. Engestrom and D. Middleton (1996) *Cognition and Communication at Work*. New York: Cambridge University Press.

Milgram, P., Drascic, D. and Grodski, J. (1990) A virtual stereoscopic pointer for a real three dimensional video world. *Interact '90*. New York: ACM Press.

Monk, A.F. and Watts, L. (1995) Poor quality video links affect speech but not gaze. *Proc. CHI Conference*. New York: ACM Press: 274–275.

Moran, T. and Anderson, R.J. (1990) The workaday world as a paradigm for CSCW design. In *Proc. CSCW'90*. New York: ACM Press.

Mumford, E. (1995) *Effective Systems Design and Requirements Analysis: The ETHICS Approach*. Basingstoke: Macmillan.

Munro, A. (1999) Place, space, inhabitants: use of space by urban tribes. Workshop position paper, *Workshop on Designing From the Interaction Out: Using Intercultural Communication As A Framework to Design Interactions in Collaborative Virtual Communities Group '99 Workshop*, Phoenix, AZ, 14 November.

Murray, D. (1993) An ethnographic study of graphic designers. In *Proc. Third European Conference on Computer-Supported Cooperative Work*. New York: ACM Press: 295–309.

Murray, J. (1997) *Hamlet on the Holodeck: the Future of Narrative in Cyberspace*. Cambridge, MA: MIT Press.

Mynatt, E.D., O'Day, V.L., Adler, A. and Ito, M. (1998) Network communities: something old, something new, something borrowed. *Computer Supported Cooperative Work: Special Issue on Interaction and Collaboration in MUDs* **7**(1–2): 123–156.

Mynatt, E.D., Adler, A., Linde, C. and O'Day, V. (1999) The network communities of SeniorNet. In *Proc. ECSCW'99*, Copenhagen, 13 September, pp. 219–238.

Nakanishi, H., Yoshida, C., Nishimura, T. and Ishida, T. (1998) FreeWalk: a three-dimensional meeting place for communities. In T. Ishida (ed.) *Community Computing – Collaboration Over Global Information Networks*. Chichester: Wiley: 55–89.

Nardi, B., Schwartz, H., Kuchinsky, A., Leichner, R., Whittaker, S. and Sclabassi, R. (1993) Turning away from talking heads: the use of video-as-data in neurosurgery. *Proc. INTERCHI '93*. New York: ACM Press.

Nash, R. (1973) *Wilderness and the American Mind*, Rev. Edn, New Haven: Yale University Press.

Neilsen, J. (1989) Usability engineering at a discount. In G. Salvendy and M.J. Smith (eds.) *Designing and Using Human-Computer Interfaces and Knowledge Based Systems*. Amsterdam: Elsevier Science Publishers: 394–401.

Neuwirth, C., Kaufer, D., Ravinder, C. and Morris, J. (1990) Issues in the design of computer support for co-authoring and commenting. In *Proc. CSCW'90*. New York: ACM Press: 183–195.

Norman, D.A. (1988) *The Psychology of Everyday Things*. New York: Basic Books.

Norretranders, T. (1998) *The User Illusion: Cutting Consciousness Down to Size*. New York: Viking/Penguin.

O'Day, V., Bobrow, D., Bobrow, K., Shirley, M., Hughes B. and Walters, J. (1998) Moving practice: from classrooms to MOO rooms. *Computer Supported Cooperative Work: Special Issue on Interaction and Collaboration in MUDs* 7(1–2): 9–45.

O'Day, V.L., Bobrow, D.G. and Shirley, M. (1998) Network Community design: a social-technical design circle. *Computer Supported Cooperative Work* 7: 315–337.

Ousterhout, J.K. (1994) *Tcl and the Tk Toolkit*. Reading, MA: Addison-Wesley.

Owens, L. and Straton, R. (1980) The development of a co-operative, competitive, and individualised learning preference scale for students. *British Journal of Educational Psychology* 50: 147–161.

Palace, The (1999) http://www.thepalace.com/.

Park, K. and Kenyon, R. (1999) Effects of network characteristics on human performance in a collaborative virtual environment. In *Proc. IEEE VR '99*, Houston, TX, 13–17 March.

Patrick, J. (1973) *A Glasgow Gang Observed*. London: Eyre Methuen.

Patterson, J.F., Hill, R.D., Rohall, S.L. and Meeks, W.S. (1990) Rendezvous: an architecture for synchronous multi-user applications. *Proc. Conference on Computer-Supported Cooperative Work*, pp. 317–328. http://www.acm.org/pubs/articles/proceedings/cscw/99332/p317-patterson/p317-patterson.pdf.

Patterson, E.S., Watts-Perotti, J. and Woods, D. D. (1999) Voice loops as coordination aids in Space Shuttle Mission Control. *Computer Supported Cooperative Work: The Journal of Collaborative Computing* 8(4): 353–371.

Penn Moo: http://ccat.sas.upenn.edu/jod/teachdemo/moo.html

Pettifer, S. and West, A. (1999) *Deva: a Distributed VR Architecture*. University of Manchester, Technical Reports in Computer Science.

Pierce, J.S., Conway, M., Van Dantzich, M. and Robertson, G. (1999) Toolspaces and glances: storing, accessing, and retrieving objects in 3D desktop applications. In *Proc. ACM Symposium on Interactive 3D Graphics*. New York: ACM Press.

Porter, D. (1997) *Internet Culture*. London: Routledge.

Preece, J. (1999) Empathy online. In *Virtual Reality: research, Development and Applications*. 4(1): 74–84.

Prinz, W. (1999) NESSIE: an awareness environment for cooperative settings. In S. Bødker, M. Kyng and K. Schmidt (eds.) *Proc. ECSCW'99: Sixth Conference on Computer Supported Cooperative Work*. Dordrecht: Kluwer Academic: 391–410.

Raybourn, E.M. (1997a) Computer game design: new directions for intercultural simulation game designers. In Developments in Business Simulation and Experiential Learning 24: 144–145. Also available at http://www.cs.unm.edu/~raybourn/.

Raybourn, E.M. (1997b) The quest for power, popularity, and privilege: identity construction in a text-based multi-user virtual reality. Unpublished Paper presented at the Western Communication Association, Denver, CO.

Raybourn, E.M. (1998a) Designing the DomeCityMOO training collaboratory: a multi-user simulation in a text-based networked virtual environment that supports non-scripted interactions toward intercultural understanding. In *Siggroup Bulletin* 19(3): 35–37.

Raybourn, E.M. (1998b) An intercultural computer-based simulation supporting participant exploration of identity and power in a text-based networked virtual reality: DomeCityMOO. *PhD dissertation.*
University of New Mexico, Albuquerque, NM.

Raybourn, E.M. (2000) Designing an emergent culture of negotiation in collaborative virtual communities: the case of the DomeCityMOO. *Siggroup Bulletin.*

Reder, S. and Schwab, R.G. (1990) The temporal structure of cooperative activity. *Proc. Conference on
Computer-Supported Cooperative Work, CSCW'90.* New York, ACM Press: 303–316.

Reid, E. (1995) Virtual worlds: culture and imagination. In S.G. Jones (ed.) *Cybersociety: Computer-
Mediated Communication and Community.* Newbury Park, CA: Sage: 164–183.

Reynard, G., Benford, S., Greenhalgh, C. and Heath, C. (1998) Awareness driven video quality of service
in collaborative virtual environments. In *Proc. CHI'98.* New York: ACM Press.

Rheingold, H. (1992) *Virtual Reality.* New York: Touchstone Books.

Rheingold, H. (1993) *The Virtual Community: Homesteading on the Electronic Frontier.* Reading, MA:
Addison-Wesley.

Robertson, G., Czerwinski, M. and van Dantzich, M. (1997) Immersion in desktop virtual reality. In *Proc.
UIST'97.* New York: ACM Press.

Robinson, M. (1993) Design for unanticipated use. In *Proc. 3rd European Conference on Computer
Supported Cooperative Work, ECSCW'93.* Dordrecht: Kluwer Academic.

Robinson, M. (1991) Double-level languages and co-operative working. *AI & Society* 5: 34–60.

Robinson, M. and Hinrichs, E. (1997) *Study on the supporting telecommunications services and applications for networks of local employment initiatives (TeleLEI Project): Final Report.* Institute for Applied
Information Technology (FIT), Sankt Augustin D 53754, Germany.

Robinson, M. and Pekkola, S. (2000) *VIVA Technical Report.* University of Jyväskylä, Department of
Computer Science.

Robinson, M., Pekkola, S. and Snowdon, D. (1998) Cat's cradle: working with other people in overlapping real and virtual worlds through tangled strands of visual and other media. *CRWIG'98 International Workshop on Groupware,* Buzios, Brazil, 8–12 September.

Robinson, M. and Pekkola, S. (1999) User communication & monitoring system for computer networks.
Patent Application (EU) 99660008.6 (US) 09/232790.

Rogers, E.M. (1995) *Diffusion of Innovations.* New York: The Free Press.

Roseman, M. and Greenberg, S. (1996) Building real-time group-ware with groupkit, a groupware
toolkit. *ACM Transactions on Computer-Human Interaction.* 3(1): 66–106.

Roussos, M., Johnson, A., Moher, T., Leigh, J., Vasilakis, C. and Barnes, C. (1999) Learning and building
together in an immersive virtual world. *Presence* 8(3): 247–263.

Ruhleder, K. and Jordan, B. (1999) Meaning-making across remote sites: how delays in transmission
affect interaction. In *Proc. ECSCW'99.* Dordrecht: Kluwer Academic: 411–430.

Rutter, D.R. and Stephenson, G.M. (1979) Role of visual communication in social interaction. *Current
Anthropology* 20: 124–125.

Sacks, H. (1992) *Lectures on Conversation,* Vols. 1 & 2 (ed. G. Jefferson). Oxford: Blackwell.

Salvador, T. and Bly, S. (1997) Supporting the flow of information through constellations of interaction.
Proc. ECSCW'97, Lancaster, pp. 269–280.

Salzman, M., Dede, C. Loftin, B. and Ash, K. (1998) VR's frames of reference: a visualization technique
for mastering abstract information spaces. In *Proc. Third International Conference on Learning
Sciences.* Charlottesville, VA: Association for the Advancement of Computers in Education: 249–255.

Şandor, O., Bogdan, C. and Bowers, J. (1997) Aether: an awareness engine for CSCW. In J.A. Hughes,
W. Prinz, T. Rodden and K. Schmidt (eds.) *Proc. Fifth European Conference on Computer-Supported
Cooperative Work.* Dordrecht: Kluwer Academic: 221–236.

Schank, P., Fenton, J., Schlager, M. and Fusco, J. From MOO to MEOW: domesticating technology for
online communities. In *Proc. Third International Conference on Computer Support for Collaborative
Learning,* pp. 518–526.

Scheifler, R.W. and Gettys, J. (1986) The X Window System. *ACM Transactions on Graphics* 5(2), 79–109.

Schiano, D. and White, S. (1998) The first noble truth of CyberSpace: people are people (even when they
MOO). In *Proc. CHI'98.* New York: ACM Press: 352–359.

Schiffler, A. and Pettifer, S. (1999) The distributed legible city. In *eSCAPE: Systems, Techniques and
Infrastructures,* Vol. 5.1. University of Lancaster: 22–31.

Scholtz, J., Bellotti, V., Schirra, L., Erickson, T., DeGroot, J. and Lund, A. (1998) Telework: when your job is on the line. *Interactions* January and February: 44–54.

Schroeder, R. (1996) *Possible Worlds: the Social Dynamic of Virtual Reality Technology*. Boulder, CO: Westview Press.

Schroeder, R. (1997) Networked worlds: social aspects of multi-user virtual reality technology. *Sociological Research Online* 2(4). http://www.socresonline.org.uk/2/4/5.html

Schulzrinne, H., Casner, S., Frederick, R. and Jacobson, V. (1996) RTP: a transport protocol for real-time applications. *IETF RFC 1889*, January (Internet standard).

Schutz, A. (1970) *On Phenomenology & Social Relations*. Chicago, IL: University of Chicago Press.

Sepusic, M., Pannoni, R., Smith, R.B., Gibbons, J., Sutherland, B. and Dutra, J. (1999) Virtual collaborative learning: a comparison between face-to-face Tutored Video Instruction (TVI) and Distributed Tutored Video Instruction (DTVI). *Sun Microsystems Laboratories Technical Report TR-99-72*. Also available at http://www.sun.com/research/techrep/1999/abstract-72.html.

Shaw, J. (1998) The legible city. In Escape: Presence and Representation in Multimedia Art and Electronic Landscapes, Vol. 1.1. University of Lancaster: 61–96.

Shen, H. and Dewan, P. (1992) Access control for collaborative environments. In *Proc. CSCW'92*. New York: ACM Press: 51–58.

Sheridan, T.B. (1992) Musings on telepresence and virtual presence. In *Presence: Teleoperators and Virtual Environments* 1(1): 120–125.

Shu, L. and Flowers, W. (1994) Teledesign: groupware experiments in three-dimensional computer-aided design. *Collaborative Computing* 1(1): 1–14.

Simsarian, K. (2000) Toward human–robot collaboration. *PhD Dissertation*, Department of Numerical Analysis and Computing Science, KTH and SICS, Kista, Sweden.

Smith, R.B. (1992) What You See Is What I Think You See. In *Proc. Conf. Computer-Supported Collaborative Learning*, published as *SIGCUE Outlook* 21(3): 18–23.

Smith, G. (1996) Cooperative virtual environments: lessons from 2D multi-user interfaces. In M.S. Ackerman (ed.) *CSCW'96: Cooperating Communities*, pp. 390–398. http://www.acm.org/pubs/articles/proceedings/cscw/240080/p390-smith/p390-smith.pdf.

Smith, G. and Mariani, J. (1997) Using subjective views to enhance 3D applications. In *ACM Symposium on Virtual Reality Software and Technology*. New York: ACM Press: 139–146.

Smith, G. and O'Brien, J. (1998) Re-coupling tailored user interfaces. In *Proc. CSCW'98*, pp. 237–246. http://www.acm.org/pubs/articles/proceedings/cscw/289444/p237-smith/p237-smith.pdf.

Smith, R.B. and Ungar, D. (1994) A simple and unifying approach to subjective objects. *Technical Report*, Sun Microsystems.

Smith, R.B. and Ungar, D. (1995) Programming as an experience: the inspiration for Self. In G. Goos, J. Hartmanis and J. van Leeuwen (eds.) *Proc. ECOOP'95*. Berlin: Springer-Verlag: 303–330.

Smith, R.B., O'Shea, T., O'Malley, C., Scanlon, E. and Taylor, J. (1990) Preliminary experiments with a distributed, multimedia problem solving environment. In *Proc. EC-CSCW'90*, Gatwick, pp. 19–34. Also in J. Bowers and S. Benford (eds.) (1991) *Studies in Computer Supported Cooperative Work: Theory, Practice and Design*. Amsterdam: Elsevier: 31–48.

Smith, R.B., Maloney, J. and Ungar, D. (1995) The Self-4.0 user interface: manifesting a system-wide vision of concreteness, uniformity, and flexibility. In *Proc. OOPSLA'95*, Austin, TX, pp. 47–60.

Smith, R.B., Wolczko, M., and Ungar, D. (1997) From Kansas to Oz: collaborative debugging when a shared world breaks. *Communications of the ACM* 40(4): 72–78.

Smith, R.B., Hixon, R. and Horan, B. (1998) Supporting flexible roles in a shared space. In *Proc. CSCW'98*. New York: ACM Press: 197–206.

Smith, M.A., Farnham, S.D. and Drucker, S.M. (2000) The social life of small graphical chat spaces. In *Proc. CHI 2000*. New York: ACM Press: 462–469.

Smith, R., Pawlicki, R., Leigh, J. and Brown, D. (2000) Collaborative VisualEyes. In *Proceedings of the 4th International Immersive Projection Technology Workshop*, Ames, IA, 19–20 June.

Snowdon, D., Greenhalgh, C. and Benford, S. (1995) What You See is Not What I See: subjectivity in virtual environments. In *Frameworks for Immersive Virtual Environments (FIVE'95)*, QMW University of London, 18–19 December.

Snowdon, D., Greenhalgh, C., Benford, S., Bullock, A. and Brown, C. (1996a) A review of distributed architectures for networked virtual reality. *Virtual Reality: Research, Development and Applications* 2(1): 155–175.

Snowdon, D., Fahlén, L. and Stenius, M. (1996b) WWW3D: a 3D multi–user Web browser. *WebNet'96*, San Francisco, CA.

Snyder, F.W. (1971) Travel patterns: implications for new communication facilities. *Bell Laboratories Memorandum*.

Sonnenwald, D.H. (1999) Evolving perspectives of human information behavior: contexts, situations, social networks and information horizons. In Wilson, T.D. and Allen, D.K. (eds.) *Exploring the Contexts of Information Behavior: Proceedings of the Second International Conference in Information Needs*. London: Taylor Graham: 176–190.

Sørgaard, P. (1988) Object oriented programming and computerised shared material. In *Second European Conference on Object Oriented Programming (ECOOP'88)*. Heidelberg: Springer-Verlag.

Space Syntax Laboratory (1997) *Proceedings of the Space Syntax First International Symposium*, London.

Spence, J.D. (1984) *The Memory Palace of Matteo Ricci*. New York: Viking Penguin.

Springmeyer, R., Werner, N. and Long, J. (1996) Mining scientific data archives through metadata generation. In *Proc. First IEEE Metadata Conference*, NOAA Auditorium, Silver Spring, MD, 16–18 April.

Stanney, K.M., Mourant, R.R. and Kennedy, R.S. (1998) Human factors issues in virtual environments: a review of the literature. *Presence* 7(4): 327–351.

Stefik, M., Bobrow, D.G., Foster, G., Lanning, S. and Tatar, D. (1987a) WYSIWIS revised: early experiences with multi-user interfaces. *ACM Transactions on Office Information Systems* 5(2): 147–167. http://www.acm.org/pubs/articles/journals/tois/1987-5-2/p147-stefik/p147-stefik.pdf.

Stefik, M., Foster, G., Bobrow, D., Kahn, K., Lanning, S. and Suchman, L. (1987b) Beyond the chalkboard: computer support for collaboration and problem solving in meetings. *Communications of the ACM* 30(1): 32–47.

Stenius, M. (1998) http://www.sics.se/ice/research/projects/escape/webplanet/.

Stephenson, N. (1992) *Snow Crash*. New York: Bantam Books.

Stevens, R. and Papka, M.E. (1999) ActiveSpaces on the grid: the construction of advanced visualization and interaction environments. *Proc. PDC Annual Conference*.

Stoakley, R., Conway, J. and Pausch, R. (1995) Virtual reality on a WIM: interactive worlds in miniature. In *Proc. CHI'95*. New York: ACM Press.

Streeck, J. (1996) How to do things with things - objets trouvés and symbolization. *Human Studies* 19(4): 365–384.

Suchman, L.A. (1983) Office procedures as practical action: models of work and system design. *TOIS* 1(4): 320–328.

Suchman, L. (1987) *Plans and Situated Action: The Problem of Human Computer Interaction*. Cambridge: Cambridge University Press.

Suchman, L. (1995) Making work visible. *Communications of the ACM* 38: 56–64.

Suchman, L. (1996) Constituting shared workspaces. In Y. Engeström and D. Middleton *Cognition and Communication at Work*. New York: Cambridge University Press.

Suchman, L.A. and Trigg, R.H. (1991) Understanding practice: video as a medium for reflection and design. In J. Greenbaum and M. Kyng (eds.) *Design at Work*. London and New Jersey: Lawrence Erlbaum: 65–89.

Surrogate (1998) The Surrogate exhibition at the ZKM Institute for Visual Media, 1 November–6 December. *Exhibition Guide*.

Tang, J. (1991) Findings from observational studies of collaborative work. *International Journal of Man-Machine Studies* 34(2): 143–160.

Tang, J., Isaacs, E. and Rua, M. (1994) Supporting distributed groups with a montage of lightweight interactions. In *Proc. CSCW'94*. New York: ACM Press: 23–34.

Tani, M., Yamaashi, K., Tanikoshi, K., Futakawa, M. and Tanifuji, S. (1992) Object-oriented video: interaction with real world objects through live video. In *Proc. CHI'92*. New York: ACM Press.

Taylor II, R.M. and Superfine, R. (1999) Advanced interfaces to scanning probe microscopes. In H.S. Nalwa (ed.) *Handbook of Nanostructured Materials and Nanotechnology*. New York: Academic Press.

Taylor, R.S. (1991) Information use environments. In B. Dervin and M. Voigt (eds.) *Progress in Communication Sciences*, Vol. 10. Norwood, NJ: ABLEX: 217–255.

Tollmar, K., Sandor, O. and Schömer, A. (1996) Supporting social awareness @ work: design and experience. In *Proceedings of the Computer Supported Cooperative Work Conference*. Cambridge, MA: ACM Press: 298–306.

Tolmie, P. (1998) *Representation - Working Document for CSCW Workshop*. Lancaster University.

Tomek, I. and Giles, R. (1999) Virtual environments for work, study and leisure. In *Virtual Reality Research, Development and Applications, Special Issue of Collaborative Virtual Environments* 4(1): 26–37.

Tornatzky, L.G. and Klein, K.J. (1982) Innovation characteristics and innovation adoption implementation: a meta-analysis of findings. *IEEE Transactions on Engineering Management* EM-29: 28–45.

Towell, J. and Towell, E. (1997) Presence in text-based networked virtual environments or "MUDs". *Presence* 6(5): 590–595.

Trevor, J., Koch, T. and Woetzen, G. (1997) MetaWeb: bringing synchronous groupware to the World Wide Web. In J. Hughes *et al.* (eds.) *Proc. Fifth European Conference on Computer Supported Cooperative Work, ECSCW'97*. Dordrecht: Kluwer Academic: 65–80.

Trevor, J., Rodden, T. and Smith, G. (1998) Out of this world: an extensible session architecture for heterogeneous electronic landscapes. *Proc. 1998 Conference on Computer Supported Cooperative Work, CSCW'98*. New York: ACM Press.

Tromp, J., Bullock, A., Steed, A. *et al.* (1998) Small group behaviour experiments in the Coven project. *IEEE Computer Graphics and Applications*.

Turkle, S. (1995) *Life on the Screen: Identity in the Age of the Internet*. New York: Simon & Schuster.

Turkle, S. (1998) All MOOs are educational - the experience of walking through the self. In C. Haynes and J.R. Holmevik (eds.) *High wired: on the design, use and theory of educational MOOs*. Ann Arbor, MI: University of Michigan Press: ix-xix.

Turner, J. and Kraut, R. (eds) (1992) *CSCW'92: Sharing perspectives*. http://www.acm.org/pubs/contents/proceedings/cscw/143457/.

Tysoe, M. (1984) Social cues and the negotiation process. *British Journal of Social Psychology* 23: 61–67.

Ungar, D. and Smith, R. (1987) Self: the power of simplicity. In *OOPSLA'87*, pp. 227–242.

Vaghi, I., Greenhalgh, C. and Benford, S. (1999) Coping with inconsistency due to network delays in collaborative virtual environments. In *Proc. VRST'99*. New York: ACM Press.

Van Buren, D., Curtis, P., Nichols, A. and Brundage, M. (1995) The Astro VR collaboratory, an on-line multi-user environment for research in astrophysics. In R.A. Shaw, H.E. Payne and J.J.E. Hayes (eds.) *Astronomical Data Analysis Software and Systems IV*. ASP Conference Series, 77.

Varner, I. and Beaner, L. (1995) *Intercultural Communication in the Global Workplace*. Chicago, IL: Irwin.

Vince, J. (1998) *Essential Virtual Reality Fast: How to Understand the Techniques and Potential of Virtual Reality*. London: Springer-Verlag.

VRML97 (1997) *International Standard ISO/IEC 14772-1:1997*, "The Virtual Reality Modeling Language".

Wallberg, A., Hansson, P., Nord, B., Söderberg, J. and Fahlén, L. (1998) The Mimoid and Blob projects. Presentation/poster at *ACM MultiMedia '98*, Bristol.

Weiser, M. (1991) The computer for the twenty-first century. *Scientific American* (September): 94–100.

Weiser, M., Gold, R. and Brown, J.S. (1999) The origins of ubiquitous computing research at PARC in the late 1980s. *IBM Systems Journal* 38(4).

Weishar, P. (1998) *Digital Space: Designing Virtual Environments*. New York: McGraw-Hill.

Wellman, B., Salaff, J., Dimitrova, D., Garton, L., Gulia, M. and Haythornthwaite, C. (1996) Computer networks as social networks: collaborative work, telework and virtual community. *Annual Review of Sociology* 22: 213–238.

Wheless, G., Lascara, C., Valle-Levinson, A. *et al.* (1996) Virtual Chesapeake Bay: interacting with a coupled physical/biological model. *IEEE Computer Graphics and Applications* 16(4): 52–57.

Whittaker, S., Frohlich, D. and Daly-Jones, O. (1994) Informal workplace communication: what is it like and how might we support it? In *Proc. CHI'94*, Boston, MA: ACM Press: 131–137. http://www.acm.org/pubs/articles/proceedings/chi/191666/p131-whittaker/p131-whittaker.pdf.

Wisneski, C., Ishii, H., Dahley, A., Gorbet, M., Brave, S., Ullmer, B. and Yarin, P. (1998) Ambient displays: turning architectural space into an interface between people and digital information. In N.A. Streitz, S. Konomi and H.-J. Burkhardt (eds.) *Cooperative Buildings - Integrating Information, Organization, and Architecture.* Berlin: Springer-Verlag: 22–32.

Witmer, B.G. and Singer, M.J. (1998) Measuring presence in virtual environments: a presence questionnaire. *Presence* 7: 225–240.

Wren, C., Azarbayejani, A., Darrell, T. and Pentland, A. (1995) Pfinder: real–time tracking of the human body. *SPIE Photonics East* **2615**: 89–98.

Yamazaki, K., Yamazaki, A., Kuzuoka, H. *et al.* (1999) GestureLaser and GestureLaser Car: Development of an embodied space to support remote instruction. In *Proc. ECSCW'99.* Dordrecht: Kluwer Acdemic: 239–258.

Yates, F.A. (1966) *The Art of Memory.* London: Routledge & Kegan Paul.

Yu, Y. and Pekkola, S. (2000) Supporting awareness of other people on the WWW: a framework and an example system. *Proc. Pacific Asian Conference on Information Systems 2000 (PACIS'2000),* Hong Kong, 1–3 June.

Zahorik, P. and Jenison, R.L. (1998) Presence as being-in-the-world. *Presence* 7: 78–89.

Zechmeister, E.B. and Nyberg, S.E. (1982) *Human Memory; an Introduction to Research and Theory.* Monterey, CA: Brooks/Cole Publishing.

Zyda, M.J., Pratt, D.R., Falby, J.S., Lombardo, C. and Kelleher, K.M. (1993) The software required for the computer generation of virtual environments. *Presence* 2(2): 130–140.

Index